D1155051

WITHDRAWN

Crime and Conflict

in English Communities

1300-1348

Crime and Conflict
in English Communities
1300-1348

Barbara A. Hanawalt

Harvard University Press
Cambridge, Massachusetts
and London, England 1979

Publication of this book has been aided by a grant from the Andrew W.
Mellon Foundation

Library of Congress Cataloging in Publication Data

Hanawalt, Barbara
  Crime and Conflict in English Communities,
  1300-1348

  Bibliography:
  Includes index.
  1. Crime and criminals—England—History—Sources.
2. Criminal statistics—England. 3. Great Britain
—History—14th century. I. Title.
HV6949.E5H35   364'.942   79-1211
ISBN 0-674-17580-8

Preface

I undertook this study with the same aims as any crime writer; I wanted to know who committed the crimes. But I was not content with knowing about a few flashy cases or well-known villains. I wanted to know about the participation of ordinary people in criminal activities. I set out to discover what types of crimes villagers committed, what goods they stole, the seasons and techniques of their crimes, the identity of the victims and the accused and their interrelationships, and the motivations for the crimes. The fourteenth century was full of calamities that might have influenced the pattern of crime: the Great Famine of 1315-1317, the Hundred Years' War, the Black Death, the alleged torture of Edward II and the coup d'état of Edward III, and the Peasant Revolt of 1381. I also sought to investigate how the dynamics of interpersonal relations within the family and the village community influenced the participants in criminal actions. And, finally, I would have liked to have found the historical Robin Hood.

In the course of my research, I have met a number of enjoyable and helpful people and have read a great deal of fine history. My first debt of gratitude is to the many historians who have found the fourteenth century as fascinating as I do and who have written excellent studies on the administrative, legal, political, economic, and social history of the period. It is because of this extensive background literature that I was able to write a book about the social history of crime in late medieval England. Sylvia L. Thrupp merits special thanks for having proposed the topic to me. It proved to be such a stimulating subject that I went on doing research and writing on it through the discouragements of periods of underemployment and unemployment. I feel especially fortunate in having had encouragement from my undergraduate professors, Peter Charanis and Margaret Hastings, as well as my graduate professor in pursuing social history when it was not yet fashionable. The staff of the Public Record Office in London was very courteous in the years I worked there. C. A. F. Meekings was especially generous in explaining the gaol delivery rolls to me and allowing me to use his own unpublished guide to the rolls. (I have retained the English spelling for "gaol" rather than Americanizing it to "jail.") J. Ambrose Raftis made an enormous contribution to my study by permitting me to use the Ramsey Abbey village reconstitution materials in the Regional Data Bank at the Pontifical Institute of Medieval Studies in Toronto. Being able to trace a group of suspects and victims in their village setting changed my whole perception of fourteenth-century crime. I felt that I could understand the participants in crime as human beings and not just as numbers.

I am very grateful to the people who helped me to make sense of the criminal statistics I compiled and who read my manuscript. Alan Abrahamse aided me throughout the project with advice on its quantitative aspects. Thomas Browder and Annette Koren helped me to computerize the data. I was fortunate to have their aid. Three criminologists gave me good insights into the final analysis of my results: James Short, Austin T. Turk, and Sheldon Messinger. I very much appreciate the criticisms that Charles Tilly gave me on the completed manuscript and also those of my inspiring colleague, Norman J. G. Pounds, who also provided the map.

I am grateful for permission to reprint here material that I originally presented in the following journal articles: "Economic Influences on the Pattern of Crime in England, 1300-1348," *American Journal of Legal History* 18 (1974): 281-297; "The Peasant Family and Crime in Fourteenth-Century England," *The Journal of British Studies* 13 (1974): 1-18; "Community Conflict and Social Control: Crime and Justice in the Ramsey Abbey Villages," *Medieval Studies* 39 (1977): 402-423; "Violent Death in Fourteenth- and Early Fifteenth-Century England," *Comparative Studies in Society and History* 18 (July 1978): 297-320.

I was aided in the completion of the project by a number of fellowships and grants that permitted me to travel to England and Toronto, to microfilm gaol delivery rolls and coroners' rolls, and to study criminology. The Woodrow Wilson Foundation, the University of Michigan, and the American Association of University Women all helped me to do the initial years of research and writing in London. A Penrose Fund grant from the American Philosophical Society permitted me to make a subsequent trip to the Public Record Office to order microfilm. J. Ambrose Raftis kindly helped along my research in Toronto through his Canada Council Grant. The American Council of Learned Societies awarded me a study fellowship for a year so that I could study criminology and quantitative methods. Indiana University was very generous in aiding the completion of the project with a grant-in-aid for research and unlimited computer time. These fellowships and grants were all deeply appreciated not only for the financial support but also for the confidence that they showed in my research.

Writing a book is often elating and often discouraging; it could not be accomplished without a number of good friends and family to help the author along. My debts to friends are too numerous to list; I only hope that I have returned some of the comfort and support they have given to me. John and Vicky Bradley, close friends and neighbors in London, provided me with a cheerful place to stay and good conversation while I was doing research. Both my parents encouraged my studies and contributed to my intellectual appreciation for my subject matter. My interest in the social dynamics of rural villages stems from time spent during my childhood in my father's birthplace in Pennsylvania. My interest in medieval English history I owe to my mother, Pearl Basset Hanawalt, who read me books on medieval subjects and told me about my medieval English ancestors. The most appropriate dedication of the book is to my mother and to these ancestors. My forebears helped to people the book both as judges and as criminals.

Contents

Tables

Figures

Crime and Conflict

in English Communities

1300-1348

Chapter One

Introduction

THE EXCITEMENT that attends the commission of a startling crime is apparent even in the bare legal accounts of the incident that survive among the criminal court records of late medieval England: "John of Apeldorfeld was indicted before William Inge and Walter of Norwich because he along with others on the night of 8 August 1313 came with arms to the monastery church at Thetford and broke into it. They killed Emery, nephew of Martin the Prior of the monastery, in the church and wounded others in the priory. They broke into the coffers of the Prior and stole his seal, a silver vase and other goods worth £20. They also took the Prior's cope and palfrey worth £10 and a certain horse belonging to Hugh, the valet of the Prior, worth £10. John comes and says that he is a clerk. Thomas, dean of Norwich, comes with letters from the bishop. The jurors say that he is innocent. He is acquitted."[1]

The morning after this terrible crime both the monks and servants in the priory must have been in a state of turmoil taking care of their wounds, notifying the coroner of Emery's death, informing local law enforcement officers of the break-in and thefts, and gossiping in the village tavern and marketplace about how near they had been to John of Apeldorfeld and his companions and how they had just avoided being struck down like Emery. They would be full of speculations about why John had broken into the church, how Emery might have escaped, and what the prior would say about the loss of his treasure and his nephew.

What is remarkable about such court records is that they contain not just a few surviving cases of outstanding brutality but thousands of criminal cases from the thirteenth through the fifteenth centuries.

Felonious actions ranging from casual theft of a few geese, to daring burglaries and robberies, to homicidal arguments are all recorded. By combining a statistical approach to this criminal court data with an analysis of individual cases and contemporary literary references to crime, it is possible to present a broad criminological study of medieval England that is both descriptive and analytic.

The problems surveyed in this book are very similar to those that a person studying crime in modern society would wish to investigate. The legal mechanisms for detection, arrest, and trial are of crucial importance. So too is the ecological setting of the crimes: the living conditions of the participants, their kinship and community ties, their means of livelihood, their power relationships, and the tensions they might resolve through criminal means. With this background one may inquire what the crimes were; how, where, and when they were committed; and who committed them. The relationship between the two participants in the criminal drama tells much about crime and about social interactions in general. With the model of Robin Hood ever present in the mind of medievalists, criminal associations and organized crime also must be central themes. The broad calamities facing the bulk of the population in fourteenth-century England—famine, overpopulation, disease, wars, private armies, and unrest in the central government—can all be studied to find their effects on fluctuations in the annual incidence of crime and changes in the types of crimes committed and goods stolen. Finally, the medievalist, like the modern criminologist, is not content to describe the phenomenon of crime but wants to know as well what motivated criminal actions and what the impact of crime was on the society.

Of primary concern are why people turned to crime and how their criminal behavior related to their social organization and their attitudes toward law enforcement. Community and familial conflicts, rebellions against authorities, and repressions by authorities could all affect the types of crimes committed and the way the law was administered. Numerous theories attempt to explain why people commit crime or settle differences through criminal means: some theories emphasize psychological or physical abnormalities; others emphasize generalized feelings of alienation from society and its laws; still others, economic and social deprivation. To the extent that the medieval records permit, I will invesitgate these various explanations and the possibility that all levels of society used crime and the judicial system as weapons in social conflicts to further their own power over others.

2

Conflict theory in sociology views law as a powerful instrument of social control. Whoever controls the law and the judicial system may use them to further their own power. In doing so those in control may be generating conflicts rather than resolving them, because their example encourages others to try to gain control over the legal system and to use nonlegal means and outright crime as weapons in the struggle for dominance. This view of the law may be more helpful in explaining the emphasis on self-help in medieval law and society than the view of the law as being essentially an instrument of conflict management, which presumes that the law is designed to prevent, minimize, or at least reduce conflicts. Since medieval English society was highly stratified and since all classes from the well-established peasantry to the crown had considerable possibilities for manipulating justice for their own ends, the applicability of conflict theory to medieval society, law, and crime is of special interest.

Many historians are now investigating crime to see if such antisocial behavior has always been the same or if new experiences such as industrialization, urban growth, and capitalism substantially changed the patterns associated with crime.[2] An investigation of crime in the Middle Ages is a useful departure point for such studies. The largely peasant, preindustrial society looked to village communities and regional authorities for daily needs and government rather than to urban centers or a national state. Such a society did not have large minority groups to be labeled as criminal subcultures, nor did it have to rely on a complicated industrial economy to either provide or withhold food. The people's livelihoods came from the soil and their own self-reliance.

Comparisons with modern crime patterns indicate that some social responses are remarkably consistent over the centuries, such as the ratio of men to women indicted for crimes. In other areas, such as the low incidence of intrafamilial crime, medieval England appears to be a different society. A historical study has some advantages over an anthropological study for such comparisons in that the roots of our present English and American legal systems and social institutions are to be found in medieval England. One is not trying to imagine criminals breaking strange taboos, but just the Anglo-American taboos against larceny, burglary, robbery, arson, receiving, homicide, suicide, rape, and petty treason.

The definition of crime used in this book is based upon fourteenth-century common and statute laws. Thus only the basic felonies just mentioned and minor treason cases such as spying and counterfeiting are included. To impose a modern definition of crime would have meant setting up artificial categories that would have defied the organization of the court roll data. More misunderstandings rather than fewer would have resulted. In any case, the medieval definition is not far from the modern one. Crimes, or more properly, felonies, were those offenses against the law of the society and its government that were so socially harmful that the victims could not be compensated through payment of a *bot* (monetary compensation). The crown, therefore, assumed the responsibility for trying and punishing the perpetrators of these "bootless" crimes by punishment to life and limb (in the fourteenth century, usually hanging). Those committing criminal acts were said to be breaking the "king's peace" to the detriment of the king and his subjects. According to F. W. Maitland, it is questionable whether the fourteenth century had a definition of felony other than a list of offenses considered criminal.[3] In forming a definition, both procedural and substantive law must be taken into consideration. In Maitland's formulation:

> (i) A felony is a crime which can be prosecuted by an appeal . . . [or by presentment and indictment in the fourteenth century]. (ii) The felon's lands go to his lord or to the king and his chattels are confiscated. (iii) The felon forfeits life or member. (iv) If a man accused of felony flies, he can be outlawed.[4]

The more concise modern definition would state that a criminal act is one that is socially harmful and for which a state-imposed penalty is legally provided.[5]

Although the modern definition of a criminal act is broad enough to encompass the medieval definition, the list of acts that could be considered criminal is much more inclusive now than then. Even the definitions of the basic felonies are somewhat different now. Modern society tends to elevate all sorts of antisocial acts to the level of felony in order to impose the most drastic punishment the law will allow; medieval society did not. The distinctions between crime and tort were not even established in the Middle Ages, for as T. F. T. Plucknett observed, "the middle ages were more intent on doing what had to be done, than on classifying ways of doing it."[6] In the Middle Ages moral problems such as sodomy, bigamy, and prostitution were matters for the church courts to regulate. Assaults, slanders, and many actions that appeared to be thefts but were, in fact, trespasses were

4

adjudicated in either manorial or town courts or were settled by civil actions in the king's assize courts. Since a study of all these different courts would have been impossible for one researcher, I have confined my survey to those matters which were considered to be criminal in the fourteenth century and were, therefore, handled in the king's criminal courts.

The kings of England continually experimented with various ways of detecting crimes and trying suspects, so that officials and courts assigned to handle these matters tended to proliferate. By the late thirteenth century and to the middle of the fourteenth century the most common courts for trying suspected felons were the gaol delivery sessions. Justices from the central courts at Westminster were sent two or more times a year on circuit to the county gaols to try the accused who were either bailed or retained in gaol until trial. Clerks traveling with the judges kept a record of the substance of each trial. The information recorded in these gaol delivery rolls includes the names and residences of the victims and the accused, the types of crimes committed, the goods stolen and their value, the place where the crimes occurred, the verdict, and the sentence. The occupation of the participants in the criminal drama, the date and time of day when the crime occurred, the arresting officer, the value of the convicted felon's personal property (chattels), and information on court procedure might also be included.

The gaol delivery justices normally had sole responsiblity for criminal matters, but occasionally the kings would use other justices or other types of commissions to do the work of gaol delivery. The king's own court, King's Bench, which traveled with him throughout the realm, often tried criminal cases. Edward II experimented with giving his justices greater powers through commissions of trailbaston. These commissions gave the justices power both to inquire into offenses and to hear the cases, rather than just to try those indicted at the lower level. All the kings tried on rare occasions to revive the general eyre (the all encompassing judicial inquiry of the thirteenth century). When the gaol delivery commission was passed to one of these other courts, the information was basically the same and has been included in the data.

Information on criminal activity exists in other rolls that were part of the king's system for detecting crime. The king's coroners kept records of all homicides and accidental deaths that occurred in their county. This material, because it comes from a court of first instance, is rich in detail and permits an extensive study of homicide. Records of indictments are not well preserved for other courts of first instance, such as leet courts, but I have sampled some of them that have been published as well.[7]

The materials preserved in the various criminal courts are so vast that I had to set some limits to the study, some resulting from the nature of the records themselves, others imposed for the purposes of this study, including the decision to deal only with rural population. The people who appear in these pages are, for the most part, the ordinary people of the countryside—peasants, village artisans, residents in market towns, wanderers, members of the clergy, and gentry—who made up about 90 percent of the population in medieval England.

Other social groups that tended to be exempt from the ordinary criminal courts appear infrequently in this study. Many boroughs had procured charters that permitted them to try their own felony cases. The city court records are not so well preserved as the national ones and present some research problems different from those that appear in the rural records. The nobility and higher clergy managed to exclude themselves from the criminal justice system, since they could use their influence in the countryside to avoid indictment. Although much of their criminal behavior will always remain hidden, a glimpse of it may be had in the trailbaston records. These records have been sampled for this study, but more research could provide further information. The shady aspect of the behavior of the higher classes is also apparent from reading the patent rolls, the close rolls, and the King's Bench rolls, where their trespasses are recorded. Nobles were also unlikely to become victims of crime more serious than larceny and burglary because they traveled about with households that might better be described as small private armies.

Gaol delivery roll data on the victims and the accused among villagers and small-town people permit a discussion of the sex of the victim and the accused, the distance they lived from each other and the scene of the crime, kinship ties within the nuclear family, some occupational information (especially for the clergy), and occasional information on private motivations for criminal acts and on victims who precipitated their own injury. Information from the coroners' rolls considerably supplements this general description of the offenders and victims for homicide cases.

The richest source of supplemental information on identity of the accused came from J. Ambrose Raftis's Regional Data Bank, which contains village reconstitution materials for more than a dozen villages belonging to Ramsey Abbey in Huntingdonshire. I was able to determine the status group and the previous village record of service, debt, trespass, assault, and other activities of more than 100 people by matching those indicted in Huntingdonshire with villagers identified in the Ramsey Abbey villages. This sample permitted me to speculate on the tensions among the status groups within the village communities and the way these tensions were resolved through crime and through the administration of criminal justice. Combining the data from these two major research efforts was particularly fruitful for understanding the dynamics of crime within the rural settlements; it permitted speculation on conflict theory in explaining the administration of justice.

In addition to information on the criminal activities of ordinary villagers, the gaol delivery rolls, with supplemental information from the coroners' rolls, provide data on criminal associations. When a group had committed a crime together, the sheriffs and justices tried to bring the accused to trial at the same time. From this material it is possible to investigate the patterns of organized crime in fourteenth-century England and even to consider the existence of outlaw kings and their bands. Certainly, no other criminal and his gang are so universally known through poetry, novels, and films as are Robin Hood and his band. Although Robin Hood did not turn up in the gaol delivery rolls, there is considerable evidence about people and bands whose criminal behavior very much resembled his. The gaol delivery rolls fail to show an altruistic side to these bandits who were in reality more of a scourge to the peasantry than a help. Household retainers of the lords also appear in the criminal courts, usually in the trailbaston sessions. They and the lords who directed their activities played a variety of roles in crime in the countryside—sometimes the medieval equivalent of white-collar criminals,[8] sometimes a primitive Mafia, and sometimes as protectors and patrons of their client peasantry. Most criminal associations, however, were composed of a couple of neighbors or brothers who would engage in one or two criminal acts together in informal associations.

Since the gaol delivery rolls only dealt with felonies, these are the only crimes studied. A full discussion of the frequency with which various types of felonies occurred, the ways in which they were committed, their seasonality, and the kind and value of goods stolen is possible from the available material.

The gaol delivery rolls cover several centuries, but they are only complete enough for this study for a period of about fifty years. They survive for the late thirteenth century in only a few counties, so that I decided to start the study with the year 1300. I also decided to terminate the major portion of the study in 1348. The Black Death in 1349 interrupted the normal judicial process, and in 1351, when the justices of the peace were finally given power to hear and determine criminal cases, the gaol delivery rolls ceased to be an accurate report of yearly incidence of indictments. The justices of the peace siphoned off an unknown number of the cases formerly heard exclusively in gaol delivery. The justice of the peace records are not well enough preserved to supplement the surviving gaol delivery rolls. For Yorkshire, Northamptonshire, and Norfolk I have used the full run of fourteenth-century records, but they are only of value for discussing the types of goods stolen, the associations of criminals, the proportion of male to female offenders, and the various types of felonies. The materials from 1300 to 1348, on the other hand, are complete enough that one may study fluctuations in the annual incidence of felony as well as the other areas of information. This relatively good run of documentation permits speculation on the types of broad social experience that contribute to crime waves.

The period from 1300 to 1348 is particularly interesting for studying the response of criminal patterns to various social, economic, and political influences. The populace of rural England was beginning to experience social and economic pressures that their forebearers had not known for a century or more. Whereas land and food had been in relatively good supply from the late eleventh century through the thirteenth century, in the first two decades of the fourteenth century the productivity and fertility of land began to decrease while population continued to increase. Combined with the struggle for food, which reached crisis proportions in 1315-1317 during the Great Famine, there were epidemics among humans and animals culminating in the Black Death in 1349.

The gradual expansion of the thirteenth century had turned into a fairly rapid contraction in the early fourteenth century, when the price of grain rose in response to shortages. Because of food shortages and famine, the population was already in decline about twenty-five years before the plague. The diminished population just before the plague had less trouble procuring food since the grain prices dropped, so that they were able to divert their profits into purchasing better equipment, luxury goods, and other items of industrial production.

Rural inhabitants also experienced foreign invasions for the first time since the Conquest. The Hundred Years' War was a direct outgrowth of the events of 1066 when the Duke of Normandy became both the vassal of the French king for his possessions in France and king of England in his own right. Relations with the French overlord had been stormy, but the fighting had been limited to skirmishes in France. When Edward III claimed the French throne by virtue of being the grandson of Philip IV, the war expanded. French pirates continually raided the English southeastern coastal towns and made inroads into the countryside. The English peasantry were not totally defenseless against the invaders; the statute of Winchester in 1285 had required all males over the age of twelve to train in arms for the defense of the realm. The militiamen on the southern coastal counties found use for this training from the 1330s on. Peasants living in Yorkshire and the northern counties experienced the problems of invasion even sooner. During the first quarter of the century the Scots united under Robert Bruce and made a number of excursions deep into Yorkshire.

The disruptions of war came both from foreign armies and from their own sovereign's armies. The royal armies were not regularly provisioned, so that they often acted as plunderers themselves. Indeed, some of their members were already known felons serving in the army to procure a pardon. Troops returning from successful campaigns or in periods of truce were often very destructive to the peace of the country; they continued to live from plunder as they had in enemy lands. Members of the Commons repeatedly petitioned the king about the roving bands of veterans and about the private armies that the nobles drew from their ranks to harass loyal subjects. Part of the inquiry of this book will center on the influence of war on crime.

Domestic crises in the king's council and problems with the succession had less direct influence on the countryside but when they led to civil war, as they did in 1322, the effects were disruptive to the region in which the fighting occurred. And who can say what influence the assassination of the king's favorites, the deposition and secretive murder of Edward II, and young Edward III's arrest of a king-maker in the bedchamber of his widowed mother had on the thinking of people who gathered in the village taverns to gossip. Did any of these events touch the lives of the people in the countryside, or were they of little consequence as long as the central administration continued to run smoothly in spite of fighting at the top? This will also be discussed in subsequent chapters.

In addition to limiting the time span covered, I limited the number of counties. I based the selection of the counties on their geographical location and on the preservation of their gaol delivery rolls. Included are Essex, Norfolk, Northamptonshire, Huntingdonshire, Yorkshire, Herefordshire, Somerset, and Surrey. These counties are representative of the various regions of England. They experienced different economic, social, and political influences during the early fourteenth century and are, therefore, good for the purposes of comparison. Sometimes a county underwent unique events that made its pattern of life and crime different; at other times all the counties experienced the same configuration in their criminal behavior.

Essex, Norfolk, and Surrey form one of the groups of counties that invite comparisons. All three took an active part in the Peasant Revolt of 1381, yet Surrey and Essex were closer to each other in their revolutionary behavior than either was to Norfolk. Their crime patterns may indicate the underlying tensions in the peasant communities that gave their participation in the revolt different twists. Essex and Surrey both bordered on London, and this proximity involved them in many unique relations with the city. People from all over England passed through their borders on their way to the capital city; criminals and honest men alike moved into the rural areas surrounding the city; and peasants took their grain and other produce to London for the city's population. Their communications and interests bound them to London. Here their similarity ended. Surrey had open-field settlement and impartible inheritance, whereas Essex had more enclosed fields and partible inheritance.[9] Norfolk also followed the East Anglian custom of partible inheritance, but had open fields. It was distinguished throughout the Middle Ages as being both one of the most populated and wealthiest counties. In the fourteenth century Norfolk developed into a major cloth producing region, and it had the ports of Great Yarmouth and King's Lynn for import and export trade. Colchester in Essex developed a woolen industry, but the period of great prosperity for Essex did not come until the sixteenth century. Essex and Surrey never had populations as large as that of Norfolk because parts of those counties were still forest area in the fourteenth century.

Northamptonshire and Huntingdonshire represent the Midlands in its various forms. Both counties had the typical open-field village and agricultural settlement plan. Huntingdonshire also had some fenland settlements similar to those in Lincolnshire and western Norfolk. Wool was produced, but little cloth was woven. Both counties grew grain, but not for export. Like Essex and Surrey, they were moderately populated. Northamptonshire was still well wooded, so some areas could not be settled. The counties, and indeed all Midland counties, had frequent contacts with each other. They were not large sized, and they were arranged in such a way that they bordered on many other counties, which made law enforcement particularly difficult because felons could ride across county lines and escape arrest. The area was known for its bands of outlaws in the Middle Ages. Northamptonshire was particularly open to wayward elements because it lay on the Great North Road. Travelers passed along this way on business north and south, troops going to fight the Scots also marched through, and the king and his court frequently stopped on their progresses.

Herefordshire might also be considered as a Midland area, but in the Middle Ages it was considerably different from Northamptonshire. It bordered on Wales and got much of its population and settlement patterns from its Celtic neighbors. The economy was based on herding, both sheep and cattle, including some transhumant herding. Since there were mountains and moorlands through the western part of the county, population could only concentrate in certain areas, so the population was fairly sparse throughout the Middle Ages. The county had been upset during the Welsh wars of Edward I, which were only recently over during the first years of the fourteenth century. Like Yorkshire, Herefordshire experienced the problems of being a border area.

Yorkshire in the Middle Ages was divided into three Ridings that spread across northern England. The West Riding resembled Herefordshire with the Celtic influence and the emphasis on herding. York and some of the other central towns developed a prosperous woolen industry using the wool from sheep on the surrounding moors. In addition to herding and wool production, Yorkshire also produced coal, lead, and iron. Population was generally sparse as one would expect on the extensive moorlands. Grain production could be profitably pursued in only a few areas of the county. Politically, Yorkshire was one of the most interesting counties in the early fourteenth century. The civil war between Edward II and the Duke of Lancaster disrupted the countryside in the southwest. The constant raids of the Scots and the presence of the English armies were very disruptive to life in the second and third decades of the century. Like Northampton-shire and the Midland areas, Yorkshire had its share of wandering outlaw bands that drew the attention of the king and the residents to the problems of keeping order in the county.

Somerset was a unique county in the fourteenth century. With the increasing use of water power for fulling cloth, Somerset became one of the chief producers of woolen cloth by the end of the fourteenth century. The Mendip hills provided rapid streams for mills and also yielded lead and copper ore. Bristol supplied Somerset with an important large port and access to the wine trade with Spain and Gas-cony. Although the settlement pattern was somewhat mixed, the county was largely composed of open-field village communities. It was moderately well populated in the fourteenth century. The nobility had their own local interests and took a particularly active role in the county, thus contributing much to the lawlessness experienced there. In general, the kings found it difficult to overcome local political con-figurations in the southwestern counties and to extend their jurisdic-tion there.

These then are the subjects, the years, and the geographical areas for which the gaol delivery rolls provide material. But how reliable are the gaol delivery rolls? Two questions immediately arise when dealing with criminological data: how complete and how accurate are the records? In order to test the hypothesis that social, political, and eco-nomic factors influenced the number of crimes per year, we must first establish that the fluctuations were not brought about by missing records, changes in the administration of justice, or increased effi-ciency in law enforcement. If the rolls are to be used to describe the pattern of crime, we must know the extent to which corruption and negligence at all levels of society influenced who was charged and which crimes were prosecuted. To keep this section brief, I have put much of the technical information about peculiarities of medieval administration in appendixes and notes. A discussion of the way in which the judicial system functioned appears in chapter 2, where it is set in its social context.

The surviving gaol delivery rolls are located in the Public Record Office in London under the classification of Justices Itinerant III (Just. 3). The series includes more than 200 separate bundles of plea rolls, files, and calendars. The calendars, which were the original records, are too sparsely preserved to be useful for a statistical study of crime. Although they are more accurate than the plea rolls, a sample comparison of the two showed that the discrepancies were not great enough to affect the results of the study. In comparing five years of calendars and plea rolls for Yorkshire, only seven additional cases appeared on the calendars, not enough to create a statistical problem. The calendars do not contain more detailed information than do the plea rolls. The files consist of odd writs, pardons, and jury lists. Their preservation is too sporadic to be of use in this study.

Records for the eight counties in this study are in different states of preservation (see table 12). Norfolk, Essex, and Yorkshire have the most complete runs with only a few years missing, mostly in the early years of the century. Norfolk with forty-six years of records out of forty-eight had 3,746 criminal cases; Essex with thirty-seven years had 2,402; and Yorkshire with thirty-nine years had 5,485. These are the counties with the largest body of data. To get information on the suspects, I counted indictments by person, that is, an offender accused of two or more crimes is counted as one indictment.[10] Likewise, if two people were accused of one crime, this counts as two indictments. The other counties do not have as good runs of records, but I selected some of them in order to have a representative county for all regions of the country. Northamptonshire had thirty-one years preserved and 1,256 criminal cases.[11] Huntingdonshire is a very small county that I added in order to utilize the Regional Data Bank. It has twenty-two years of records and 301 cases. In identifying eighty-nine of those charged with crimes in the Ramsey Abbey villages in the Data Bank, I was working with 30 percent of the criminal cases preserved. This makes conclusions drawn from this material a fairly reliable sample. Herefordshire and Surrey have moderately well-preserved records. Herefordshire had twenty-three years and 991 criminal cases; Surrey had twenty-nine years and 575. The records for Somerset were the least numerous—only eighteen years, but 1,135 criminal cases. The whole of the southwest circuit does not have complete records because the commissions were issued to local justices who kept them in their own possession.[12] The total number of cases in the eight counties for 1300-1348 is 15,891. With the added cases from Norfolk, Yorkshire, and Northamptonshire for the years 1349-1398 the total number is 22,417.

Unless otherwise noted, the figures in this book are based on indictments, not on convictions, although it is recognized that the indictments were not always accurate. Mistakes were made in transcription of cases to the gaol delivery rolls, and some indictments were false. But the indictments had to be plausible in order to be recorded, and most crimes had been committed even if by people different from those indicted. Furthermore, the sample size of this study is so large that small variations would have no significant influence on final figures.

Loss of records and experiments with other forms of administering justice account for gaps in the gaol delivery series. The history of the rolls explains many of these breaks. During the trial the sheriff's calendar of indictments was used to conduct the proceedings. The clerk entered the results of the trial on the calendar along with the description of the value of forfeited goods or any point affecting the delivery of the prisoner.[13] The calendars then went into the keeping of the senior justice of the session who was responsible for having a clerk make a copy to be deposited with the Exchequer.[14] In practice the enrollments were handed on from one justice to the next as the personnel of the commissions changed.[15] Some justices were conscientious about the records; but the Exchequer often had to ask for the rolls, even pressing the heirs of a dead justice for them.[16]

The loss of rolls could occur at any point in this process or during the succeeding centuries of storage. In 1381, for instance, the peasantry destroyed some rolls as a symbol of their revolt.[17] A clerk in Northampton ironically lost some rolls in a robbery on the king's highway.[18] Many rolls never were deposited, and some were destroyed by the mice, the elements, and misguided archivists.[19] Some gaps simply indicate that the sessions never took place.[20]

In order to use the records to determine the annual incidence of crimes, it is necessary to know as nearly as possible where the records are incomplete. Appendix A discusses the ways to detect and compensate for gaps in the records. For the purposes of this book I concluded that all years with two or more deliveries may be considered complete. Years with one or no deliveries have been excluded on the grounds that records are probably missing, unless there is evidence to the contrary.[21] Experiments with other devices for compensating for missing records did not improve greatly upon simply using the raw data.

Extending power to administer criminal law to justices other than those for gaol delivery periodically drew off cases. If the drain was fairly constant, then it had little effect on the annual incidence of reported crimes. But irregular removal of cases from gaol delivery might be sufficient to explain fluctuations in the number of crimes per year recorded in the rolls. Courts that occasionally tried felonies included eyre, King's Bench, trailbaston, oyer and terminer, leets, and peace sessions. The eyres, King's Bench, and trailbaston all held regular gaol delivery sessions from time to time, but these sessions have been included in the data.[22]

Oyer and terminer commissions had limited criminal jurisdiction covering only serious crimes or those committed against high ranking persons. Their usual business was trespass cases. They were never issued at regular or frequent intervals in the fourteenth century, but rather to meet dangerous situations as they arose.[23] A survey of the patent rolls shows that there were usually only one or two oyer and terminer commissions per year for each county. Of these, some are enrolled along with the gaol delivery records and have been included in this study.

The leet courts and private franchisal courts drew off some cases that would normally be included in gaol delivery, but these represent a constant drain of cases and do not cause fluctuations in the number of cases coming in each year. A miller who stole grain from his customers, for instance, might get off with a fine in leet court rather than being taken to gaol delivery if his action was considered to be a trespass rather than a felony. The published Wakefield manor court rolls and the Ramsey Abbey rolls from the Regional Data Bank show that very few felony cases were tried in the manorial courts.[24] Some of the leet courts had the right of *infangthef*, that is, the power to hang a thief caught red-handed or with the stolen goods. By the fourteenth century the crown had discouraged *infangthef* and had even encroached on the rights of those lords who had retained the power to hear crown pleas in their liberties. Most of the criminal cases that were prosecuted, therefore, came into the king's courts.

Of all the rival jurisdictions, the keepers of the peace pose the greatest problems in using gaol delivery information for a study of the annual fluctuations in the amount of crime. In 1329, 1332, and 1338 the keepers of the peace were granted the right to try the cases indicted before them. To test the effects of granting judicial powers to the keepers of the peace (thus making them justices), the years when peace cases were excluded from gaol delivery have been compared with a table of the annual incidence of crime in the eight counties (see appendix B). This comparison shows that the number of crimes per year dropped only in 1332 when the keepers were given the power to determine cases for only the month of February. In 1329 and 1338, the number rose despite the cases drawn off by peace sessions. Thus, if the cases tried in these sessions are added to those of gaol delivery, it serves to augment an already existing rise. After 1351 the gaol delivery rolls become unreliable for an analysis of annual incidence of crime because the justices of the peace held their own sessions regularly.

We may assume, then, that most criminal cases ending in indictment appear in the gaol delivery rolls and that competing court jurisdictions cannot explain the fluctuations in recorded crime. These yearly differences might, however, reflect changes in the methods of apprehending criminals or in the efficiency of existing law enforcement officials rather than an actual increase in the amount of crime. Modern criminologists like to point to police reforms and public concern campaigns as being chiefly responsible for what is perceived as crime waves. Was the same true in the fourteenth century? In appendix C I have again used the methods of comparing changes in law enforcement to a table of the number of crimes per year. The comparison renders inconclusive results. The number of cases per year does sometimes rise following a reform, but this is not always true. Sometimes the number in one county rises while it falls in another. Furthermore, some peaks on the graph do not coincide with administrative changes. Further difficulties arise because at times the authorities were exercising extended powers without specific permission.[25] Usually, increases coincided with periods of social, economic, and political crises as well as with reforms, so that it is difficult to assess which had the greater influence. It seems unlikely, however, that huge increases in court business in 1315-1317 could be caused by a new policing measure alone. The period of greatest public concern about crime was the 1330s, but this was a low point for criminal indictments. While attempts at reform may help to explain some of the fluctuations, they are not the only explanations nor, perhaps, the most satisfactory ones.

Another possible cause for fluctuations is the effect of corrupt officials who either suppressed cases or falsely indicted people. So serious was this problem in nineteenth-century England that J. J. Tobias based his refusal to grapple with criminal statistics largely on this ground.[26] Corruption was certainly rife in medieval England, but it is unlikely that it could have caused significant fluctuations in the number of cases brought into court. Those participating in the criminal justice system were unsalaried or had inadequate salaries, so that everyone assumed that the officials were corrupt. Only a long run of honest officials would make any significant change in the number of crimes reported.

Heavy reliance on the appeals of approvers, felons who turned state's evidence and named their accomplices, might have brought abnormal numbers of cases into court. The use of approvers seemed to run in cycles of popularity. In order to assess their influence on the number of cases brought into court each year, I plotted the number of crimes per year in Norfolk both with and without approver cases (see figure 22). This graph shows that, although the approver cases do add a considerable number of cases to the totals during the years 1320-1330 and 1346-1347, they tend to follow the same pattern as the other cases. For this reason I have included the approver cases in my calculations of the number of cases per year.

A caution that should precede all criminological studies based on court records is that such records include only cases for which a suspect has been detected, indicted, and arrested. Many cases are never reported because they are settled out of court, because they are never detected, because they are concealed through personal concern for the culprit or through failure of witnesses to report a felony, or because the suspect has disappeared. Court records, therefore, never give the true volume of crime; they are only an index to the amount of crime and to fluctuations in that amount.[27] Furthermore, they are more reliable for homicides where the evidence is harder to conceal than they are for other types of crimes.[28] They are probably least accurate for minor thefts.

Many modern criminologists and those studying the history of crime refuse to use trial records because of the incompleteness of the sample. John Bellamy dismissed the whole body of gaol delivery evidence with the statement that "an accurate assessment of incidence of criminal misdeeds . . . may never be possible."[29] I have chosen to use the rolls in spite of their problems because otherwise I feel that one can only make impressionistic statements about crime that are sure to be full of value judgments. The failure of the subjective method in the study of crime is amply apparent in the work of both Bellamy and Tobias. Comparing their work with the studies of L. L. Robson and Eric H. Monkkonen one can quickly see the advantages of making an effort to cope with criminal court records.[30] Furthermore, a quantitative approach is the only viable way to deal with such a large body of evidence. Although there are errors and gaps in the records, there are also ways to compensate for them. The sample for the study is sufficiently large that minor information losses would not be crucial. Since the sample is drawn from eight very different counties, local variations can be detected in the trends being discussed. Used together with information from literary sources and outstanding individual cases, it is possible to discuss crime in both its quantitative and qualitative aspects.

A severe limitation in employing gaol delivery data is that there are no population figures for early fourteenth-century England, so that criminal data cannot be expressed in crimes per 1,000 population.[31] To partially compensate for not being able to talk in terms of the percent of the population affected by crime, I have used modern comparisons extensively. This helps to put the facts and figures in a readily comprehensible framework. The device of comparison is purely for the sake of giving perspective; it cannot be taken as an absolutely reliable indicator of stability or change in crime patterns over the centuries because laws and punishments are somewhat different and society is not the same now as in the fourteenth century. Still, the comparisons are suggestive for gaining a better understanding of medieval society and for detecting new lines of research for modern criminology.

The sources for this study, particularly the gaol delivery rolls, contain a wealth of information both to describe crime and criminals and to investigate various hypotheses about patterns of crime. Since fluctuations in annual incidence of crime are not explainable solely through a drain of cases to other jurisdictions or increases in efficiency in law enforcement, the possible influences of political unrest, wars, invasions, overpopulation, famine, and industrial growth may be investigated. Further evidence for the influence of these events on crime may be found by looking at the changes in the types of crimes committed and the variety of goods stolen over the period. The ways in which crimes were committed, the organization of criminal associations, and the interrelationship of the participants in the criminal drama may be analyzed on the basis of the court roll evidence. These rolls also show the biases, prejudices, and intercommunity conflicts that took place in the administration of justice. The crimes the communities felt must be punished and the people they punished reveal much about tolerances and intolerances among ordinary rural dwellers in fourteenth-century England.

Chapter Two
The Social and Judicial Context
of Fourteenth-Century Crime

MEDIEVAL KINGS were more capable of analyzing the ills of the body politic than of treating them: "Forasmuch as from day to day, robberies, murders, burnings be more often committed than they have been heretofore, and felonies cannot be attainted by the oath of the jurors which had rather suffer felonies done to strangers to pass unpunished, than to indict the offenders of whom great part be people of the same country, or at least because, if the offenders be of another country the receivers be of the neighborhood . . . our lord the king, for to abate the power of felons, ordains a penalty in this case, so that from hence forth . . . they shall not spare any person nor conceal any felonies."[1]

In issuing this great prescription for purging crime and disorder in the countryside, Edward I not only established the basis for future administration of criminal justice but also perpetuated the tradition of the over optimistic reformer. Even the English Justinian could make little headway against crime in a society that openly accepted its presence as part of everyday life. Members of the king's council, representatives to Parliament, royal justices, officers of the peace, and the people of the shires all accepted crime as endemic to the human condition. The chronicler Matthew of Paris observed as keenly as did his sovereign that society was all too accepting of the inconveniences of crime because the people were themselves too much involved in illegal gains to report or punish offenders. "What wonder? The whole country-side was after the same mould, and theft was universal."[2]

Concern about the prevalence of disorder and felony was expressed in every quarter and by every class. The king promulgated statutes against lawlessness, undertook administrative reforms, and tried to rid himself of corrupt officials, while Commons pleaded for better law enforcement and punishment of corrupt officials. Lords kept household retainers to protect themselves against felons, but rural people complained bitterly that the lords' household troops were chiefly responsible for the violence. Justices pointed out that criminals brutalized and bullied them so that they could not do their work, while everyone accused the justices of selling justice like cows and punishing innocent men who could not pay them for acquittals. Peasant jurors would acquit their neighbors even after repeated criminal acts so that, when the jurors themselves were caught, their neighbors would do the same for them. While the members of the different estates in medieval England would have agreed with the Anglo-Saxon Chronicler that in a well-ordered realm "any honest man could travel over [the] kingdom without injury with his bosom full of gold, and no one dared strike another, however much wrong he had done him,"[3] they showed little interest in doing their part to aid the king in keeping the peace.

Complaints about the prevalence of crime, its increase, and the failure of proper authorities to deal with it are a part of the Western tradition of social griping. Such complaints seem to play as important a role in the expression of social discontent as crime itself. The problem for the historian is to unravel the counteraccusations, dramatic stories, and exaggerated figures from what was actually going on in the society at the time. Obviously, the place to start is the social and judicial context in which crimes occurred.

THE STRUCTURE OF THE RURAL COMMUNITY

The popular concept of medieval social organization is that it consisted of a mass of undifferentiated serfs cruelly dominated politically and economically by the nobility and the king and subject to rigid moral restrictions by the clergy. If this picture of medieval society is true, then the only tensions in society that would have produced criminal responses would have been those between the classes. One would imagine nobles plundering and murdering the peasants and they in turn ambushing nobles and clergy or supporting the exploits of some sturdy spokesman of their class, a Robin Hood. While the criminal records do show tensions between the three estates, most of the crimes were among the villagers and townspeople themselves. As a group they made up about 90 percent of the population and were as socially stratified and concerned about status differences as the working class of a modern industrialized country.[4]

The physical environment of the peasants varied somewhat depending upon the part of England in which they lived. Both the customs of the people who settled the area and the geography of the region influenced settlement and housing patterns.[5] The traditional division that has been made for the medieval English countryside is that between the champion (or open-field) country and the woodland. The champion country was settled in nuclear villages surrounded by large, open fields in which the peasantry held strips of land. The woodland, on the other hand, was closer to the modern family farm with settlements spread out in individual enclosed landholdings. Champion was the most common settlement and agricultural pattern in medieval England, so it is not surprising that most of the counties in this survey fall into this group. Huntingdonshire, Northamptonshire, and most of Norfolk, Surrey, Yorkshire, and Somerset had open fields and nucleated villages. Essex and Herefordshire, however, had more woodland-type settlements. Although the champion predominated, there were areas such as the moors of Somerset and Yorkshire, the Weald of Surrey, and the forest of Northamptonshire that never had this form of agriculture because they were unsuited for it. Other places, such as Surrey and Norfolk, were already beginning to be enclosed.[6] The division of settlements and agricultural patterns into champion and woodland is important because the two patterns influenced the social interactions of the peasantry.

The main features of champion country settlements are still readily observable in the English countryside, for centuries of cultivation have etched them on the land. Looking at the fields from a prominence, one can still see the washboard ridges and furrows of the strips; aerial photography shows them even more clearly. The open fields, two or more to a village, could be as large as several hundred acres. They were divided into strips for cultivation rather than cultivated as one large field. The strips were of various sizes depending upon the shape of the fields, the contours of the land, and the amount of plowing that could be done in one day. The peasants held strips in all the fields so that they could rotate their crops from one field to another. In the fall after harvest the first field was allowed to remain fallow and the village stock grazed on the stubble. The second field was then plowed and planted with the winter grain crops; in the spring the third field was plowed and planted with the summer crops. The working year followed the cycle of plowing and harvest. Neighbors worked side by side in their strips in the fields, often cooperating on the plowing by putting their animals together to form a plow team. They also worked the lord's land, which often was scattered among the peasant holdings in the open fields. Villages also had meadows, timber stands, and wastelands. The meadows provided hay to keep the livestock over the winter, and the wastelands and forests provided additional grazing, wood for fires and building, wild fruits, and wild animals poached from the lord's preserve.

The amount of land that each family held in the open fields varied considerably, depending not only upon the initial holding granted to the family but also upon their success at producing heirs, marrying women with land, farming profitably, and buying and selling land. While the standard holding for purposes of measurement was the virgate, roughly thirty acres, only the most fortunate peasants held this much land. The disparities in landholdings in the community led to a distinct social structure and to social tensions.

The plan of the villages differed somewhat from region to region in accordance with the function the village performed. In some of the herding areas village houses were arranged around a square where the cattle could be kept. Market towns might be organized around a market square. More typically, however, houses were clustered along the road passing through the center of the village. Such villages had a haphazard arrangement of streets and alleys in a vaguely radial pattern. By no means was there a necessary coincidence of the boundaries of a manor and a village. A manor could include a number of villages, and sometimes villages were split between two or more manors. For the purposes of this study, the village is more important than the manor, since the village was the unit responsible for the local administration of justice.

In their villages the tillers of the open fields had houses and plots of land for a garden and keeping animals. The plots were enclosed by walls or ditches and contained a house, outbuildings, kitchen gardens, and often an outside oven and well. Some houses doubled as shops and taverns. Supplemental occupations included blacksmiths, millers, bakers, potters, thatchers, carpenters, and weavers. The village women brewed ale, and some ran taverns as well. In addition to the villagers' homes, there was, of course, a church and residence of the priest and perhaps a residence for the lord of the manor or his officials.

The population of the villages ranged from 50 to 600 inhabitants, depending upon the amount of common land and the soil fertility. Since there were no regular census returns or parish records for the four-teenth century, it is impossible to determine the exact size of the villages. Various studies have attempted to estimate population using manorial court records, poll tax rolls, and so on. The average village population seems to have been between 150 and 300 inhabitants. Only market and fair towns would have had as many as 1000 inhabitants.[7]

The common fields of the champion country with their interspersed strips and emphasis on cooperation in regulating the use of the fields and pasture required that the inhabitants of the village live in con-stant, close contact with one another. Medieval England has been aptly described as "a world of neighbors."[8] To regulate their lives the villagers developed village bylaws covering day-to-day living prob-lems. Nevertheless, arguments about equal labor in the fields, boundary disputes over strips, trespasses with animals, stealing of crops, and jealousies over success were inevitable. In *Piers Plowman* the dishonest peasant (Avarice) describes the types of cheating in the common field: "If I went to the plough I pinched so narrowly that I would steal a foot of land or a furrow, or gnaw the half acre of my neighbour; and if I reaped, I would over-reap, or gave counsel to them that reaped to seize for me with their sickles that which I never sowed."[9] These disputes were routine matters of the manorial courts where they appear as suits for trespass, slander, wrongful gleaning, destruction by animals, assaults, debts, and disputed property rights.

Although the woodland type of agricultural settlement also had vil-lages that grew up around churches, manor houses, monasteries, and markets, the more typical settlement pattern was hamlets or individual farms. Individual or extended families worked their fields and put up fences or dug ditches around them. The countryside in places such as Essex and Kent, had the appearance of small, modern farms with their hedges, square fields, and clusters of buildings. As in the champion country, the same factors determined the size of holdings, which by no means were equal.

The traditional view of the medieval peasantry emphasizes the legal distinction between the villein (serf, on the Continent) and the free peasant. In practice these distinctions made little difference in the community. The significant differences among the peasantry were along less complicated lines; the "haves" and the "have nots." The "haves" held most of the land (whether in free or unfree tenure) and were able to hold in their family the chief village offices. Those holding thirty or more acres, the virgaters, were the most prominent

23

members of the village. The semi-virgaters held half the requisite acreage. Those below the semi-virgaters held only a few acres and had a cottage in the village.

The wealthier members of the community were not necessarily the free ones. Some of them were, but the lines became blurred with intermarriage and buying and selling of land. The same family could hold land for which they would have to perform the traditional work services as well as holding land free of these services. Sometimes one branch of the same family would be free and another not.[10] Contrary to expectation, also, the smaller holders and cottagers were more likely to be free than were the large landholders. They were the more mobile group in the peasantry, since profitable holdings did not bind them to one region or one village. They traveled about and settled where the prospects of employment looked best.[11] If the distinction among the different groups in the village by free or unfree status is inadequate to describe the divisions, so too is the distinction by landholding. The cottagers might only have a small piece of land, but if they also practiced a lucrative craft or trade, they might be among the wealthier villagers.

The most subtle differentiations of status in the village communities were indicators of prestige—those outward signs that modern sociologists call status symbols. Undoubtedly, these indicators often were clothing, housing, and horses and cattle. But, as the work of J. A. Raftis has shown, they also centered on control of the village offices. Dominating village governing responsibilities was more than an empty symbol of power. Those who were jurors, capital pledges, ale tasters, woodwards, reeves, and beadles, had considerable real control over the daily lives of villagers who could never hope to aspire to this group. Raftis found that the top group in the village (the primary villagers or A families) was composed of important local freemen and villeins. They were wealthy, having a virgate of land or a comparably lucrative trade or herds, and they were able to maintain family continuity and power over several generations.[12] As jurors in the manorial court they indicted people for trespasses, failures to perform work, and assaults and were responsible for determining the guilt and innocence of the indicted. They also judged private suits of debt, trespass, land disputes, slanders, and so on. At the hundred level or at the coroners' inquests they indicted people for felonies. Capital pledges headed their tithing group and guaranteed the behavior of its members. The ale tasters tested the quality of the ale and imposed fines when it was bad. The woodward regulated the collection of wood from the village woodland; the reeve looked after the administration of work on the lord's demesne land; and the beadle was the usual pledge for trespass cases. In these offices the primary villagers could regulate the lives of their less fortunate neighbors. They were an unpaid but powerful village oligarchy.

Those below this village elite are more difficult to classify. Raftis and his students have worked out various possible classifications for them.[13] I prefer to use the broad classifications of primary, secondary, and intermediate (or A, B, and C families). The secondary villagers were smaller landholders, not as wealthy as the primary villagers, but they certainly supported themselves from their land. They might even occasionally hold one of the coveted village offices. Their families had considerable continuity of village residence. Below this group were the intermediate villagers. They might have a cottage in the village or live as servants with the more prominent villagers or have a trade such as tinker that gave them greater mobility. Mostly they made their livings by hiring themselves out as laborers to the primary villagers or to craftsmen. Some of them had several generations of continuity, but they might also wander out of the village within one generation.

The distinctions between the three status groups caused conflicts among them. Secondary villagers coveted the power of primary villagers and resented their use of power. Intermediate villagers distrusted both groups above them for they were dependent upon them for their employment and for their treatment in court. The primary group, the village oligarchs, could easily be petty tyrants in using their social position to their own advantage unless strictly controlled by the customs of the manor. Customary village bylaws and traditions did much to check potential conflicts as did the need for community cooperation in agriculture for the sake of survival.

A unifying force in the society was the identity of the villagers with their community. A variety of institutions and customs emphasized community loyalty. All males twelve years of age or older (except clergy, nobility, and their household servants) were still, in the early fourteenth century, bound into tithing groups. Members of the group were legally responsible for reporting one another's misdeeds at the biannual view of frankpledge. If a person came from outside to settle in the village, he had to become a member of a tithing. This action gave a very immediate sense of who belonged and who was an outsider. Another community activity that indicated the boundaries

25

of membership was the perambulation of the village fields. This annual ceremonial walk established the village's distinction from the neighboring village. Frequently there were competitive games, such as football, between villages. Finally, there were cases in which the community acted together against the attempts of the lord to impose further labor services or monetary payments upon them, or times when the community would act as a militia against an outside invader.[14]

The feeling of community on the part of all status groups was a strong and useful bond for survival in the face of outside threats. One way to guard the bonds was to be suspicious of outsiders. Anyone lingering in the village had to find a villager, usually a prominent one, who would insure the good behavior of the visitor. The Anglo-Saxon rule had been that the first night a stranger, second night a guest, and third night a member of the household.

All communities had strangers wandering into them: people from neighboring villages, laborers looking for work, merchants, tinkers, pedlers, ecclesiastics, soldiers, and nobility. Some of these came to buy and sell goods, but others came to steal, trespass, exploit, or even murder. Some who passed through were beggars, transients, felons, and members of outlaw bands. Indeed, *vagabundus* often meant a person fleeing from a crime.[15] Strangers were a catalyst for criminal interactions. They either precipitated criminal activity or were the most obvious scapegoats for communal wrath and, therefore, were likely to be indicted on suspicion or to get involved in tavern brawls. The prosecution of strangers, whether guilty or not, confirmed the sense of village community.

Family as well as community was important for a villager's identity. Much of the routine of work, social interaction, and survival were bound up with other residents of the household. A physical description of the houses can be constructed largely on the basis of criminal records. The coroners' rolls have incidental information on the interiors and exteriors of the houses, and the goods stolen indicate the moveable chattels in them. The most common house construction for fourteenth-century England was a wooden frame consisting of curved uprights made of timber and a ridgepole running through the house, the cruck-type house. The plan resembled a modern A-frame or a slightly curved modification of it. The roofs were thatched or covered with sod. The walls between the supporting uprights were made of woven twigs covered with layers of mud, known as wattle and daub. The doors were of timber, the small windows were covered with wooden shutters or with canvas. So insubstantial were these dwellings that thieves often did not bother to enter by windows and doors but broke through walls instead. Sometimes these houses had modifications to their basic structure. If the uprights were sufficiently tall, there would be a second floor. Another modification was the long house with its series of uprights. Part of the long house was used for keeping stock. Such an arrangement was an odorous but efficient way to use the heat generated by the livestock for warming the family living quarters. Only a few areas had stone houses, but very few of these were for the peasantry in any part of England. Not until the fifteenth century did domestic architecture begin to improve.

Inside these houses the atmosphere was as cramped and "ful sooty" as the house that Chanticleer's owner inhabited.[16] Depending on the size of the house there were one or two rooms downstairs and a storage area upstairs, or maybe another room. The fireplace was usually an open hearth in the center of the room. With small windows and only a hole in the roof for the smoke to escape, the interior was often smokey. Fireplaces with chimneys were not a regular feature of domestic architecture even in wealthy homes until the end of the fifteenth century.[17] The straw or rushes covering the floors created a fire hazard. The rooms were sparsely furnished with a table, benches, chairs, a cradle, and beds. The household goods that appeared in the burglars' bundles included spoons, knives, trivets, pots and pans of brass, wooden bowls, sheets, blankets, canvas, cloth, cheeses, bacon, bread, and perhaps tools and other items connected with a cottage craft. Personal items such as clothing and jewelry were also stolen from these houses. Because the houses were so cramped and provided so few comforts, most activity took place outside.

The size of peasant households has been the subject of considerable discussion among historians. Josiah Cox Russell estimated 3.5 persons per household, but H. E. Hallam, working with more complete census data, placed the size at four people in the rather densely populated fenland of Lincolnshire. Both Russell and Hallam found that the nuclear family predominated, although in the fens of thirteenth-century Lincolnshire there were instances of single households and extended families.[18] The coroners' rolls give some information, particularly in burglary or house fire cases, on the number of people living in a household. The evidence is not entirely reliable because some members of the household, particularly young children, might have escaped attack from the burglars and therefore are not listed. Nevertheless, the Bedfordshire coroners' rolls, which are among the most detailed, show that the late thirteenth-century rural household was far from being a static unit.[19] The sample is a small one, twenty-five cases, but it indicates that the household size was upward of 3.5 persons and that there were a variety of household types. Just over half the households were nuclear families, but extended families with the husband's mother living with her son or two brothers or sisters living together were also present. Men and women also lived alone or with children. Servants lived in some of the houses with the nuclear family.[20] In counties such as Norfolk and Essex, which had partible inheritance, there may have been more extended families than there were in Bedfordshire, which had impartible inheritance.

The inheritance pattern in a region could have profound effects on intrafamilial relations. George C. Homans investigated some of the implications of partible inheritance for Norfolk. He argues that the policy of dividing up family holdings among all the surviving heirs meant that the land became divided into parcels too small to secure an adequate living for the cultivators and their families. To provide for themselves, people often sold their land or supplemented their income with cloth production; hence the early development of the woolen industry in Norfolk.[21] In other parts of England the custom of impartible inheritance either through primogeniture or Borough English (the youngest son or the one designated by the father inherited) might have encouraged the sons who were not going to inherit to plan careers in towns, in the army, or even in crime.

Even with the continual need for agrarian work in order to survive, there was time for leisure and conviviality. The luxury of the weekend was unknown, but Sunday was a day for some respite from work. Also, the yearly calendar was punctuated with a variety of religious feast days and pagan-rooted celebrations at the end of harvest. Sunday drinking started in the morning for the less devout members of the community who skipped Mass. Glutton in *Piers Plowman* is a good example:

> But Breton the Brewster bad him good morrow,
> And asked him with that whither he was going:
> "To holy church," said he, "to hear the service,
> And so I will be shriven and sin no longer."
> "I have good ale, gossip: Glutton, will you try it."[22]

Glutton went to the tavern and drank through to evensong. Others joined the early drinkers at the tavern after Mass. Drinking spilled out into the village green where there was also dancing. In addition to Sunday relaxation, marriages and funerals were customarily celebrated by feasting and ale drinking. There were also outdoor contests such as football, wrestling, knife games, and shooting at targets. Hunting, which was in fact poaching on the lord's preserve, was a favorite pastime.

A normal day's travel was a radius of five miles.[23] But villagers sometimes traveled farther to fairs, shrines, or the great city of London. Trips to the local market town, sometimes once a week, offered an opportunity to sell surplus agricultural or craft products and to buy those items of manufacture that could not be produced in the villages. It was also an opportunity to learn what was going on in London and the world. In the marketplace and taverns the villagers heard about the Scottish invasions, the battles of the war with France, the murder of Edward II's favorites, and the disappearance of the king himself. They exchanged information about the condition of peasants on other manors, about rebellions, about opportunities to serve in the king's armies, and about possible apprenticeships for sons. Plays, entertainments, religious spectacles would also be available. Villagers traveled much more than has traditionally been assumed. If it were not for this exposure to the world, books such as *Piers Plowman*, plays and ballads of the late Middle Ages, and even the Peasant Revolt of 1381 would not have been possible. In spite of robbers on the road and thieves and counterfeiters in the marketplace, trips to the towns were worth the effort.

Townspeople had a more varied environment than did those living in the countryside. Many of the market and fair towns, such as St. Ives, resembled overgrown villages with agriculture still the main occupation of the inhabitants and the status of the people still partially that of villeins. In other towns, such as Lynn and Leominster, there was more differentiation of occupation, with many of the inhabitants making their living as craftsmen, servants, hostlers, bakers, butchers, administrators, sailors, merchants, prostitutes, thieves, and fences. Although life in these towns was more diverse, it was not necessarily better than that found in the countryside. Coroners' roll evidence from London and Oxford for the early fourteenth century shows that housing was cramped; more people lived in tenements than in individual houses. Craftsmen and shopkeepers lived in their shops. Family size was smaller, with more single people.[24] The towns could not maintain a stable population without migration from the country. For children not inheriting land, the towns provided opportunities for making a living, both honest and dishonest. To the towns also came beggars, the lame, and the sick hoping for charity from the well-endowed town churches.

The towns, like the villages, were socially stratified. Lay and ecclesiastical lords might have a residence in the town. Their administrators and the king's officers, merchants, and members of the clergy made up another rank. Craftsmen, shopkeepers, victualers, and so on followed, progressing through the laborers, apprentices, and servants to the sick and the beggars.

Villagers and residents of the smaller towns had ties to their lords, be they lay, ecclesiastical, or royal overlords. Even with the best of lords, the relationship between the lord and his tenants was filled with tensions and distrust on both sides. The free tenants were hardly exempt for they had to pay rents and, because of the convenience of the manorial court and lack of other alternatives, they took their disputes to the lord's court as well. The manorial court not only enforced the village bylaws but also was a tool for punishing those who did not honor their commitments to the lord. The custumals, records of fees and services owed on the manors, stated the number of days a week peasants owed to the lord for service in his fields, workshops, and kitchens; occasions on which they could be asked for extra work; money or goods they owed on feasts; money they owed for marriage of a daughter or the career of a son in the clergy; entry fines for taking a new piece of land; and the livestock that had to be given as heriot when the peasant died. As if the financial and work obligations were not enough, their personal behavior was also restricted. The wood they used to heat their uncomfortable homes was obtained "by hook or by crook" from the lord's woods; women discovered having sexual relations before marriage paid a fine; grain could only be ground in the lord's mills, not in hand mills; at the lord's command the peasants had to provide hospitality for him and his officials; and the quality of the bread and ale was tested and taxed. Almost all aspects of a peasant's life could be turned to the lord's profit in or out of court.

The meetings of the manorial court, more than any other event of the tenants' life, brought home the control the lord exercised over the peasantry. At least twice yearly all males of villein status—and most freemen—over twelve years of age attended the sessions or paid a fine. At the sessions all infringements of manorial rules were presented, land transactions were recorded, and fines were collected. In sum, the manorial court was a time when the lord or his designated official could review the behavior of the tenants and make a profit from the fines imposed. It was also a time when the village oligarchs could impose restraints on their own group and those below them, for infringements of the village bylaws, trespass, debt, and slander cases were tried as well.

The relationships between the lord and the peasantry were complicated and ambiguous. The villagers with their strong community identity, self-government, and own leaders often rose in minor revolts against their lord. The lord had to insure his control over the peasantry, who considerably outnumbered him. The lord's officials, his steward and bailiffs, kept an eye on the villages so that unrest could be detected early and stopped. In addition the lord collected around him a group of armed retainers who made up his household or "baron's council" (also known as his *familia* or *meinie*). The lord's household served a variety of functions, including checking accounts, surveying the work of the stewards and bailiffs, waiting upon the lord, and serving as his bodyguards and personal ruffians.[25] The household retainers dressed in the livery of their lord and ate at his table.

The lord's household could be both a terror and a benefit to the villagers. When a peasant defaulted on payments or revolted, it was the lord's household that would be the ultimate source of discipline. Members of the household could enter a tenant's house, take his goods, and imprison him with impunity. On the other hand, if the lord wished to look after the interests of his peasants, he would use his household to punish their enemies. On balance, the practice of livery and maintenance, or "bastard feudalism," was a strain on the countryside and one of the great obstacles to providing public justice in the late Middle Ages.

The Church played a large part in the lives of all villagers. Church services and festivals marked the days of the week and the seasons of the year, church bells marked the hours of the day, and the sacraments of baptism and marriage and burial Masses marked the villagers' progress through life. The church was usually the best-constructed building in the village. It dominated the skyline. Within its walls could be held village festivities, meetings of the manorial court, and even the whole population of the village in times of war. In the eyes of the villagers, however, the Church was not always a benevolent influence. They regularly paid one-tenth of their incomes, the tithe, to the Church, so they were always reminded of the cost of maintaining the building and the clergy. Many villagers lived on ecclesiastical manors where members of the clergy were as exacting landlords as were the lay lords. The local priest was a formidable rival of the primary villagers for village power. Like the lay lords, the ecclesiastical lords maintained armed households that often contributed to disorder in the countryside and discomfort for the villagers. Throughout the fourteenth century there was increasing anticlericalism and criticism of the worldly Church. The villagers of fourteenth-century England were among the critics and eventually vented some of their hostility by becoming Lollards.

The countryside of fourteenth-century England contained a number of different interlocking social groupings. For the most part the groups worked well enough together so that food was produced; rents, tithes, and taxes were paid; trade carried on; towns grew; and kings reigned over the land and extended their bureaucracy throughout the country. But just because fourteenth-century England was not in a state of anarchy, it cannot be assumed that all went well among the different groups in society or that the king had complete control over either his subjects or his justice system. When community tensions errupted into crime, the whole society agreed that the king had the ultimate responsibility for returning stability to the system and punishing offenders.

The Criminal Justice System

The criminal justice system and the social system of the villages were bound together closely. The villagers had the primary responsibility for insuring the good behavior of their neighbors and for identifying, pursuing, catching, imprisoning, and trying felons. While the custom of the realm and the political theory of medieval Europe dictated that the king was the fountain of justice and the person with the ultimate authority for keeping the "king's peace," in England it had been the custom since Anglo-Saxon times for the king to delegate much of the responsibility to his subjects. To increase the efficiency of citizen participation in law enforcement and to insure that the king had ultimate control over it, the villagers were organized into various units of local government, each unit having its appropriate official.

The structure of local criminal jurisdiction was not a neat pyramid; its institutions were a combination of Anglo-Saxon custom, Norman feudal concepts, and various administrative experiments of the twelfth through fourteenth centuries. The administrative division of the country was the county or shire, which was divided into hundreds, which, in turn, were divided into vills or townships. In the early years of the fourteenth century a further division, the tithing group, was still important, but as it declined other institutions such as the vills (villages) and the justices of the peace took over its functions.[26] The officials at the different levels included a sheriff, coroners, and keepers or justices of the peace for the county as a whole, bailiffs in the hundreds, constables in the vills, and capital pledges in the tithing groups.[27]

The responsibility for detecting a felony and naming the suspect fell on the lowest of administrative units—the tithing groups and the vill. The most ancient method, which was still in use in the fourteenth century, was the hue and cry (*hutesium et clamor*). To initiate it within the vill, anyone coming upon evidence of a felony, such as a body, a house broken open, or a person in the act of theft, had to rouse the neighbors in pursuit of the suspect.[28] Pursuing a suspect was often dangerous for the villagers. For instance, John son of Peter of East Lexham followed the hue and cry when his neighbor, Emma wife of William Rook, raised it over a robbery. The robber, John Ballok, attacked John with a sword so that he had to defend himself with his axe.[29] John Ballok was killed in the encounter, but if the villagers had captured him alive, they would have had to guard him in the village or take him under guard to the county gaol.[30] Either option was risky and expensive for the villagers. They would have to take time from their work to prevent his escape and, if he had a gang supporting him, they would have to fight off a rescue attempt. When the suspected felon managed to escape beyond the borders of the hundred, the villagers had to notify the authorities in the next hundred to take up the pursuit.

The royal government made frequent attempts through statutes to increase the efficiency of local peacekeeping units. By the Assize of Arms in 1181 all males in tithing had to be armed and prepared to use their weapons in following the hue and cry.[31] The Statute of Winchester in 1285 consolidated the vills' duties by requiring all walled towns to shut their gates from sunset to sunrise and to place a watch at the gate. The watch arrested all strangers attempting to pass at night.[32] The king reconfirmed the statute in 1331 and made the constables of the vill responsible for its enforcement.[33]

The most common way to bring suspects to trial was through indictment in the sheriff's tourn at the view of frankpledge rather than through the hue and cry. Twice a year the sheriff made a tour (hence "tourn") of his county, visiting each hundred and holding a view of frankpledge to insure that all men were in tithing groups. In addition he heard presentments of criminal activities in the hundred. Again the tithing group and the vill were indispensible, for they made the presentments. The members had to report all felonies committed by or against them and any occurring in their neighborhood. Sometimes the vills made the presentments rather than the tithing groups.[34] Vills and tithing groups paid fines to the king for failure to report crimes.[35] In Wakefield a vill was amerced because it concealed the theft of 9s. in silver and one-half stone of wool for nine years.[36] Not everyone in the village had to attend the view of frankpledge; the capital pledge or reeve and four men from the vill along with the constable were usually enough.

A jury of twelve men from the hundred, a grand jury, heard the presentments.[37] While the vills were supposed to present all cases in which there was suspicion of felonious behavior, the system allowed for a good bit of abuse. People could be falsely accused of crimes to get them incarcerated and punished. The duty of the jury was to try to sort out the false accusations and decide if the evidence presented was sufficiently convincing for indictment.[38] If they did decide on indictment, the sheriff instructed the bailiff of the hundred to make the arrest.

Although the sheriff held the tourn and heard the presentments, the bailiff carried out the ordinary administrative tasks associated with criminal justice in the hundred. He attended the sheriff's tourn, was present at the coroners' inquests, arrested those indicted and took them to gaol, collected fines, distrained chattels of suspects, delivered writs, and impanelled juries both for indictments and trials.[39] The bailiff's task was not always an easy one. For example, the bailiff of Rydale in Yorkshire, who went to arrest John Annotsen of Ness and nine other men indicted for larceny, was wounded, maltreated, and finally decapitated by the gang.[40] Bailiffs saw that they were well compensated for their risks. They were either royal appointees or else made a contract with the sheriff in which they undertook to pay a certain amount for the office and carry out the requisite duties. They derived their own pay from what they could charge or extort in office.[41]

The detection and indictment procedure was slightly different in homicide cases. The king directed each county to elect four coroners from among its knights so that a royal official could arrive at a homicide case within a day or two of the discovery of the body.[42] When villagers discovered a body that showed evidence of unnatural death (death by misadventure, homicide, or suicide), they notified one of the coroners. The coroner ordered the hundred bailiff to summon a jury of the vill and several neighboring vills for an inquest into the cause of death. The coroner then viewed the body and noted all wounds that might have caused the death. If there was suspicion of felony in the death, the coroner requested the jurors to name suspects and then directed the bailiff to arrest them. When the circuit justices came to deliver the county gaol, the coroner attended and brought his records from the inquests.[43]

The policing methods described so far would seem to favor the felons. Unless the villagers caught felons red-handed during the hue and cry, the felons had ample warning that they were suspected of crimes and could easily escape between the time of indictment and arrest. The royal government was aware of the inefficiency of the system and experimented with new county officials during the course of the fourteenth century. The keepers of the peace (later called justices) were one of the many governmental experiments in keeping order. Until 1307 the keepers were to help the sheriff to enforce the king's peace and the Statute of Winchester.[44] During 1307-1308 they received the additional powers to arrest malefactors and to pursue them from hundred to hundred and from shire to shire.[45] The government hoped that this power would facilitate the capture of disturbers of the peace who crossed jurisdictional lines that bailiffs and members of the vill could not cross. During Edward II's Scottish campaign the keepers were also empowered to hold inquiries into felonies by sworn inquest and to arrest suspects.[46] The purpose of this measure was to eliminate the time between indictment and arrest that made it so easy for notorious bands of felons to escape.[47] Sometimes the keepers of the peace were given judicial powers, but their usual role in criminal justice in the first half of the fourteenth century was sworn inquests and arrest.

In addition to community indictment of suspects, individuals could bring charges against suspects as the victim of a crime or by becoming a king's approver (turning state's evidence). In a private appeal the victim or the next of kin of a murdered person could come to the county court and bring suit against the person or persons suspected of committing the crime.[48] In an appeal of rape the woman had to appear before the coroner and show through torn clothing and wounds that she had resisted the rapist.[49] The advantage of private appeal was that the victim could get back stolen property rather than lose it to the crown. The hazard was that the appealer who lost was fined. For instance, Thomas the Shepherd accused John Dish of stealing a sheep. The jury acquitted John and Thomas was imprisoned until he paid a fine.[50]

The king's approver was a felon who confessed his guilt and named the people who had aided him in committing the crimes. A suspect usually turned approver in gaol or during the trial when it looked as if he would be convicted. He then called for the coroner to record his confession and the names of his accomplices. After the appeals the coroner instructed the sheriff to arrest the people named. The approver was maintained in prison at the king's expense until the trial.[51]

The attraction of becoming an approver was that it prolonged the prisoner's life and perhaps even gave him time to escape or to get a pardon from the king.[52] John Kyronn, for example, appealed a number of people for crimes that were never committed. It took two years for the sheriff to check out the false appeals.[53] If a substantial number of those appealed were convicted, the approver might be allowed to abjure the realm.[54]

Jurors obviously did not trust the testimony of approvers for only 9 percent of those they appealed were convicted. Approvers were hanged as confessed felons as soon as someone they appealed was acquitted. Perhaps another reason why the jurors did not trust approvers was that they often made their appeals under duress. The gaolers and sheriffs might torture some unfortunate inmate of the gaol to appeal wealthy people or enemies of the sheriff so that they could make a profit from the accused who would pay to get out of gaol or to quash the charge. This practice was so common that approvers frequently testified in gaol delivery that they had been tortured to confess.[55] William Challe accused two gaolers in York Castle of forcing him to become an approver by applying "pirwynkes" to his fingers.[56] In spite of the unreliability of the approvers, the government continued to encourage their use because their appeals were often the only way to identify members of established criminal bands. During the 1320s the great increase in approver cases almost looks like a concerted government effort to encourage their use.[57]

The sheriff and his bailiffs had to track down and arrest suspects once they were appealed or indicted. The arrest process was not always easy because suspects had ample time to escape. Some felons went immediately to churches where they sought sanctuary so that they could abjure the realm. To procure the right to abjure they had to stay in the church continuously forty days and forty nights. The villagers guarded the church to see that the suspects did not escape.[58] Before the end of forty days the coroner came, took the confession of guilt for the crime and an oath from the person that he would abjure the realm. The coroner designated a port for his departure; gave him a cross to identify his status on the way to the coast; and set a time limit for getting there. If he exceeded the time or if he left the road, he could be killed or brought to gaol delivery and hanged.[59] John son of Nicholas le Woodward of Cheddar was found wandering around Wells after he had abjured the realm at Cheddar and was assigned to go to Lyme. Since he had left the king's highway, he was hanged at gaol delivery.[60] Many abjurors must have been luckier than John and been able successfully to hide their identity and live in another area.

Other suspects who avoided arrest simply went into hiding immediately and became outlaws. If the accused failed to appear in county court for four consecutive sessions to answer charges, he was outlawed.[61] Originally outlawry meant that the person was outside the law and could be killed outright if he were found.[62] Although the law still stood in the fourteenth century, most outlaws were either arrested, if found, or procured pardons.[63] Capturing a notorious outlaw was every bit as exciting in fourteenth-century England as on the American frontier. When John of Lincoln defied arrest for various murders, William of Slingesby and others formed a posse and tracked him down. They found him sheltered in a house, which they sieged and broke into. The outlaw was killed in the struggle.[64] Another outlaw, Hugh le Prest, was dragged out of his hiding place and beheaded after a pursuit involving the sheriffs and posses of two counties.[65]

After arrest the accused had to be incarcerated or bailed until trial. Usually the prisoner was taken to the county, municipal, or franchisal gaol, or occasionally to one of the central gaols such as Newgate, Fleet, or the Tower of London.[66] These fourteenth-century gaols warranted their evil reputations. Prisoners were kept in crowded, damp dungeons underground or in rooms in the castle towers. One case in particular gives insight into the conditions. Richard Sapling came before the justices of gaol delivery in August 1308 and presented a piece of parchment with the king's seal attached. He claimed that the parchment was his charter of pardon but that during the winter he had been kept exposed to the elements in the north tower and that "during that time his charter was in water except for the case of the seal."[67] Not surprisingly, coroners' rolls indicate frequent death from "gaol fever" and starvation.

The sheriff was responsible for the upkeep and staffing of the gaol. Gaolers, like bailiffs, paid the sheriff or owner of the franchisal gaol for the office. As the gaoler received little or no salary, he sought his remuneration in charging prisoners for their meals, bed linens, and the privilege of wearing lighter irons.[68] Wealthy prisoners could buy comfortable accommodations from the gaoler, but for the ordinary villager the period of waiting in gaol for trial was very expensive. For the poorer prisoners, charitable gifts of food were all that stood between them and starvation.[69] At the sentencing most of the felons had no chattels; even a moderate wealth could be quickly consumed in gaol.

Other abuses of the gaolers, besides torturing prisoners into becoming approvers, frequently appeared in the records. Female prisoners were at the mercy of gaolers and other prisoners, for the common cells were mixed. Thomas Porter, gaoler of Richmond gaol, was accused of adulterous rape of a woman prisoner. The rape was adulterous because she was in his care.[70] Falsely appealed prisoners were often willing to pay the gaoler high prices to stay out of gaol or to be comfortable in it. Some gaolers were so accommodating to the wishes of their more violent or wealthier prisoners that they were willing to help them escape from gaol for the right amount of threats or money.[71]

Fortunately, the time spent in gaol was usually brief. If the justices came every four months to deliver the gaol as they were supposed to, then at most only a third of a year was lost, depending, of course, on when the suspect was arrested. In 18 percent of the cases the suspect was tried the year of the crime; in 31 percent, a year after the crime; in 15 percent, two years after; and in 10 percent, three years afterward (see appendix D). The other 26 percent were tried anywhere from four to ten or more years after the crime for which they were charged was committed.

Although the usual judicial lag was short, the time in gaol could be cruelly lengthened for the least occurrence out of the ordinary at the trial. The most common cause of delayed trial was the default of a hundred jury or an official. Some suspects might be bailed at this time, but many were returned to prison. If the jurors had to come from another county, the process could take years. One of the most frustrating of these cases was that of William of Leake who was taken on suspicion of stealing a horse that he had actually bought legally at Boston fair in Lincolnshire. It took two years for the Lincolnshire jury to come to Norwich and confirm his story.[72] Richard Sapling spent at least seven winters in Norfolk Castle while the authenticity of his water-damaged charter of pardon was being checked in Chancery.[73] Since he disappears from the rolls, it is impossible to say whether the search was finally successful or whether he eventually succumbed to the same dampness as his charter.

Fortunately for the accused, gaol was not inevitable, for granting of bail or releasing people on mainprise (to sureties) was very common. By the Statute of Westminster I (1275) anyone who was not accused of a heinous crime such as homicide or treason could be bailed.[74] To be bailed the accused had to find sureties who undertook responsibility for his appearance at the trial. If he did not come, the sureties were amerced. The sheriff, who had control over the granting of bail, often ignored the statutory limitation on eligibility. Commons deplored the havoc that bailed murders, robbers, and other malefactors raised.[75]

Those accused people who were finally caught and put into custody were tried at a gaol delivery session. Circuit justices, appointed by the central government, traveled from county to county and from gaol to gaol trying those accused of felonies. Three writs were necessary to set in motion the machinery for a delivery. A writ commissioning justices to deliver specific gaols was issued through letters patent.[76] The sheriff received a writ *de Intendendo* in a letter close that ordered him to prepare for the coming of the justices. And finally, the appointed justices sent a writ, *venire facias*, in the king's name giving the sheriff full instructions about the date of the delivery.[77] New writs to commission justices of gaol delivery were not issued for every regular session. A writ could be valid for several years unless one of the justices was removed from the commission.[78]

Although the central government made several attempts to regulate the frequency of gaol delivery by statute, in practice the number of deliveries per year depended upon the amount of business and upon the administrative efficiency of the central government. By a statute in 1299, gaol delivery, like assize, was to be held at least once a year but not more than three times a year.[79] In 1330 another statute placed the minimum at three times a year.[80] Both these statutes went unobserved, although, normally, the justices did come two to three times a year in the vacations of the central courts. Thus there were spring, summer-autumn, and winter deliveries.[81]

Statutory law also attempted to regulate the personnel of the commissions. The statute of 1299 required that the same justices who took assize should also deliver the gaols while they were in the county.[82] In terms of the qualifications of the judges this meant that they were experienced central court justices who either had a formal legal education or who had a great knowledge of the law. These requirements were often set aside, and local men had to be relied upon to take up the commission.[83] Statutes also required that the judges should not be property holders in the county where they were hearing pleas so that they would be more impartial.[84]

The sessions of gaol delivery usually took place in the county castle or the town hall of the city where the gaol was located.[85] Most of the preparation for the delivery rested with the sheriff and his staff. As soon as he received notification of an impending delivery, the sheriff prepared the calendar of cases to be tried and made a public proclamation of the day of the delivery so that all whose duty it was to appear would be at court. He also impanelled hundred juries and notified the coroners, bailiffs, and franchise officers to be present.[86]

On the day of the sessions the justices sat on the bench while the prisoner stood at the bar to be tried. The court must have been very full, for all the county officials were present in addition to the twelve to twenty-four men from each hundred who made up the trial juries. When the prisoner stood at the bar, the indictment against him was read out from the sheriff's calendar or the coroners' roll. The judge then asked him how he wished to plead. The accused had several options—he could refuse to answer the charges; deny his guilt and ask for a jury; claim benefit of clergy; confess his guilt and become an approver; or ask to prove his innocence by combat if his appealer was an approver.

By far the most common choice was for a jury trial:

[The accused] comes and being asked how he wishes to acquit himself thereof denies the [particular felony] consent, company, all felony and whatever is against the peace, etc. And for good and ill puts himself therefore on the country.

The sheriff then called a jury of twelve men from the hundred in which the crime was committed. The accused could challenge, without showing cause, any number of jurors less than thirty-six, or three whole juries.[87] William Strangbowe, who was accused of murdering Alainore de Bello Monte at Skerynyng and her servant and of stealing 60s. from them, refused three juries. The judge returned him to prison.[88] The refusal of juries raised a problem because the juries acted as witnesses; the accused might clear himself by refusing the maximum number. But the rejected juror might still influence the jurors selected or be consulted as a witness.[89] The jurors gave a unanimous verdict from their knowledge of the case. Witnesses might be called upon to testify or the accused might offer an alibi, but the jurors were to make their inquiries before they came to court.[90] Because of this dual role of juror and witness, it was possible for the indictment jury and the petit jury to have the same personnel or for the victim to be on the jury.[91] In addition to deciding on guilt or innocence, the jurors might suggest extenuating circumstances that would permit the person to be pardoned or excused. On the basis of the jury's evidence, the justices of gaol delivery consulted and passed sentence on the accused and specified the punishment or returned the person to gaol for further information.

Justice was swift on the day of the trial. In a sample of six deliveries of Norwich Castle gaol an average of forty-six persons were tried per day. These six deliveries were carefully selected—they all were followed immediately by a delivery of Norwich City gaol so that the beginning and end of the delivery could be determined exactly. Assuming that the justices worked at the most ten to twelve hours a day, a normal day's load of forty-six cases would allow about five to seven cases per hour or about fifteen minutes per case. The highest number of people tried per day was seventy-one in the famine year of 1316 when on March 15-16 one hundred forty-two people were tried. The swiftness of justice gave the jurors a large role in the trial process, for the judge had to rely almost entirely on their knowledge of the case and of the reputation of the suspect.

If the allegation of crime came from an approver, the accused could demand the right to a trial by combat. Armed with shields and clubs pointed with iron, the two combatants met on the field before the judges. The accused denied the charge word for word. The approver repeated the accusation and swore that it was true. The fight then commenced until one was killed or cried "craven." Whoever cried "craven" was hanged. If the approver won, he would confront another man he had appealed or he would be hanged on the strength of his confession of guilt.[92] One approver, Galfred Chalener, refused to fight when the man he appealed asked for a duel because he claimed that the fight would be unfair since he lacked two fingers. The judge upheld his objection and the accused went before a jury.[93]

The accused might also stand mute before the justices and refuse to plead. In such cases the judges returned him to prison *ad dietam* or under *peine forte et dure* until he died or agreed to plead.[94] The author of *Vita Edwardi Secundi* gives a vivid description of the process:

> When [the suspect] was brought before the justices, questioned and accused of many crimes, he did not answer. He was therefore thrust back into prison at the discretion of the judges to undergo his sentence. The customary punishment, indeed, for those mute of malice is carried out thus throughout the realm. The prisoner shall sit on the cold bare floor, dressed only in the thinnest of shirts, and pressed with as great a weight of iron as his wretched body can bear. His food shall be a little rotten bread, and his drink cloudy and stinking water. The day on which he eats he shall not drink, and the day on which he has drunk he shall not taste bread. Only superhuman strength survives this punishment beyond the fifth or sixth day.[95]

Usually the person who stood mute gave in and agreed to plead. Matilda Mese stood mute when she was accused of breaking into the house of Alice, niece of the vicar of Depsham, and taking goods valued at 40s. She was returned to gaol where she gave in under torture and was convicted in the following session.[96] The only advantage of dying under *peine forte et dure* rather than hanging was that the heirs got the accused's possessions rather than the crown. Standing mute was very uncommon: only 0.8 percent did so.

Indicted members of the clergy could claim the rights of benefit of clergy before going before a jury. The prisoner had first to prove that he was a clerk, either by a literacy test, by appearing in proper tonsure and habit, or by having an ecclesiastical representative—an ordinary—come to court with notice from the bishop that the accused was a member of the clergy in his diocese. Clerical privilege extended to all persons who received orders and covered all cases but high treason.[97] Thus even students and others who had only entered the lowest ranks of the Church were excluded from punishment by the king. The cleric was tried by the jury and, if convicted, was released to the care of his ordinary. The king detained his chattels until the convicted clerk could purge his offense in the bishop's court.[98]

For lay people as well there were ways to stay the hangman's noose either permanently or temporarily. Children under twelve years of age could expect the charges against them to be dropped because they had not reached the age of reason and could not be expected to distinguish right from wrong in their actions. The insane were pardoned for their criminal actions for the same reason, and people who killed by misadventure (accident) or in self-defense could expect a pardon.[99] Serving in the king's army or foreign wars for a year was a way for known felons and outlaws to procure a pardon. Increasingly, the abuse of selling pardons became a problem. Usually only men could get pardons for military service, but Alice daughter of Roger de Walton was pardoned "in consideration of her having for a long time followed the king . . . in Brittany."[100] Few pardons appeared in gaol delivery; only 1.5 percent of all those tried were pardoned (only 5 percent of these were female).

Since canon law prohibited killing unborn children in the womb of a convicted felon, pregnant women could delay execution until their babies were born. The court did not accept the woman's word about her condition, but appointed a jury of matrons to examine her. If they confirmed her pregnancy, she was returned to prison until the child was born. One woman, Matilda Hereward of Brandiston in North-amptonshire, was able to prolong her life at least a year and a half by being pregnant every time the justices came to deliver the gaol. She and her husband were found guilty of larceny in the delivery of June 21, 1301. They were sentenced to be hanged, but she was returned to gaol until her child was born. Again on September 25, 1301, she was returned to prison because she was pregnant. Likewise the justices found her pregnant on January 15, 1302, June 5, 1302, October 26, 1302, and January 22, 1303.[101] After that date there is a gap in the records, so that we do not know the ultimate fate of Matilda. Since her husband had been hanged in 1301, one assumes that the mixed prison conditions must have made repeated pregnancy possible—indeed, perhaps impossible to avoid.

The court dealt quickly with those who could find no way to delay punishment. The felon's movable chattels and the proceeds from his land for one year became the property of the king. The usual punishment for convicted felons was hanging (94.9 percent of those convicted were hanged), which took place within a couple of hours after conviction or at the most a couple of days.[102] Some lucky people were saved by friends or fellow gang members even at this late moment in heroic rescues from the gallows. People who committed treason—spying, counterfeiting, killing one's lord, or for women killing their husbands—were treated to an aggravated form of capital punishment. Men were drawn behind carts to the gallows and then were hanged (0.6 percent of those convicted died in this manner) and women were burned to death (again 0.6 percent of the convicted). If the value of goods stolen in a theft was under 12d., custom provided a number of minor punishments. The person might be found guilty but released *sine die* (1.8 percent of the convicted were released without cause for punishment). Sometimes the justices would sentence the person to the pillory (0.6 percent of the convictions).[103] Other times the person would be sentenced to a day in prison for each penny worth of goods stolen or the justices would decide that the person had already been sufficiently punished by pretrial imprisonment.[104] Only 0.7 percent of the convicted had prison sentences. The barbarous punishments of mutilation, which were common in Tudor England, were rare in the fourteenth-century records.

In summary, the most common way of detecting felons was through an indictment made by the villagers in the sheriff's tourn, at the coroner's inquest, at the sworn inquest of the keeper of the peace, or before the bailiff of a liberty granted the right to take presentments. After indictment the sheriff or one of his subordinates, the hundred bailiff, or the keeper of the peace arrested the accused, if he had not already fled. Arrest without previous indictment could be done in the village by hue and cry if a felon was caught red-handed and by the keeper of the peace if the suspect was of notorious reputation. Suspects could also be arrested on the accusation of the victim or of an approver. If the accused avoided arrest or failed to appear in court, he was outlawed. While awaiting the arrival of the gaol delivery justices, the suspects were either kept in gaol or held on bail. The justices of gaol delivery were appointed by the crown to travel in circuits and try the felony cases in the county gaols. Usually, the suspects had a trial by jury with the jurors collecting evidence and deciding on the guilt or innocence of the accused. The judges passed sentence on the basis of their evidence. Throughout the process from detection through sentencing the villagers played a major role in deciding which of their neighbors would be indicted and which ultimately would be hanged. Their attitude toward law enforcement and their tolerance of felonies are, therefore, essential to know in order to understand the social context of fourteenth-century crime.

SOCIAL ATTITUDES TOWARD LAW ENFORCEMENT AND CRIME

Modern historians have been quick to condemn the medieval kings, officers of the law, and jurors for failing to enforce the laws against felons effectively.[105] It is an easy conclusion to reach, for certainly our society would not tolerate the prevalence of crime and the overt corruption of justice that existed then. Historians reinforce their conclusions with references to statements such as are found in the Statute of Winchester quoted near the beginning of this chapter and the numerous petitions from Commons. Having made an essentially ethnocentric value judgment on the state of the king's peace in the countryside and further indicated the horrors of disorder in the Middle Ages, they leave the topic without asking why there was corruption at all levels and why people were willing to tolerate such a high level of lawlessness. Certainly, the populace was not ignorant of the law or of their obligations in regard to its enforcement.

England in the Middle Ages had the reputation of being the most violent country in Europe and also the one where people most enjoyed protracted lawsuits. Surviving records show that probably both descriptions are justified. From the lowest manorial court to the king's courts at Westminster the interest in pleading and the ingenuity and legal knowledge of the plaintiffs and defendants is obvious. The legal knowledge also appears in popular literature such as the Robin Hood ballads.[106] The English language became increasingly enriched in the fourteenth century with legal terms such as to "allege" and "deny" and to "rely" on the "gist of the matter."[107] In spite of the prevalence of legal knowledge, crime went unpunished and the kings and people complained. It is obvious that simple inefficiency cannot account for the lawlessness or public opinion would have brought about a change. Rather, the corruption and inefficiency served a variety of useful functions in the society.

The peasantry, craftsmen, and townspeople left little direct evidence of complaints about official corruption and bad justice, but we know something of their opinions from the literature they were familiar with and their actions in the revolt of 1381, when justices were attacked and their rolls destroyed. A Latin poem of the early four-teenth century put the problem thus: "The lawful man shall be put in prison; the thief who ever does wrong shall escape." In another place the common man's feeling was "Jack Trewman doeth you know that falsness and gyle havith regned to long, and trewth hath ben sette under a lokke, and falseness regneth in everylk flokke. No man may come trewthe to, but he sing 'dedero' [bribe]." In sermons preachers told the poor man, "Iff he goth to the law there is no helpe; for trewly lawe goys as lordship biddeth him."[108]

The gentry and the knights of the shire also had their complaints. The "Tale of Gamelyn," which was so popular that Chaucer used it later in the century, spoke of the problems of the knights and gentry who were dispossessed of their land and found that the justices and sheriffs would do nothing to help them. Gamelyn finally got justice only by attacking the judge at the session and taking his place.[109] In a fourteenth-century poem, "The Outlaw's Song of Trailbaston," the speaker complains of the use of law to frame him and the impossibility of getting a fair judgment in his case because of corrupt justices and sheriffs. The only choice left to him, a member of the upper class, was the greenwood and outlawry.[110] The gentry and knights also expressed their dissatisfaction in Parliament through various pleas to the king to keep order in his realm.

Was the justice system as corrupt as literary evidence indicates? Ample official records demonstrate that, from the king down to the lowest peasant, justice was sold or subverted for particular interests. Control over the justice system also guaranteed financial rewards and opportunities to dominate others socially and politically.

Although it was important to fourteenth-century English kings to keep the countryside of England peaceful and to gain as much revenue as possible from the criminal justice system, they often compromised. While they needed to have peace at home and money for foreign wars, the kings also needed troops for their campaigns. This gave rise to the abuse of granting pardons to known felons who would serve the kings in their wars. After all, the felons were skilled in arms and known for their brutality. But after the campaigns the felons returned to England where they formed criminal bands and lived by plundering the coun-tryside. The kings also would have liked to stop the growth of the nobles' private armies, but they had to rely upon them, as well, to support their foreign wars. The kings understood very well the com-plaints of Commons when they petitioned for the removal of corrupt justices, sheriffs, and gaolers,[111] but the officials were not salaried and the kings and the rest of the society assumed that the officials should have some profit from their offices to make them worthwhile.

The kings' circuit justices bore the brunt of bitter satire and heartfelt lament. John Bromyard, one of the most biting satirists, said that the bench was the fastest way to become a wealthy man.[112] One of his best known satires, which exists in several forms, was the story of a judge who received an ox from one of the litigants before the trial. The other side gave the judge's wife a cow. On the day of the trial, the judge favored the latter. The angry litigant whispered into the judge's ear, "Thou oxe, speke for me as thou hyetest me!" The judge replied, "The oxe may not speke, for the cowe wyle not sufferyn hym!"[113] In a political song, "On the Venality of Judges," a writer complains that not only the judge has to be paid but also his clerks, messengers, ushers, and so on. Some people, according to the author, are more successful than others at having their civil cases decided: beautiful and noble women, the wealthy who can pay for justice, the nobles who can use their influence and their private armies. But the poor will have to follow the judge all around the circuit hoping for a chance to have their case heard.[114] These themes appeared in the Robin Hood legends and in the tale of Gamelyn as well.[115] The charges are not mere literary exaggerations, and they apply to both civil and criminal cases. The biographer of Justice Scrope found that the judgeship did make him a very wealthy man.[116] In 1340-1342 there was so much public pressure on the king that he had to fine three of his most renowned justices— Willoughby, Shardelowe, and Inge—for taking bribes. They were all back in their positions within two years.[117]

Political songs and satires also accused sheriffs of corruption.

Who can tell truly
  How cruel sheriffs are?
Of their hardness to poor people
  No tale can go too far.
If a man cannot pay
  They drag him here and there,
They put him on assizes,
  The juror's oath to swear.
He dares not breathe a murmur,
  Or he has to pay again,
And the saltness of the sea
  Is less bitter than his pain.[118]

Again, the songs do not exaggerate what the records tell so well. Sheriffs could quash indictments or grant bail for a fee, stop legitimate appeals of felony, force prisoners to become king's approvers and make false appeals, and indict innocent people who would pay to have a packed jury. They could also quash writs, forge them, or refuse to receive them.[119] Those who complained about the sheriff could easily face indictment, expensive jury service, or confiscation of their chattels.

The sheriff's clerks and minor appointees were also corrupt. The peasants felt particularly bitter about these officials because they were drawn from their own ranks and should have been more sympathetic.

> Oh, the sheriff's clerks!
>   Needy folk at first,
> Poor like others, suffering
>   From hunger and thirst;
> But when they get a bailiwick
>   How they grow and swell!
> Their teeth grow long, their heads grow high,
> Houses, lands, and rents they buy,
>   And pile up gold as well.
> They scorn their poor neighbours,
>   They govern by new rules,
> That is reconed wisdom now
>   In our modern schools.[120]

The bailiffs had charge of impanelling juries. Through this office they had considerable direct control over who would be on a jury and what the final verdict would be. A bailiff could also make profits when he distrained the animals of felons, for he could drive them away to his own house and sell them or let the felon's family keep them for a price. The sheriff's and bailiff's clerks also had opportunities to collect bribes for their services.[121]

The king's particular watchdogs in the counties, the coroners, were also corrupt, although they were suspected less frequently than other officials.[122] The coroners were the only elected county officials. Apparently the office was sufficiently profitable from bribes that candidates made large gifts to obtain the post.[123] The coroners were supposed to serve free, but often they would charge the villagers anything from ls. 6d. to 6s. 8d. to hold an inquest. They could also undervalue the suspect's chattels and keep part for themselves. Probably their most profitable income was from bribes to quash indictments made either at the inquest or from an approver's appeals. Bribes for this service were £1.[124]

Bribes to officers of the peace were well worth it, if one could thereby stay out of prison. In the "Outlaw's Song of Trailbaston" the writer says that he paid 40s. to the sheriff to avoid prison and that many people choose to live as outlaws rather than languish in prison.[125] The wretched conditions in the county gaols and the malpractices of the gaolers justified these fears. People were so terrified of gaolers that jurors very seldom found gaolers guilty of the mysterious deaths in gaols or the claims of approvers that they had been tortured.[126]

People of all ranks complained about corruption, but did little themselves to rectify it because they could use the justice system to aggrandize their own local power. The magnates of the realm might complain that justice was better the century before when they tried criminal cases in their seignorial courts. But, in fact, they had about as much power through their manipulation of the king's justice. The *quo warranto* proceedings of the late thirteenth century emphasized to the magnates that the king, not themselves, had the power to try criminal and civil pleas. The king might dispense with their franchisal rights, but he could not eliminate their domination of the judicial system in their own districts.[127] Using tactics of jury intimidation, bribery, armed trespasses, protection rackets, and taking over the local judicial system for entire regions, the magnates were able to increase their own power and wealth.

Getting an indictment against a powerful noble was almost impossible. When John Gan testified at the assize against Lord John de Mandeville, Lord John sent two of his household retainers to Gan's house where they assaulted him and broke his arm "as a warning to others."[128] If maltreatment or bribes did not persuade the jurors, then the lords turned their attention to the justices. Roger son of Lord Robert de Brent, two of the Hywis brothers, and three other men wounded and maltreated one of the justices of assize who was holding the sessions at which they were finally indicted.[129] Justices responded to gentler means of persuasion than physical assault. In a very modern sounding letter a justice wrote to a young noble that, "for the love of your father I have hindered charges being brought against you and have prevented execution of indictment actually made."[130] If neither love nor money could stop a case, then the noble might try to stop the session altogether. Sir Roger Swynnerton of Staffordshire and his supporters closed the doors of the hall where the county court was being held and threatened to kill the sheriff if he tried to start the session.[131] Another way to halt a case was to prevent a victim from testifying in court. Sir William Bradshaw appeared at court with sixty armed men and prevented Cecilia le Boteler from bringing an appeal against him.[132]

The gentry, seeing through the example of the magnates that holding office could be used to consolidate local prestige and insure success in private legal suits, pushed for a greater part in county government. The members of the Commons continually urged the kings to extend the powers of the keepers of the peace and make them justices of the peace so that they could hear and determine cases in addition to taking indictments. Gratifying the wishes of Commons was rather like turning over the care of a herd of sheep to the wolves. The members of Parliament who were active in petitioning the king to enforce the laws or reform abuses of justice were themselves in some cases people with criminal records. Some members even had been indicted for homicide and robbery.[133] Edward II was the first to crumble to these demands and, not surprisingly, the deterioration of government is often dated from his reign.[134]

By 1351 when the justices of the peace were established, the gentry had won their battle. They used their powers over criminal and civil law as a weapon of local politics. They could throw their enemies into gaol, possess their goods, or pack a jury to convict them.[135] The magnates found that it was very helpful to secure the appointment of their followers among the gentry to the office of justice of the peace. From that position they could work for the magnates. The feudal relations between the gentry and the magnates of late medieval England were no longer reckoned in terms of land and fighting service but in terms of money and power brokering within the justice system.[136] In the first half of the fourteenth century, the gentry were still struggling to get the office of justice of the peace recognized, so that their chief influence was still through the more traditional lines of coroner and other such county offices.

With the corruption of justice from the judges down to the lowest clerk, and with the drive of the magnates, knights, and gentry to control as much of the judicial system as possible, one might assume that the peasantry would be helpless victims of power-hungry superiors. While they sometimes were, two social instruments mitigated some of the effects: (1) they could put themselves under the protection of one of the power brokers, and (2) they could manipulate the judicial system for their own ends. In the realignment of social connections in the later Middle Ages, I argue, not only the traditional relationship between the magnates and knights and gentry changed from the old feudal bonds but the relationship between the lord and peasant also changed. The growth of royal justice at the expense of seigneurial justice meant that crimes of peasants were no longer tried in the lord's court and many civil pleas involving peasants were also reserved for the crown. But the king's officers of justice were often so corrupt or the system so slow that the peasantry could not be sure of speedy or fair treatment. Many peasants found it expedient to put themselves under the protection of a local lord who could call upon armed household retainers to rectify the problems of his client. Thus there developed in late medieval England a patron-client system that anthropologists would find typical of many peasant societies, historical and contemporary. The magnate acted as a power broker between the peasant (his client) and the government.

Records of special inquiry (trailbaston) into the function of justice abound in examples of the patron-client relationship. Lord Adam de la Ford was indicted for receiving and protecting Walter le Moch of Edyngton, a runaway serf of John le Waleys. Walter paid Lord Adam two marks for his aid. Apparently Lord Adam had done this before because the indictment goes on to say that he is a "common maintainor and protector."[137] Other times the villagers would need protection in the hundred or royal courts. Hugh le Franne, who was accused of robbing a man of two horses, gave Lord Simon de Montacute one hundred sheep to procure an acquittal through jury intimidation.[138] When Lord John Fitzwalter of Essex was unable to stop the indictment and arrest of his client, he sent his men to rescue him from prison before he could be tried.[139]

One of the most complicated and interesting cases of the patron-client relationship comes from the west Midlands. Walter Pukerel of Clun in Shropshire was a tenant of the Earl of Arundel and a cattle dealer. When thieves stole four of his oxen and drove them off to Worcester market, Walter pursued them closely. He arrived just after the oxen were sold to three butchers, but Walter recognized their hides in the butchers' shops. Walter immediately went to the city bailiff to demand justice. The bailiff assured him that he would look into the matter and sent for the three butchers. He offered to give them time to destroy the hides if they would give him the price of the four oxen.

Walter had no case without the hides and had to return home in anger. Revenge came through Walter's lord. When merchants from Worcester next came to Clun to buy stock, the Earl of Arundel's bailiffs captured them and would not allow them to return until they compensated Walter for his stolen oxen.[140]

The peasantry did not always rely on powerful patrons, for the judicial system relied ultimately on villagers and townspeople to identify, indict, and try suspects, which gave ordinary citizens ample opportunity to use the system for local social control and to enrich themselves through corruption. Jurors were easily bribed by the accused. Sometimes just providing the jury with a lavish dinner on the day of the trial was sufficient.[141] The satirist Bromyard relates an amusing tale. When a justice "enquired of his jury, according to the custom, whether they were all agreed, one of them made answer—'No, because each of my fellow jury men has received forty pounds, and I have only received twenty.' "[142] Villagers might also make money from felons in other ways. For example, local officials in Wakefield took goods from prisoners they were escorting to gaol.[143]

Manipulation of the judicial system through jury service gave the village oligarchy, the A families, a powerful weapon for dominating their villages. Some historians have argued that jury service was shunned and that the task fell to the poorest in society who could not afford to bribe their way out.[144] This might have been true of some jury service such as trailbaston, but more recent work has shown that the jurors for normal criminal cases were drawn from the elite families of the villages and towns and that the right was carefully kept in these families for generations.[145] The position of juror was such a powerful one that it would not be lightly given up. Prominent families used jury service to help each other out of scrapes with the law. The instructions to the justices of eyre in 1278-1279 show that the king was aware of the practice: "Whereas we have been given to understand that certain malicious persons in many counties of our realm, to serve their own ends, being more prone to evil than to good, have presumed to make certain detestable confederacies and evil plots amongst themselves, taking oaths to each other to uphold the cause of their friends . . . in pleas . . . coming up in the courts, by deceitful conduct on assizes, juries and recognitions . . . and in like manner, to grieve their enemies, and where possible to discredit them."[146] Edward I repeated the complaint in the Statute of Winchester.

The data collected from the Ramsey Abbey villages confirm these complaints. An analysis of who was punished by status in the village shows the use of the judicial system as an elaborate system for warning and punishing in varying degrees. For minor infringments of community bylaws fines in the local courts or expulsion from the village were sufficient punishments. The jurors could increase the punishment by indicting people for criminal offenses that would necessitate the accused finding sureties for bail and making a trip to the county town for trial or supporting themselves in prison until trial. The most severe punishment was convicting the person at the gaol delivery sessions. The uses of these types of social control mechanisms are apparent in the court rolls. For instance, in the village of Wistow in 1333 Ellen Kelenach, an intermediate villager (C family), was expelled from the village after a career in petty thefts that went back to 1309. Her daughter, Joan, began a similar career in 1334, but the villagers apparently would not tolerate a similar pattern so she was indicted for felony in 1335 and brought to gaol. She was ultimately acquitted because the value of the theft was so small.[147] The case is a good example of the escalation of the type of punishment employed.

Indictment was a convenient punishment for primary and secondary villagers. Since they held considerable land in the villages, they could not be expelled from the villages as easily as an intermediate family. Their position in the power structure of the village made it very difficult for the villagers to hang them. The jurors knew the people well; they had been neighbors and their parents had been neighbors; they were probably related by kinship ties. But the villagers did have to have some mechanism of reprimand; the indictment and arrest procedure provided a method that was financially punishing and inconvenient without going to extremes. Of the thirty-four primary villagers indicted and tried in the Ramsey Abbey villages, only two were convicted; only six out of the thirty-seven secondary villagers were convicted. Eight out of the eighteen intermediate villagers, however, were convicted.

Status determined punishment as well as conviction. Only one prominent villager was hanged—John Gere who confessed his crime and became an approver. The other prominent villager convicted was a member of the clergy who was released to the bishop. Of the secondary family members convicted, three were hanged, two pardoned, and one sent to the pillory. The intermediate group was treated more harshly—five were hanged, two released because of the low value of the goods stolen, and one pardoned. "As it is saide in olde proverbe— 'Pore be hangid by the neck; a riche man bi the purs.'"[148]

The jurors were biased in their judgments not only according to the status of the accused but also according to residence. The jurors convicted 37.5 percent of the strangers (normally the Ramsey jurors convicted only 18 percent of the suspects) and gave only two of them the benefit of the doubt by declaring them *sine die*. If an outsider committed larceny, he was almost sure to be convicted. The greater number of convictions for strangers no doubt reflected the feeling of village unity and xenophobia, but the jurors also simply found it easier to condemn people to hang whom they did not know personally. In theft cases involving an outsider, recovery of goods would be difficult, so that this type of property loss had to be discouraged more forcefully than thefts within the village.

Some families and individuals had a tendency toward aggression and criminal behavior that offended community standards. These people had numerous fines for assault or small thefts and trespasses in the manorial court rolls. Although all prominent villagers were aggressive in these matters, those who were unusually violence-prone tended to be indicted and sometimes convicted as well. William Bird of Warboys, who was tried for homicide in 1348, seems to have come from an exceptionally aggressive family.[149] His own record was a series of trespasses and having the hue raised against him. Other relatives—Simon, Richard, Michael, and Christine—all had long records of hue, assault, and theft. Since they were all contemporaries, the village must have had its fill of the bad Birds and punished William.

The Ramsey jurors and all other jurors in this study treated some categories of people differently. The most notable distinction was between men and women. Women were indicted less frequently than men (one woman to nine men) and acquitted more readily. Men were convicted in 22.8 percent of the cases, about the same as the overall conviction rate of 22.9 percent. But only 12.3 percent of the women indicted were convicted. In the county by county breakdown, Norfolk, Northamptonshire, and Essex were particularly lenient to women.[150] The male jurors obviously did not take women's role in crime seriously or thought that, if caught, women deserved special consideration. Their attitude was the precursor to that of modern jurors who also acquit more women than men.[151]

While women were singled out for generous treatment, the clergy was given notably worse treatment—63.6 percent of them were convicted. This high conviction rate of the clergy would seem to indicate blatant anticlericalism on the part of the trial juries, but alternative explanations caution against this conclusion. When jurors convicted a lay person, they knew that he would probably be hanged. But members of the clergy would not be hanged; their retrial in ecclesiastical court would end with a penance at most. The conviction rate for clerks may indicate what the real conviction-acquittal pattern would have been in the society if the jurors had always given their honest opinion on guilt or innocence. Alternatively, if many professional criminals took the precaution of joining lower orders of the clergy or of learning to read in order to avoid hanging, then perhaps the juries were convicting these people as notorious criminals regardless of their clerical status, thus causing an increase in the overall conviction rate for clergy. When one looks at organized crime and the larger gangs, one is struck by the number of suspects who successfully pleaded benefit of clergy.

An upward trend in conviction rates over the fifty-year period could, perhaps, provide a better argument that jurors were basically anticlerical, since the laity of England were becoming increasingly anti-clerical as the century wore on. The data do show a gradual increase in the percentage of clerics found guilty. The percentage of convictions for 1300-1319 was 60 percent; it had risen to 75.4 percent by 1330-1348. Such evidence might indicate growing anticlericalism among lay jurors, but if so, it only indicates that they were convicting more clerics rather than indicting more. The convictions for clergy did not rise out of proportion to the increased guilty verdicts of laity during the same period. Furthermore, some of the increase may represent laymen using reading to obtain clerical benefits, for the literacy test became more acceptable for proving clergy toward the middle of the century. At the same time it became more common to enter the plea for benefit of clergy after conviction by the lay courts rather than before the trial.[152] Thus the acquittal-conviction ratio for the latter part of the period could be unreliable, showing an increase in convictions simply because there was a decrease in the number of known clerics acquitted. In spite of the greater number of clerical convictions, there is insufficient evidence to conclude that anticlericalism influenced the jurors' verdicts.

Information on other occupational groups in the gaol delivery rolls is too sparse to make generalizations about the jurors' attitude toward them. Butchers, millers, servants, craftsmen, sailors, shepherds, and others are mentioned, but what evidence there is indicates that the jurors were not likely to convict them any more frequently than the norm. Nobles, on the other hand, were almost uniformly acquitted. For example, all the nobles and their *familia* indicted in the Somerset trailbaston sessions in 1305 were acquitted, pardoned, or fined.

The conviction rate for people committing crimes with the aid of others was the same as the ordinary conviction rate. Of the counties, only Surrey showed a marked concern, by convicting 35.1 percent of the members of criminal associations (normally that county convicted 27.1 percent of those they indicted).

The reluctance of the jurors to convict suspected felons has puzzled historians. In the overall average of the eight counties only 22.9 percent of the suspects were convicted. There was a considerable county by county difference. Norfolk was the only county that convicted about a third of the people tried (32.8 percent). Huntingdonshire (27.2 percent convictions), Surrey (27.1 percent), Northamptonshire (26.9 percent), and Essex (25.3 percent) formed a group close in pattern to Norfolk. They were all near to London or fairly closely tied to London by the road system. In addition to being close to the seat of government, they had more stable conditions economically and politically than the other three counties. The drop in convictions is very noticeable the farther the county is from the capital. Hereford juries convicted only 18.1 percent of the suspects, Somerset 17.3 percent, and Yorkshire 13.7 percent. These fringe areas were more unsettled during the fourteenth century than the center of the country. Herefordshire was on the unruly Welsh border, and Yorkshire experienced direct attacks from the Scots. In the southwestern counties there was some threat of invasion from France, but the peculiarity that was more likely to account for the low convictions was that the southwestern circuit was less under the control of the central government and more subject to the domination of local interests. The unstable conditions in the border counties made them more subject to local power as well.

Most historians have assumed that the dearth of convictions reflected the high degree of corruption of the system.[153] To be sure, laxness and corruption abounded. For instance, even in Yorkshire the convictions rose from 14 to 20 percent when the judges of King's Bench held the gaol delivery sessions. But even allowing for considerable corruption, it must be explained why medieval society was

willing to have so many criminals in its midst when in modern societies the conviction rate is so high: 87.4 percent of those tried for
felonies in the United States and 83 percent in Britain.[154]

The kings complained that the jurors' sympathy for the suspects or
their fear of reprisals from friends of the condemned led them to tolerate crime in their midst rather than risk their lives convicting known
criminals. The primary villagers were very reluctant to condemn each
other to the gallows. They might have wanted to convict notorious
outlaws and high-handed knights and gentry, but they would have
been afraid to do so. But in spite of the fact that the villagers convicted
so few suspects, they went on arresting and trying them. Although the
fines for failure to report crimes were low and the possiblility of concealing them was fairly great, the villagers did not let up on indictments. Jurors had learned to use the indictment procedure for rep-
rimanding offenders rather than for hanging them. Undergoing the
expense and inconvenience of the judicial process was in itself a punishment, so that there was no need to convict all people indicted—especially one's neighbors.

The most crucial factor influencing the low conviction rate and the
use of indictment as punishment was that the sole punishment, hanging, was too severe to fit the popular attitude toward crime. Reducing
the seriousness of an offense or simply acquitting the suspects are
common responses of citizenry when they feel that the punishments
do not fit the crime. In late eighteenth-century England, when jurors
had to work with basically the same laws as were in force in medieval
England, they reduced the value of goods stolen so that the convicted
person could be imprisoned or transported rather than hanged.[155]
Medieval jurors responded to the problem by acquitting the suspects
after indictment. Again, modern figures give a perspective on the
problems of the medieval judicial system. Of the 87.4 percent of
people convicted in U.S. District Courts, 78.7 percent pleaded guilty
and only 8.7 percent were convicted by the courts.[156] The medieval
system did not have any mechanism to encourage people to confess
guilt without becoming an approver. In all the cases for this study,
only one person confessed his guilt without becoming an approver:
Robert le Bakere of Sewelle confessed to stealing a purse worth 3d.,
but since it was under 12d. he was only sent to the pillory.[157] The
punishments were too inflexible to permit either the jurors to convict
readily or the felons to confess. It is for this reason that the conviction

Table 1. *Acquittals and convictions in five-year averages for all counties, 1300-1348.*

	ACQUITTALS		CONVICTIONS		TOTAL
Years	N	%	N	%	%
1300-1304	47	82.5	10	17.5	100
1305-1309	33	86.7	5	13.3	100
1310-1314	22	81.5	5	18.5	100
1315-1319	91	74.0	32	26.0	100
1320-1324	54	79.4	14	20.6	100
1325-1329	37	82.2	8	17.8	100
1330-1334	41	87.2	6	12.8	100
1335-1339	20	71.4	8	28.6	100
1340-1344	35	77.8	10	22.2	100
1345-1348	41	77.4	12	22.6	100

rate of 63.6 percent for the clergy may represent what the jurors really thought of the guilt of the suspects when they did not have to decide to hang them.

From looking at the percentage of convictions in five-year intervals (see table 1), trends emerge that might reflect popular concern over the lack of law and order. From 1300 through 1314 the number of convictions was slightly below the mean. The number of indictments was also generally low during this period. Between 1315-1319, the period of famine and political disturbances in the central government, the number of indictments rose dramatically and the percentage of convictions rose to 26 percent. Convictions steadily decreased in the period 1320 through 1334, although indictments were on the average higher than they had been before the famine. Indictments dropped in the period 1335-1348, but convictions remained somewhat higher than usual, climbing to 28.6 percent in 1335-1339 and then decreasing slightly.[158] All eight counties registered their concern in that five-year period through increased convictions. The period coincided with petitions in Commons about the amount of lawlessness in the countryside and pressure on the king to use existing officials more effectively and to extend powers for the keepers of the peace (see appendixes B and C). The higher conviction rate probably represented a general mood in the countryside that the amount of crime was reaching an intolerable level and that both the jurors and the king would have to take more stringent measures.

Table 2. *Acquittals and convictions for the different types of crimes for all counties, 1300-1348.*

	ACQUITTALS		CONVICTIONS	
Crime	N	%	N	%
Larceny	4,356	77.6	1,261	22.4
Burglary	2,906	69.0	1,808	31.0
Robbery	1,201	69.4	529	30.6
Homicide	2,667	87.6	379	12.4
Receiving	872	94.6	50	5.4
Counterfeiting	41	53.2	36	46.8
Arson	116	76.8	35	23.2
Rape	70	89.7	8	10.3
Treason	4	13.3	26	86.7
Total number	12,233		3,632	

A more sensitive indicator of the jurors' attitude toward crime is the types of crimes for which they were more likely to convict suspects (see table 2). Perhaps because the king's interests rather than local ones were so closely involved, jurors readily convicted those committing treason. Although there were only thirty cases of treason in the whole sample, 86.7 percent of them ended in convictions. Treason of this sort included spying and murder of one's master. Only three counties had problems with spying (see figure 1)—Norfolk because of its major ports, Northamptonshire because it was on the Great North Road to the wars with Scotland, and Yorkshire because the Scots invaded it. Even Yorkshire, which normally was lax in its punishments, convicted 62.5 percent of the spies. Norfolk, the "law and order" county, convicted all charged with treason. Counterfeiting, which was also treasonous, was a highly punished offense: of the seventy-seven counterfeiters, 46.8 percent were convicted. Not only the king's interest was involved in counterfeiting but also that of the tradesmen and merchants who would be cheated. In a fair town such as St. Ives or a port such as Lynn, the local jurors could not afford to be lenient toward purveyors of false coins. Furthermore, counterfeiters were usually strangers to the area who would not have a patronage system to protect them or friendships to hinder the decision to hang them.

Suspects accused of committing property crimes through ambush, stealth, or under the cover of night were the next most likely group to

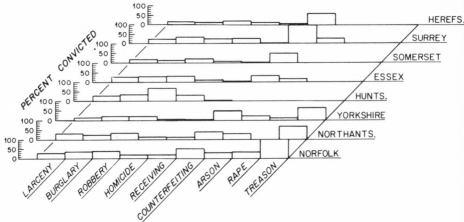

Figure 1. *Percentage of convictions for the different types of crimes in the eight counties, 1300-1348.*

be convicted: burglary suspects were convicted in 31 percent of the cases and robbery suspects in 30.6 percent. All but Surrey and Yorkshire ranked robbery as the crime after treason and counterfeiting that should be punished most frequently. Huntingdonshire jurors convicted 66.7 percent of the robbery suspects. Burglars and robbers won the special disapproval of the jurors for several reasons. Modern studies indicate that the public fears these crimes more than most. Robbery is a personal, physical assault or threat of it, and burglary is an invasion of privacy of the dwelling place as well as a property crime. Both are usually more profitable than simple larceny. Medieval people added another dimension to their dislike of burglars and robbers—a strong sentiment against stealth in personal confrontations. Burglars who attacked in the night or robbers who lay in wait for unsuspecting travelers came at their illegal gains indirectly when the owner of the goods was most vulnerable. So feared and despised were robbers that in the manor court of Ingoldmells, people could successfully sue for slander if they were called "robbers."[159] Participants in violent property crimes were sometimes organized bandits or outsiders, who, if caught, were deserving of punishment and were not people who had claims of friendship on the jurors. Furthermore, the clergy were frequent participants in violent property crimes and their conviction rate was generally higher. Arson was also frequently punished (23.2 percent of the 151 cases). Arson was very similar to robbery and burglary in that it was done by stealth and often by organized bands.

Larceny was the most common crime that the jurors dealt with. Their convictions for it were average (22.4 percent out of 5,617 cases), with a few regional variations. The jurors of Northamptonshire and Surrey convicted those accused of larceny as frequently as robbers. These two counties might well have had more transient thieves than other counties: Surrey because of its proximity to London and its location on roads leading to the southern ports; Northamptonshire because of the fluidity of the criminal population in the Midlands. The jurors would, therefore, be convicting more strangers and vagabonds. The value of goods stolen in larceny was often small, and the people charged were most frequently neighbors of the jurors or they found patrons in the locale, thus assuring acquittal.

Jurors rarely convicted receivers of stolen goods—only 5.4 percent of 922 people indicted were found guilty. Receivers were mostly known members of the community who were receiving relatives and friends, and most accusations of receiving came from approvers whose word was always suspect to jurors.

In punishing crimes against the person the medieval jurors were lenient. Very few rapes were prosecuted (seventy-eight for the eight counties) and of these only 10.3 percent ended in conviction. Homicide was common in the medieval criminal statistics, amounting to 19.2 percent of all felonies (3,046 cases) but only 12.4 percent of those accused were convicted. Homicide most often grew out of arguments between neighbors. The jurors would have known the people involved and probably the reasons for the argument. Aggressive behavior was common in defense of one's honor and rights. If a neighbor was killed in the course of such an argument, the jurors could understand and acquit. Indeed, they were often so understanding that they found reasons not to bring an indictment.[160]

From these figures one might conclude that medieval jurors put a low value on life and a high value on property. It would seem that jurors wished to discourage property crimes, especially violent ones, but were quite willing to let homicide and rape pass virtually unpunished. Comparisons with modern figures do not help, for, while they show that in both periods larceny is the most frequently convicted crime and rape the least frequently, the differential in types of punishments and presentment of evidence makes any conclusion impossible.[161] Medieval jurors were sentencing all suspects to the same type of punishments, so that their convictions represent their attitudes toward the different types of felonies.

The types of goods stolen and their value also influenced the conviction-acquittal ratio, but these were closely tied to the types of crimes committed. Thefts involving household goods and clothing ended in conviction in 34.6 percent and 37.6 percent of the cases, respectively. This closely parallels the convictions for burglary and robbery, which are the crimes in which they were most likely to be stolen. Convictions for stealing cloth and industrial products such as equipment and valuables were fairly high as well for the same reason. Thefts of foodstuffs such as meat and bread and thefts of livestock ended in convictions in roughly a quarter of the cases. If the livestock is further divided, those stealing horses were more likely to be found guilty (29.2 percent) than those stealing sheep, cattle, and pigs (20.5 percent, 24.3 percent, and 21.1 percent, respectively). Again, horses were more valuable animals and were often part of the take from a robbery. Jurors tended to overlook thefts of grain and poultry (13.9 percent and 14.7 percent, respectively) because they were of low value and were usually stolen through simple larceny.

Jurors treated thefts of greater monetary value more seriously. Only 17.7 percent of thefts involving goods worth 12d. or under ended in convictions. From 1-10s. the convictions rose to 25.6 percent; from 11-12s. they were 22.3 percent. Thieves stealing goods worth over £1 were convicted in 23.5 percent of the cases. Again, the more valuable goods were stolen in burglaries and robberies. The jurors were concerned not only with the type of crime but also with the amount of damages the victims sustained.

A number of factors help to explain the apparent laxness in law enforcement. Most groups in society derived some benefits, either financial or political, from the corruption of justice. The whole of the medieval English legal system seems to bear out the contention that "law is power" and "that the availability of legal resources is in itself an impetus to social conflict because conflicting or potentially conflicting parties cannot risk the possible costs of not having the law—or at least some law—on their side."[162] The kings controlled their subjects and made money from their forfeited chattels through running the judicial system. The lords of the manors controlled many aspects of their peasants' lives and made money from offering them protection or fining them when they broke manorial rules. No less so did the primary villagers use their control over the indictment and trial procedure to establish themselves as power brokers in their villages.

Austin T. Turk's observations fit the medieval pattern when he suggests that "the presence of law encourages its use by parties hoping to improve their positions by methods relatively less dangerous or costly than nonlegal power struggles to dominate the law."[163] All parties tried to gain control through manipulation of the system. The fight for control over the instruments of law enforcement leads, Turk argues, to "the party with greater legal as well as non-legal power [increasing] its edge over weaker parties, even to the extreme of excluding the weaker altogether from access to the legal arena, cutting him off from even the opportunity to advance his claims and defend his interests 'legally.'"[164] The primary villagers did cut off the intermediate villagers and to a certain extent the secondary ones from participation in the legal system of the villages. The gentry tried to get exclusive local control through the office of the justice of the peace, and the magnates and the kings vied for control of the law for whole counties and regions of England. All tried to exclude other parties from power. By the end of the fifteenth century it was apparent that the king would finally dominate the legal system, but this was not as obvious in the first half of the fourteenth century. In the Middle Ages the fight for dominance was a violent one in which crime might be used as well as the court system. For those people who felt that they could not insure their power position in the courts, the only solution that remained was personally to right the wrongs done to them through violence or through stealing items they thought were owed to them.

Conflict theory is attractive in explaining the corruption of justice and the emphasis on self-help in medieval society, but other factors were also influential. The acquittal rate was so high because the punishment for conviction was too severe. There also seemed to be mutual agreements not to convict in order to avoid reprisals within the villages. But, in order to understand the toleration of the population for the corruption of justice, it is necessary to know what impact crime had on society. The frequency of crime is bound to be a determining factor, although complaints about increases in crimes are often simply a political device that has little to do with the real danger the average citizen suffers from loss of property or life. If people can live most of their lives without experiencing a felony, then they can afford to be tolerant. If the amounts they lose in theft are negligible, then they will not feel the need to punish. Attitudes toward law and order also depend upon who the suspects are and what their relationship with the victim is. Individual motivations of suspects, extenuating circumstances such as war or famine, general disillusionment with the political and judicial system can all influence the attitude of the public toward law enforcement.

Chapter Three

The Crimes:

Definitions, Patterns, and Techniques

MEDIEVAL KINGS and their subjects were well aware of felonious behavior. As lawmakers, jurors, or poets they accurately described the techniques of committing crimes. Indeed, probably quite a large proportion of the population, including lawmakers and enforcers, had participated personally in criminal acts. The gaol delivery and coroners' rolls provide much information on the frequency and seasonality of various types of crime, kinds of goods stolen, place of the incident, and so on. In conjunction with literary sources, they also give an accurate picture of the techniques of crime. Modern criminology has provided models for the systematic study of patterns in different types of crimes.

Broadly defined, the felonies described in the fourteenth-century records fell into two categories—crimes against property and crimes against the person. Property crimes included larceny, burglary, robbery, arson, and receiving stolen goods, while personal crimes were limited to homicide (including suicide) and rape. Robbery and rape often fell between the two categories because both often combined physical assault and property loss. In addition to the felonies, gaol delivery also handled minor treason cases.

Traditional legal history has tended to rely upon the treatise writers such as Bracton, Britten, and Littleton and the Year Books to sort out the confusions of definition and legal practice. But these writers with their veneer of Roman law and the compilers of the Year Books were somewhat removed from the actual practice and application of the law in the fourteenth century. The precedents they were establishing for a small, learned group were much more influential on the course of justice in the sixteenth through the eighteenth centuries when other legal commentators and judges read them and applied them to the system of justice. In the fourteenth century, villagers made the decisions on whether to indict a suspect and, ultimately, they were responsible for collecting and weighing the evidence and reaching a verdict. It was the "twelve good men and true" in the hundred with the help of the sheriff, bailiff, or coroner who made the daily decisions that influenced the lives of those who appeared for trial in gaol delivery. These established peasants and gentry made their decisions without recourse to the treatise writers or the Year Books.

In the fourteenth century, the actual trial was subordinate to the process of pleading. The forms of indictment were not stereotyped into the forms they would eventually take. Instead, they had about them "the brevity and businesslike curtness of the real Middle Ages when hard-pressed officials were too busy to indulge in verbosity, and when the indictment was a rough and ready instrument of law rather than a game of skill for special pleaders."[1] In their own words the jurors told the incidents of the case, including extraneous information about them such as that they happened at night or on the king's highway or that the burglars entered through the wall. This information made little difference in hanging the felon—the punishment could not be made more severe because the thief stole at night—but it did reflect the jurors' particular condemnation for the act and does provide information on the patterns of crime. The indictments, then, "contain language which makes it evident that they are the spontaneous expression of the juror's attitude towards criminal law, very little influenced by the academic conservatism of the professional lawyer."[2]

LARCENY

Larceny, the felonious act of taking and carrying off goods, was the most common crime in fourteenth-century England, comprising 38.7 percent of all felonies (see table 3). Since many trespasses might actually have been larcenies and since larceny is usually the most underreported of all the felonies, the cases appearing in gaol delivery are probably only a fraction of those committed.[3] All counties reported similar levels of larceny (see table 4). Norfolk, Essex, Huntingdonshire, Herefordshire, and Somerset were all near or below the mean while Yorkshire, Northamptonshire, and Surrey were slightly above.[4] The variations may represent both different opportunities for larceny from county to county and local differences in legal definition. The greater importance of herding in Yorkshire's economy may have in-

Table 3. *Indictments for the different types of crimes for the total data, 1300-1348.*

Crime	N	%
Larceny	6,243	38.7
Burglary	3,818	24.3
Robbery	1,640	10.5
Homicide	2,952	18.2
Receiving	976	6.2
Counterfeiting	79	0.6
Arson	120	0.8
Rape	79	0.5
Treason	45	0.2
Total	15,952	100.0

creased the opportunities for larceny of cattle and probably explains the higher percentage of larceny there. Herefordshire also had substantial herding, but the jurors tended to define even the driving off of animals as robbery.

The basic element in the law of larceny is that goods must be feloniously carried off (*felonice furavit*). Sir James Fitz James Stephen stated this simple dictum in a more sophisticated fashion when he argued that three conditions have to be present: (1) fraudulent intent to misappropriate property, (2) property that can be misappropriated, and (3) actual misappropriation of property.[5] This broad definition could cover all sorts of thefts, but burglary and robbery are treated separately as distinct felonious actions involving more than absconding with another person's property. For convenience, theft is used as a generic term for misappropriation of property, but larceny has a more specific meaning. Larceny is the simple process of taking and carrying away (as the jurors say in the indictment) goods for which the thief can make no claim of ownership. Larceny is divided into grand and petty larceny. The dividing point in the fourteenth century was 12d. or one shilling worth of goods. The distinction was made apparent by the different punishments: hanging for grand larceny; some lesser punishment, such as pillory, for petty larceny.[6]

Fourteenth-century law also restricted theft to only certain property. It had to be property to which the wronged possessor had a clear title (thus distinguishing larceny from trespass, which it often re-

Table 4. *Indictments for the different types of crimes for the eight counties, 1300–1348.*

Crime	Norfolk N	%	Northants. N	%	Yorkshire N	%	Hunts. N	%	Essex N	%	Somerset N	%	Heref N	%	Surrey N	%
Larceny	1,382	36.9	574	45.7	2,365	43.1	112	36.7	779	32.4	398	35.1	391	36.8	242	42.1
Burglary	1,180	31.5	177	14.1	1,046	19.4	23	7.5	713	29.6	350	30.9	193	18.2	136	23.6
Robery	431	11.5	124	9.9	285	5.2	21	7.0	392	16.3	149	13.1	175	16.5	63	11.0
Homicide	491	13.1	297	23.7	1,311	23.9	84	27.5	319	13.2	186	16.4	179	16.7	85	14.8
Receiving	180	4.8	58	4.6	324	5.9	61	20.0	178	7.4	31	2.7	103	9.7	41	7.1
Counterfeiting	22	0.6	9	0.7	27	0.5	4	1.3	4	0.2	2	0.2	10	0.9	1	0.2
Arson	22	0.6	13	1.0	49	0.9	0	0.0	18	0.7	5	0.4	6	0.6	7	1.2
Rape	6	0.2	0	0.0	49	0.9	0	0.0	5	0.2	13	1.2	6	0.6	0	0.0
Treason	30	0.8	4	0.3	11	0.2	0	0.0	0	0.0	0	0.0	0	0.0	0	0.0
Total	3,524	100.0	1,057	100.0	5,210	100.0	305	100.0	2,408	100.0	1,134	100.0	1,063	100.0	575	100.0

sembled); it could not be wild things in nature or undomesticated animals (*ferae naturae*); it had to be moveable (land could not be stolen according to the law). Furthermore, the law made no clear provision for calling theft by fraud, confidence games, or extortion a larceny.⁷ Thus the Canon in *The Canterbury Tales* who persuaded people to part with goods and coins in exchange for a promise to convert them to gold through alchemy was not punishable through felony laws. The types of goods that could be stolen and the ways in which they were stolen thus limited the definition of larceny in medieval law.

Medieval jurors knew these basic provisions of the law and distinguished larcenies from other property crimes accordingly. In addition, the records they left show their concern with the time of day, the place, the type and value of goods stolen, and even the determination of the thief in overcoming such obstacles as doors, closes, gates, and windows.⁸ The jurors' concern with these additional aspects of simple larceny makes possible a detailed study of the behavior patterns that accompanied this type of theft.

Larceny had a distinct seasonal pattern that reflected the routine of agricultural work—the fallow, planting, and harvest periods. This seasonality had both economic and social explanations. Larceny is an offense that covers as many criminal settings as there are goods and victims. Some thieves, such as pickpockets or prostitutes, rely on social contacts for their thefts, while others, such as cattle rustlers, wait for the cover of night or periods when goods are poorly guarded. From December through April, the lean months of living on reserves, little was lying about in the open to steal. There were no mature crops and no fruits on trees, and the autumn butchering had diminished livestock. Grain, meat, and even the remaining livestock would be safely kept in houses or barns. Furthermore, there were fewer social contacts during the cold weather, so that thieves who thrived on these conditions were hindered. The lack of opportunity for larceny is reflected in the distribution of larcenies—only 21 percent of the annual larcenies were committed during this fallow period.⁹ In May through August, when planting was in full swing, early crops were ripened, replenished herds were out grazing, and the population was busy in the fields and less able to keep a watchful eye on possessions, the number of larcenies rose to include 34 percent of the annual total. The highest period for larceny was the months of harvest and butchering, September through November, when the rural population was scrambling to make winter provisions. These busy, fruitful, and tense months had 45 percent of the annual larcenies, with November having the most larcenies of any month.[10] Opportunities for picking up unwatched goods were best in these months when all available help was in the fields, grain was in sheaves, and hams and sides of bacon were not yet stored. For the thieves seeking social contact for their thefts, the flush of harvest meant that market towns and taverns were full.

For the substantial villagers—most of the suspects appearing in gaol delivery came from this group—planting and particularly harvest seasons were times of bickering over debts, crops, and disputed property. Actual larceny and accusations of larceny were frequent. In chapter 2 I quoted Avarice in *Piers Plowman* describing his technique for gleaning crops from his neighbor's strip. Suspicion of theft naturally arose with the strips lying so close to one another in the common fields. Villagers took precautions against theft at harvest, placing servants or corn reeves in fields to guard against larceny of crops. In one instance, two paupers set upon one such guard and tried to overpower him so that they could steal grain. He killed one of them in self-defense and the other fled.[11] After the harvest was over, most areas of England permitted gleaners to go into the fields to pick up the grain that had escaped harvesters. Those who began to glean before the crops were in could be fined or expelled from the village or the offense could be prosecuted as larceny in the king's courts. For instance, Agnes of Weldon and her three children were accused of stealing eight sheaves of grain worth 4d. at harvest time.[12]

While literary references indicate a general awarness that larceny was seasonal, they also suggest that professional thieves knew no season. In the thirteenth-century German poem about the peasant youth, Helmbrecht, who became a thief, the poet speaks with condemnation about the lack of seasonality of professional gangs.

> Wolfsgaum's another comrade. He,
> No matter what his love may be
> For cousin, uncle, aunt—or whether
> It be February weather—
> Leaves no thread upon their form
> Man or woman, to keep them warm,
> Or even cover up their shame.[13]

Another comrade was described as carrying out his pillaging "whether it be cold or warm."[14] Modern professional thieves also make crime a year round occupation. To villagers struggling in the lean months of late winter, thefts at that season must have seemed particularly pernicious.

Larceny also followed a daily pattern. The sample cases indicate that for the most part thieves observed a four day work week starting on Monday and reaching a high point on Thursday. Friday, Saturday, and Sunday saw a substantial drop in the number of thefts. Since medieval society did not observe the weekend as a holiday, but only Sunday, the daily pattern of theft is difficult to explain. There is no reason to assume that people were guarding their property more on Friday through Sunday than on the other days of the week. Modern thieves tend to work up from a low on Sunday to a high on Saturday.[15]

The types of goods stolen indicate the techniques used in larceny and often reflect the seasonality of the crime. Livestock were the most common valuable items in the peasant economy, so it is not surprising to find that they were also the most commonly stolen items, accounting for 65.9 percent of the booty (see figure 2). They were among the easiest possessions to steal since driving or leading off animals required no physical strength and no particular knowledge outside the ordinary rural experience. Eighty-three percent of all livestock thefts occurred through larceny. Young Helmbrecht boasted of how simple such larceny is.

Many a farmyard I shall gut,
And if my man is gone that day,
I'll drive his stock off, anyway.[16]

Often the thief would not even run into the barrier of a farmyard but would find cattle at pasture. The villagers, of course, employed shepherds and other herders to guard against theft.

The kinds and number of animals stolen varied considerably. Horses, the most valuable of the animals, were stolen most frequently: 36.2 percent of the livestock thefts. Sheep were more plentiful, but they comprised only 30.7 percent of the animals stolen. Cattle accounted for 26.9 percent, and the most common animals, pigs and poultry, for only 3.4 percent and 2.8 percent respectively. Much of the poultry theft would be under 12d. and, therefore, not be reported, and pigs were not attractive because they would not fetch a high price for the thief.

The number of animals stolen at one time very much depended upon the kind of animal. Over three-quarters of the horse thefts in-

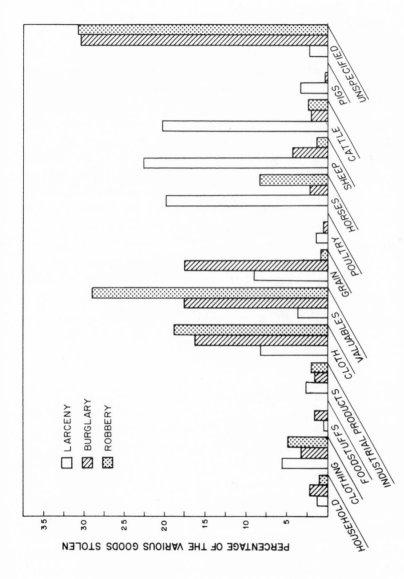

Figure 2. Percentage of the various goods stolen in larceny, burglary, and robbery.

volved one horse. Horses were not so plentiful that they would be kept in herds. And because of their value, they were carefully guarded. Very rarely were horse thieves lucky enough to steal three or more horses at a time. Cattle rustlers stole single animals in about half the instances and two or more in the other half. The cattle stolen included plow oxen, bulls, milk cows, and steers. Cattle were very valuable for the peasant economy but were more likely to be kept in village herds than were horses, and hence it was easier to steal more than one at a time. Sheep were grazed in large herds sometimes amounting to several hundred animals, particularly in the moor areas. Sheep thieves, therefore, stole the animals in fairly large numbers at one time. Over three-quarters of the thefts involved two or more animals, and in one-half of these the thieves made away with five or more sheep. Only 14.6 percent of the thieves stole one sheep. Almost all the recorded pig and poultry thefts involved more than one animal because these animals were not so valuable and the thieves would probably not even be indicted unless they stole enough to be equal to a shilling value.

Gangs usually participated in stealing large numbers of animals because of the herding problems. For instance, Stephen of Knaplock and his associates stole six oxen and forty sheep.[17] But a single thief could isolate several sheep in a large pasture without help. John Wyryng went into the common marshland pasture in Huntingdonshire called "la Mersh" and stole four sheep from the village herd.[18] Such thefts were easy since the flocks strayed and the shepherds slept, or such was the case when Mak stole the sheep in the *Second Shepherds' Pagent*. Mak says on the verge of the theft:

Now were time for a man that lacks what he would
To stalk privily then unto a fold . . .

Was I never a shepherd, but now will I lere.
If the flock be scared, yet shall I nib near.[19]

Livestock was an easy target for theft, even for an inexperienced animal handler like Mak.

Some animal thefts were more sophisticated. In the medieval French comedy *Peter Quill's Shenanigans*, the shepherd stole sheep from his master by a method he described to his lawyer, Peter Quill.

Well, the truth is, I gave some of them [sheep] a knock between the ears, and would you believe it, they fainted away and then dropped dead, even the healthy ones. But I'd let on like they'd died on the scab, just so's I wouldn't get blamed. "Come on," says my employer, "better get rid of the animal so it won't contaminate the others." "Right," says I. But being that I know what the disease really was, I carved 'em all up for my table.[20]

Such thefts of livestock as well as some of the other techniques of theft to be described might be prosecuted in either criminal actions or as trespasses.

Grain presented more difficulties than livestock for thieves. Only 8.1 percent of all larcenies involved grain. The season for stealing grain from fields was limited to the harvest period. A large quantity had to be stolen to be worth the effort. After the grain was harvested, it was stored in barns or houses so that simple larceny was not as readily possible. Furthermore, to carry off a substantial and profitable quantity of grain required a cart or animal, which would be too visible for stealth. Most grain thefts were in small quantities and were often committed by women.

The theft of items normally stored in houses or barns generally posed a problem for thieves and often required cunning and skill in acquiring them without resorting to burglary or robbery. Household goods, clothing, foodstuffs, valuables, money, and cloth comprised only 23.8 percent of the items stolen in the course of larceny. Of these, the most commonly stolen item was cloth, 10.3 percent.[21] Some of the cloth may have been stolen outside the house in the process of cloth-making such as drying the fabric. This would require no more skill than clothesline thefts. Most thieves who stole from houses bided their time until the owner was out on an errand and then walked in and carried off the goods. Thomas Tolly entered the house of Aleyn Syger of Hoo and walked off with one lute and a litany worth 4s.[22]

Cunning was required in many larcenies. For instance, John Rate bought 110 boards from John Cussing; when he picked them up he stole fourteen more. Another petty thief furtively sheared sheep of their wool.[23] Other thieves were careful in their selection of victims, choosing those who could not resist their thefts. One woman stole from lepers who were maintained by charity outside the doors of various Norwich churches. They were surprisingly prosperous victims, having cloth worth 20 to 40s. A man in Norfolk entered a chapel where a body was laid out for a funeral and stole two "bandekynes" of gold from the coffin valued at £10.[24] A common ruse, which could end in murder, was for the potential thief to come to a village and beg for a night's lodging for the sake of charity. During the night the thief would steal the goods from the house. If the thief killed or wounded the occupants, the case became a robbery as are the two coroner's cases cited here. But they illustrate the technique. In one case a husband and wife let in a man and a woman for the night. They ate together and then went to bed. In the night the felons rose and killed the family and stole their goods. In another case a woman let in an unknown pauper who opened her doors to his gang during the night.[25] Sometimes the roles were reversed in this type of theft. Thomas son of John le Waleys led an unknown man from Bristol to his house where he gave him a meal and bed and stole his clothing worth 10s.[26]

Although such ruses often ended tragically, medieval society found the duping of larceny victims a subject for mirth. In *The Chicken Pie and the Chocolate Cake* two beggars overheard a self-important pastry cook tell his wife that he would dine with friends in town and that he would serve them a feast that he prepared himself. He instructed his wife in the password that the servant he would send for the food would use. The beggars came to her with the password and stole the food.[27]

Cutpurses, the precursers of pickpockets, were by far the most skilled thieves. Medieval men and women carried their money in purses attached by thin straps to their belts or girdles. In order to steal the purses, the thief had to cut the straps and take the purse without the owner's knowledge. The fourteenth-century cutpurses' techniques were probably the same as those of thieves in Tudor England. Part of the gang created a disturbance that distracted the attention of observers and the victim, while other members cut purses or picked up goods.[28] One can easily imagine these tactics being used when a gang including Thomas of London, John son of Thomas Adam of St. Edmunds, Agnes his wife, William Cristine of Lincoln, and Agnes le Brewester took two boxes of silver from the tavern of Richard le Basoun at Boston. Another gang from diverse parts of the country were rounded up in Great Yarmouth on a number of charges of purse cutting.[29] A light-fingered purse cutter might work on his own in public places where the victim's mind was already distracted. Langland warned in *Piers Plowman* that pickpockets and cutpurses frequented taverns.[30] The marketplace was also a prime risk area for cutpurses. Even church was not safe. Robert le Bakere de Shewelle took one purse containing three pence in the church of St. Botulph in Norwich presumably during the service when his victim's thoughts were not on such worldly possessions.[31]

It would be desirable to determine the role of purse cutting in the total larceny pattern, but few cases were reported in gaol delivery because the value of the goods was usually under 12d. The two gangs just mentioned would indicate a mobile body of cutpurses traveling around to major towns and markets, but it is difficult to assess whether these constituted as large a part of the criminal population as they did in Elizabethan England and later.

Although larceny was the most prevalent crime in medieval society, it did not provide the rich rewards of burglary or robbery (see figure 3). Valuable cattle, horses, and sheep could be driven off in fairly large numbers, but the ordinary thieves tended to steal one at a time for their supper tables or own use. About a third (32.1 percent) of the larcenies were 12d. or under, 38.1 percent were from 1 to 10s., and 15.3 percent were from 11 to 20s. Only 14.5 percent of the larcenies exceeded £1. The low value of the spoils indicates much about the pattern of larceny in medieval society. Because it generally required little skill and no great physical risks or strength, it was attractive to ordinary villagers who might commit only a few felonies in their life-

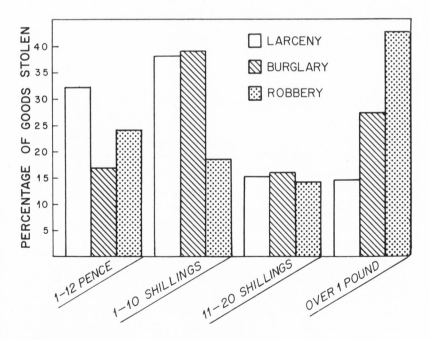

Figure 3. *Percentage of goods stolen by value in larceny, burglary, and robbery.*

time. Indeed, 45.4 percent of all larcenies were committed in the suspect's own village or within a five-mile radius. Another 15 percent of the suspects traveled only six to fifteen miles (see table 7). Simple need, or greed, or a fortuitous opportunity could lead villagers or vagrants to commit larceny.

For the most part, the larceny could be committed in the open where there were either few observers (50.8 percent in fields) or in a street or market area where the observers would be distracted (11.7 percent) (see figure 4). Only 18.6 percent of those committing larceny actually entered their victim's home to steal.[32] With the exception of cutpurses and a few other thieves, larceny seems, therefore, to have functioned as a supplemental income. The more serious criminals sought the higher valued goods that could only be gained through burglary and robbery.

BURGLARY

Burglary, the act of forcibly breaking into a structure with the intent to commit a felony, was one of the three most common crimes in fourteenth-century England, comprising 24.3 percent of the total felonies. But the prevalence of burglary varied widely from county to county. The East Anglian counties—Norfolk and Essex—both had a high concentration of burglary (31.5 percent and 29.6 percent respectively). Somerset was also high with 30.9 percent. Three other counties had about 10 percent less (Yorkshire 19.4 percent, Herefordshire 18.2 percent, and Surrey 23.6 percent). The two Midland counties, Northamptonshire and Huntingdonshire, were very low with 14.1 percent and 7.5 percent. The high percentage of burglaries in East Anglia may be tied to both the inheritance system and to the population density. Local variations in legal definitions may have influenced the distribution of burglaries particularly in East Anglia and the Midlands, but none of the other counties are grouped in any logical geographical or cultural patterns. The percentages of types of crimes in the different counties is only a rough indicator, since a county might have just as many burglaries per 1,000 population but more or less of another crime.

The term "burglary" (*burglaria*) rarely appears in fourteenth-century criminal records.[33] Instead, the law differentiated burglary from larceny by insisting on felonious breaking into a structure and carrying off chattels (*felonice fregit domum et felonice asportavit* or

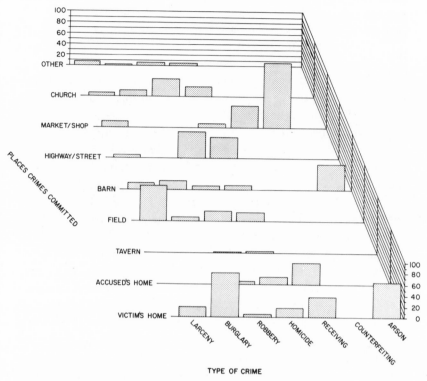

Figure 4. *Places where the various crimes were committed.*

felonice furavit). During the course of the fourteenth century the act of forcefully breaking into a structure with intent to commit felony was sufficient to declare the act a burglary; it was not necessary to actually carry off goods.[34] With very few exceptions the burglary cases appearing in gaol delivery courts involved both the acts of breaking in and of carrying off goods. As for the goods stolen the same considerations on the value of the chattels and the nature of the chattels applied to burglary as they did to larceny.

One characteristic that distinguishes the medieval definition of burglary from the modern one affects the criminal statistics. In the modern definition those cases where the victim is in the structure broken into and suffers from physical assault, threats of violence, or actual homicide are classed as robbery in the first two instances and as homicide in the last. This distinction arose partly from a decision that in compiling the *Uniform Crime Reports* crimes involving more than one felonious act should be recorded according to the rank order of seriousness. Thus homicide, rape, robbery, and burglary are classed in descending order so that a burglary involving a higher ranked crime would be recorded under that crime.[35] In the common law tradition this was not true; the cases make clear that the indictments included charges of both homicide and burglary (wounding and assault were not felonies) and they have been so counted in this study. The situation was far from clear in the Middle Ages, for occasionally terms indicating robbery crept into the records. For the purposes of categorization I have used the simple description of breaking and entering for burglary. Homicide accompanied burglary in only 1 percent of the burglary cases in gaol delivery. Many more involved wounding, but this information was seldom recorded.[36] For the most part, however, burglars tried to avoid contact with the property owners as the seasons and time of day of burglaries indicate.[37]

Because the burglars were in pursuit of goods normally kept in protective structures, their pattern of theft differed substantially from that found in larceny, especially in the crime's seasonality. Burglary reversed the pattern of larceny. While goods were readily available during the planting and harvest seasons, the number of burglaries was low. When the products of the harvest were stored and the amount of goods lying around diminished, burglaries increased. From November through February 50 percent of the burglaries occurred. The rest were scattered through the remaining eight months. Economic desperation on the part of poor burglars would account for some of the winter burglaries because food was scarce and locked up and casual employment in fields was not available. More professional burglars might have preferred the long winter nights as providing more cover.[38] Among modern burglars there is a slight preference for the winter months.

Burglars, like thieves, had a four-day work week. Monday had the highest number of burglaries at 24 percent and Sunday had the lowest at 7 percent. Between Monday and Thursday 73 percent of the burglaries occurred. As in larceny, there is no immediate explanation for this distribution. In the twelfth century the Chruch had tried to bring peace to southern France by imposing the Truce of God, which encouraged the nobility to limit fighting and wars to Monday through Thursday. But it is unlikely that thieves felt bound by this archaic rule. The modern burglar follows the work week of his victims, entering their homes on weekdays when they are at work and their offices on weekends when they are home.[39] Medieval burglars were apparently not as systematic, although they did take advantage of the absence of occupants in the fields or church to break into their homes. Burglaries involving gangs and violence almost always took place at twilight or at night, when people were in their houses either asleep or eating supper so that encounters between the victims and felons were likely.[40]

Most fourteenth-century burglars selected residences for their targets (69.8 percent of the cases).[41] Since the home doubled as shop, workshop, and barn in some homes, one would expect this figure to be high (see figure 4). Barns figured in 14.1 percent of the instances and churches in 8.3 percent.[42] The wattle and daub construction of houses made them easy targets for burglary. Doors and windows were barred from the inside, but only the wealthiest homes had outside locks. For those who wished to keep their valuables and money safe, the only solution was a strong box made of oak or maple, girded with iron, and locked with a padlock. Boxes such as these appear in the case descriptions in gaol delivery rolls.

Modern criminologists classify burglary techniques as skilled (lock picking), semi-skilled (prying, pass key, breaking lock), or unskilled (breaking into a structure through a door or window).[43] In the fourteenth century few burglars needed to become skilled since there were so few locks. But Helmbecht mentions that one member of his gang was particularly skilled at undoing locks.

> Wolfstrussel, he's a man of skill!
> Without a key he bursts at will
> The neatest-fastened iron box.
> Within one year I've seen the locks
> Of safes, at least a hundred such
> Spring wide ajar without a touch
> At his approach! I can't say how.
> Horse, ox and also many a cow,
> Far more than I can tell about,
> From barn and farm he's driven out;
> For when he'd merely toward it start,
> Each lock would quickly spring apart.[44]

Such skilled lockpickers did not appear in the records, but some of the cases of breaking into strong boxes may have involved this technique. For instance, Henry Payn, sailor on the ship *La Nicholas* out of Scarborough, broke into the chest of William Cut of Scarborough, a merchant on the same ship, and stole £30 15s. in pence and £10 in gold florins. Considering the close quarters of the ship, he may well have picked the lock rather than risked the noise of breaking into a heavy chest.[45] Other thieves simply broke into the chests. The type of damage inflicted upon the chests can be seen today in Durham Castle where a medieval chest that had been burglarized is on display. The only identifiable semi-skilled burglary in the records involved two petty thieves indicted in Wakefield tourn for having a false key made for the Parson of Birton's cellar from which, on two occasions, they stole bread and a girdle.[46] Despite the scarcity of cases involving skilled and semi-skilled burglars, they must have been common for statutes speak of felonies done by "drawlacches" as a major problem.[47]

For the most part, burglars were unskilled, for no particular talents were necessary to break into most medieval houses. The laddermen or "second-story men" provide good examples. One man in Norfolk climbed up a ladder to the top window of a house. When he got there he discovered that he was too large to enter the window and the window was too small to extract the goods he wanted to steal.[48] A Bedfordshire burglar ran into problems with his plan as well.

> On 17 March 1317 John le Long came to Maud Bolle's house at Dean, took a ladder, climbed up the house, burgled and entered it and took a ham. As he left with it Maud saw him and raised the hue, and through fear of the hue he fell from the house with the ham and thereby died.[49]

Even using a ladder was a more sophisticated technique than many burglars employed.

A common way of entering a house was simply by pushing in the wall or using a heavy instrument to break it in. For instance, "on the night of 22 January felons and evil-doers came to William Bevetoun's house at Farndish, broke a wall on the west side with a plough-share and entered."[50] Other thieves broke down doors to enter.

> At twilight on 23 April 1271 felons and thieves came to the house of John Reyd of Ravensden at Ravensden, while John, his wife Maud and his servants Walter of Astwood and Richard Pikhorn were sitting at supper, entered by the door towards the court-yard on the west side and immediately assaulted John, striking him on the head near the crown to the brain, apparently with an axe, and to the heart with a knife, of which he died immediately. They wounded Maud on the right side of the head, almost cut off her left

hand, heated a trivet and placed her upon it so that they left her almost dead. They tied Walter and Richard up and then robbed and carried away all the goods of the house.[51]

The amount of violence against the inhabitants in this case is appalling but indicative of the mentality of some felons. Burglars often did not take time to gag and tie their victims, but silenced them permanently instead. The streak of sadism in the felony was characteristic of the Middle Ages.

Violence in burglary usually occurred during unsuspected confrontations with the victims, in cases involving a feud, or when daring and armed gangs perpetrated the burglary. Since local people committed most of the burglaries—34.1 percent were from the same village and 21.2 percent from only one to five miles away—surprise confrontations were unusual. Everyone in the village knew the habits of everyone else and would know when a house was left unguarded. One Northamptonshire man went to a neighbor's house and broke into it when he knew that the husband and wife were in church. The two daughters of the house, aged eight and three, were there alone, so he had to kill them both to silence them while he stole the goods.[52] In a Bedfordshire case the inquest notes that "unknown evildoers came and broke into the house of Jordan de le Hulles of Wilden at Wilden while he was away, wounded his wife Agnes, killed his eight-year-old daughter Emma and then carried away all the goods of the house."[53]

Burglary on a large scale required prior planning to be successful. An unguarded house or one in which little resistance would be encountered were the most attractive sites. Gangs might observe the habits of their target households, or rely on an informant, or pick up stray information in a tavern or market. Once they selected a target they needed a plan of action. For instance, the burglars who broke into a house at Astwick in Bedfordshire assigned some of their gang to break down the wall, steal the goods, and kill the occupants if necessary. Others were detailed to stand guard outside and frighten off anyone who tried to interfere. The plan worked well, for when one of the occupants escaped and raised the hue, the thieves on the outside were able to ward off the pursuers thus permitting them all to escape. Another gang of burglars guarded against pursuit by cutting their victims' leg sinews.[54]

Bands of burglars often made their night's work more profitable by committing a series of burglaries in one village.

On the night of 17 Nov. 1269 felons and thieves came to a house in Roxton in which there were 2 girls, Margaret and Alice daughters of Ralph Bovetoun, broke a wall, entered, and robbed and carried away all the goods of the house. They then went to the next house in which Maude del Forde and Alice Pressade, both of Roxton, were staying, broke its west wall, entered, found Maud in her bed and immediately struck her above the left ear so that her brain issued forth and she immediately died; struck Alice on the top of the head, apparently with a "Denech" axe, so that she lay without speaking and died the same night; and then carried away all the goods of the house. Next they went to the house of John the Cobbler of Roxton, broke its east door and west windows, entered, immediately assaulted John, striking him on the head to the brain, which issued forth, apparently with a "Denech" axe, and in the stomach apparently with a "fauchoun," so that his bowels issued forth; they then took him from the house into the street and immediately killed him there. They also wounded John's wife Alma and his daughter Agnes in their heads apparently with an axe, in their bodies near their hearts with a knife, and in their hattrels and arms so that their lives were dispaired of. Another daughter Alice, who was in the house ran and hid between a basket and a chest. They also struck John's servant, Walter of St. Neots, above the left ear so that he fell as if dead. They then robbed and carried away all the goods of the house. Alice, who had hidden in the house, first found John dead, raised the hue, which was followed, and found pledges.[55]

This series of violent burglaries had been very well planned by people with inside information on the contents of the houses they robbed. The wife of John the Cobbler, before she died, identified those present as a servant of the Prior of Newnham, certain men who had collected tithes for the Prior of Cauldwell in Roxton the previous harvest, and glovers from Bedford. She was taken to gaol after some of them were arrested and identified them as the culprits.

Burglaries were more profitable than larceny (see figure 3). Only 17 percent of the burglars indicted stole less than shilling's worth of goods. Most made much larger profits: 39.3 percent stole 1 to 10s.; 16.1 percent stole 11s. to £1; and 27.6 percent stole goods worth more than £1. Burglary was not only more profitable than larceny but also the types of goods stolen differed (see figure 2). Cloth, valuables (money, jewels, plate), and grain dominated the pattern of the burglaries. These were items that were apt to be kept locked up. Much of the plate came from church property and cloth came from private residences that doubled as workshops and warehouses. The burglar's take also included slightly more household goods and food than did that of the thief. Burglars stole less livestock than those committing larceny and they tended to steal only one or two animals.[56] Since the animals were kept outside most of the time and since only 14.1 percent of the burglaries occurred in barns, one would not expect many animals to be stolen. Curiously, burglars stole sheep much more frequently than horses or cows and even managed to steal fairly large numbers of them. The sheep must have been rounded up and kept in closes or barns, perhaps at shearing time in the spring.

ROBBERY

Robbery has always been considered to be one of the most sinister crimes. It is a surprise attack, usually by a stranger, on both the victim's person and his property. In burglary, larceny, and homicide, more often than not the victim knows the felon and may even have some role in precipitating the felony.[57] But in medieval England only 9.9 percent of the accused robbers lived in the same town as the victims. An additional 20.7 percent lived within a five-mile radius. Most robbers came from more than fifteen miles from the scene of the crime, with 49.1 percent coming from another county (see table 7). Homicide occurred with robbery in 7.8 percent of the robbery cases.[58] Despite the low incidence of robbery—10.5 percent of all crimes—the jurors convicted the violent strangers who perpetrated it more frequently than other suspects.

In Herefordshire and Essex, robberies accounted for 16.5 percent and 16.3 percent of all felonies respectively. Somerset was not far behind with 13.1 percent. Norfolk (11.5 percent), Surrey (11.0 percent), and Northamptonshire (9.9 percent) were closest to the overall average (see table 4). Huntingdonshire had only 7.0 percent. Despite its tradition of highwaymen committing robberies on lonely moors and at treacherous passes, Yorkshire had a mere 5.2 percent. As in other property crimes, local differences of definition may account for some of the differences in percentages for the different counties.

The amount of wealth conveyed on the king's highways was the major determinant of the number of robberies. Essex and Surrey had more robberies because of the number of wealthy travelers—merchants, administrators, clergy, nobility, soldiers, and others—coming to London for business or pleasure. In Herefordshire, Essex, and Norfolk cloth transported along the roads was a favorite target for robbers. Hereford was a chief access town to the middle of Wales. Communications between the two areas meant that valuable goods and money passed through Herefordshire. The border area was an ideal shelter for outlaws preying on this traffic. Yorkshire was sparsely settled and had few wealthy travelers. But because it was ideal terrain for robbery, some of the most spectacular robberies of the fourteenth century took place there.

Robbery is the theft of property through physical violence to a person or threats of violence that will force a person to give over his property. In the fourteenth century the term *robator*[59] or a variation was sometimes used, but more generally the indictment used the verb *depredare* or *spoliare*.[60] The same rules of felony applied to robbery as to larceny, that is, the goods had to be valued over 12d. and not be *ferae naturae*. In 1348, however, the royal judges of Westminster declared that all robbers would receive capital punishment regardless of the value of goods stolen.[61] This legal pronouncement brought the definition of robbery in line with that of burglary, which stated that simple breaking and entering, even if nothing was stolen, was sufficient for indictment.[62] Homicide that occured along with a robbery was charged against the suspect separately as in cases where burglary ended in the victim's murder.

Robbery was distinguished from both burglary and larceny in the techniques it involved, the types of goods the robbers sought, and the people who became robbers. While burglary and larceny largely involved unarmed local people, robberies were committed by outsiders skilled in the use of weapons such as swords, bows and arrows, and battle axes. The robbers, looking for high-profit items to steal, were not deterred by the possibility of violent encounters with their victims. If armed at all, their victims had only a knife or staff and were no match for robbers wielding the weapons of warfare. The robber most resembled the burglars who committed acts of physical violence against household residents. Indeed, there was little distinction between the two types of activity. Most gangs, such as that to which Helmbrecht belonged, committed both.

The type of goods stolen and the places where robberies occurred show that robbers have changed little over the centuries (see figures 3 and 7). Traditionally the robber is an impatient thief who does not want to wait until goods are left unguarded. Nor does he want to risk being caught in a house during a burglary. He does not want to ex-change easily recognized goods for money, but would rather have the money directly.[63] Valuables or money were taken in 29 percent of the robberies and cloth in 18.9 percent. Such items could be readily dis-posed of without the owner identifying them. Both horses (8.5 per-cent) and clothing (4.9 percent) were also common items for the rob-bers, being obvious goods to take from travelers. Because robbers usually selected lone victims, they most often acquired only one horse in a robbery. Clothing, even used clothing, was very expensive in the Middle Ages. A cloak or supertunic could be worth from 10s. to over a pound depending upon the traveler's wealth. Robbers also stole sheep and cattle, but they had no interest in low-value goods such as poultry, pigs, grain, and food.[64]

The risks of robbery were great, but so too were the profits (see figure 3). An astonishing 43.1 percent brought in £1 or more, 14.1 percent got 11 to 20s., and 18.5 percent got from 5 to 10s. Consider-ing the normal loot in robbery and the risks involved, it is surprising to find that 24.3 percent of the robberies were worth a shilling or under. No wonder the justices decided to punish the act of robbery regardless of the value of the goods stolen.

Robbers, unlike burglars and thieves, did not keep to a distinctive seasonal pattern. It was always open season on the highways for the victims of robbery. Only a slight decrease, not great enough to be significant, is noticeable in robbery for the colder months. In the weekly patterns, however, robbers followed the distribution of those committing larceny and burglary. Monday through Thursday were the high points (70 percent of the robberies) dropping down on Friday and at its lowest on Saturday and Sunday. Again, this is the reverse of the modern pattern. Market days might have been expected to bring out more robbers who would stop people traveling to and from the markets. But Sunday, a day with few robberies, was the most popular market day. Other market days were scattered during the week. Twilight was the most common time of theft, since it provided the cover of darkness, but where there were few observers on the road, travelers were vulnerable at any time.

Highways or streets were the most frequent sites of robberies (39.6 percent of the cases). This is also true of modern robberies.[65] Churches (28.1 percent) and fields (15.6 percent) were the next most frequent sites. Residences, both of the victims and the accused, also figured in robberies.[66] The kings were well aware of the problem of robbers lurking about the highways, as is indicated in the Statute of Winchester: "It is commanded that the highways leading from one market town to another shall be broadened, wherever there is ditch or underwood or bushes, so that there be neither dyke, tree, nor bush where a man may lurk to do hurt."[67] The danger of highways and byways was also noted by Langland in *Piers Plowman.*

> Outlaws in the Wode, and under banke lotyeth,
> And many uch man se, and good merk take,
> Who is bihynde and who bifore, and who ben on horse,
> For he halt hym hardyer on horse, than he that is a fote.[68]

The techniques of robbery varied very much depending on the number of people involved and the type of goods to be stolen. One well-armed person or a group of people could accomplish simple highway robbery. A coroner's inquest gives the details of the lone robber's technique.

> At twilight on 25 April an unknown felon was standing among the blackthorns below Putnoe by the king's highway at Putnoe in the parish of Goldington, when brother Ralph the Carpenter, a wood-seller, came with Henry the Hayward, a servant-boy. They wished to go to their lodging at Putnoe, but the felon [armed with a bow and arrow] stole a good coat of "blanket" and 4d. in coin from brother Ralph and a coat of "rosset" from the said hayward and then ordered them to go home. They went to their lodging and immediately raised the hue, which was followed. The neighbourhood came, pursued the felon, found him below Putnoe wood fleeing with the stolen goods and tried to arrest him, but could not because he defended himself with a bow and arrows and would not surrender. Therefore brother Henry le Granger's servant Peter slew him in flight.[69]

Apparently this robber threatened his victims at a distance with a bow and arrow and had them disrobe.

Other robbers, usually working in groups, knocked out their victims, bound them, or killed them before robbing them. For instance, one man was on his way to the mill when he was set upon and bound by a group of unknown felons; another group of villagers were coming from St. Neots fair when they were beaten and robbed.[70] One outraged peasant complained about Helmbrecht and his gang:

> Me and my wife he once roped in
> And stripped us to the very skin—

Took every garment we had on;
So now he is my proper pawn.[71]

The planning in these cases was minimal compared to the elaborate, well-organized robbery carried out in 1342 by Sir Robert Rideware and Sir John de Oddyngesles against some Lichfield merchants who were carrying spices and textiles worth £40 to Stafford for market. Sir Robert and two of his men seized two servants and two packhorses with goods and took them to the priory of Lappeleye where Sir John was waiting with his supporters. They divided the spoils and then withstood an attack by the bailiff.[72]

Rather than taking goods from victims on the highway, robbers might take the victims themselves and hold them for ransom. Sometimes such cases were treated as trespasses rather than felonies. Two famous cases in the early fourteenth century have received considerable attention from historians. The ransoming of Sir Richard de Wylughby, a King's Bench justice, involved the concerted efforts of the Folvilles,[73] the Coterels,[74] Sir William de Coventry, and a number of lesser gangs in the West Midlands. The risk in robbing such a highly placed figure was great but worth it since the ransom paid was 1,300 marks. Another famous robbery and ransoming which gave England a bad reputation was engineered by Sir Gilbert Middleton. Sir Henry Beaumont was traveling to Durham with his brother, the bishop-elect, and two cardinals who were papal representatives on a peacemaking mission to the Scots. Sir Gilbert and a gang composed of northern gentry robbed the cardinals and took the Beaumonts to Sir Gilbert's castle at Mitford, where they were released after paying ransoms.[75] Bishops were good targets, for they traveled in expensive style. Nineteen men were accused of holding up Thomas Percy, elected and confimed bishop of Norwich, and his traveling companions in 1355.[76] Other gangs were after less high rewards than could be collected from a bishop or the king's justice. John son of Thomas Whit of Harpham seized Richard Randolf on the king's highway at Hontoncotes and imprisoned him until he paid 8 marks.[77]

Robbery, more than larceny and burglary, required planning because the robbers had to assume personal physical risk and calculate ways of making sure that the victim and not themselves would come off the worse for the confrontation. One of the most popular forms of robbery was to hold a pass or bridge on the main road that travelers had to use; they could not escape the ambush. The advantages of this technique were that the personnel required for success was minimal and that there was less need for prior knowledge of the travelers' movements. For instance, John Spryng was accused of holding a pass at le Regarth in the park of Newburgh and robbing one chaplain of 8s. 5d., four men of Brunne and Rotse of 9 marks, and one man of £10.[78] William of Norton and Hugh son of John le Servant of Newton Wakefield were convicted of holding a pass at Berngestan for four days and robbing William Mabotson of Wynbelton of 1s., John of Rockwell of clothing worth 3s., Robert of Berton of money worth 5s., and Nicholas of Chirlekeld of money worth 22s.[79]

Women occasionally were part of gangs, but their role was not specified. They might have been used as decoys to encourage travelers to slow down and engage in conversation. Hugh of Nuttle and Lucia, his concubine, formed one such association at the pass at Emmethorp Rye in Yorkshire and robbed various people there. Isabel daughter of Stacie of Rudham was accused along with her husband and four other men of holding Hertfordbridge in Norfolk and committing robberies there.[80]

Some gangs of criminals even held ports, towns, and gates to cities and robbed the inhabitants. John of Allerston and John Scot of Whitby and others were charged with holding the port of Whitby, robbing two men, stopping ships and sailors, and generally endangering the lives and property of the people in the town.[81] Scarborough was held twice in the fourteenth century by armed robbers who fortified the town and robbed the citizens.[82] Allies of the Duke of Lancaster held Harrowgate and Bilton and robbed people coming through the gates.[83]

Markets and fairs were also good targets for well-organized robber gangs. William of Coventry and his gang held up the market of Foxele and then proceeded to rob the manor of Lord Richard of Foxele.[84] More petty attacks at fairs are cited in the Wakefield court materials where, for instance, William son of Nicholas Carter charged John de Heton with assault and the loss of cheese and beer from his stall.[85]

Norfolk's geographical location on the treacherous sandbars of the Wash gave her felons an added specialty in robbery—attacking grounded ships and carrying off their cargoes. Henry Stake of Woodrising appealed Robert Boidyn of Yelverton and others of killing thirty-six men in a ship called *St. Edmund* in a place called Le Nes near Hunstanton. They took wax, leather, oil, and timber valued at £3,000.[86] Others robbed at sea or when boats were in port. Walter of

Osborn and Adam son of Richard of Saham, John Brydand, and others were accused of murdering a woman and a foreign merchant in a boat at sea on the coast and taking cloth worth £40. They were all found guilty but produced pardons from the king for their service against the Scots.[87] The gang of Roger of Stone and John Robel robbed boats in port.[88] One man, John Crame, a mariner from North Yarmouth, took a leper boat that was moored at Yarmouth.[89]

Robbers also entered the homes of victims, attacking them and taking their goods. Rather than breaking into the structures as a burglar would, the robbers used ruses similar to those used in larceny cases to gain entry. Both the technique of these bands and the impact they could have on a village is apparent in this case from Bedfordshire.

> Towards vespers at twilight on 1 Sept. 1267, 6 thieves came to Honeydon in the parish of Eaton Socon, found a boy Philip son of Roger Golde, who was coming from his father's fold, beat, ill treated and wounded him, and forced him to lead them to Ralph son of Geoffry of Honeydon's house and called to Ralph to let them in. Ralph recognized Philip and opened the door. The thieves entered, assaulted, wounded and then bound Ralph, killed his mother Denis and his servant William of Roxton and then robbed the whole house and took away all its goods. From there they went to William Courtepie's house, broke it, assaulted and badly wounded William with swords, axes and anlances and stole the goods of the house. From there they went to the house of Margery Levot, widow, and killed her with swords. From there they went to Mathew le Messer's house, assaulted, beat and wounded him, struck his wife Isabel, breaking her left arm and took away the goods of the house. From there they went to Roger Golde's house, and Roger, hearing the great noise of the slain and wounded; immediately took his wife and boys and hid in the croft; the thieves entered his house, robbed it of all its goods and took them away. From there they went to William of Lodday's house, bound him and took away the goods of the house. From there they went to William Motte's house in Goodwick, wounded William, left him for dead and then burned his house; he died before prime on 5 September, having had the rites of the church. At length Philip, Roger Golde's boy, who had been captured at the fold, escaped from the hands of the thieves and raised the hue.[90]

In another case the victim's charity led to his robbery and murder. Reynold le Wyt heard a poor boy, aged 8, sitting outside his house crying for lack of a home. When Reynold came out of his house to comfort the boy, thieves jumped him and struck a blow to his head that killed him. They then entered his house, assaulted his family, and stole his goods.[91]

Robbers also enticed victims to their homes rather than trying to gain access to the victims' homes. One approver, Hugh le Mareshal, claimed that he and Juetta la Hayward of Bodenham killed a Coventry merchant in her house and stole money from him worth five marks. They disposed of the body in the water at Lugge.[92] Juetta may have been a prostitute, but no reference is made in this or other cases of prostitutes stealing in the course of their profession. There are cases in the London coroners' rolls of prostitutes bringing men into their rooms and then murdering them. Presumably they could have robbed them as well.

Extortion, the extraction of money by threats of violence, was sometimes recorded as a felony. Its position in criminal courts was ambiguous. Extortion was basically considered to be a trespass and, therefore, a matter for civil jurisdiction, but there were occasions when extortion threats came into the criminal courts, especially with special oyer and terminer or trailbaston sessions. For instance, Lord Robert son of Payn kept a gang that roamed the countryside beating and wounding victims and then warning them to pay a sum to avoid such attacks in the future. They managed to extort from one mark to £2 from five victims for a total of £6 9d.[93] Gangs such as the Coterels in the west Midlands found that they had sufficient reputation for murder, beating, robbery, and mayhem that the fear of their reputation alone was enough for extortion. In one case members of the Coterel gang went to the home of Robert Fraunceys at Hardstoft and demanded 40s. Fraunceys was so terrified that he left his house and did not return to live there for a long time.[94]

ARSON

Arson, the willful burning of structures and goods belonging to another person, was very rare in the fourteenth century. Only 0.8 percent of all crimes were arson cases. Furthermore, there was very little county to county variation.[95] There were too few arson cases recorded for a seasonal or daily analysis of the felony. Since there was no insurance on structures, burning a building was only destructive and not profitable. The only way to make money on arson was through extortion. Other motives for arson were revenge, punishment of the victim, or insanity. In the few cases in the records the arsonists burnt the victim's home in 62.5 percent of them and his barn in 37.5 percent.

Arson cases involving an insane person are rare. The jurors did, however, recommend that Thomas of Ipswich, a stranger to the Ramsey Abbey area, be pardoned for burning the Rector of Ripton's barn because he was insane.[96] He may have been a pyromaniac or he could have attacked the Rector's property because of a supposed grudge.

The motivation in revenge arson cases is likewise very unclear. Sometimes arson followed a robbery of the property and other times no goods were taken but the property loss was substantial. For instance, John Wolmer of Rockland was accused of burning a barn belonging to Robert Peper that contained grain worth 100s.[97] No reason for this destruction was given. This case looks like a private matter between the victim and accused, but sometimes there were so many different people involved that the action might have been a concerted community punishment of one of its members or possibly of an officer of the village's lord. Thirteen men in Norfolk were accused of burning the house of Alexander le Deken of Needham in 1301.[98] In one case the motivation for the revenge arson was given. Lord Simon de Montacute employed Luke le Little and his gang to break the millstones and burn the mills of three jurors who testified against Matilda Simon of Chard, a woman under Lord Simon's protection.[99]

The threat of or actual use of arson in procuring money or services through extortion appears in some detail in the records and shows a range from simple amateur extortion to very sophisticated, professional efforts to collect money. The most simply planned was that of Richard the Smith of Werloley and John son of Nyk who came at night to the house of William the Grave. They threatened to burn him and all his goods unless he gave them a silver mark and a tunic. William opened his window and gave them 2s. 4d. and a tunic worth 3s.[100] Two other men were much more demanding; they required 4s. 4d. redemption from immediate destruction of the house and its owner and subsequent payments of 4s. 4d.[101]

A few spectacular cases are preserved in which elaborate plans were made involving considerable division of labor. It was perhaps for this reason that in the 1360s instructions to the justices of the peace specifically told them to take sureties from men who threatened arson or bodily harm.[102] The techniques of extortion for either property damage or physical violence described in the robbery section are similar to those used in arson cases. Someone would write the threatening letter to the intended victim, a carrier would deliver the letter, perhaps "tourchmen" would be employed to set the fire or threaten to do so, and arrangements would be made for the money to be delivered to another carrier. A few examples will show this process in practice. The Coterel gang sent a threatening letter to William Amyas, mayor of Nottingham, instructing him to pay the sum of £20 or else all his possessions outside Nottingham would be burned. With the letter Amyas received half of an indented bill. He was to pay the money to a carrier who would present him with the other half of the indented bill as identification.[103] The reputation of the Coterels was sufficiently villainous that they did not have to burn the property to show that the threat was serious.

In a Kent case a gang broke into Lord John de Cobham's manor and set fires in his barns. We have some idea of the cost of "tourchmen" of this sort from a Yorkshire case in which a man paid two arsonists 6s. 6d. to burn a mill.[104] The wages were high, but the men risked being charged with the crime themselves. The Cobham fires had followed an unsuccessful attempt to get Lord John to pay £400. The extortionists instructed him to send two or three of his men and horses with the money to a place called Kynlyne Crouch on the high hill near Aylesford. To indicate his agreement, he was to dispatch his bailiff to Chatham chapel at High Mass as a sign. Since the bailiff did not appear, the arsonists burnt Lord John's goods. They had also sent a letter to the bailiff urging him to advise Lord John to comply. When indictments were brought some men were cited for the actual arson; a member of the clergy, Master Henry de Nortwode, for consenting to the act and writing the letters; a canon of Leeds for carrying the letter; and several other men for consent and conspiracy.[105]

The rarity of arson cases in fourteenth-century gaol delivery rolls is understandable. Although fairly large sums of money might be procured through threats of arson, the planning of such extortion was complicated and required specialized personnel. Furthermore, influential victims were likely to treat it as a civil case or get a writ of oyer and terminer for a special inquiry. For the bulk of the offenders, who were looking for smaller rewards, larceny, burglary, and even robbery were more direct ways of procuring money.

Receiving

An important concern for felons who stole property was disposing of the goods and hiding themselves from their pursuers. Receivers of stolen goods and suspected felons are necessary elements in the criminal behavior pattern both in the fourteenth century and now. Yet very few people, 6.2 percent of all felons, were indicted for receiving. With the exception of Huntingdonshire, the percentages of indictment for receiving varied little.[106] The high percentage in Huntingdonshire, 20 percent, could indicate that the fairs of St. Ives and St. Neots attracted more felons with goods to dispose of, but more likely it is attributable to the small sample for the county, which probably throws off the data.[107] Seasonal and daily patterns are not available for receiving.

Receiving of stolen goods or known felons has been ignored or only briefly mentioned by most legal historians largely because the treatise writers ignored the problem.[108] In the surviving justice of the peace indictments the jurors seemed far more concerned about the offense than the chief justice of the session.[109] The gaol delivery cases give some indication of the ambiguity toward receivers. Approvers appealed most of the receivers appearing in gaol delivery rolls. The credibility of these confessed felons was very low in any case and even more so when they named receivers, so that most suspects were acquitted. The wealth of detail that is often given about the activities of receivers leaves little doubt about their actual existence. The approvers often told exactly what they had gotten in exchange for the goods and where they had taken them. All the information was duly recorded in the gaol delivery rolls, but the jurors went on acquitting suspected fences.

Receivers usually worked out of their own homes (66.6 percent) or in the marketplace (33.3 percent). The scene of the transaction depended upon who the receiver was. A woman receiving her felonious husband would obviously be in their home.[110] But even professional fences used their own homes as a base. A husband and wife bought clothing and six ells of cloth from a thief in their home and a woolen cloth worker bought seven ells of cloth in his home-shop.[111] Other fences bought in their shops. Robert Bayl, a confessed thief, claimed that he disposed of his goods regularly to goldsmiths in Hereford city.[112] Butchers also were prime receivers, especially for stolen animals.

Agnes Pegere of Thornes stole two sheep from William Maynard, sold them to Peter de Acom and John le Leche, butchers, and afterwards William Maynard came to the house of the butchers and knew the sheep; but what he knew therein is not known.[113]

Usually what the owner recognized in the butcher's shop was the hide and the head of the animal.

To conceal the identity of stolen goods, the thief either had to dispose of them at considerable distance from the crime or had to convert them into a form in which the owner would not recognize them. With livestock, the most obvious solution was to convert the animal into a variety of chops, roasts, and stews. Many thieves stole for their own suppers, as did Mak in the *Second Shepherds' Pagent*. Because they did not have time to kill the sheep before the shepherds discovered them, Mak and his wife tried to disguise it as a baby in a cradle.[114] When a person was caught on suspicion of theft with hides in his possession, he probably had eaten the meat and was on the way to a market to sell the hides. Thieves whose interest was not in filling their immediate needs of hunger would sell the animals to a butcher or another receiver of stolen goods for cash. Jewelry, plate, and cloth were also readily convertible into other forms and found a quick market among goldsmiths, clothiers, and less specialized receivers. For instance, one approver found a mercer willing to buy one pound of red silk and vellum.[115] The mercer would have little trouble converting these items into other goods.

Removing the stolen goods far from the scene of the crime before finding a buyer was a good precaution. Taking goods across the county line was advisable because they were then hard to trace. Philip Coke stole a cow in Bedfordshire and sold the meat at Rothwell in Northamptonshire, and Richard Mariot stole nineteen cows and oxen in Everton, Huntingtonshire, and sold them in Ely, Cambridgeshire. Robert Crowe of Rothwell stole two pigs at Brampton and sold the meat at Rothwell, four-and-a-half miles away. John de Modewell of Brampton burgled a mill in Haxelberth from which he stole grain and flour worth 16s. and sold it in Arthingworth, three-and-a-half miles away.[116] Although these cases were all from Northamptonshire, other counties show similar patterns. In Herefordshire, the thieves tended to take their goods to Hereford or Leominster where there seem to have been regular receivers. In Huntingdonshire St. Neots fair had a number of receivers. These established centers for receiving may indicate a thriving black market for some goods.

Those receivers who were not obviously amateurs receiving members of their own families and their loot seemed to have developed techniques to get the best products and to avoid detection. They probably also had a fairly wide reputation. One receiver ranged over several counties and many miles. Hugh le Turill was from Cringleford, Norfolk, and was convicted for receiving a horse in that village, another horse in Rickingall, Suffolk, twenty-one miles away, and a third horse in Cambridgeshire, forty miles away.[117] Some receivers appear to have been organized into groups. For instance, Christine Hewish, Margery Brendel, Felicia Kyngman and her daughter Colette, John son of Matilda la Frie, his brother Richard, and William son of John de Bruges were indicted as a group for receiving the goods from a robbery done by Henry Capus.[118] One wonders what type of organization they had for disposal of the goods. Was there a Flemish connection through John de Bruges? One man, Richard de Wormbridge, was a resident of Hereford city and was called a "common receiver of thieves and purse cutters."[119] Whether or not he was guilty of this is immaterial to the fact that the indicting jurors of Hereford knew that there were people who made their living as fences.

Fences never paid the thief the full value of the goods, for they made their profits from paying less and selling at the full market value. In all the transactions recorded in the gaol delivery rolls, the thief got half or less than half the value of the stolen items. Helmbrecht's father warned his son that he would come to sell his ill-gotten loot for even less than half if he was hungry.

> Do you, dear child, eat of it [meal cake] too,
> Before you go so far that you
> Exchange your stolen oxen when
> You're hungry, for a paltry hen.
> Each week day mother she can make
> The best of soups and no mistake!
> Fill up your maw with that! 'Twill aid
> You better than to give in trade
> For someone's goose your stolen horse.
> If you will only take this course
> You'll live in honor, son like me,
> No matter where you chance to be.[120]

In desperation, no doubt, thieves like Helmbrecht did sell their goods for paltry sums or exchange them for food.

A few examples will give an idea of the fences' profits. A Yorkshire thief described what his various fences gave him: he sold one pound of red silk worth 18s. for 7s., seven ells of cloth worth 11s. for 5s., eleven ells of cloth worth 9s. for 3s., six ells of cloth worth 6s. for 3s., clothes worth 6s. for 3s., a stone of pork meat worth 8d. for 3d., seven ells of cloth worth 5s. 1d. sold for 3s. Northamptonshire fences drove even harder bargains. A rochet worth 16d. sold for 7d., cloth and a robe worth 16d. sold for 6d., clothing worth 8s. sold for 2s., a horse worth 30s. sold for 5s., sixteen sheep worth 32s. sold for 3s., sixty sheep worth 4 marks sold for 1/2 mark, twelve oxen worth £6 sold for £3, and church vestments worth 20s. sold for 10s.[121]

Not all felons nor their receivers were involved in selling goods; some of the felons simply sought food, drink, and refuge from the law. Henry of Oldfield, a clerk, was found guilty of receiving the felons Philip le Drous, Henry and Reginald his brothers, and William of Oldfield. The crown must have been very serious about insuring the continued good behavior of this clerk because he was released to the bishop only after paying £100 to the crown.[122] The receivers did not always take in felons with good will. When the Rideware and Oddyngesles gang collaborated on a robbery they sought shelter in a nunnery. The prioress refused to let them in but they broke in and helped themselves to the amenities of the place.[123] Members of the nobility and upper clergy, who regularly received and protected felons, were probably employing the felons in their own schemes or as part of their household.

HOMICIDE

People regard homicide with both fear and tingling curiosity. It is no less fascinating to study it in the fourteenth century than in the present day. Indeed, the comparisons between the two increase the interest and indicate that the pattern of homicide has changed, perhaps more than for other felonies. The reason probably lies in the nature of the crime itself. Homicide is most often an act of passionate anger, which is usually only possible between people who know each other well and have reason to argue.[124] If the range and type of people with whom people are likely to come into potentially homicidal conflict changes, so too will the pattern of homicide. If attitudes toward taking human life in protection of honor or property change, then the role of homicide in the overall crime configuration will alter as well. In some respects, therefore, an analysis of homicide indicates not only how criminal behavior has changed but also how social interactions have altered over six hundred years. But comparison with modern studies of homicide, even for primitive societies, can only be suggestive of the change for many other factors can influence the figures.

Homicide may be studied in more depth and with more accuracy

than other felonies because the coroners' inquests, the court of first
instance for violent deaths, have been preserved as well as the gaol
delivery rolls.[125] Northamptonshire has one of the best series of coroners' rolls, which includes seventy years from 1300-1420.[126] This
series has 1,307 cases (575 homicides, 716 misadventures, and 16
suicides). H. E. Salter's collection of Oxford city coroners' rolls from
1296 to 1393 includes twelve complete years of records yielding 100
cases (68 homicides, 40 misadventures, and 2 suicides).[127] R. R.
Sharpe's calendar has eight complete years of London rolls for 1300-
1340 with 205 cases (145 homicides, 58 misadventures, and 2 suicides).[128] The two series of printed borough records have the advantage of being a reliable report of the number of violent deaths in the
cities in the years that they cover because borough coroners kept only
one roll between them. The county records are not as dependable
because individual coroners often kept their own rolls.[129]

At the beginning of the fourteenth century virtually every homicidal act—the killing of one person by another—was culpable except
for those connected with the enforcement of the peace; accidental and
self-defense slayings, which were pardonable; and a variety of other
cases where extenuating circumstances, including insanity and the
minority of the offender, could lead to the recommendation of a pardon.[130] All other cases of homicide were punishable by hanging
whether or not they were done with malice aforethought. The word
"murder" was used in two senses in the fourteenth century. Initially,
the meaning was a specific one connected with the fine of *murdrum*,
which the community was to pay when a Norman was found slain and
the slayer was not caught. This law had been introduced by William I
to protect the conquerors and was not removed until 1340, long after
the need for it had ceased to exist. But the word also came to mean a
particularly heinous crime involving secret slaying or malice aforethought.[131] This second meaning was not given statutory recognition
until 1390 when murder was distinguished to mean those killings involving a willful act of *par malice prepense*. The distinction between
murder and manslaughter did not come until the sixteenth century.[132]
The coroners' rolls, then, include both manslaughter and murder cases
and do not draw a distinction between them, except in accidental
death, self-defense and other pardon cases.

Homicide was the third most common crime prosecuted in England;
18.2 percent of all cases appearing in gaol delivery were homicides.
This is a very high percentage compared to the United States in 1965

when only 0.4 percent of all crimes were homicides.[133] Some counties had more homicide cases than others (see table 4). The wild north and Midlands counties deserved their reputations in the fourteenth century, for Yorkshire had 23.9 percent homicides, Northamptonshire had 23.7 percent, and Huntingdonshire had 27.5 percent. Herefordshire and Somerset also were fairly rough with 16.7 percent and 16.4 percent respectively. The more settled counties in the center of England had fewer homicides (all near to 13 percent). Considering that the population was sparse in Yorkshire and Huntingdonshire, the amount of homicide was very high.

Because the records for homicide are more accurate than for any other crime, it is possible to speculate on the number of incidences of homicide in the population. L. O. Pike threw caution to the winds in that delightful polemical style of nineteenth-century crime writers and, based on eighty-eight cases for 1348 from Yorkshire and a guess at the population of England at the time, calculated that

> If it were possible to conceive society in the same state now as then, there would be four thousand four hundred simple murders per annum, in addition to all the horrors of brigandage and private war. [This is compared to 250 cases per annum in the 1860s in England.] In other words, the security of life is now at least eighteen times as great as it was in the age of chivalry.[134]

Modern studies in medieval demography have shown that estimates of total population have too wide a margin of error to be used for arriving at an accurate crime rate. Certainly, a homicide rate for Northamptonshire is out of the question since both population and homicide statistics are suspect. A cautious estimate might be made using the more reliable coroners' roll data from London and the probable range of 35,000 to 50,000 for the pre-plague London population.[135] In the eight years of London coroners' rolls of the first half of the fourteenth century, there was an average of eighteen homicides per year. A glance at the *Uniform Crime Reports* for 1965 shows that, normally, a city in the United States with a population range of 25,000 to 50,000 has two homicides per year.[136] Expressing the London figures in homicides per 10,000 population gives a homicide rate of 5.2 to 3.6 per year. Compared to more modern annual homicide rates, these are strikingly high: Miami had the highest homicide rate of any American city in 1948-52 with 1.5 per 10,000 population; among Uganda tribes in Africa the highest rate was 1.2; in Ceylon the highest rate was 0.7; and in modern Britain, 0.05.[137]

So common was violent death from homicide that in medieval London or Oxford the man in the street ran more of a risk from dying at the hands of a fellow citizen than from an accident. There were 43 percent more homicides than misadventures in London and 26 percent more in Oxford. In rural Northamptonshire the percentage of homicidal deaths was only 10 percent lower than accidental deaths.[138]

The seasonal pattern of homicide in rural Northamptonshire generally followed the agricultural calendar. The period of high homicide was March through August, when 59 percent of the homicides occurred.[139] The gaol delivery rolls give exactly the same breakdown, and statistical tests confirm that these figures are significant. In the modern pattern of crime, which shows an increase in May through September, the peaks in homicide are attributed to changes in social activities.[140] The social activities associated with the spring and summer months in medieval rural England could have produced potentially homicidal tensions. Between March and May, competition for food remaining from the previous harvest would be at its greatest. The stresses arising from food shortages would have been aggravated during those months and the succeeding ones by the planting and harvesting of crops. Arguments over land, debts, and trespasses were most crucial during this period. Finally, there was more social contact among villagers at this time than during the fall and winter because of the longer daylight hours and the necessity of working close together in the common fields. Those fields must have been very bloody indeed during those six months because 60 percent of the misadventures occurred during that period as well.

The importance of social activities associated with seasonal labor becomes clearer when the seasonal homicide pattern of Northamptonshire is compared with those of London and Oxford. The Oxford cycle seemed to follow the academic calendar rather than the agricultural pursuits or warm weather: summer was the low homicide season while December through June were high. Both the increase of population with the students in town and the traditional tensions between town and gown contributed to the distribution of homicide in Oxford.[141] London, on the other hand, reflected very little seasonal variation showing only a slight tendency for both homicide and misadventure to increase in the summer months.

Although city and country differed in the monthly distribution of violent death, they followed a very similar pattern in their daily deaths. Sunday was the day of murder in medieval society. In Northamptonshire 21 percent of the homicides occurred on Sunday with

Saturday and Monday catching the spillover with 15 percent each. The information from the gaol delivery rolls indicates a similar pattern. In London, the Sunday total was 38 percent with Monday having 20 percent; and Oxford had 23 percent on Sunday, but its highest was 29 percent on Saturday. Again, social customs played the most likely role in the daily distribution of crime. With paychecks coming on Friday or Saturday and drink flowing most freely on those days, modern murder figures are highest on the weekends.[142] Medieval society did not know the weekend, but did recognize Sunday and some saints' days as having at least some hours of rest, drinking, sports, and fights. Perhaps it was the lingering effects of the Sunday drinking or argument that made Monday high in homicide as well.

If Sunday was the day to kill, evening to night was the time. The medieval designation of time is rather rough, but it did distinguish the canonical hours and the natural divisions of sunrise, sunset, and night. Vespers to midnight were overwhelmingly homicide hours. In Northamptonshire 86 percent of the killings occurred during this period with the bulk of them happening after nightfall. In Oxford these hours brought fatal attacks to 96 percent of the victims. In London 90 percent of the homicidal attacks fell in those hours with a peak being reached at the hour of curfew. The twilight hours were times of drinking and social contact in taverns and night was the time favored by surreptitious killers such as burglars, robbers, and ambushers. This preference of the murderer for the cover of darkness is a long tradition, for in modern homicide as well 80 percent of the murders occur between 6:00 P.M. and 12:00 A.M.[143]

Weapons that pierced or cut were the most common murder instruments, causing 73 percent of the deaths.[144] Medieval men routinely carried some sort of knife or dagger on their persons, so it is not surprising that knife wounds caused 42 percent of the fatal deaths. The ready availability of knives is apparent in almost all self-defense cases. To give but one example:

> On Sunday 22 March 1332, John Wikynes was leading his mother on a horse across a field to Grymmesbury hospital when Robert de Beruglby, a miller, set his dog on John and knocked John to the ground. While the dog pinned John down, Robert prepared to hit him another blow with his staff. John drew his knife and killed Robert.[145]

As the case indicates, the staff was also a common weapon. Little John of the Robin Hood gang was not alone in his proficiency with the quarter staff, for 27 percent of the deaths were attributed to this weapon.[146] The bow and arrow was a surprisingly unpopular weapon in homicides despite the great tradition of the English long bow and the advantages of being able to kill a victim at a distance. But most medieval homicides occurred in the course of an argument rather than resulting from either long-standing hatreds or malice aforethought. The bow and arrow was typically the weapon of ambush rather than of man to man fighting.

About a third of all homicides in rural society and about a quarter of the urban ones occurred in a house, usually that of the victim. Most domestic murders and homicide/burglaries took place in the home of the victim. Tavern fights figured in only 7 percent of the murders. Robbery accounts for practically all slayings in the woods and some of those on the king's highway. But for the most part, medieval society engaged in social contacts on the streets and in the fields. In London, 61 percent of all homicides took place in the streets. Often matters directly related to the use of the streets instigated the homicide. A boy was beaten to death by a couple of apprentices because he was selling eels in front of their shop and throwing the skins on the ground.[147] In rural society as well, the village streets were social gathering places for business, drinking, games, and a variety of other contacts with neighbors and strangers that had the potential of ending in homicide. In the majority of cases, however, the fields were the setting for rural homicides. The gaol delivery information shows a slightly different pattern from the Northamptonshire coroners' rolls. Highways and streets were the most common location (30 percent), followed by houses (27.1 percent), churches (15.7 percent), and fields (12.8 percent.)[148]

SUICIDE

Suicide, *felo de se*, was technically a felony even though a person could not stand trial for successfully accomplishing it. I found no cases of people being tried for attempted suicide. Killing oneself was considered a felony both because of the religious prohibitions against self-destruction and because the king had the same rights over a suicide's land and chattels as he did over those of a regular felon.[149] Only if the person was judged to be insane at the time of the death were his lands and goods safe for his heirs. Considering the profit the king could derive, it is surprising that suicides were not reported more frequently in the coroners' rolls. Suicides comprised only 1 percent of all cases in the coroners' rolls (3 percent of the combined homicidal and suicidal deaths.) The percentage increased somewhat in the Tudor period to 5 percent of all violent deaths.[150]

There is a temptation to look at the very low percentage of suicides and find that Durkheim was correct in his study on homicide and suicide; that suicide will be greater in industrialized society where anomie is greater. The close knit village community appears, he suggests, more capable of coming to the aid of the depressed person and preventing suicide.[151] This explanation is, however, not necessarily the most obvious one for the dearth of suicides in coroners' rolls. While there may have been more community support and less feeling of alienation, the community was also probably active in concealing the suicides. The vast majority of those cases of suicide mentioned in the rolls involved hanging. Hanging would be almost impossible for the local jurors to call either an accident or a homicide, but, since 40 percent of the accidental deaths involving adults were drownings, they could have concealed suicide by claiming the person drowned accidentally. People certainly did drown themselves. Those cases in gaol delivery where the insane were said to have attempted suicide through drowning before they committed homicide heightens suspicions that the record is incomplete. The community may have been ignorant of the motivation for drownings, but it is more likely that they purposely concealed those suicides that they could. The absence of suicide notes in a largely illiterate society made the task easier. Community feeling would be with the surviving family. If the jurors declared the death an accident, the family would be able to inherit the property. Furthermore, the body would be properly buried in the churchyard rather than at the crossroads with a stake through the heart or outside the hallowed grounds of the church.[152]

The mode of death and, in some cases, the motivation for death were recorded, but suicides were so infrequent that no seasonal or daily pattern is discernable. Although it is certainly possible that drowning was the most characteristic form of suicide, hanging was the most frequently reported one. For instance, John Bretton of Wardon hanged himself from a beam in his house on March 24, 1334.[153] Sometimes the scene of the hanging was away from the family in the seclusion of the barn or in a tree. The suicide of Agnes wife of John le Smithesson of Middleton is reported in more detail than most. The jurors say that she went at night "with malice aforethought to a tree in her husband's close and climbed it. She tied a rope around a branch of the tree and the other end around her neck and hanged herself."[154]

There were some recorded cases of drownings. Hugh Beaufitz, the jurors claimed, drowned himself in the river flowing through Weston field and feloniously killed himself.[155]

Men and women committed suicide with equal frequency and showed no preference for one form of death over another. Suicide was usually committed in the evening or at night. Those hanging themselves chose their homes or barns most frequently.

The motivations for suicides were seldom given unless the person was insane. Poverty does not seem to have been a motivation in the recorded cases. This is consistent with the modern pattern in which there are more suicides among the upper status groups in society. When the chattels were listed, they showed most victims to have had sufficient wealth to live comfortably. For instance, Hugh de Brethale of Geytington was found to have grain worth £20, sheep worth 9 marks, and oxen, cows, steers, mares, horses, colts, and pigs worth 11 marks.[156]

Domestic troubles might have motivated some of the suicides. Isabel wife of John Aylgard and her husband were going to town when he inquired if she had been sure to cover the fire in their house. He then ordered her, apparently rather roughly, to return to the house and put it out. She committed suicide in the house when she returned.[157] This selection of a suicide site within the house may indicate that there was a desire on the part of the perpetrator to make members of the family uncomfortable by the death and to insure that they would be the first finders of the body.

Some of the cases resulted from depression over specific circumstances. For instance, a man arrested for larceny was being led across a bridge on his way to gaol. He broke loose and jumped off the bridge into the river.[158] Given gaol conditions, the suicide is understandable. One particularly poignant case comes from Worcestershire. A tenant of the Earl of Glocester was ordered to take land on servile conditions. He drowned himself in the River Severn.[159]

Those cases where the jury could definitely declare the person to be insane at the time of the suicide indicate readily identifiable cases of extreme depression and mental illness. The Oxford jurors, for instance, said that Henry de Bordesle "had long been sick with diverse diseases, and on Saturday before the said Monday he took a knife and smote himself in the belly, for he was as it were mad; and afterwards he lived until the Sunday and then died of his wound."[160] A Bedfordshire woman was also described as ill at the time of her suicide and murders.

103

On 15 June 1316 Emma le Bere had an illness called "frenesye" (*sic*. frenzy) and was lying down, but rose from her bed, took an instrument called "boleax" (*sic*. bole-axe, a large axe) and cut the throats of John, Helen, Felise, and Maude the son and daughters of John le Bere. Immediately afterwards she hanged herself in her house on a beam with two cords of hemp.[161]

Such overt sickness was, however, the only psychological explanation that jurors would permit themselves in analyzing suicide. It was similar to the criteria used for pleading insanity in homicide.

RAPE

Rape is a particularly important crime to study in the fourteenth century because it was first elevated to the position of a true felony in 1285 by the Statute of Westminster II, just fifteen years before this study begins to survey the records. As this law became the basis of our modern rape law, its implementation is of great importance for understanding our own law. The law of 1285 made it possible for presentment jurors to indict men for rape rather than putting the burden of appeal on the victims. It also made the punishment for rape the same as for all other felonies. Prior to 1285 rape along with mayhem (wounding) were considered illegal attacks on persons but in the case of rape the punishment was castration.[162] In practice few rape cases were tried and those that were ended in acquittal or some concord with the victim such as a fine or marriage.[163] The comparatively recent formulation of the rape law meant that legal opinion on the definition and prosecution of rape cases in the countryside was confused in the first half of the fourteenth century.

The act of rape was loosely defined as violent sexual assault on a woman (*vi concubuit*) against her will and against the peace (*contra voluntatem ipsius A. et contra pacem*). In order for the act to count as a rape, coitus apparently had to be completed. Cases were dismissed or degraded to trespasses or finable offenses if there was only violent assault and attempted rape.[164] Unnatural sexual acts came under ecclesiastical court discretion rather than that of secular courts. The Statute of Westminster II also distinguished abduction of women with the intention to sexually assault them and to take their property or their husband's property as a felony that could be tried at the king's suit.[165] Although the statute implied that this was a separate offense from rape, it will be considered with rape in this section.

The administration of Westminster II added further interpretations to the law of rape. The statute gave women forty days to appeal a case of rape and name the felon. The time limit was set to prevent women from appealing men for rape months later, perhaps when a child was born. Even before forty days were up much of the evidence proving she had resisted the rape—wounds, bruises, and such—would have disappeared. As in modern courts, the onus of proof was put upon the victim if she initiated the charges. Rape cases could also come into the courts through the regular process of indictments. In practice, indictments depended upon the condition in society of the victimized woman. If the woman involved was a young girl, a virgin, or a noble or very high status woman, indictment was likely. But if she was of low status or some slur could be put upon her, the jury would not indict or the case would end in acquittal.[166] There seemed to be strong sentiment that men should not even be indicted for rape unless the victim was a virgin and even then the low incidence of indictment indicates that opinion was not strong about punishing rapists.[167]

In the first half of the fourteenth century few rape cases were prosecuted. They constituted only 0.5 percent of all felony cases studied. Huntingdonshire, Northamptonshire, and Surrey had no reported rapes, but Somerset had 1.2 percent and Yorkshire had 0.9 percent, or slightly above the mean. This figure is in fact very close to the 0.9 percent of felonies in the United States.[168] Looking at the progessive application of the law over the century in Norfolk and Yorkshire, it appears that jurors only gradually became aware of the new felony and the conditions necessary for indictment. In the first half of the century Norfolk, which was usually more aware of the fine points of legal process than the other counties, had only 0.2 percent cases of rape or 0.1 incidence a year. Yorkshire had 0.8 annual incidences of rape in the first half of the century. These figures completely changed in the second fifty years of the fourteenth century. Norfolk jumped to 2 recorded rapes annually and 5.4 percent of all cases. Yorkshire, already high, went to 3.4 incidence per year and 3.6 percent of all crimes. In other words, it took about sixty-five years for the new rape law to be implemented in the countryside.

The prosecution of rape cases was often tied to a charge of accompanying burglary or robbery so that the rape may have been an incidental charge to that of property loss. Because the medieval definition of burglary was breaking and entering with the intent to commit a felony, if the rapist broke into his victim's house and raped her but did not take any of her possessions, he would still be charged with burglary, as was a man who broke into the house of Isabelle daughter of William de Brakenbergh and raped her.[169]

In general the value of goods taken in rape-robbery and rape-burglary was fairly small unless the felon stole goods from the victim's father or husband. One rapist-burglar got £ 20 from the husband.[170] In some cases the initial intention of the offender was probably theft, but, given the opportunity, he also raped the woman of the house. When a woman was alone on the highway, usually only her clothing and immediate possessions, which usually were of small value, were taken.[171] Widows were sometimes the exception to this rule for they might have substantial unguarded property. One widow was abducted with £ 10.[172]

Rape in the Middle Ages, as now, was underreported. Who can say how many masters raped servants or lords raped peasant women? Andreas Capellanus advised noblemen to do just that in *The Art of Courtly Love*.

> If you should, by some chance, fall in love with a peasant woman, be careful to puff her up with lots of praise and then, when you find a convenient place, do not hesitate to take what you seek and to embrace her by force. For you can hardly soften their outward inflexibility so far that they will grant you their embraces quietly or permit you to have the solaces you desire unless first you use a little compulsion as a convenient cure for their shyness.[173]

Rape could be a prelude to marriage, particularly when there was initial resistance on the part of the victim or her family. How large a role this played in medieval marriage customs cannot be determined, but cases do appear in which the woman later married the rapist.[174] The only readily documentable cases of using abduction and rape for marriage occurs among the upper classes and is really heir and heiress snatching. Children and widows of tenants-in-chief were valuable commodities. In a number of cases in the Patent Rolls guardians of abducted women and children asked for a commission of oyer and terminer against the abductors. For instance, William Coleman complained that a gang broke into his house at Carleton in Lincoln and abducted his daughter, Juliana, against her will and without his consent and married her off.[175] This type of abduction and marriage was typical for male children as well, so that it is not a sex-specific offense.[176] Some women consented to their abductions. Eva, recent widow of a tenant-in-chief, William Paunel, agreed to be abducted and married to Edward de St. John. He, however, was accused of rape because she married him without the king's consent. He had to pay a fine for the marriage.[177]

Because rape was so rarely reported, there is insufficient data for working out the monthly and daily distribution. The distance the rapists lived from their victims is also difficult to ascertain from the meager data. The reported cases, however, do permit a study of fourteenth-century rapists' techniques and the place of the crime.

Although a statistical analysis of the meeting place of the offender and victim is not possible with the scanty data, individual cases show that the settings of rape tended to be fields, or in the case of burglary or abduction the victim's or the accused's house. The attempted rape of a young girl in the fields is illustrated in a coroner's case.

> After nones on 24 May 1270 Emma daughter of Richard Toky of Southill went to "Houleden" in Southill to gather wood. Walter Gargolf of Stanford came, carrying a bow and a small sheaf of arrows, took hold of Emma and tried to throw her to the ground and deflower her, but she immediately shouted and her father came. Walter immediately shot an arrow at him, striking him on the right side of the forehead and giving him a mortal wound. He struck him again with another arrow under the right side so into the stomach. Seman of Southill immediately came and asked him why he wished to kill Richard, and Walter immediately shot an arrow at him, striking him in the back so that his life was despaired of. Walter then immediately fled.[178]

Cases in gaol delivery also report the rape of girls in houses, in a barn, as on the Prior of Watton's estate where the offender found his victim, and in the woods, where a forester raped his victim.[179]

In the robbery and rape cases on highways or streets the rape might take place at the meeting point or the victim might be removed. Two men, one a marshall, robbed William Ciry of 100s. in goods and raped his wife, Matilda, on Mikelgate Street in York City.[180] The records do not indicate that they dragged their victim to an alley but rather that the act occurred on the street. In other cases, however, the victim was abducted to another location, perhaps the home of the offender, before the rape occurred. Such was the case with Joan wife of Richard Bakon de Markington who was taken to Claton Grange, twenty-four miles from her home, and detained there.[181] In another case, the woman was carried from the meeting place in Ripon to Thirsk, which was ten miles away.[182] In burglary cases as well, the woman might be raped in her house or abducted. Walter Gaselyn and Isabella his wife complained that a gang had abducted her at night when she was alone in her house in Somerset. They took her goods and threw her over a horse and carried her into the forest of Dene where they detained her.[183]

The question that arises continually for modern rape is the amount of physical harm done to the woman and the amount of resistance the woman should or does exhibit.[184] Some information is available from medieval cases to describe the rape victims' resistance. The London coroners' rolls have two cases where the woman's resistance led to her death. In one case the man accosted his victim in a churchyard at twilight. He wanted to have intercourse with her but she refused. Apparently she put up a considerable resistance because he eventually killed her with a knife.[185] The king's poulter pursued another intended victim until he had chased her as far as the Thames. She jumped into the river to avoid him and was drowned.[186]

Ordinary wounding was seldom mentioned in the court cases because the law said explicitly that force had to used to qualify the act for rape and in any case, assault and wounding were not felonies in themselves and so would not be mentioned in criminal records. One case does mention that the woman was wounded as well as raped. In this case the victim may have been particularly young or more than usually battered.[187] Hugh Fitz Henry, a local notable, was charged with the rape of Maud, daughter of Ingreda Scot of Ingelton. The jurors said that Hugh was passing through the village of Ingelton one day when he saw Maud standing in her mother's doorway. He ordered two of his servants to seize Maud and take her to his manor house in the village. She put up a considerable fight by clinging to the doorway and raising the hue and cry, but she was dragged off. The jurors maintained that once at his house, she voluntarily submitted to him. It is questionable what sort of resistance she could possibly have made in his manor house, but the jurors simply charged him with a trespass of abduction and suggested a heavy fine of £100 on the condition that "the king accept it."[188] Obviously, the jurors were afraid to convict a local lord.

The medieval play *Robin and Marion* centers around the attempted abduction of Marion and is indicative of both the techniques of the rapist (who seems to have read Andreas Capellanus) and the resistance of the victim. The knight in the play comes upon Marion, a shepherdess, looking after her flocks in the fields. He suggests that they go into the woods but she refuses.

Knight: And yet, my lovely, wouldn't it be fine to ride with me into the wood and play a delightful game with me?
Marion: My lord! Take your horse away! He almost hurt me. Robin's horse doesn't rear when I follow his plow.
Knight: Be my sweetheart, shepherd girl; give in to me, do.[189]

The knight persists, however, and eventually swings Marion up on his horse and carries her off. She raises the hue and cry and Robin returns to the village to get his friends armed with pitchforks, clubs, and so on. Marion, in a rather unconvincing manner, manages to talk her way out of the rape situation and Robin is, therefore, not called upon to attack a nobleman.[190] Resistance to rape in the Middle Ages, then, could be a physical resistance or talking the rapist out of the act.

The techniques of rape were similar to those of robbery, abduction for ransom, or burglary, in that they often reflected some planning and involved some violence. When a vicar set out to procure the object of his desire, Agnes Manusel, he banded together with his servant and another woman for the abduction. Only the vicar engaged in the actual rape; and the other two were named as auxiliaries.[191]

Multiple rape situations also appear in the gaol delivery rolls. Those women who were abducted for a considerable period of time were usually taken by one or two men. Two men took Agnes Spiller of Shelton and kept her for a week.[192] In another case the rapist took his victim to his place, and the jurors could only say that she was kept there "a long time."[193]

Gang rape has come into prominence recently as being part of an initiation ritual for youth. Both historical studies and modern ones indicate that the gang leader initiates the rape and has the role of the "magical seducer." The rape situation is seen as a proof of manhood.[194] The medieval records do not indicate that the gang rapists were teenagers or young, for they do not give ages. Another pattern of gang rape does, however, emerge from the records. There are many instances of gang rape reported both in the early patent rolls and later in the gaol delivery rolls of cases in which the victim was a widow or wife of a titled gentleman or wealthy merchant or gentry. I suggest that these were revenge rapes. Not only were the rapists carrying away the wealth of their male victim in a robbery or burglary, but they also were humiliating him and calling his prowess into question by raping his wife. In other cases the rapists seemed to intend revenge on a dead man by raping his widow. The rape, robbery, and abduction of Walter Gacelyn's widow appears to be this type of case as does the rape of Agnes, widow of Master Robert de Abberford at Parlington, by nine men.[195] The attackers are all named and so must have been well known to the victims in these cases as one would expect if they were their husband's associates or enemies.

Rape, although newly a felony in the fourteenth century, had already taken on the characteristics that have persisted to the present day: the character of the victim determined the indictment and conviction, and the crime was seldom prosecuted. The motivations and techniques of rape have also changed little except for the revenge rapes and rape-marriages of heiresses.

TREASON

Petty treason and a few cases of high treason came under the jurisdiction of gaol delivery courts. The most common cases, forgery or counterfeiting, would not be considered treason under present law, nor would the killing of a husband by a wife or of a lord by one of his men. But these were treasonous acts in the fourteenth century and were distinguished by special punishment even if they were indicted and handled in all other respects like ordinary felonies. The core of treason was that it represented a betrayal: of the king, of the lord and master.

Incidences of treason were few compared with the overall pattern of crime. The average percentage of counterfeiting, the most common treason charge, was 0.5 percent. Only Huntingdonshire with 1.3 percent had more counterfeiters than the other counties.[196] Only a few women were accused of killing their husbands, and very few men were accused of killing their lords. Only 0.2 percent of the cases were spying, and, as we have seen, these were in Northamptonshire, Yorkshire, and Norfolk.

The rarity of the treason charges is explainable. Warfare against the king was not made a treasonable offense in statute law until 1352, thirty years after Edward II innovatively used treason as a way of punishing such people as Sir Gilbert de Middleton.[197] Feudal vassals were assumed to have the right to fight their lord if they felt that he had broken the feudal contract.[198] The kings of England who were fighting their overlords in France could hardly dispute that. The few cases of a peasant killing his lord or a woman killing her husband are understandable because of the lack of opportunity for a peasant to risk killing his lord and the low participation of women in homicide in general. Forgery and counterfeiting were infrequent because of the great skill they required compared with other treasons and most felonies. Then, as now, the forger was among the elite of the criminals. This section will deal primarily with counterfeiting and forgery as the other treasons will be dealt with in other chapters.

The successful forger or counterfeiter needed artistic ability, perhaps writing skills, and organization. Counterfeiting was a skilled art in which a cast had to be perfected and gold or silver melted and debased so that the coins looked like real ones. All this required special training, time, and some capital investment in bullion, lead, and instruments. In fact, Peter of Swaffham was convicted for having the counterfeiting instruments alone, not for having any false money.[199] The counterfeiter also had to have some way of exchanging the bad coins for either goods or real money. Mere clipping of coins, which required less skill than counterfeiting, was also practiced.

Insufficient evidence makes a study of the seasonality of the counterfeiters impossible and, indeed, there is no reason to assume a seasonality. Their criminal opportunities came in cities, on market days, and at fairs. In Huntingdonshire most of the counterfeiters were caught in or near St. Ives Fair. A large regional or international fair was one of the best places for counterfeiters to distribute their coins. International ports such as King's Lynn, Yarmouth, and London also attracted counterfeiters.

Because the best areas for disposing of counterfeit coins were fairs and cities, counterfeiters were a particularly mobile group of criminals. One of the most interesting cases of counterfeiters' mobility was that of two Flemish traders, Jakim du Dam and his son William, who were taken in Lynn with £11s. 8d. in counterfeit money and 2s. 4d. in good money. Jakim confessed to the crime immediately, but William put himself on the country.[200] Usually the counterfeiters just crossed county lines with their false coins. One large group that was picked up in St. Ives came from Boston in Lincolnshire. William of Boston and his wife Alice, Adam le Barbur of Lincoln, and Peter Peitnin were all indicted for having false money. A man found with 12d. in false money in Yarmouth had come up from Essex to dispose of his coin.[201]

Since counterfeiting required some aid in processing and in distributing the coins and since counterfeiters had to be mobile, it was not unusual for them to work in association with others, particularly members of their own families. A woman could be quite useful in spending false money for goods in a market. The most elaborate of these familial groups was Richard of Cosby's family of counterfeiters, which included him and his wife, one son, two daughters, and a granddaughter.[202]

Forgers required some of the same skills as counterfeiters because they too had to duplicate seals, make casts, and have the appropriate instruments, wax, and parchment. Medieval documents were authenticated by seals so that if one copied the king's seal, it was treason. In addition to copying the seal, forgers would also have to know how to copy the handwriting on the documents and sometimes master the particular wording used. T. F. Tout has described other methods of medieval forgers that included cutting a seal off another document and copying the wording, writing, and seal from an authentic document.[203] Although forgery was widespread for charters of rights and ownership of land, it was often not prosecuted as a felony in these cases, for the crown was satisfied to procure their rights through civil proceedings. Only small-time forgers, therefore, came into the gaol delivery rolls. Peter of Hertford and William Hermite were accused of fabricating the king's seal on a charter of pardon in Yorkshire.[204] Nicholas de Hawstead was accused of having copied the king's seal and attaching it to a commission.[205] Unlike counterfeiters, forgers did not have a problem of disposing of their frauds. The forgeries were usually intended for a specific purpose.

This description and analysis of the types of crimes committed, their seasonal and daily fluctuations, the value of goods stolen in property thefts, and the techniques of crime indicates some marked patterns that contribute to an understanding of the relationship of crime to medieval rural society. The seasonality of crime shows that it was closely tied to the agricultural flow of life. Homicides and thefts were high in the planting and harvest seasons when tempers and social contacts reached their pitch and when goods were lying in the fields for the taking. Burglars chose the winter months when goods were locked up in houses and barns. Homes, fields, and streets were the most common places for crimes of all sorts to occur. All property crimes followed the inexplicable schedule of Monday through Thursday, but homicide concentrated on Sunday, the sole day of relaxation. The property crimes were all lucrative, but a comparison of the value of goods stolen with types of crimes shows a strong association between the amount of risk and the profits: robbery was the most risky and most profitable, larceny the least. The types of goods stolen also varied with the form of property theft. The techniques of the criminals were direct and relatively unsophisticated. Little skill was needed to break into walls or rob people at sword point. Counterfeiters, forgers, and cutpurses were the most skilled among the felons. Differences in county crime patterns were associated with the particular economic conditions or geographical location that made some types of crimes more or less feasible. The seasonality, prevalence, and techniques of crime affected the total crime pattern as did the identity of the victims and the accused, their interrelationship, and the importance of professionals and organized crime.

Chapter Four

The Suspects

 I T IS EASIER to find out how the system for arresting and trying suspects worked than to identify who the suspects were. After analyzing the keepers of the peace, Bertha Putnam inquired about the identity of the breakers of the peace: "Who were the burglars, robbers, and murderers . . . the sleepers by day and wanderers by night and what was their political, social, and economic status?"[1] Medieval literary traditions present several criminal models: the nobility as represented in the Herward poems; the bandit as typified by Robin Hood and his merry men; and the ordinary small-time thieves such as Chaucer's millers who stole a bit when the opportunity was right. Not surprisingly, the criminal justice system was most successful at catching ordinary thieves and murderers. Therefore, villagers predominated in the criminal population as they did in society at large. The suspects were for the most part village worthies like Chaucer's millers, who moved into and out of crime as need and opportunity dictated.

The problem of describing why these people deviated from a normal law-abiding life while others of their class did not or why they were so unfortunate as to be detected when their equally criminous neighbors were not is a central issue to criminology. Attempts to classify and predict criminal behavior have produced a mass of explanations ranging from physical and psychological characteristics to social alienation to denying that there is criminal behavior except in that society labels certain people or groups as criminals. The nature of historical sources precludes certain areas of investigation such as physical typologies and psychological profiles of known criminals, but it does permit some investigation of the suspects' identity and how this influenced their participation in crime. Differing types of criminal behavior will be discussed in terms of the suspects' sex, age, wealth and status, occupation, and, in scattered cases, mental abnormalities. The gaol delivery rolls provide data on the sex of the accused, the age (if the accused was a minor), the occupation only in rare cases unless the accused pleaded benefit of clergy, and, only occasionally, the wealth and status of the accused. For homicide suspects the coroners' rolls provide supplemental information. Comparing the names of those who appeared in gaol delivery with those who paid the lay subsidies of 1327 and 1333 provides some information on wealth. Trailbaston sessions and commissions of oyer and terminer in the Patent Rolls give valuable insights into the nobility's criminal behavior. But the most important source of information on the wealth and status of the accused comes from comparisons of the Huntingdonshire gaol delivery suspects with the people in the Ramsey Abbey village reconstitution materials in the Regional Data Bank. The Ramsey manorial court materials are arranged in longitudinal studies of individual villagers and families associated with the economic, political, and social life of the villages. For a sample of eighty-nine suspects, it is possible to discuss the felon's identity. The combination of the different types of court rolls makes it possible to put together a profile of those tried for criminal offenses in fourteenth-century England.

The Sex of the Suspects

The role of women in crime has remained remarkably consistent from the fourteenth century to the present. In the fourteenth century, with some minor county to county variations, the suspect was female in 10 percent of the cases. Somerset and Yorkshire had a lower proportion of women suspects while that for Norfolk was somewhat higher.[2] In Elizabethan Essex, 250 years later, women still comprised only 10 percent of those tried.[3] In modern Britain the ratio is 1:7.4, and in America in 1955 the ratio was 1:8.[4] The stability of the sex ratio of those tried in criminal courts raises speculation on the roles of men and women in our Western cultural tradition and the influence this had on criminal behavior and the functioning of the judicial system. Is the chivalric literature an accurate portrayal of the gentle, passive nature of women, or do they commit just as many crimes as men but get caught less frequently?

Two basic arguments have traditionally been advanced to explain the female/male crime ratio: nature and nurture.[5] With the current interest in equality for women, the nurture argument has gained prominence. At the turn of the century W. A. Bonger stated the position rather quaintly: "[Women's] smaller criminality is like the health of the hothouse plant; it is not due to innate qualities, but to the hothouse which protects it from harmful influences."[6] Women, according to the nurture argument, are barred from crime as they are from other areas involving aggression because of the way they are reared and the constraints that male-dominated society puts on their social behavior. The criminality of women is certainly linked to the definition of sex roles in society. For instance, the extreme sex-role differences in tribal Africa give a ratio as high as 900:1; in prewar North Africa it was 3,000:1.[7]

Since the Western European and, by extension, the American ratio has changed so little until recently,[8] the role of women in Western society has probably also altered little since the Middle Ages. No systematic or exhaustive study has yet been done on women in medieval society, but the evidence indicates that women had mixed roles then as now.[9] Although peasant women worked primarily in the home and men did the heavier work with equipment, both worked in the fields at planting and harvest.[10] Women appear in the manorial court records as property owners, brewers, bakers, weavers, and plaintiffs and defendants in business matters. The continuity of both the percentage of women tried for crime and their role in society would suggest that the two factors are linked, especially since women are taking an increasing part in crime now that they are challenging their traditional role in society. But the stability of the sex ratio over so many centuries could, on the other hand, be taken as evidence for a biological difference between men and women that makes women less aggressive and more submissive to the law. Until further research has been done in genetics and psychology and further statistics are available on the changing crime patterns concurrent with changes in the role of women in Western society, there can be no conclusive answer to the nature versus nurture controversy.

Criminologists have also argued that women commit as many crimes as men, but that they are apprehended less frequently. One reason given for this assumption deserves mention only so that it may be dismissed: that women are more successful at concealing crimes than men are. The idea that women's criminality involves deception is found in one of the first books on women's antisocial behavior,

Malleus Maleficarum, published in 1487. According to the witch-hunting authors, women were prone to deceit, lies, and concealment because

> There was a defect in the formation of the first woman since she was formed from a bent rib, that is, a rib from the breast, which is bent as it were in a contrary direction to a man. And since through this defect she is an imperfect animal, she always deceives.[11]

The fear of women as felons-on-the-sly appears in modern works as well, particularly those which try to explain female crime in terms of female sexuality.[12] Solid evidence that women conceal crime more successfully than men is lacking, especially for the Middle Ages. It is usually argued that women conceal homicide by poisoning, but poison and stealth in homicide were rare in fourteenth-century England. The other charge is that women commit more infanticide than men, but again fourteenth-century data do not support this claim. In other felonies the opportunities for concealment were as good for men as for women. To suggest that women committed as many crimes as men but concealed them is to say that women succeeded in hiding 90 percent of their crimes!

In the Middle Ages, as is the case today, women were convicted less frequently than men. This leniency of the male-dominated judicial system toward women undoubtedly extended to indictments as well, so that of those people suspected, fewer women than men would ultimately be tried. The ratio of women to men committing crimes as derived from the court records is not, therefore, totally accurate, but the discrepancy is not so great that one can assume that women committed just as many crimes as men. Thus women did commit fewer crimes. The problem of an instinctual or cultural explanation for this fact remains the central issue in discussing female criminality. Indeed, the fact that the male-dominated judicial systems in the Middle Ages (and now) treated women with special consideration is a further indication that women's role in Western society is assumed to be non-criminous. Women adopted the self-perception that they should not take the initiative in crime. When confronted with a female felon, the male jurors and law enforcement officers assumed that she could not have done the deed or that if she had she should not be hanged.[13]

An analysis of the types of crimes men and women committed in the Middle Ages further indicates the importance of the perpetrators' sex

Table 5. *Males and females tried for particular crimes for all counties, 1300-1348.*

Crime	MALES		FEMALES		
	N	% of all males indicted	N	% of all females indicted	% of females in each crime
Larceny	5,357	35.8	527	32.4	8.9
Burglary	3,789	25.3	471	28.9	11.0
Robbery	1,737	11.6	93	5.7	5.1
Homicide	3,074	20.5	235	14.4	7.0
Receiving	701	4.7	266	16.3	27.5
Counterfeiting	58	0.4	23	1.4	28.8
Arson	146	1.0	12	0.7	7.6
Rape	80	0.5	0	0.0	—
Treason	34	0.2	0	0.0	—
Total	14,976	100.0	1,627	100.0	

in their criminal profile. It also sheds much light on women's role in medieval society as well as their participation in crime.

For both men and women the illegal acquisition of property was the dominant criminal motif (see table 5). Men committed most of the property crimes, but a comparison of the popularity of the various forms of property crime gives some interesting results. Men were indicted for 91.1 percent of all larcenies, but of all the felony indictments for men 35.8 percent were larcenies and of all the females indicted 32.4 percent were for larcenies. Contrary to the modern pattern, then, men and women involved in felony showed about an equal interest in simple theft. But even in the modern figures, women participate in more shoplifting so that they too are arrested most frequently for larceny.[14] Medieval England had few shops and stalls, and most of these were only open on market days so that this form of theft was limited. Furthermore, both men and women shoplifted. By the eighteenth century increased industrialization and urbanization seem to have already changed the pattern of female crime, for women were indicted more frequently for larceny than they were in the fourteenth century.[15]

Burglary is one of the most notable areas where medieval women seemed to be more aggressive than modern women. Women were charged with 11 percent of all burglaries; it was the second most popular felony among the women suspects at 28.9 percent. Only 8.1 percent of the women arrested today are accused of burglary.[16] Were medieval women stronger than modern women, medieval houses weaker, or has women's social role changed? The construction of medieval houses was so insubstantial that a woman as well as a man could break in a wattle and daub wall with a sharp instrument. Furthermore, the goods they were interested in procuring—clothing and household goods—could best be stolen from houses. Unlike in the eighteenth or twentieth centuries, these items were not readily available through shoplifting. But, not surprisingly, in 46.6 percent of their burglary cases women acted with an accomplice, usually a male. Matilda, sister of Richard ad Fres, had the help of Robert of Pinkney of Westmorland and William of Strickland, clerk, in the burglary of a house in Bagby in Yorkshire.[17] With or without accomplices, medieval women seemed to be more aggressive in property crime patterns than are modern women.

Although robbery is very much a male crime both now and in the Middle Ages, women also played an active role in it. Of the men indicted 11.6 percent were charged with robbery and of the women, 5.7 percent were.[18] Robbery falls between a personal assault and a property crime so that women's role in it needs analysis. Women were not skilled in the weapons of war that were most often used in robberies. Their role was probably that of decoy among a gang of male robbers. Indeed, in 84.2 percent of the robbery cases for which women were arrested, they had male accomplices. Alice le Frensche and her husband, William, and a third associate robbed and murdered a foreign Hospitaller on the king's highway and stole 10 silver marks from him.[19] But some women did successfully rob on their own.

The goods that men and women stole and their value also indicate the difference in their crime patterns. Men stole more valuable goods than women: 20.1 percent were worth over £1 while only 8.8 percent of the women's thefts were (see figure 5). In the thefts of goods worth 11-20s., the same pattern continued with men having 12.3 percent of their thefts in this group but women having only 6.8 percent. Women's thefts were generally of low value with over half of them (53.9 percent) falling at 12d. or under. Men's thefts in this range were 41.5 percent. Women also stole a greater percentage of goods in the 2-10s. range (30.5 percent) compared to men (26.1 percent). The dif-

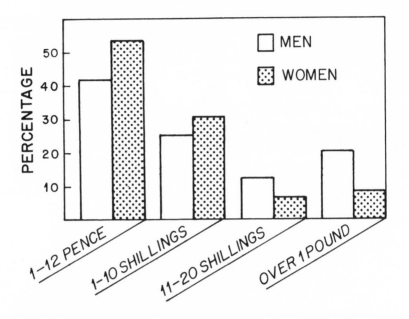

Figure 5. *Value of goods men and women stole.*

ferences in the value of goods stolen between men and women is due
in part to the greater participation of males in the more profitable
crimes of robbery and burglary and in part to the types of goods that
they stole.

Both women and men showed a marked preference for stealing
livestock: 47.1 percent of the male thefts and 23.6 percent of the
female thefts (see figure 6). Women stole slightly more sheep and
poultry than men and fewer horses. Since many horses were taken in
robbery in which women did not participate as frequently, this is an
understandable split. But the size of beasts did not deter women from
stealing cattle and horses. They were just as competent at herding
these animals as men.

On the whole, however, female thefts seemed to be directed more
toward household concerns. They stole grain in 21.5 percent of the
cases, while men stole it in only 11.7 percent. These thefts were often
small and done during harvest. Women also stole such useful items as
clothing and household goods more frequently than did men (14.6
percent compared to 6.9 percent). Twenty-three percent of all the
goods women stole was cloth compared to 14.6 percent for men.
Considering that most cloth was stolen in burglary and robbery,
women obviously had strong inclinations to steal this item when they

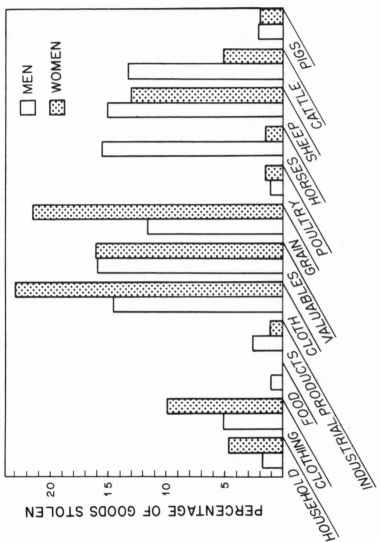

Figure 6. Comparison of the types of goods men and women stole.

did commit these crimes. Men showed a greater interest in stealing industrial products than women (2.6 percent compared to 1 percent). Both sexes stole valuables in the same proportion.

The analysis of the types of goods women stole is perhaps a more sensitive indicator of their role in society than the types of property crimes they committed. Their marked preference for stealing items of immediate household need indicates that their preoccupation was with the home. Not only were they more involved with the clothing, feeding, and furnishing of their households, they probably knew better than the men what items their neighbors had that would be worth stealing.

With women's sights directed toward care for family and home, one would expect that female participation in crime in time of famines would increase substantially. There was a slight tendency toward a higher proportion of women indicted in the first quarter of the century when famine conditions were frequent. Between 1300-1325 women committed 11.6 percent of the crimes. After 1325 and the easing of pressure on food supplies, women committed 9 percent of the crimes.

The only crimes in which women played a larger than usual role were counterfeiting (28.8 percent of all people indicted) and receiving (27.5 percent). Women and men alike usually had criminal associates in counterfeiting. Women's role in these gangs may have been trading the money in market for goods. Since the society did not suspect women of criminal behavior, their more innocent image would make them more successful at passing off counterfeit coins than men would be. Counterfeiting played a slightly larger role in the overall female crime pattern than it did in the male one (1.4 percent of all felonies committed by females compared to 0.4 percent for males).

Receiving was a crime in which women might be expected to participate more frequently. With men committing substantially more of the crimes, their wives, mothers, and daughters would necessarily have to receive them at home with their stolen goods. Again, women's crime pattern indicates a more passive role in the society. Of all the crimes for which females were indicted, 16.3 percent were for receiving compared to 4.7 percent for males. Women might be innocent victims in receiving cases, because they were unable to refuse shelter to felonious male family members. The sister of John Benne of Ormesby who received her brother after he had broken into a house and stolen goods worth 100s. may have fallen into this category, but perhaps she got a cut in the value of the goods.[20] Many receivers were butchers, goldsmiths, and others who carried on semi-professional receiving, but both women and men seem to have been professional receivers. A woman in Wakefield had the reputation of being a regular receiver of malefactors.[21]

Men dominated the felonies that involved physical violence. We have already seen that they played the major role in robbery. They also were indicted for all the rape and abduction cases. Occasionally a woman would be an accomplice, but this was rare. Rape, as we have seen, was not very frequently prosecuted in the first half of the fourteenth century so that only 0.5 percent of the male suspects were indicted for rape.

Men were charged with 93 percent of the homicides, but the breakdown of indictments of all males and all females for different types of crimes shows that while 20.5 percent of the men indicted were charged with homicide, thus making it the third most likely crime for males, 14.4 percent of the females were suspected, only slightly less than for receiving. The coroners' rolls give an even more detailed picture of the sex breakdown of the suspects. Of the 575 homicide inquests preserved for fourteenth-century Northamptonshire, 99 percent of the suspects were male. In the university city of Oxford men committed all 68 homicides. The more urban centers of London produced more female suspects: 7 percent of 145 cases. Modern figures show a slightly greater percentage of women arrested for homicide.[22]

If the lack of physical strength were the crucial factor in women not committing more homicides, then we would expect to find that they were more heavily involved in assaults and woundings that were not fatal to their victims. Evidence of assaults from the Wakefield court rolls for the first half of the century showed that of the 632 assault cases, women committed only 11 percent. While this was higher than their homicide record, it is not as high as the modern participation of women in assault.[23] One might also argue that medieval women like modern ones turned their aggressions toward themselves in suicide rather than to committing homicide. But in the few suicide cases recorded, men and women committed *felo de se* equally. Medieval women were less physically aggressive than medieval men and somewhat less prone to personal violent attacks than modern women.[24]

Luke Owen Pike, writing in the nineteenth century, claimed that medieval women were more likely to be concentrated in nonviolent property crimes because medieval weapons such as swords, battle axes, and staffs required too much brute force for them to wield. Only with the gun could the female come into her own in violence.[25] The weaponry of medieval England did determine to some extent the predominence of men in physical violence, for it required both skill and strength to use the most common weapons of medieval homicide: the knife and staff. The men spent part of their play time as boys and recreation time as adults in games involving weapons. But women also knew how to use weapons that could inflict mortal injury and chose those with which they were most familiar: knives and hatchets. Their daily household routines made them very skilled with these two weapons. The coroners' rolls show women using knives in 53.8 percent of their homicides and hatchets in 30.8 percent. Women virtually never used battle weapons such as the staff, sword, bow and arrow, lance, or battle ax, or other equipment such as hammers or pitchforks. Both men and women might beat a victim to death. For instance, one woman in Northamptonshire whipped her ten-year-old son to death in a fit of anger.[26] One might assume that women would select victims such as children or other women who could be more easily overpowered, but in 68.4 percent of the coroners' inquests and 81.6 percent of the gaol delivery cases women killed men. Women usually did not undertake a violent crime without an accomplice. In 64.4 percent of their homicides another person aided them, with a male being the accomplice in 52.9 percent of the cases.

Women had accomplices in 46.8 percent of all of their felonies; men in 39 percent of their felonies. Men drew their associates from other family members in 5.5 percent of the cases; women in 19 percent. The male suspects, it seems, had more social contacts outside the family that could turn into criminal associations. The family member associated with also shows a different pattern of socialization. Women acted with their husbands in 66.7 percent of the cases, whereas men chose their wives as accomplices in only 22.4 percent of the cases. To men, their brothers were more usual companions in crime: 45.6 percent chose siblings compared to only 9 percent of the women. For both men and women, parents were often the entree into crime. Of those people indicted with associates, 25 percent of the men and 19.2 percent of the women were in parent/child associations. The husband's parents were slightly more likely to corrupt their daughter-in-law than the other way around: 2.6 percent of the women were tried with their husband's family as opposed to 1.3 percent of the men who were tried with their wife's family.

For the most part, men dominated the organization of criminal associations, but they were not the only instigators of violent gangs. Agnes and Maud Pikhorn were accused of inciting and concealing felons who robbed and tortured a village family.[27]

Fourteenth-century legal practice did not assume, as did that of the sixteenth century, that married women were incapable of full and voluntary participation in criminal acts without their husbands' coercion.[28] Married women faced equal liability for hanging if they acted with their husbands.[29] Isabel daughter of Stacie of Rudham was the exception rather than the rule when she was found guilty but excused on the grounds that her husband coerced her to help him and four other men in various robberies at Hertford Bridge.[30] Concubines who did the same thing certainly received no such consideration. Lucy, concubine of Hugh de Nuttle, was convicted for aiding Hugh and for holding the pass at Emmethorp Rye.[31]

Whether married or single, women played a substantially different role in crime than men did, and these differences point to different processes of socialization for men and women. Women took a less aggressive role in crime in general and also in the particular types of crimes. The evidence from the gaol delivery rolls favors the nurture rather than the nature argument on lower female participation in crime. The crime pattern of the medieval female offenders indicates dependence upon the family or other males and an interest in crimes that would benefit their households and families. There were, of course, the Moll Flanderses of their age as well. Alice Garlic of Great Houghton single-handedly stole one horse worth 10s. and robbed three different men of clothing.[32]

THE AGE OF THE SUSPECTS

People in medieval England were, for the most part, ageless as far as the records are concerned. Ages were given only for children under twelve because they were excused for their criminal acts. Once a child reached the age of twelve, he was considered to have full adult responsibility and could be hanged for his crimes. The age of reason in the Middle Ages coincided with the age of bearing arms, for at twelve the child was to be counted in the tithing and was expected to defend the realm in the militia if necessary.[33] Specific ages for suspects over twelve are seldom available. However, generational information can be reconstructed from the Ramsey Abbey materials.

Juvenile delinquency and the criminal behavior of people under twenty-five occupies much of the concern of modern policing efforts, but this age-group is difficult to identify from the medieval records. Some cases, however, seem to be so identifiable in modern terms that the reader is tempted to assume that little has changed. Consider, for example, the case of a young man who panicked when his girlfriend's kinsmen discovered them together in a haystack.

> Well into the night of 30 March 1270 Simon and Richard, sons of Hugh the Fisher of Radwell, came from the house of Hugh's daughter Alice towards that of their father in Radwell and wished to cross the court-yard of Robert Ball of Radwell, in which Simon son of Agnes of Radwell and Juliana daughter of Walter the Fisher of Radwell were lying under a haystack. Simon immediately arose and struck Simon the Fisher on the top of the head to the brain apparently with an axe, so that he immediately died. Richard, seeing this, raised the hue and fled. Simon the felon immediately fled and Juliana with him.[34]

Another typical experience of the juvenile delinquent is that of John son of Hugh de London. He came from a prominent family in Ramsey, in fact his father was a bailiff. He went through a spurt of manorial court complaints and in 1353 was indicted and acquitted of a burglary.[35] This was his last brush with the law. By 1380 he was a stalwart member of the village community and occupied the position of juror. We have already cited the case of the young Kentish noble whose indictment was quashed because his father was the judge's friend. These cases simply indicate that some of the patterns of crime that we have come to regard as part of juvenile delinquency existed in the Middle Ages, but they do not give any hint of the extent of juvenile crime.

The proportion of crimes involving teenagers and young adults can probably never be known exactly, but two conflicting hypotheses about their probable involvement deserve consideration. If, as Philippe Ariés argues, children were valued only for their productive role in society and passed quickly from childhood to the responsibilities of adulthood, then the whole concept of "juvenile" and hence "juvenile delinquency" would be invalid.[36] In a society that does not recognize and does not provide opportunity for the behavior associated with delayed adult responsibilities, it is not so possible to have the modes of expression, antisocial as well as social, that are associated with this age-group as it is in a society such as our own that places great emphasis on these years of psychological development.

Following this argument, juvenile delinquency could not exist in the Middle Ages because there were no juveniles. The opposing hypothesis, however, maintains that human behavior is fairly constant and that biologically and psychologically the stage of juvenile must be passed through on the way to adulthood regardless of the practices of the society.

The age structure of medieval Europe before the Black Death makes this second hypothesis particularly interesting to pursue. The best demographic evidence on age structure in the early fourteenth century indicates that society was largely composed of young peoples with the bulk of the population being under the age of thirty-five.[37] Thus a very large proportion of the population would have fallen into the age-group of teens through the early thirties, which tends to be the age-group most prone to participation in crime. In all modern Western European and American criminal statistics, being young and being male are the most consistent conditions associated with the risk of becoming a ciminal. In a society where this group is very large, there will be more crime. This would help to explain the general lawlessness in the countryside of medieval England. If medieval teenagers behaved like modern ones, then their large numbers would be partly responsible for the great number of simple larcenies and burglaries. The high number of homicides in medieval society, which is so difficult to explain, might result from a heavy demographic concentration of young men between the ages of 25 and 35, which is the dominant age-group in modern society committing homicides and acts of personal violence. Crime is much less prevalent the older the age-group, except for crimes of skill such as counterfeiting and forgery.[38] Very possibly, then, a key to understanding medieval crime lies in the youthfulness of the population.

The records are somewhat less obscure about prejuvenile crime. Children do appear in both the gaol delivery rolls and in the coroner's inquests, but infrequently. Much of the disciplining of the very young was certainly done informally by the victim, the child's family, or the community, so that actual charges were seldom brought. One case in London is indicative of community attitudes toward disciplining delinquent children. A boy, age six, ran into a shop and stole a piece of wool by grabbing it and putting it under his cap. Both his mother and the woman who ran the shop were present. The shop tender hit the boy under his ear so violently that he died from the blow. The coroner's jury said that the death was accidental and did not even indict the woman so that she would have to stand trial and get a pardon.[39] Apparently, the matter was considered so routine that the coroner did not question the jurors on their decision. The delinquent child could also be dealt with at the manorial level. For instance, Thomas Fernoule sued Adam the Waynwright because his dogs, at the instigation of his children, killed a sheep of his worth 2s. He also claimed that Adam's children broke a hedge so that Adam's sheep trampled Thomas's crops.[40] The father, not the children, was held responsible for making good the damages.

Those children who were brought before gaol delivery rather than being disciplined locally usually committed some sort of theft and were near the age of twelve. For instance, John son of Reginald of Dalling, eleven years old, and Thomas son of Robert of Kempstone, nine years old, were found guilty of the burglary of Adam de Walpole of Lynn's house and of stealing a box with silver in it.[41] Sometimes the children were brought in as accomplices of adult criminals. John son of Adam de Happisburgh was accused with his father of stealing two pieces of wax worth 5s. 2d. in Ormesby. The father was convicted and sentenced to hang, but the son was excused because he was only nine years old.[42] The immunity of children from punishment must have tempted parents to use their children for criminal purposes. Of all the suspects accused of committing crime in associations, the parent-child relationship accounted for 4 percent. Parents, therefore, played some role in introducing children to criminal techniques.

The other charge that could bring children into the central court system was homicide. In most cases, the homicides were accidental slayings connected with an older child's learning to use weapons. For instance, John son of Ralph Puch of Tilbrook, age ten, fled from the neighborhood when he shot an arrow at a target on a dunghill and hit a young girl, age five, instead.[43] Two Northamptonshire boys, age ten and nine, were watching sheep and playing with staffs when one killed the other.[44] Aside from children such as these and the probable role of juveniles and young men in the overall crime pattern, the age of the suspects remains tantalizingly obscure.

Wealth and Status

The great majority of the suspects were peasants and residents of the villages and small towns in the countryside. As we have seen, they were not a class of undifferentiated serfs, but rather they had three

basic status groups: the primary villagers (A families), who controlled
the village governance; the secondary villagers (B families); and the
intermediate villagers (C families), who worked for the primary and
secondary villagers. Comparing the gaol delivery rolls to the Ramsey
Abbey materials made it possible to identify eighty-nine of the villagers by status and previous village activities. The sample is a small
one but very illuminating of the dynamics of crime and of the village
communities.

The most interesting fact to emerge from the identification of the
status of the suspected felons in their villages is that main families
(primary and secondary villagers), not the dregs of society, dominated
the criminal courts with 79.8 percent of the people tried. Other
sources confirm this conclusion. The coroners' rolls show that the
average wealth of those indicted for homicide in Northamptonshire
was 10s. 4d. (there were 248 people for which specific information on
the value of their chattels was available). In Leicestershire as well the
murderers were landholders and well-off.[45] In the urban setting the
middle ranks of the community, tradesmen, provided 51 percent of
the homicidal elements.

Those who possessed at least 10s. of movable property were sufficiently wealthy to be taxed in the lay subsidies of 1327 and 1333.
Comparing the names of the suspected felons with those listed on the
lay subsidy rolls also provides some information on their wealth. The
task is a difficult one, however, because for real accuracy the name of
the suspect and his residence must correspond exactly to the entry on
the subsidy rolls. Of the 171 suspects appearing in gaol delivery between 1327 and 1347 in Huntingdonshire, only 37, or 22 percent,
could be identified with complete certainty as having paid a tax. This
figure is probably a gross underrepresentation because of problems of
identification and of widespread cheating in reporting taxable goods.[46]

Although the gaol delivery rolls list the chattels of those hanged, the
information is not reliable. The average value of the chattels was only
1s. 5d., and most cases conclude that the felon had no chattels. One
cannot conclude from this sort of evidence, as R. B. Pugh did, that the
felons were destitute.[47] Family and community tried to hide the wealth
of suspects from the king's officials or even take it before they arrived.[48] For instance, Holne township was amerced 6s. 8d. because the
man assigned to take a prisoner to Wakefield gaol stole a jacket, hood,
and sheet from him.[49] Furthermore, as Pugh points out in his book on

prisons, the prisoners were often maintained in gaol on the value of their own chattels so that the final value of chattels was bound to be small.[50]

Despite the deficiencies of the gaol delivery rolls, the other sources of evidence indicate that a substantial portion of those appearing in gaol delivery were members of the more established, landholding peasantry.

The Ramsey village oligarchs, the primary villagers, comprised 38.2 percent of the indictments (thirty-four people). In spite of their involvement in peacekeeping as jurors and capital pledges, their high incidence of felony indictments is not surprising. In the village studies of Broughton and Holywell-cum-Needingworth, the primary families far outstripped the other groups in semicriminal acts of trespass, raising the hue, assault, and so on.[51] Meier Helmbrecht of the peasant epic also came from this class. As prominent land and chattel holders and as officials they had a wide range of potentially criminal interactions with both fellow villagers and outsiders. Often these prominent villagers had a considerable record for trouble-making before and after the indictment. For instance, John de Broughton was tried and acquitted for homicide in 1302.[52] In the five years prior to that time he had nineteen pleas, five trespasses against neighbors, and four work defaults. After the trial he went back to his usual aggressive pattern, adding assault and defamation charges. John de Broughton was not only a prominent villager but was also the leading member of his family. Fifteen out of the thirty-four primary villagers accused of crimes were the leading members of their families.

The secondary village families, like their betters, were well enough established economically to have a number of social interactions and to pursue their disputes aggressively in court or in crime. They were involved only slightly less frequently than primary families in trespass, assaults, and other antisocial acts in the villages.[53] But they were indicted for felonies somewhat more frequently—41.6 percent of those accused, or thirty-seven people. The chief family member was indicted for felony in eight of the cases. For instance, Hamon of Holywell, who was accused of larceny in 1337, was the chief member of his family; ten years before he had paid 2s. on 30s. of movable goods in the lay subsidy of 1327.[54]

The most dramatic drop in appearance in gaol delivery comes with the intermediate group of villagers: only 20.2 percent of those identified. Their opportunities for aggressive economic and social interaction with other members of the community were limited because they possessed little property and they did not serve in village government. In the manorial court rolls they were cited for being received out of tithing and for minor infractions such as wrongful gleaning. A typical example of an intermediate villager indicted for felony is Richard Tynker of Hemingford Grey. He was tried in 1329 for stealing grain from a barn. The case ended in acquittal when the jurors said that he had only stolen grain worth 5d.[55]

The participation of the three status groups in crime is not meaningful unless one knows the proportion of the village population each group composed. Arriving at an accurate picture of the size of each group is difficult, because the manorial rolls do not deal with women and children as regularly as with men, nor with transients as much as with permanent residents. While the primary and secondary villagers would be very visible in bringing suits to the manorial court, the intermediate villagers probably either could not or were actively discouraged from doing so. For Holywell-cum-Needingworth and Broughton 34 to 48 percent of the people appearing in manorial courts were primary villagers, 24 to 41 percent were secondary, and the rest intermediate.[56] If these figures are an accurate measure of the membership in the different status groups, then each group committed crime roughly in proportion to their numbers in the population. There may, however, have been more intermediate villagers in both crime and the population than are indicated.

Opportunities for crime were influenced by a person's status group, which also influenced the types of crimes committed. The single most common crime for all status groups in the village, 40 percent of all crimes, was homicide (see table 6). Primary and secondary villagers committed the bulk of these. Their economic and social contacts made violent interpersonal relationships more readily possible. They were, for example, more likely to get into disputes over crops and boundaries during the course of work in the common fields. A case illustrative of the main families' involvement in homicide is that of Ralph le Somet of Thering who killed Richard of Woldweston in self-defense. Ralph's mother, Christine, had bought a cow from Richard in the town of Thering. When she did not pay the 20s. owed to him, Richard tried to repossess the cow. Ralph resisted this forceful effort and Richard attacked him with a sword. Ralph killed him in self-defense and was pardoned.[57] Other evidence such as that from the coroners' rolls confirms the domination of the upper status groups in violent physical

Table 6. *Distribution of crimes by the status of the accused in the Ramsey Abbey villages, 1295-1350.*

CRIME	PRIMARY	SECONDARY	INTERMEDIATE
Homicide	12	17	8
Burglary	6	15	1
Larceny	8	9	7
Receiving	7	7	2

assault. In Broughton the prominent families were responsible for thirty-five out of thirty-seven cases of assault.[58] Secondary families committed 43 percent of all the homicides and the primary families 36 percent. While it is tempting to interpret this discrepancy as hostility on the part of a grasping, upwardly mobile group, the difference is slight and may result from the small sample size or the greater number of secondary villagers in the community. More significant is the large role that homicide played in the crime pattern of intermediate families (44.4 percent of all their crime). Violent death was a mode of social behavior common to all types of villagers. As we will see in the next chapter, the selection of victims in violent death indicates the lines of social tension in the villages.

The types of social interactions of the different status groups is more apparent in property crimes than in homicide. Larceny played the largest role (39 percent) among the intermediate group.[59] Because this group had little land and no guaranteed employment, the motivation for these thefts often must have been economic. Joan Kelenach of Wistow is a good example of larceny among this fringe group. In 1353 she was accused of three larcenies in Wistow involving the theft of geese. The value of the stolen goods was very small, so she was acquitted of all three charges.[60] Life must have been difficult for Joan and her mother, who also appears in the manorial records, for they were repeatedly cited for wrongful gleaning.

Primary and secondary village families concentrated their property crimes in burglary. While 23 percent of the charges against them were for larceny, their burglary record was more notable. Only 6 percent of the charges against intermediate villagers was for breaking and entering compared to 16 to 19 percent of the main families. Burglaries required more planning and a greater knowledge of where valuable goods might be found. Burglary also involved more valuable goods, which were more likely to appeal to primary and secondary villagers, who were not looking for food and other subsistence items.

Receiving was far more common among the primary and secondary families than among the intermediate families for obvious reasons: they had the money to pay for stolen goods and they also hired laborers, some of whom would have criminal records. Not only were the main villagers frequently indicted for receiving in the gaol delivery records, but they also were charged on the manorial level with receiving people out of tithing.[61] The wealthier peasants often hired people from the wandering labor force and were charged with receiving them. Villagers who received professional bands such as the Coterels probably did so in exchange for protection, money, or for the commission of some private quarrel of their own.[62]

In addition to the regular village residents, outsiders appeared in the village and committed crimes. The outsiders were a very mixed group. The most obvious were people from neighboring villages who had contacts with the local residents in trade, marriage, trespass, debts, and so on. Raftis has analyzed the appearance of outsiders in manorial records and found that the majority were from main families in neighboring villages.[63] Since the main families were most likely to have more than local economic and social contacts, one would expect their mobility to be greater than intermediate families. At least some of the outsiders, however, were vagabonds, transients, and criminal bands. Preindustrial society has long been characterized as having a large wandering body of poor and vagabonds begging, looking for work, and committing crimes. While this was certainly a feature of sixteenth-century England, the extent of the transient population in pre-plague fourteenth-century England is not known. As long as the frankpledge system worked well before the Black Death, there was probably not a large transient problem. Gaol delivery evidence would tend to support this hypothesis, since most of the crime was local in nature and the people indicted have fixed residences.

Our analysis of crime, however, showed that crimes such as robbery and counterfeiting tended to be committed by outsiders. In the Ramsey sample, none of the villagers committed robbery or counterfeiting. Other evidence of the presence of outsiders comes from the coroners' rolls. Of the 575 surviving homicide inquests in Northamptonshire, the jurors said in 107 cases, or 19 percent, that the suspects were "strangers," "unknown thieves," "bands of thieves," and so on. This figure represents unsolved homicides and would include both wandering felons and undetected local people. But often the cases are specific. For instance, in Bedfordshire some "unknown strangers" lodging in an empty house in the village in 1317 argued among themselves and a homicide occurred. The villagers did not know their names and the strangers fled after the murder. In another case the victim was a wanderer known only to the community as "Swetealys." She had lived with one of the villagers for a brief time before the murder.[64] Some counties had more transients than others. A comparison of Norfolk and Northamptonshire shows that Norfolk, being a more settled county and having neighbors on only two sides, had only 14.7 percent of her suspects come from another county. Northamptonshire, on the other hand, was a long narrow county in the heart of the Midlands. There was a good bit of gang activity there and the Great North Road brought a fair number of transients through the county. People from other counties were more common among Northamptonshire's suspects: 37.5 percent of those indicted. Not all these were transients or criminal bands; they might come from a neighboring village just over the border. The total number of all types of crimes transients committed or indeed the size of the transient population cannot be estimated.

Occupations of the Suspects

Tilling the soil was the most common way of making a living in the Middle Ages, but some villagers either supplemented agricultural pursuits with a trade or craft or made their living solely from them. The pursuit of particular crafts often gave rise to special opportunities for crime. Folk custom and proverbs have long reflected the suspicions with which craftsmen were regarded in the peasant community: "Many a miller, many a thief"; "Put a miller, a tailor, and a weaver into one bag, and shake them. The first that comes out will be a thief"; and the German proverb, "Millers and bakers do not steal, they buy the booty."[65] Do the criminal records for the fourteenth century support these slurs on various occupations? The occupation or social rank of the accused did not become part of the official record until a statute in the reign of Henry V, a century after this study.[66] The occupations mentioned in the fourteenth-century records appear to be only randomly recorded by way of further identifying the suspect. The only occupation recorded with regularity was clergy, because they were allowed to plead benefit of clergy. Aside from clergy, the small sample of other occupations makes any generalizations tentative rather than conclusive.

Sailors appearing in port areas such as Yarmouth were suspected of having committed crimes in connection with their trade. We have already seen such typical examples as John Crame, mariner in North Yarmouth, who was accused of taking a boat belonging to the lepers and Henry Payne, "saylor," who was accused of breaking into a chest on board ship and taking £30 15s. in sterling pence and £10 in gold florins.[67] Sailors worked under the handicap of being strangers in the places where they were charged and, therefore, were naturally objects of suspicion to local jurors. One sailor, for instance, was taken on suspicion for having 40 florins. He claimed that he was acting for his master in Yorkshire, but the jurors returned him to prison so that they could make inquiries about him and his purpose in Yarmouth.[68]

Shepherds were also liable to suspicion, for they were entrusted with the care of livestock other than their own and were accountable for missing animals. The owners might well assume that the shepherds stole them or acted in collusion with a gang. Of the sixteen shepherds mentioned by trade in gaol delivery, two-thirds were suspected of stealing sheep and one-third cattle. Of course, their trade may only have seemed relevant to the indicting jurors if they had stolen animals. Counties in which herding played a greater role in economic life probably had a greater number of shepherds involved in theft.

Receiving was the common vice attributed in literature to millers, butchers, and cloth workers because they all had a ready way of converting the stolen product—grain, livestock, and cloth, respectively—into unrecognizably altered goods. But like the rest of the population, they seemed to concentrate on thefts. They did have a tendency to steal goods related to their trade, although, again, the jurors may have suspected them of such thefts. In the cases in Norfolk four out of eleven tailors were accused of stealing cloth, six out of ten butchers took livestock, and eleven out of twenty-eight millers took grain or mill equipment. For instance, Robert Eve and William Thugh, millers, were accused of stealing mill parts including sailcloths for windmills valued at one half mark and one horse and grain. Robert Eve became an approver and appealed five other millers for taking mill parts.[69]

Tradesmen often had common interests related to their crafts that led to crimes other than larceny and receiving. The widow of a weaver in York accused sixteen tailors of killing her husband.[70] The tailors may well have been dissatisfied customers of a dishonest weaver who sought an extralegal revenge. The widow certainly thought it was plausible but had to pay 5s. in fines when they were acquitted. The London coroners' rolls record various homicides resulting from trade rivalries and even small riots brought about by clashes between the apprentices of different trades.

Servants, who play such a large role in crime in later centuries, are seldom mentioned in rural crime. Their crimes were distributed among the various felonies with some tendency to be high in robbery. They were often indicted with their masters as part of a gang. In the London coroners' rolls 25 percent of the suspects were servants. Their thefts reflect their trade in that they tended to steal household goods and valuables.

The clergy, the only occupational group about which reliable statistical information is available, followed a path of crime largely unrelated to their profession. Because of their literacy, one would expect to find them frequently as forgers, or because of their pastoral duties they might be indicted for receiving felons or booty, but instead they were heavily involved in robbery and such crimes. The explanation lies in the broad definition of clergy and the abuses of the plea of benefit of clergy.

Members of the clergy were charged with 4.4 percent of all felonies. There was very little variation from county to county,[71] with the slight differences perhaps representing differences in the clerical population. A Norfolk historian suggested that medieval clerks of his county acquired their reputation for criminal behavior because there were an overabundance of churches with inadequate livings so that the parish clergy were forced to supplement their livelihoods through thefts and fraud.[72] Unfortunately, we do not know the number of clergy in fourteenth-century England, so the percentage of those charged with felonies cannot be known.

It is the types of crimes rather than the amount of crime that demonstrates the uniqueness of the clerical record. On the whole, the clergy concentrated on the more violent property crimes. The clergy were suspected of robbery far more frequently than laymen: 26.9 percent of all their crimes compared to 11.6 percent of those of laymen. Burglary was also a common crime for clergy, but they were 10 percent less likely to be charged with larceny. Their record was comparable to that of the laity in receiving, counterfeiting, and arson. They tended to direct their efforts to the more dangerous, but more profitable, property crimes. In homicide their record paralleled that of laymen. One might expect that, because of the celibacy required of clergy, they would be more likely to participate in rape. The records show only a slight tendency in this direction that cannot be taken as significant given the small number of rapes reported.

There are several possible explanations for the predominance of clergy in violent property crimes. Many of the clergy, like the nobility, had their basic sustenance provided for through their benefices or livings. They were not likely to need and, therefore, to steal through simple larceny, such items as grain, household goods, clothing, and stray pigs and poultry. The valuables and livestock from which they would want to profit would best be acquired through burglary and robbery. A comparison of the types of goods clergy and laymen stole confirms this assumption. Valuables comprised 37.3 percent of all the goods clergy stole compared to 15.9 percent of the thefts of laymen (see figure 7). Horses accounted for 21.6 percent compared to 15.6 percent for laity. Because of their heavy emphasis on robbery, they also stole more clothing than laymen. Ordinary and cheaper goods were seldom part of their loot.[73] The profits from their thefts were also greater: 35.1 percent of the clergy got goods over £1 whereas only 20.1 percent of the laymen did.[74]

High paying robbery was usually done by gangs. Clergy often led the gangs or provided the core leadership. They also had an entree into the gangs of the nobility, for many of the clergy—vicars, chaplains, rectors—mingled socially with the nobility either because the nobles provided them with their livings or because they were the younger brothers or relatives of the local lord. The Folville gang, for instance, counted among its members a brother who was beheaded in his own churchyard where he had been both rector and criminal for twenty years.[75] Felons who joined such bands or those with a professional bent might have joined the clergy or learned to read in order to avoid hanging if convicted for one of their burglaries or robberies. The prominence of clergy in violent property crimes might simply represent a shrewd professional class of criminals.

Clerical offenders came from almost all levels of clerical life. A statistical breakdown is not feasible since the particular title is not often given. The highest clergy to appear in the rolls were the Abbot of Egleston and the Abbot of St. Agatha in Richmond who were appealed by an approver for receiving two horses and sixteen oxen. They were acquitted.[76] Secular clergy—*capellani, rectores,* and *pres-*

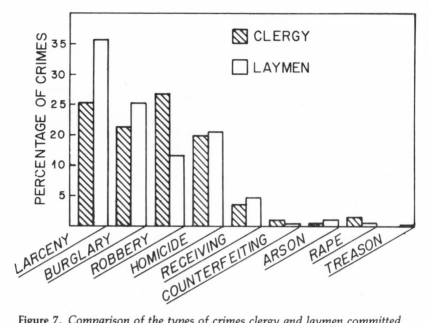

Figure 7. *Comparison of the types of crimes clergy and laymen committed.*

byteri—were frequently accused of committing robbery, burglary, and homicide as was Richard Herbert, chaplain, who robbed William de Brodish, vicar of Snareshill, of clothes, money, and a horse worth 44s. and stole cloth worth 10s. from the treasury of St. Edmund church.[77] Members of monastic houses also appeared in gaol delivery. Two Yorkshire monks, Hugh de Herternegg and David Scot, were accused of larceny and receiving livestock.[78] One Augustinian monk in Norfolk, Brother Robert de Weybridge, was accused of killing Prior Humprey of St. Mary's in Weybridge.[79] Students can be found with great regularity in the Oxford and Cambridge coroners' and gaol delivery rolls. Those in the lowest orders of clergy who could marry appear frequently accompanied by their wives who were also facing criminal charges. In one case the jurors would not accept a plea of clergy on the part of a local clerk because they said that he had a wife in Leicestershire and another one in Norfolk and that because he was a "bigamous clerk" he was not entitled to benefit of clergy.[80]

THE NOBILITY: A COMBINATION OF WEALTH, STATUS, AND OCCUPATION IN CRIME

The nobility must be considered separately from the peasants, tradesmen, craftsmen, and clergy for their wealth, status, and occupation were intimately bound up together and with their pattern of criminal behavior. This close connection between the occupation of the upper class and their crime pattern led me, in an earlier exploration of the problem, to call them "fur-collar criminals" and to compare them with white-collar criminals who are the deviants of the elite social class today.[81] The nature of upper-class crime was sociologically analyzed by Edwin H. Sutherland in his study, *White Collar Crime*, as "crime committed by a person of respectability and high social status in the course of his occupation."[82] If allowances are made for differences in occupation of a modern corporation executive and a medieval noble, the concept of white-collar crime proves useful in forming a more general understanding of crime among the social and governing elite of a society. It also helps to explain what appears to most historians of the fourteenth and fifteenth centuries to be an inexplicably great amount of violence and antisocial behavior on the part of the nobility. If they are seen as simply exploiting for criminal purposes their occupations as warriors, local government administrators, and managers of landed estates, then their behavior is much more understandable.

Crime among the upper classes was the first area to attract the attention of historians trying to answer Putnam's query about who the murderers, burglars, and robbers were that the king's justice was trying to capture.[83] The nobility and gentry seemed to be the logical place to start because public documents such as the statutes and the petitions of the Commons placed the blame for the crime problems on the nobility, their gangs, and those whom they protected. With a few examples of notorious noble bandits to draw from, the authors concluded that they had found the felons the government was trying to catch in its judicial machinery. As Hilton concluded, "members of the gentry families appear with such considerable frequency, in proportion to their numbers, that disorder appears almost to be a by-occupation of the class."[84]

Certainly, all evidence points to the nobility using the privileges of their social position to pursue illegal careers, but they do not necessarily appear in the criminal court records with great frequency. Only fifteen were identified by their titles in the gaol delivery data for this study.[85] In a court of first instance, Kent keepers of the peace indictments of 1316-1317, only four out of the seventy-seven people indicted were nobles, and they either never came to trial or were acquitted.[86] The reason for their low appearance was because of their class. Not only did their status protect them from being brought into the regular criminal courts, but also part of their criminal pattern was subversion of justice, particularly stopping cases against themselves and their supporters.

The criminal behavior of the upper classes in rural society was preserved in the accounts of chroniclers, since their involvement in crime was more sensational news than that of the peasantry. It also appeared in the patent rolls often in the form of commissions for special sessions of oyer and terminer and as special sessions of gaol delivery held under a commission of trailbaston. Medieval governments are hardly to be faulted for failing to catch the well-born criminal in the regular judicial procedure, for modern governments as well tend to deal with white-collar criminals in special commissions and in civil courts.

The nobility form such as unique group in the pattern of rural crime that both the membership in the class and the term "crime," as it applied to their activities, must be defined. The distinctive badge of the nobility in their dress was that they and their families were allowed to wear miniver fur decorations on their collars and robes. Edward III's sumptuary legislation regulating the wearing of miniver fur drew the line between the noble and the non-noble at the rank of esquires or gentlemen who could claim to have land and rents yielding 200 marks or more per year.[87] The very existence of the sumptuary legislation indicates that a law was already needed to draw distinctions within a class whose composition was changing. Many a rising gentleman and many an ancient and noble family who did not have such a large income were considered noble by both themselves and their contemporaries, even if Edward III would only have them wear squirrel collars. McFarlane pointed out that the baronage represented only the "upper level" of a large category of established people of honorable family and ancient wealth who were considered noble by medieval standards.[88] This group ranged from the wealthy and ancient gentry in villages to the great magnates. The distinguishing features of the class were nobility of birth and a particular set of social values. There were, of course, great differences in the rank and income of those within the class. These differences are reflected in differing patterns of criminal behavior.

The crimes that members of the nobility were likely to commit must be defined, for, by and large, they do not fall within the usual medieval category of felonious acts. Although nobles might commit an ordinary felony, they were more likely to direct a follower to do it or to use the prerogatives of their class to extort land, money, and chattels or to influence the course of justice. The distinction between crime and tort did not exist in medieval English law, so that a noble attacking a manor house and carrying off goods might be accused of trespass on some occasions, felony on others, and even treason depending upon whose house it was. In this study I treat cases as criminal if the society defined them as such and brought them within the criminal justice system.

In his study of white-collar crime Sutherland eliminated the ordinary felonies from his categories of upper-class criminal behavior because acts such as homicide, robbery, and rape were rare among this group and were not connected with their occupation. In the Middle Ages, however, warfare was part of the occupation of the upper classes and murder and pillage (robbery and burglary) could be work-related crimes. The barons and gentry of medieval England were involved in some notable murders such as the beheading of Piers Gaveston, the sadistic execution of Edward II, and numerous homicides in connection with private warfare and civil wars. These acts ranged from treason to vague feudal rights of revenge and private war to execution of the ruler's orders. Such homicides were directly related to the position of the noble class in their capacity as military and political leaders. Members of the higher nobility had little occasion to stain their hands in ordinary homicide involving disputes with the lower classes, because their household retainers could be ordered to take the necessary steps. For example, after dinner on May 13, 1301, Sir Ralph Porthos of Polebrook sent two of his men to John of Weldon's house in Polebrook to bring him to Sir Ralph's court dead or alive. They killed him and brought back ten shillings of his instead. In this murder Sir Ralph was an instigator and receiver but not a murderer.[89]

Members of the lower nobility and gentry were more likely than the higher nobility to participate personally in occasional robberies, burglaries, homicides, and larcenies as heads of criminal bands or members of a magnate's household. The activities of these lower ranks of nobility were so bad in 1331 that a special complaint was made in Parliament about them.[90] Part of the reason for the gentry's criminality may have lain in their worsening economic position in the late thirteenth and early fourteenth centuries.[91] Under these circumstances, some of them may have turned to crime to keep up their standard of living. Robbery and burglary certainly paid well for those knights who brought together a gang for that purpose. We have already seen that Sir Robert Rideware and Sir John Oddingseles got £ 40 for their ambush and robbery of merchants. But this was a small affair compared to the thirty-eight-member gang of Sir John de Colseby and Sir William Bussy who were able to take goods amounting to £ 3,000 in various property crimes.[92] These knights did particularly well in crime considering that the average value of goods stolen by persons tried in gaol delivery was £ 1 5s. Like the clergy, knights could rely on their estates or upon receivers for their daily bread so that they tended to steal items of larger value and to commit burglary and robbery as opposed to larceny. Even when the nobility did carry off foodstuffs, they thought in larger terms than their next meal. Lord Robert de Mangleyes sent four of his men to carry off no mere side of bacon, but five stones of meat.[93]

From the highest to the lowest level of the nobility, receiving was the most common felony. Although the barons such as Lord Robert de Mangleyes and Sir Ralph Porthos did not do their own hatchet work, they did shelter and protect their criminal henchmen. When the justices came to Somerset in 1305 to make special inquiries into criminal activities, they found that Lord Simon de Montacute, Lord Robert son of Payn, Lady Juliana la Brett, and Lord Robert de Brente were all suspected of receiving felons as were the high churchmen of the region.[94] None of these peers had taken part in the felonies, but they were accused of inciting the deeds and of sheltering the culprits, who were often members of their households.

For most of the nobility, particularly those above the rank of knight or gentry, simple felony was not as profitable as a number of other illegal activities more closely related to their position in society. As maintainers of armed households, owners of estates, and governing officials through manorial and royal commissions, the nobles could make abuse of their powers very profitable. The rewards for illegal actions might be collectable in tangibles such as goods, money, and land or in intangibles such as extension of power over tenantry or noble neighbors.

The nobles blurred the lines between collecting legitimate rents and services and actually looting their tenants' possessions. For instance, Lord Robert son of Payn and members of his *familia* forced Richard Seger of Raunton to pay twenty marks or be evicted from his tenement and Sir Ralph le Cort ordered his household to expel his miller or burn the mill.[95] Both these cases could have involved tenants who defaulted on rents and hence the actions of their lords would have been legitimate, if unsavory, by our standards. The jurors dismissed charges against a knight and his son for breaking into a man's house and taking his goods because the victim was the knight's serf who was in arrears on rent.[96]

The nobility used the techniques of extortion like a crude protection racket. The victim was beaten and then required to pay money to buy protection from future assaults and possible homicide. In other cases, as we have seen, the gang of gentry had sufficient reputation for violence that they only needed to send their proposed victim a letter informing them of their danger and the amount they should pay the bearer to avert it. Extortion techniques could be used to settle land disputes as well as to gain money. Two brothers in a venerable Somerset family had a dispute over land in which Thomas de Hywis took John de Hywis to his home and tied him up until he drew up a charter of enfeoffment for his brother and paid £200.[97] As we saw in chapter 2 the nobles used these same techniques in subverting justice for their own ends and those of their clients.

Traditional historians have tended to identify with the king in the constitutional struggles that led to a centralized state and monarchical control along Tudor lines.[98] These historians regard the magnates as "overmighty subjects" who took the law into their own hands and made illegitimate attacks on the royal authority. In fact, the politics of the time was closer to the model of feudalism and localism than the Tudor absolutism that was still two centuries away. Local people were used to turning to local lords for protection in a primitive form of Mafia and, unfortunately, were also all too accustomed to being oppressed by them on occasion as well. The nobles, for their part, were used to dispensing justice, administering their own estates, and raising armies with little interference from the central government. The kings seemed to be willing to accept the illegal actions of their nobility as natural. Rather than trying to eliminate this form of crime they tried to regulate it.

For the most part the kings avoided direct confrontation with the nobility in their courts because the royal judicial system was likely to back down in the face of threats from the nobility. It was to the king's advantage to recruit the upper classes to peacekeeping commissions of various sorts where they could use their propensities for war and management in the service of the king. Edward I effectively removed

Robert son of Payn from his criminal activities and his *familia* after the 1305 trailbaston sessions by sending him to Gascony on a commission of oyer and terminer.[99] Other nobles were summoned to serve in foreign wars. The Folvilles and Coterels served in Scotland and returned to become law-abiding citizens.[100] Only if all else failed did the king confront nobles with their misdeeds. Lord John Fitzwalter had dominated the judicial system of Essex for years with the aid of his household. Edward III tried a number of expedients to stop Fitzwalter's criminal activities including recruiting him for the seige of Calais, but he finally threw him into the Tower and confiscated his lands. After Fitzwalter spent about a year in prison, the king pardoned him and then "sold" his estates back to him. Fitzwalter lived on for ten more years, but he was so busy buying back his estates that he had neither the time nor the money to maintain a band of felons again. Ten years of Pipe Rolls benignly enter payments to the king from his "dear and faithful" John Fitzwalter.[101] While the nobility contributed much to crime in the countryside, particularly to organized crime, the king's judicial machinery was not really designed to trap them. They were not the "sleepers by day and wanderers by night" the king was after unless he was being unrealistic about his judicial system.

THE INDIVIDUAL OFFENDERS

For a small group of offenders the motivation for and the types of crime they committed had little to do with their social position. They were the criminally insane, those who came from violence-prone familial environments, and those particularly violence-prone individuals. Social background, wealth, or occupation had little to do with their involvement in crime, rather it was caused by their psychological state, either environmentally or physically produced.

Alcohol is an intoxicant traditionally associated with crime, particularly with homicide, because it releases aggression and is often used in the social atmosphere of the tavern or of a friend's home where social contact is already heightened. Beer played a large role in the life of the peasantry both in the home and tavern, but the traceable influence of drinking on homicide suspects in both rural and urban society was low. The drunken brawl figured in only 4.3 percent of rural homicides, and the tavern was the scene of a murder in only 7 percent of the cases.

Some families and individuals whose records can be traced in both the manorial courts and in gaol delivery appear to have been particularly criminous either because of the environment within the family or possibly because of an inherited physical or psychological characteristic. The Kelenach women of Huntingdonshire, whom we have cited before, are good examples of the chronic theft record of intermediate villagers. While it might be argued that these women from the poorer elements of the peasant community were driven by economic need to careers of petty theft, generations of offenders are found in the main village families as well. Although all the prominent villagers were prone to aggressive behavior, a few stood out as being unusually obstreperous. William Bird of Warboys and his family were one such group. As we mentioned in chapter 2, they must have gone beyond community toleration because one member was eventually indicted for homicide. Other families also produced criminal types. Nicholas atte Welle of Wood Hirst and his family had a history of assault, hues raised against them, leyrwite, and offenses against the lord and their neighbors before Nicholas was indicted for receiving in 1342.[102] Robert Careless of St. Ives, charged with burglary and homicide in 1339, came from a family with a history of assault stretching back to 1300.[103] In another case an individual seemed to have a particularly aggressive tendency that ended in his death rather than that of one of the people he assaulted. John le White of St. Ives was killed in a tavern fight that he had started himself and that had provoked his intended victim to self-defense.[104] Prior to the fatal fight White had a record of five assaults; two of which were in 1328, and had the hue raised against him twice in 1332. The criminal behavior of these people was distinct from other members of the village communities, but the exact causes of their more frequent criminal participation are not apparent from the rolls.

Another aspect of individual criminals that occasionally appeared in the records was their mental state at the time of the crime: criminal insanity. The plea of insanity required a particularly full description of the cases from the jury, since it was on the basis of their evidence that the king issued pardons. The jury's testimony included a full description of the crime, evidence of the nature of the abnormality, and the length of time before and after the event during which the accused was deranged. Like a minor, the insane felon was declared guilty of the offense but, because he was innocent of felonious intent in committing it, he was not hanged.[105] If the plea of *non compos mentis* successfully ended in pardon, then the king, lord, or city took the chattels of the insane into their keeping and provided a living for

145

him from them. If he returned to his reason at a later date, his chattels were restored to him.[106]

The juries normally described the deranged criminal as *non sanae mentis, non compos mentis, non sana memoria, amentia, furiosus, lunaticus, dementia, sine sensu et ratione humana*, and *insanitas*.[107] Medical science at the time attributed mental disorders to three causes: physical, as with rabies and fevers; mental, as with melancholia; and spiritual, as with demonic possession.[108] Usually, the juries did not attempt to analyze the causes of the mental disorder but simply described the symptoms. The most common proofs were attempted suicide, violent or irrational behavior, and abnormal behavior in conjunction with sickness.

Attempted suicide was one of the most common preludes to a frenzied homicide. The suspect would try to drown himself, but would be saved by those who came to rescue him. He might then kill one of those who saved him. Such was the case of Seman, son of Henry Thedlef, who tried to drown himself in the sea at Yarmouth. When John, son of Robert of Rollesby, and others stopped him, he killed John in a fit of violence.[109]

Fits of violence, accompanied by irrational behavior, were another common indication of insanity. The irrational behavior was not simply failure to conform with the normally accepted standards but, rather, completely nonsensical actions. For example, Andreas Friday was declared mad because he cut down all the trees on his property and then stuck them into the ground again expecting them to grow. During this fit of madness he committed a theft for which he was put into prison. Here he again became violent, attacking the other prisoners and tearing his clothes with his teeth.[110] John, son of John Spynk of Winterton, was considered a lunatic because, prior to killing William, son of John Winterton, he entered the church of Winterton, spat on the images, and then became violent, wounding several men in the church.[111] According to the juries, fits of insanity often occurred during the crescent of the moon. They even said specifically which phase of the crescent—the waxing or the waning of the moon. Robert Angot, who had been periodically insane for twenty years, became vexed with his fury during the waxing of the moon.[112]

Sometimes the jury testified that the accused had been sick with fever before the crime and that this had brought on a fit of violent frenzy during which he killed someone, usually in his family. One particularly pathetic case of this sort was Margery, who killed her husband William Martyn during a fit arising out of an acute fever. Becoming violent she took a knife and fatally wounded her husband on the head. After William died, she raised the hue and cry but had no sense (*nulla . . . sensum intellectum*) of what she had done. She remained in bed in a wild state for fifteen days thereafter so that her friends had to bind her. She recovered her reason as the disease abated.[113] In a similar case William Frer killed his daughter Alice and John, son of William Wikocson, after he had been sick and become demented.[114]

The length of time during which the accused appeared to be insane before committing the crime varied considerably, but apparently it was necessary for legal purposes that the person be insane both before and after the crime. The jury testified that Richard Sharp of Maltby, who killed his wife, Agnes, had been *non compos mentis* all the forty-four years of his life and particularly in the two months before and one month after the crime.[115] Another long-term mental illness was that of Robert Angot, whom we have already mentioned as having seizures during the crescent of the moon. He had been a lunatic for twenty years, but he had enjoyed lucid intervals during that time.[116] Margery, cited in the paragraph above, had been sick with fever fifteen days before she killed her husband and fifteen days after. In another case, the suspect had been deranged only eight days before and eight days after the crime.[117] At least one of the accused was only temporarily insane and fully regained awareness of his terrible act. This was Robert, son of Elene de Normanby, who had been mad for three weeks before he killed his daughter Elizabeth and John, son of Simon. Six weeks after the deed he returned to sanity and realized what he had done—"*maxime lamentabat et in dies lamentat.*"[118]

In the majority of the cases the insane person committed homicide, although there were also a few thefts and one case of arson. Of the fourteen homicides, nine were of parents killing their children, two were of a husband or a wife killing his or her spouse, and five were of insane people killing their caretakers or people who tried to bind them. One mother, Margaret, widow of Mark le Waleys, killed her two sons, Thomas and Robert, and her daughter Anastasia on St. Valentine's Day 1329. Earlier that day she had tried to commit suicide by throwing herself into a ditch filled with water. After her neighbors prevented her, she returned home and killed her children.[119] Children killed by their demented mothers were often very young. Juliana Motte of Killingbury drowned her one-year-old son John in a spring.[120] Another mother, Margery, wife of William Cabot, killed her two-year-old daughter Agnes with a knife and forced her four-year-old daughter Matilda to sit in the flames in the hearth.[121] We have already mentioned the two cases in which a man and a woman killed their respective spouses. Of the insane killing their caretakers or the people who tried to bind them, there are several examples. One was John Soliz who had become dangerously insane. His neighbors, including the victim, Roger Godsman, went to John's house to bind him. Roger cornered John in the attic but John picked up a hatchet and killed Roger with it.[122] By far the most hideous crime in the rolls was that of Robert Angot's killing his caretaker Thomas de Riston and William Maillie, who had come to Thomas's rescue. During one of Robert's periods of intermittent insanity, he grabbed a knife from Thomas and stuck it into Thomas's hand. William Maillie heard him cry out for help and came to his aid, but Robert was able to resist their efforts to bind him. He stabbed William in the chest and afterward beat Thomas on the testicles until he died.[123]

In three cases thieves were pardoned because of their insanity. Andreas Friday, whom we have already mentioned as cutting down his trees and replanting them, was accused of taking a horse. John Elnene of Swaffham, a lunatic, was accused of stealing wool worth 2s. Hugh Godware and his brother Henry stole money from several houses. Henry was hanged, but the jury claimed that Hugh was *non sanae mentis*.[124]

A case of arson in which the accused was declared insane was that of John, son of William, son of Kenneth de Nasserton, who burnt down the home of Robert Dreny of Duffeld; the fire consumed 40s. worth of goods.[125]

All the cases of mental disorder described in the rolls seem to have been the sort that would be readily recognizable to the average person: abnormalities as obvious as attempted suicide, bizarre behavior, and motiveless violence. Although the cases read very much like modern cases of criminal insanity, there is not enough evidence in the rolls to identify them with modern categories of mental illness. We can, therefore, only suggest the types of mental illness they might be. Some murders of children or of family members may have been done by manic-depressives who thought that the loved one would be better off dead than living on in a miserable world. A suicide attempt often accompanies such crimes. Nursing mothers sometimes suffer from a manic-depressive state in which they kill their children.[126] Crimes accompanied by suicide attempts may also be symptoms of paranoia, particularly the religious form,[127] or even of schizophrenia.[128] Some of the very violent crimes, such as Robert Angot's murder of his caretaker, may have arisen out of schizophrenia. Although it is not possible to analyze with certainty the variety of mental illness from which these people suffered, it is obvious that the jurors had a good knowledge of what criminal insanity involved and what type of evidence would be acceptable for it in court.

Were all insanity cases genuine or were there instances of malingerers trying to get pardoned for a crime they were known to have committed? There was certainly a benefit to be gained in appearing to be insane. The guilty person was not only pardoned but also had his chattels returned to him if he regained his sanity. In spite of the advantages of pleading insane, all but one case were accepted as genuine by the court. In the case of John, son of Agnes Clochun, who became an approver and then claimed in court that he was *non sanae memoria* at the time of the appeals, the coroner testified that he had been in good health and sound mental condition at the time.[129] The jurors apparently did not suspect malingering in other cases or knew the background of their neighbors too well for a fraud to be successful. Because of this knowledge, malingering was unlikely to occur without the jurors' connivance. Could the jurors then have helped a friend make a plea of insanity? The extreme rarity of the plea of insanity—about one case in every thousand—makes it unlikely that the jury was busily making up pleas of *non sanae mentis* for friends in trouble. It was probably so easy to get the jury to comply in giving a favorable verdict either by threats, bribes, or use of influential connections that it was unnecessary to resort to a plea of insanity.

Assuming that these people were actually insane, what happened to them after they received pardons? From the cases in the rolls we know something of the keeping of the insane. Robert Angot had both parents and an aunt living at the time of his trial who testified that he had been insane for twenty years. Apparently he did not live with them but was in the charge of the caretaker whom he murdered. Richard Sharp of Maltby, who killed his wife, also lived separated from her, for the record says that he took an axe to the place where his wife was living.[130] The rolls do not say who paid for the care of these people. If they had insufficient personal income, then the family and friends were responsible for their keeping. Occasionally they were kept in gaol if they were too violent to be kept at home.[131] They were also kept in hospitals along with others ill with normal diseases or in leper hospitals.[132] The family and friends of the person sometimes undertook to treat him, usually by taking him to a shrine noted for healing. A window in Canterbury Cathedral shows an insane man being dragged by his friends to the shrine of St. Thomas. He is tied with ropes and is being beaten with birch rods. In the second scene he appears in his right mind giving thanks.[133] Whipping was not uncommon as a treatment to bring the deranged to their senses.[134] If Robert Angot received this type of treatment from his caretaker, then perhaps the madman had his reasons for murder.

The man in the street in the reigns of the three Edwards might have had his imagination caught by the violent acts of the insane and feared to find himself in a plight similar to that of Isabel Climne who was grabbed by her hair in Great Yarmouth and nearly strangled with her hood until she killed the madman who was having his crescent-of-the-moon fit.[135] But, in fact, the ordinary citizens should have looked for attack from people very similar to themselves. The offender would be male in 90 percent of the cases. In property crimes there was a somewhat better possibility that the suspect would be a woman, especially if clothing, food, or household goods were involved. If the property crime were robbery or if the assault were homicidal, the assailant would probably be male and possibly a member of the clergy, a knight, or member of a magnate's household. Most likely, the suspect would be in his teens or early twenties. In about three-fourths of the cases he would be a neighbor and well known to the victim. Aside from the violent property crime of robbery and to a lesser extent burglary, which attracted outside thieves, the suspects were largely from the established village families who ranged in wealth from near gentry level to day laborers. In summary, then, the "sleepers by day and the wanderers by night" may have been no more sinister than the prominent and respected villager next door. At least those caught by the justice system and tried for their crimes were of this sort.

Chapter Five

The Relationship

between the Victim and the Accused

CERTAIN SEGMENTS of the population in the Middle Ages, as is still the case, were more likely to become unwitting victims of crime than was the general population. Women and children were particularly vulnerable to assault because of their relative physical weakness and because of social attitudes toward them that made them vulnerable to certain crimes, such as rape of women and infanticide of unwanted children. The old, ill, handicapped, and drunk were also easy targets of crime. And the attraction of wealth to thieves needs no more modern criminologist than Langland who pointed out that "Riches are the root of robbery and of murder."[1] Still, the most probable victims were fellow villagers who themselves could just as readily have been the perpetrators of the crimes.

The relationship between the victim and the accused is seldom a random one—of the victim being in the wrong place at the wrong time. The perpetrator of the crime usually knows his victim personally or at least knows a great deal about him or her. If the crime is premeditated to gain a particular end for the offender, then he will have to know, as does the hunter, the habits of his prey in order to stalk them successfully. Or if the attack comes in a moment of passion, it will usually be against a victim who can arouse such destructive anger in the aggressor. The close connection between the victim and the perpetrator is often described as a doer-sufferer relationship. This "duet frame" in criminal cases has long been recognized in rape and homicide.[2] If an adult woman consents to a rape, then her attacker is not culpable before the law. A person who incites an enemy to homicidal anger has contributed to his own murder. Other, more subtle relationships between the victim and the perpetrator, such as that between a thief and his victim, are harder to investigate. Yet modern criminology has become increasingly interested in the role of the victim in inciting crime, calling this new area of inquiry "victimology"[3]

Medieval society and its laws also reflected a concern with differentiating the types of victims and the possibility of the victim's culpability as well as that of the perpetrator. The most apparent cases of victim precipitation in medieval records appear in homicides where the victim initiated the aggression and the slayer had to kill in self-defense. But the society also expressed concern about the less obvious cases where psychological aggression rather than physical violence led to assault. So common was this interest that it entered into one of the medieval love ballads, "Lord Thomas and Fair Annet." Thomas and Eleanor had been in love for many years, but Thomas decided to marry the wealthy "nut-brown maiden." Eleanor, obviously outraged by this breach of faith, went to the wedding in her finest clothing and commented to Lord Thomas:

"Is this your bride?" Fair Ellin she sayd,
  "Methinks she looks wondrous browne;
Thou mightest have had as fair a woman
  As ever trod on ground!"[4]

This taunt was sufficient provocation for the bride to kill Eleanor and for Lord Thomas to kill his bride.

While homicidal attacks were open to speculation, romantic and legal, evidence of the victim bringing about attacks on his property were muddled in both law and social reactions. Arson, of course, could be a direct response to a wrong committed by the victim to the perpetrator, but for other property crimes this was not necessarily true. A man's goods might be stolen by a spiteful neighbor or one who genuinely thought that the goods belonged to him. But the law accommodated such property cases through trespass actions and fines. For the most part direct victim participation in crimes or any prior relationships between the victim and the accused cannot be traced and probably often did not exist.

THE SEX OF THE VICTIMS

The proportion of males to females who became victims of crime was exactly the same as that for those indicted for crimes: nine to one.

County to county variations were slight. The breakdown of the types of crimes by the sex of the victim is inconclusive, except for rape where the victims obviously were women. Arson cases are too few to analyze by the sex of the victims. Counterfeiting, receiving, and treason did not cite individual victims. Men were victims in 88.9 percent of the larcenies, 84.9 percent of the burglaries, 95.8 percent of the robberies, and 82.3 percent of the homicides. In the more complete coroners' roll data, 94 percent of the homicide victims were male in Northamptonshire, 96.5 percent in heavily clerical Oxford, and 90 percent in London.

Women were less apt to be found in situations conducive to becoming victims. They were not actively engaged in the heavy work in fields and shops and therefore were less likely to become the victims of homicidal arguments related to these activities. Women infrequently traveled with valuable chattel and animals, so that they were rare victims of robberies. But the naming of victims was often inaccurate because it reflected the bias of a male-dominated society. Usually the male head of house was declared the victim in property crimes because males owned most of the moveable property. Even if the property belonged to the wife, the husband was likely to be cited as the victim.

Like modern criminal court records, the gaol delivery rolls recorded only a select population of rape victims. Only innocent and virginal or titled and high-status rape victims could expect to have their day in court. In Yorkshire, for instance, a man was convicted for raping Agnes daughter of William Neilesone and Isabel daughter of Simon Gregesone who were both only 14 years old.[5] Widows who were not under some man's protection were common targets for rape. If a rapist were after profit as well as sex, then a wealthy married woman or widow would be his victim in rape/robbery or rape/burglary. For instance, a married woman from Stambourne in Essex was abducted and raped by a man who carried her off to Cambridgeshire and stole goods worth £10 from her.[6] I have also suggested that sometimes the motivation for gang rapes of high-status widows or married women was to humiliate their husbands. It was a method of social retribution that men could use against other men to indicate that the victim's protector was too impotent to guard her honor.

The medieval rape cases show that some were victim-precipitated or at least accomplished with the victim's consent. Some rapes were ruses to enter into marriage. Other victims were merely seeking pleasure.

Alice wife of John Kyde of Wakefeud was abducted by night by the servant of Nicholas, the parish chaplain of Wakfeud, on the chaplain's horse and by his command, and with the women's consent; she was taken to Alysbiry, with goods belonging to her husband, to wit, 11d. taken from her husband's purse; three gold rings worth 18d.; a cup of mazer 12d.; a napkin, 12d.; a towel, 6d.; a gown, 6s. 8d.; a new hood taken from her husband's pack, 12d. and many other things unknown. Afterwards Alice returned to her husband.[7]

THE AGE OF THE VICTIMS

The victims' age influences how they are victimized in crime and the means that are used. In modern crime infants and young children are usually killed with different weapons than are able-bodied men. Adult males in their thirties predominate among the homicide victims and among those of burglaries and robberies as well. These patterns of age and crime have a continuity from the Middle Ages to the modern period, but the particular social conditions of the Middle Ages also produced divergent patterns.

The problem of infanticide in preindustrial Europe has received widespread attention recently from both demographers and historians of crime. The infant, like the young of any animal, is the classical victim who can neither precipitate its own murder nor defend itself against murder. The vulnerability of the young child to death from disease and accident is also extremely high, so that detecting murder from other causes of death is difficult, particularly in the Middle Ages when infant mortality was 30 to 50 percent and medical autopsies minimal. Infanticide was, therefore, more easily concealed than other types of homicide.

For fourteenth-century England, infanticide presents something of a mystery. A combination of the homicide cases in gaol delivery and in the coroners' rolls yielding a sample of over 5,000 cases revealed only three instances of infanticide. In a Norfolk case, Alice Grunt and Alice Grym were indicted for having drowned a three-day-old baby in a river at the request of Isabel of Bradenham and her son and daughter. They were acquitted.[8] Whose child it was and why Isabel and her family were so anxious to be rid of it is not made clear. Likewise in a Huntingdonshire case, Juetta Morning was acquitted for the death of an unknown infant, not assumed to be hers.[9] In the third case, the jurors of Oxford city said that a baby girl, one-half-day old, was carried downstream and they knew nothing about the father or mother. They concluded that the child had not been baptized because the navel was not tied.[10] In two of these cases the mother apparently was not directly responsible for the deaths of the infants and in the third case there is no information. Perhaps the women committing the murders were midwives, but this too is not spelled out.

Why were there only three reported infanticides? Part of the explanation may lie in the ambiguous attitude of the law toward infanticide. A statute law against mothers killing their illegitimate children was not passed until 1623.[11] Before that time, secular law dealt with the problem in a variety of ways. In the two cases cited above, the offenders were tried by the ordinary criminal court procedure, but this may have been because they were not the mothers of the infants. Hurnard found that the "woman who killed in child-birth was sometimes held responsible and could sometimes receive a pardon for her actions."[12]

The Church was more adamant than was the secular government that those who committed infanticide should be brought into ecclesiastical courts and should do penance for their acts if they were found guilty. Synodal legislation and books of penance in England both contain admonishments against child-murder and prescribe suitable penances and spiritual exercises for the people responsible.[13] The Church was well aware of the methods of committing and con-cealing infanticide. Parents were told not to sleep with their children because they might smother them in the night (often called "over-lay-ing"); not to leave their children alone because they might wander off and drown or meet with some other injury; and not to place the children too near the fire.[14] The Church, however, did not seem to pursue their concern with infanticide; R. H. Helmholtz found very few instances of the ecclesiastical courts hearing such cases.[15] Further-more, the Church apparently did not rank the prosecution or punish-ment of those who killed children any higher than many other moral offenses they had jurisdiction over, for the punishment for child mur-derers was about the same as for those who committed sexual offenses.[16]

The pastoral injunctions about the care of children were certainly well-founded, for they are directed at the types of accidents that commonly killed children. With children under twelve being involved in 17.5 percent of all violent deaths recorded in the coroners' inquests of rural Northamptonshire and Bedfordshire (247 children out of

1,409 cases), it seems plausible that at least some of the accidental drownings and burnings of children might have been concealed infanticides. Among the accidental deaths of infants in our sample (48 cases) there were no reported cases of over-laying but 50 percent of the infants died from fires and 22 percent from drowning. Was this neglect or premeditated murder? At least one attempted drowning case was intentional. John son of Adam de Routonstall threw his son into a well and held him down with felonious intent but was stopped before he could succeed in drowning the child.[17]

One of the more consistent patterns associated with infanticide is that female children are killed more frequently than male.[18] The coroners' rolls, however, show that in Northamptonshire the percentage of accidental deaths of boys under twelve was much higher than girls—63 percent of all accidental deaths among children were male. The close similarity to modern accident figures where 63 percent of all accidental death victims fourteen and under are males seems to indicate that this consistency has more to do with child development than with infanticide.[19] In the age group of one year and under twenty-eight boys died compared to twenty girls. While this is a lower percentage than the overall comparison, the discrepancy should not be taken as an indication that female children were killed. Again the modern accident figures indicate that the degree of excess of male deaths is lowest in infancy and increases with age.[20] Even if the accident figures do conceal infanticide, there is no evidence that females were more frequent victims. We really do not have sufficient information on the legal position of women or social attitudes toward them yet to conclude that medieval society valued women less than men and, therefore, tended to kill female babies.

There remain two possibilities to explain the low incidence of infant victims: (1) that infanticide was a widely accepted practice and, therefore, society largely ignored it, or (2) that infanticide was not widely practiced for a variety of reasons. Infant mortality may have been so high that there was no need for widespread infanticide; the need for laborers in the fields was so great that all additional hands were welcome; or the society may not have put a stigma on illegitimacy either because of laxness of marriage customs or because of the need for workers. Neither of the two hypotheses can yet be substantiated. With more knowledge about the economic circumstances of the bulk of the population and more systematic use of folk and other literature a better knowledge of society's opinion of infanticide might be possible. For instance, illegitimacy might well have been discouraged by the wealthier elements of the peasant communities who were concerned with keeping both their lines of wealth and their power in the community under clear title. But to the members of the intermediate group, the presence of more children would mean more helpers to bring in an income. Because their diet would be poorer, however, fewer of their children would be likely to survive.

No doubt growing children could be an unwelcome burden on a family with limited livelihood. One has only to note the lament of Mak in the "Second Shepherd's Pagent."

> I thought Gill began to croak and travail full sad,
> Well-nigh at the first cock, of a young lad
> For to mend our flock. Then be I never glad;
> I have two on my rock more than ever I had.
> Ah, my head!
> A house full of young tharms, (bellies)
> The devil knock out their harns! (brains)
> Woe is to him as has many bairns,
> And thereto little bread.[21]

But Mak does not suggest that he is going to do damage to the children himself. There is fourteenth-century chronicle evidence, however, suggesting that parents did kill their children in famine time.[22] Such evidence is suspect because the chronicler might have been using a literary form to indicate the terrible suffering in the Great Famine of 1315-1317, but one is reminded of the Chinese peasant woman in the *Good Earth* who suffocated her newborn infant during a famine. Considering the problems of overpopulation of Malthusian dimensions that England faced, it is remarkable that there is not more mention of infanticide, particularly in the years of grain shortage.

Children over one year old were also seldom victims of violence. In the gaol delivery records only 2 percent of all homicides involved children under twelve. Some of these children were killed in accidental slayings and some in the course of burglaries. For instance, a two-year-old boy was killed by William son of Richard of Finchdon as William was shooting arrows at a target. The child suddenly wandered out of a door into the path of the arrows.[23] Direct homicidal assaults on children were, however, rare. We have already mentioned the mother who whipped her eleven-year-old son to death in a fit of anger and the London shopkeeper who killed a six-year-old thief with a blow on the ear. This type of assault was not premeditated nor were those of insane mothers or fathers who killed their children. Only 0.3 percent of all homicide cases in the gaol delivery rolls involved insane mothers killing their children. There is, therefore, very little evidence that either family or society in general hated or preyed upon children.

The ages of victims over twelve are difficult to establish except for homicide cases. Some of the coroners, for no apparent reason, did begin to record the victims' ages in the middle to late fourteenth century.[24] The mean age of the homicide victims was 36.8 years—a distribution only slightly older than the modern one.[25] Three of the victims were teenagers, fifteen in their twenties, forty in their thirties, nineteen in their forties, twelve in their fifties, seven in their sixties, and three in their seventies. Since the motivation for the homicides was mostly arguments, probably centered around crops and property, men in their thirties and forties were most likely to be involved for they were in their contentious years when they were consolidating their landholdings and social position in the community. They would have to defend these from other, perhaps younger, men who were also trying to make their way. Since a large part of the population were in their twenties and thirties, the homicide age, the dominant role of homicide in the medieval crime pattern is understandable.

Most of the older men and women in the sample were killed in the course of a robbery, burglary, or premeditated attack. For instance, unknown felons knocked John Pekot, Parson of Old Church, aged sixty, off his horse one night.[26] Some older men started arguments and became classic victim-precipitation cases. Roger Schorsbery went to Richard Hunte's house and began to call him a thief and attacked him with a fork. Richard defended himself with a staff and killed Roger. Robert Fulmesby did a very similar thing and was killed by the person he had gone to assault.[27] They were pursuing a pattern of aggressive encounter that was part of the normal social interaction for medieval males, but they were unable to win the fight. Perhaps when they were younger men, the outcome had been different.

Criminal Interactions in the Family

One of the most striking aspects of medieval crime is that intrafamilial relationships produced very few felonies. The remarkably small role that violence played in the medieval family is in direct contrast to the modern victim-offender relationship and speaks both to the problem of tensions that gave rise to crime in medieval

England and to the relationships within the family. Of all cases brought into gaol delivery only 0.7 percent were cases of one family member transgressing against another. In 92 percent of these cases the felonious action involved homicide, but this was only 2 percent of the total homicides tried in gaol delivery. Even in the coroners' inquests the family played a very small role. Of the 554 cases of homicide recorded in the Northamptonshire coroners' rolls in the fourteenth century only 8 percent were intrafamilial homicide. In contrast, 53 percent of all murders in modern England involve intrafamilial actions.[28]

It might be assumed that the medieval family was contentious, but that their arguments seldom developed into felonies or homicides. But if one looks at the percentage of family members active in disputes with each other in manorial courts, even there disputes between kin are rare. Of the 2,774 cases tried in the first half of the century in the courts of Wakefield and Ingoldmells only sixty cases, or 2 percent, involved members of the same family. At this level the family cases predominated in assault (56.7 percent of the family cases) rather than debt or trespass (40 percent).[29] In other words, intrafamilial crime was rare, but when one family member did commit a crime against another, it tended to be of the most violent kind.

In all court rolls—coroners', manorial, and gaol delivery—only the closest relationships were entered; that is, only spouses, parents and children, and siblings. Occasionally uncles, cousins, and grandparents appeared, and sometimes consanguinity can be detected by the coincidence of the last name. Although it is impossible to establish with absolute certainty that even all the closest kinship ties were recorded, there is good evidence to indicate that probably the majority were. Kinship ties were used extensively for identification purposes even when last names became more common. The intrafamilial crimes took on a special significance that made it more likely that the jurors would mention the relationship in the court. Finally, information on familial relationships would be useful to lords' and king's officials who confiscated the goods of the felon's immediate family. Family members probably tried to settle nonhomicide cases out of court, which would remove some of the thefts. Even assuming that some data are missing, the discrepancy between the modern and medieval figures for intrafamilial crime is so great that problems of recording data cannot be the sole explanation. Furthermore, the records are sufficiently adequate for investigating the percentages of different family members most frequently involved in conflict with each other.

The line of homicidal tensions within the family show definite patterns of conflict. In homicide cases in both the gaol delivery rolls and the coroners' rolls the tension between spouses was most likely to lead to fatal aggravations—55.5 percent in gaol delivery rolls and 39.2 percent in the coroners' rolls (see figure 8). In almost all these cases the wife was the victim of the husband's violence, which is consistent with both the general pattern of female victimization by males and with the modern pattern of intrafamilial homicide. The other major point of conflict within the family was in the parent-child relationship: 31.6 percent in gaol delivery rolls and 21.7 percent in the coroners' rolls. Next in magnitude came the sibling quarrels with 11.4 percent in gaol delivery and 21.7 percent in the coroners' rolls.

Although the husband-wife quarrels predominated in homicides, nonfatal disputes in manorial courts show a somewhat different picture. The sibling rivalry predominated with 66.6 percent of the familial cases in manorial court. The parent-child conflicts were next with 18.4 percent, and the spouse discord accounted for only 5 percent of the cases. Again, the pattern was for husbands to be the assailant, brothers fought brothers in sibling cases, and in the parent-child disputes the pattern varied from court to court. Children acted against their parents on the manorial level whereas in the homicide cases the parent was more likely to be the killer of the child. Although the step-child/step-parent relationship was not specifically delineated in the records, other evidence suggests that this nonblood tie was particularly prone to conflict.

The motivations for disputes between different members of the family were not always recorded in the court rolls, and, on the whole, must be inferred from the documents or reconstructed from a combination of manorial rolls and trial records. Many areas where modern criminology can point definitely to a cause and effect relationship in producing intrafamilial tensions, such as psychological conflicts, medieval records are inadequate for anything but speculation.

Arguments over land that led to assaults, homicides, and property disputes are a logical starting point for discussing potentially criminal tensions within the peasant family, for land was the basis of the peasant economy. In the manorial records, land disputes were second

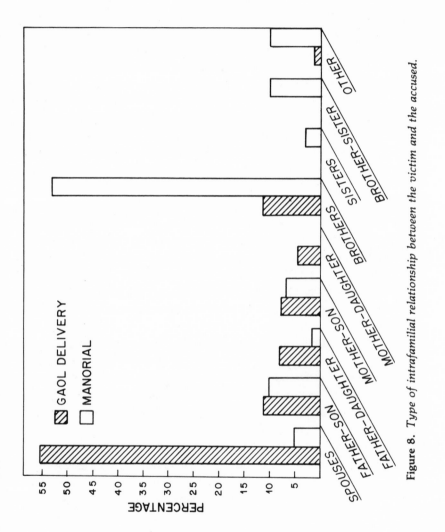

Figure 8. Type of intrafamilial relationship between the victim and the accused.

only to assaults as a cause for court action between kin, but as we will show, many of the assaults and even homicides in the total population also had their origins in quarrels over land or other property. The kinship ties that occurred most frequently in land quarrels were brother against brother. The disputes are numerous, but only a few examples need be cited to show their genesis. Since the reading of their father's will, Robert and Thomas le Parker had been arguing over a piece of land that their father had left to Thomas. Robert decided to force Thomas into a settlement. On the day of the murder he had taken two of his kinsmen to Thomas's house. Abducting Thomas to his own house, Robert locked the door and began to threaten Thomas with a knife. Thomas tried to escape, but finding the door locked, he seized the knife from Robert and killed his brother in self-defense.[30] Evidence from the manorial courts gives a background to this particular type of dispute. For instance, in Ramsey village the Porthos brothers, John Major and John Minor, were identified not only as belonging to one of the main families but as having had disputes with each other that appeared in manorial court. In 1333 these disputes between the brothers finally ended in a homicidal attack in which one brother was killed.[31] It is noteworthy that this is one of the few cases in manorial court where brother attacked brother and where the dispute actually led to homicide.[32]

Tensions arising over the division of land between brothers are probably endemic to peasant societies. It has been estimated that in the Chinese peasant communities the longest duration of harmonious family land usage was usually two generations. After that, arguments between brothers would force a breakup of the family holdings.[33] Such tensions were not limited to the peasant families but were notable among all levels of the society in the Middle Ages. At their worst they led to civil wars or more minor wars and land seizures among the nobility. In areas with partible inheritance brothers frequently quarrelled over the division of inheritance and the working of the land. For instance, in Norfolk and Essex, where all brothers inherited under the laws of partible inheritance, instances of brother killing brother comprised 14.3 percent of the intrafamilial crimes. In Yorkshire and Northamptonshire, which had primogeniture, only 7.3 percent of intrafamilial homocides involved this relationship. The tension between brothers shows up also when one compares the kin who joined together to commit crimes. In Norfolk and Essex only 20.7

percent of the family criminal associations were brothers, but in the two primogeniture counties 39.5 percent were brothers. These figures should be taken only as indicative rather than conclusive because of the small size: 42 intrafamilial cases and 87 familial criminal associations in Norfolk and Essex and 42 intrafamilial cases and 514 criminal associations in Yorkshire and Northamptonshire.

Other familial connections produced disputes over land. The widow was often the victim in this type of argument. For example, Alice widow of Adam Broun sued Richard Broun in Wakefield court because, she complained, he "deforced her of her dower in a house, a garden, and an essert called Ryding." Richard claimed that he bought the land from her husband. The dispute had already gotten out of hand by the time it reached court for widow Alice also accused brother Richard of taking a chest worth 2s., of assaulting and beating her seven years ago, and of sundry other trespasses.[34] One of the most fascinating cases of land inheritance and murder comes from a Midlands village. It spans two generations and deals not only with land but with the psychological relations between a mother, her son, and her second husband. Emma Mabyll belonged to a prominent village family in Wigston. She married John Baker and had a son by him called Richard. When she married Adam de Sutton she had inherited a piece of freehold property. Adam must have persuaded her to sell the freehold rather than giving it to her son by her first marriage. On the night of November 13, 1390, probably in front of his mother's house, Richard lay in wait for Adam and killed him with a staff before his mother's eyes.[35]

If one combines court actions such as debt, trespass, and arguments over chattels in one category—property disputes—these form 33.3 percent of familial disputes in manorial courts. Once again, it is likely that many assaults and homicides were generated out of arguments over movable property. As in land disputes they were more common among siblings than other kin relationships. Such was the case between the Pees brothers, Robert and Thomas, who reached a court settlement over a trespass at Wakefield court. Apparently it was not mutually agreeable, because several months later they were again in court on charges of assaulting one another.[36] In a coroners' roll case in Bedfordshire, such an argument ended in homicide.

At dawn on 31 Dec. 1268 Henry and William, sons of Richard the carpenter of Goldington, quarrelled in their father's house in

Goldington about a halfpenny, which one of them had lent the other, and went forth quarrelling to the outer door. William then struck Henry on the head with a crab-apple staff so that he fell.[37]

Property disputes could end in felonies of robbery and burglary as well as homicide. For instance, four female relatives killed and robbed William Elyot, chaplain of Dalling, of goods worth 20s.[38] Those related to each other by ties of kinship, however, were not more notably engaged in litigation or arguments over land and property than were other people appearing in manor courts. During the Great Famine of 1315-1317 the amount of property actions increased in both familial and nonfamilial cases. In the struggle for survival, external tensions could drive a family apart as well as a community. One wonders if, in some cases, there was not the feeling that in times of crisis charity should begin at home and that, if it were not forthcoming, it could be forcefully acquired. Perhaps this explains why the four Elyot women killed the chaplain and robbed him at the height of the famine in 1316.

Between husbands and wives as opposed to siblings, land and property were less likely to be a problem than were arguments over children and daily chores, the frustrations about daily life, and sexual jealousies. Although examples can be found of all these motivations for homicide between spouses, they cannot be ranked from the most common to the least common because of insufficient evidence.

From the chivalric tales of Tristan and Iseult to the numerous fabliaux, some of which Chaucer repeated in the Miller's tale and the Reeve's reply, medieval literature dwelled on adultery cases. The problems of adultery would normally come before ecclesiastical courts, which were responsible for handling matters of morals and marriage, but the village community could intervene and any cases involving property or physical damages were a matter for secular courts. For instance, John Kenward of Hepworth was summoned into Wakefield manor court by Master Ralph of Coningburgh to account for living adulterously with Alice daughter of Simon de Hepworth and for driving his wife from his house.[39] The fines in these cases leave no doubt that the matter was serious. John Kenward paid 6s. 8d. for not appearing in court. Another man accused of living with a harlot was fined 40s. Women as well as men were cited for their wayward lives. The wife of Thomas de Langsfeld not only committed adultery with John del Risseleye but also took goods belonging to her husband to John's house.[40] Tempers were bound to flare in these types of situations, and there are indications in the circuit court records and in coroners' inquests that adultery could lead to homicide. John Edwyne of Weld and Emma, the former wife of William le Carpenter and concubine of John Edwyne, were both convicted in Huntingdonshire for the murder of William. They were not poor people in the community, since the crown was able to confiscate 13s. 6d. from him and 27s. 5d. from her in movable property.[41] More commonly, however, it was the husband who killed the wife and/or the lover. Robert le Baurserman killed John Doughty when John came to his house at night while Robert was asleep and had a secret rendezvous with Robert's wife. When Robert awakened and found his wife was not at his side but with John in the other room an argument ensued in which John was killed.[42]

Long-standing incompatibility and the problems of separation and child support seemed to enter into the homicide cases as well. Often the recorded residence of the husband and the wife in homicide cases indicated that they had been living apart before the murder. In a few cases the problems were more explicitly spelled out as in this argument over child support.

> On the night of 29 March 1271 Walter le Bedel of Renhold came to the house of his wife, Isabel daughter of Reynold, in Ravensden and asked her to come with him to Renhold to get a bushel of wheat which he wished to give her for her boys, and she went with him. When they reached "Longemead" meadow, he immediately struck her over the left ear apparently with a knife, giving her a wound three inches long and in depth to the brain . . . and afterwards threw her into "Ravensbrok" stream.[43]

Since divorce was virtually impossible and annulment rare in ecclesiastical courts, the tensions of marriage could be prolonged and therefore increase the potential for a murderous solution to marital difficulties.[44]

Incompatibilities between couples also arose from brutality or from an inability to deal with outside frustrations except by beating spouse or children. Although the husband beater received attention in church sculpture and in the culture of the Middle Ages, the homicidal beatings generally involved the husband killing the wife. For instance, a village reported to the coroner that a man, whose wife was found dead, should be considered as a suspect because they knew that he was a chronic wife-beater.[45] On occasion the community would intervene before a murder occurred. In Wakefield in 1331 Thomas son of John

Kenward had to find sureties "that he will be reconciled with Agnes his wife and will treat her well."[46] In another case the battered wife called out to her brother to save her from her husband's blows. The brother rushed in and permanently stilled his brother-in-law's up-raised fist with a hatchet blow.[47] The reasons for the beatings are not given in the texts.

Bouts of uncontrollable anger may have arisen from the frustrations of a life in which there were few other outlets. Maxim Gorki's dialogue between two Russian peasants is instructive.

> "You may have many reasons for it, but it's not your wife's temper that causes you to treat her so unwisely. The cause is your own un-enlightened condition." "That's just so," exclaimed Yakoff—"We do indeed live in darkness as black as pitch."—"The conditions of your life irritate you, and your wife has to suffer from it . . . She is always there ready to your hand, she can't get away from you." Thereupon Yakoff turns to the other man and says: "Stop! You beat your wife also, don't you?" "I'm not saying I don't, because I do. How can I help it? I can't beat the wall with my fist when I feel I must beat something." "That's just how I feel," said Yakoff.[48]

Although medieval data are insufficiently complete to substantiate the suggestion made by Gorki, modern data indicate that in cases where the wife did kill the husband, the husband very often brought on his own demise by an intolerable brutality not explainable in terms of the wife's behavior toward him.[49] In none of the cases of pardon for self-defense slayings did I find one in which the wife made that plea as an excuse for killing her husband. The self-defense plea was, perhaps, impossible since a wife killing her husband was considered to have committed a treasonous offense.

Latent psychological motivations could have accounted for homicides among other members of the family as well as spouses, but the documentation is rare. Nevertheless, speculation on the subject is inevitable and must be included if only to indicate how little real evidence there is. One cannot help but observe that a half-penny was a very small amount to justify the murder of one brother by another. Sibling rivalry may have been the real cause of the crime. The setting of one such murder in their mother's house also hints at a sibling rivalry with deeper psychological motivations.[50] Another classic area of jealousies was that of the step-parent and step-children. One particularly brutal case indicated the depth of such feelings. Raymond le Tailur and his children by a previous marriage cut the throat and shins of Emma, Raymond's second wife.[51] The low percentage of parent-child murder seems to indicate that if Oedipal conflicts were present, they were seldom expressed homicidally.[52]

Ascribing psychological motivations for intrafamilial violence in the Middle Ages is risky because of the nature of the evidence. Not only is there little discussion in the documents of motivations for homicides, but also on the whole the medieval family seems to have been remarkably free from the violence that characterizes the modern nuclear family. It is this aspect of their crime pattern, rather than the motivations for the little crime that did occur, that deserves further attention. Even the problems of overcrowding in the two-room medieval houses did not appear to produce the homicidal manifestations that it does in today's overcrowded families. Did medieval families know the secret of congenial cohesiveness that has been lost to the modern family or were the families such loose emotional structures that one would have less cause to kill a brother than a neighbor? The relative commoness of bigamy and the informality with which marriage contracts could be arranged might lead one to believe that the family was a fairly loose institution in which emotional bonds might be transitory and not as deep as those with the community. On the other hand, the work of Raftis and his students has indicated that among the main village families there was great concern about keeping families cohesive so that property holdings and consolidation of political power in the villages could be maintained. Threats to the breakup of family holdings or the possibility of illegitimacy were all treated as serious issues by the main villagers. Even when one looks at the participation of families in crime, the chief area of their importance was in associations of criminals where they cooperated in crime rather than criminally attacked one another.

The explanation for the low incidence of crime in medieval families must await further evidence on the structure and relationships within them and the crucial factors in homicidal relationships. Modern criminology has shown that the victims of homicide will most often be those with whom the accused has an intense personal relationship. If this relationship seems not to be present among family members in the Middle Ages, was it with neighbors instead? In a close rural community many neighbors would be related to each other by kinship ties. It is possible, as in some of the African tribes, that not the nuclear family but uncles and in-laws produced the homicidal tensions.[53] If one looks at the felonious relationships with neighbors and acquaintances as compared to the family, it would seem as if the homicidal tensions within medieval society were centered on struggles for dominance in the community and the violent settling of disputes with those who lived close to the accused but not with him or her.

NEIGHBORS AS VICTIMS

The village community of medieval England was not the close knit cooperative unit that historians have often depicted it to be. Much has been said about the high degree of mutual assistance needed in the villages to get the plowing done, the spirit of cooperation involved in sharing the open fields, and the unity of the peasantry in the face of over-exacting landlords and their officials. Too little attention has been given to the tensions and antisocial behavior that could arise out of these same areas where cooperation has been assumed: whose field got plowed first, where did one strip end and another begin, who benefited from resisting the lord and who from supporting him. The medieval village communities, far from always cooperating on matters of village economics and politics, were often divided. These divisions tended to be along the lines of the different status groups composing the community. The criminal records clearly show that villagers were more likely to suffer felonious attack from neighbors, friends, or acquaintances than from strangers, family members, or from a lord.

The relationship of the victim and the accused in terms of their acquaintance with each other may be roughly shown by analyzing the geographical proximity of the victim and the accused. For this purpose, a sample of 1,862 cases was taken from Norfolk and Northamptonshire, two counties with fairly different patterns of crime, and the distances between the residence of the victim and the accused were plotted (see table 7). In almost half the recorded cases (46.3 percent) the victim and the accused must have known each other, for 28.8 percent came from the same village and 17.5 percent from within a day's round of business, which was five miles.[54] These people would have had frequent contacts with each other in both work and relaxation. An additional 9.8 percent, living six to ten miles from each other, would also have known each other. Those living eleven to fifteen miles from each other, 6.3 percent of the cases, might have had some previous contacts and at least been acquainted. For over fifteen miles or when the victim and the accused were residents of different

Table 7. *Distances the victim and the accused lived from each other by type of crimes.*

MILES	LARCENY N	%	BURGLARY N	%	ROBBERY N	%	HOMICIDE N	%	ARSON N	%	RECEIVING N	%	RAPE N	%
0	187	30.1	180	34.1	32	9.9	96	33.0	6	35.3	34	45.9	1	33.3
1-5	95	15.3	112	21.2	67	20.7	43	14.8	2	11.8	7	9.5		
6-10	57	9.2	45	8.5	38	11.7	36	12.4	3	17.6	4	5.4		
11-15	38	6.1	23	4.3	28	8.6	15	5.1	1	5.9	12	16.2		
Over 15	79	12.7	76	14.4	46	14.2	37	12.7	2	11.8	2	2.7	1	33.3
Another county	165	26.6	93	17.5	113	34.9	64	22.0	3	17.6	15	20.3	1	33.3
Total	521	100.0	528	100.0	324	100.0	291	100.0	17	100.0	74	100.0	3	100

Evidence from Northamptonshire and Norfolk. In the four counterfeiting cases, the victim and the accused lived in different counties.

counties, a prior acquaintance becomes more problematic unless they lived in a border area or in a market town and had frequent contacts with the outside. This group accounted for 37.6 percent of the cases.[55] In the bulk of the cases, therefore, the victim and the accused lived sufficiently close to each other that they would have been acquainted. Medieval crime would thus seem to be predominantly a neighborhood affair.

A word of caution must be added before accepting the essentially neighborhood quality of crime. Mobile felons could come into a village or lie in wait in ambush on a highway, do their evil deed, and be gone before the cumbrous process of arrest got underway. The coroners' inquests often concluded that the identity of the suspect was unknown. Frequently, it was only the testimony of an approver or the suspicious behavior of the felon that brought him to trial. For example, Adam Buleyn of Wood Dalling appealed Benedict son of Walter of the same for robbing and murdering William Eidard at Lincoln.[56] Without the approver's story it is improbable, given the law enforcement system of the day, that the authorities in Lincoln would know who killed William nor would Wood Dalling know that two of its residents committed a felony in another county. In other cases the fact that a poor man was carrying goods of a value beyond what he could purchase led to his arrest.

Even assuming that outsiders were often undetected while a neighbor was more likely to be, the nature of crime in general and the habits of medieval society indicate that the bulk of crimes would be committed against those whom the accused knew. While we now know that medieval society was more mobile than historians assumed in the past, most of the population tended to move within a small radius or did not move from their lands unless they had to do so. Furthermore, even in the modern crime pattern the victim and the accused usually live in the same area or know each other well.

The mobility pattern for the different types of crimes is a further guide to the relationship between the victim and the accused. Homicide, larceny, and burglary were typical crimes among the villagers but robbery, rape, and counterfeiting tended to be committed by people who traveled more than five miles to commit their crimes. In a third or more of all larcenies, burglaries, homicides, and arsons the victim was a fellow villager of the accused. Receiving is usually a victimless crime, but the two people entering into an agreement about disposing of stolen goods were often from the same village and same

Table 8. *Percentage distribution of motives for homicide (from coroners' rolls evidence), 1300-1415.*

MOTIVE	NORTHAMPTONSHIRE	LONDON
Argument (unspecified)	51.3	47
Domestic dispute	0.9	3
Revenge	0.6	21
Property dispute	3.7	4
Drinking	4.3	6
Self-defense	7.2	1
Jealousy	0.6	6
Accident	1.7	3
Robbery	24.5	5
Official	0.9	2
Insanity	0.3	0
Malice aforethought	3.7	2
Other	0.3	0
Total percentage	100.0	100
Total number	347	112

family (45.9 percent). Those who lived from one to five miles from the suspects followed the same pattern. The predominance of robbery among the more mobile felons indicates that robbers were more likely to be in gangs that roamed whole territories. The number of rape cases is small and statistically unreliable. The tendency toward greater mobility for rapists comes from the rape-abduction cases.

Since murder is most frequently a crime of passion, it is not surprising that the victim and the accused should come from the same village or within a short distance of each other. In the coroners' roll evidence, which is more accurate than gaol delivery since it gives the identity of suspects whether they have been arrested or not, 46 percent of the murderers and their victims came from the same village, 17.5 percent from one to five miles away, and 17.5 percent from six to ten miles. An additional 19 percent came from more than ten miles.[57] The pattern from the gaol delivery evidence was similar. The types of motives given for the homicides in the coroners' rolls indicate the areas of conflict within the community (see table 8).

The impression the coroners' inquests give is that of a society in which men are quick to give insult and to make good their point or defend their honor with a resort to arms and physical violence. About 60 percent of all rural homicides and 84 percent of all urban ones were said to have arisen over some sort of argument. In about half these cases the jurors assigned no specific cause to the argument.

Jealousy, revenge, domestic and property quarrels, and even malice aforethought played a remarkably small role in the perpetration of murders. The apparently trivial nature of arguments leading to homicide cannot be dismissed as mere reporting deficiencies on the part of coroners because in modern criminal statistics as well there is a similar pattern in the distribution of motivations.[58] Of course there is always a problem in classifying motives or isolating the final cause of a murder. The following case is illustrative.

> It happened at Ylvertoft on Saturday next before Martinmass in the fifth year of King Edward that a certain William of Wellington, parish chaplain of Ylvertoft, sent John, his clerk to John Cobbler's house to buy a candle for him for a penny. But John would not send it to him without the money wherefore William became enraged, and, knocking the door in upon him, he struck John in the front part of the head so that his brains flowed forth and he died forthwith.[59]

On the face of it, this is a property dispute, but the small value of the goods and the ferocity of the attack suggest a deeper hostility between the actors in the homicidal drama.

Although underlying motives for arguments are difficult to discover from the court records, the monthly pattern of homicide indicated that perhaps some of the tensions centered around planting and harvest, those areas where historians traditionally have claimed that there was a high degree of cooperation. Since, as we saw in chapter 3, the homicides in rural society were highest in the most intensive period of agricultural activity, it would seem that these functions in the society produced a high degree of tension within the community. This hypothesis is further supported by a sample survey of data that indicated that homicides related to robbery, domestic quarrels, official killings, and drinking were spread fairly evenly over the various months but that unspecified arguments, property disputes, and revenge homicides were highest in summer and harvest periods. The location of the homicidal disputes in the rural communities provides further evidence of the relationship of homicidal tensions between neighbors and the agricultural calendar: a third of them occurred in the fields.

While thefts and burglaries were easier when the thief knew both the location and the value of the goods, detection was also more likely. Thieves who stole near to home ran a great risk of being caught. The face and hide markings of sheep and cattle would be familiar to the owners as would any household goods or clothing. A villager who was suddenly two bushels short of grain would have little difficulty in detecting who was suddenly two bushels richer. In cases of dire economic need, considerations of capture would be secondary to the alleviation of extreme want, but many of the accused were not in economic need. Indeed, as we saw in the last chapter, many were from the wealthier peasantry. They may have assumed that they could dispose of the goods at a market away from the village and profit that way. But some of the thefts may be more indicative of tensions within the community rather than the lure of the profit motive. In other words, property thefts may have been a tool of social conflict within the villages. If this hypothesis is true, then the local nature of crime could partially be explained as purposeful illegal acts for the sake of punishment or revenge on neighbors.

In order to trace this sort of relationship between the victim and the accused, the combination of gaol delivery and Ramsey Abbey manorial court records was again used. In addition to the material on the status of the accused that has already been discussed, it is possible to positively identify and ascribe a status in the communities to forty-three of the victims. Of these, twelve were from the primary villagers, eighteen from secondary families, nine members of the clergy including the Abbot of Ramsey, and only four came from intermediate peasant families. When those indicted in gaol delivery were compared to those appearing in the lay subsidy rolls, twenty-five out of sixty-seven or 37 percent of the victims were identifiable as sufficiently wealthy to pay tax and hence be members of the main village families.[60] Although the sample is too small to be conclusive, a comparison of the status of the victim and the accused indicated that there was a distinct pattern of victimization and that it was related to status differences between the parties in crime.

The primary villagers chose their victims from those above them on the social scale, the clergy, from their own rank, or from the secondary villagers. They did not commit crimes against intermediate villagers. The thefts from clergy or from the Abbot of Ramsey are explainable in part because their property would be the most valuable in the neighborhood and hence the most tempting to the already well-off primary villagers. But, as we will see in the section on interclass crime, thefts from the Abbot may have had a revolutionary edge to them. Some of the aggression against the clergy, however, was of a local disciplinary nature. The most striking of these cases occurred in 1332 in Godmanchester. Twenty men of the town—eleven primary and nine secondary—killed John de Revely, a parson in neighboring Huntingdon.[61] The association in his murder was a distinguished one. For instance, Geoffrey Manipeny was not only one of the wealthiest members of the community but also served as baliff at the time of the crime. The group was one used to acting together, for they often appeared in the court rolls of Godmanchester in trespasses, debts, marriage settlements, and land transactions. The indictment made it clear that the attack was a premeditated and a collective concern: William Colyon and Andrew Bonis were indicted for the actual murder while the other eighteen were accused of aiding and abetting it. It is possible that the initial intention had been an assault to convey a warning rather than murder. Such practice was common in the eighteenth century, when as in the fourteenth century, the discipline could go too far.[62] What John de Revely did to deserve such severe warning is not spelled out in the records. Most likely this and other attacks on the clergy did not arise out of anticlerical feelings but out of conflicts involving the clergy in their roles of landholders, businessmen, and powerful neighbors in the villages. Their interests in the villages on all three levels was bound to conflict with that of the prominent villagers and lead the latter to exert their dominance through crime. The clergy were virtually immune, because of their status, to being brought into the local courts and there was a certain risk in bringing them into the royal courts.

Primary villagers also had disputes among themselves that they sometimes settled through criminal means. In homicides, particularly those that arose over property disputes and trivial arguments, their victims were most commonly members of their own status group. Some of their thefts also indicate that crime and court procedure were both used to pursue fights. A complicated case of this sort is illustrative. John Edelyne brought a private suit against John le Glovere in gaol delivery accusing him of the burglary of his house in Magna Paxton and of stealing there seven ells of russet-colored woolen cloth worth 7s. The jurors determined that the cloth never belonged legally to John Edelyne but belonged instead to John le Glovere who regained the cloth after the trial. John Edelyne's attempt to steal the cloth through the courts was bold, if foolhardy, for he was fined for bringing a false suit.[63] There is little indication that the primary villagers stole from each other unless there were the extenuating circumstances of a dispute over goods.

Attacks on secondary villagers by primary villagers may sometimes have been a weapon for social leveling in which the object was not only illegal economic gain but also rivalry or punishment of the secondary villagers. Three prominent villagers, Robert West of Woodhirst, William West, and William Edward, stole three sheep worth 6s. from Nicholas le Porter of Woodhirst, a member of a secondary village family.[64] The possibility that this theft was undertaken to keep a lower villager in his social and economic place is suggested by the collusion among the three men of primary status to deprive a secondary villager of valuable livestock. Further evidence is found in the position of one of the accused. Robert West had been a capital pledge and reeve of the village and may have been settling old scores with the victim. In cases such as this one, the accused may have purposely wished to be detected in their crime as a way of indicating the power the primary villagers had over the secondary villagers. The risk for the primary villager would be minimal for, although he would be indicted for these illegal acts, he would be bailed before trial and assured of acquittal.

The use of felony against those just above and just below them in social status was valuable to the primary villagers, but they did not need to use crime to discipline intermediate villagers. Hence, no intermediate villager was found to be a victim of a primary villager in this sample. The primary villagers' control over the local administration of justice and the village bylaws gave them all the control they needed over the more transient elements in the community.

Secondary villagers found their chief victims in their immediate social superiors, the primary villagers, and among themselves. Aside from the nine secondary villagers from Godmanchester who aided in the murder of the parson, they did not attack the clergy nor the intermediate villagers. The conflict between the primary and secondary village status groups is one of the best documented in the manorial courts as well as in gaol delivery. In Broughton alone, conflicts between these two status groups accounted for 93 out of 121 cases that came into the manorial court.[65] Thefts from prominent families were undoubtedly motivated in part by the simple fact that they had goods worth stealing. For instance, Laurence Baldwin and John Bernard, his brother, stole two calves from Thomas le Barker who had been a constable in Ramsey before the theft.[66] The calves were valuable property, but the two brothers may have had other resentments against the former constable. Since the secondary villagers did not steal from the clergy but from their immediate superiors in the village, the use of crime as a social weapon to express and further the aggravations between the two groups is suggestive of conflict. The lower group had cause to resent the dominance of the primary village families because that clique controlled the village offices and juries that extracted fines and labor from them. Since they were seldom selected for one of these powerful positions, they had few formal ways of expressing their resentment. Thefts, slander, and assaults seemed to have filled this need.

In homicide the secondary villagers were most likely to pick targets within their own status group. A good example is John le Lord who paid 6d. in the 1327 lay subsidy and who murdered Robert le Clerk whose family paid 14d.[67] Again, this pattern of homicide is consistent with the general pattern of fatal arguments within the community.

The intermediate group selected the two status groups immediately above them in the village as their victims. They did not seem to prey on each other or if they did the jurors did not consider the matter worth prosecuting in the royal courts. Economic need was, of course, a motivation for many of the thefts. For these families who had few chattels and no secure means of support, the obvious targets for theft would be the rich members of the village. But economic need alone did not determine the crimes of this group. In six cases of murder by intermediate villagers two victims were primary villagers and four were secondary villagers. This pattern of homicide suggests bitter conflict with the main village families that found expression in direct violence. The main villagers could literally deprive them of their livelihood. They had little hope of receiving fair treatment in manorial court, which the primary villagers dominated, and no hope of achieving primary or secondary status themselves.

Although it may not be argued that all crimes, even those that occurred locally, were committed either to preserve dominance in the community or to take revenge for undue subordination, the tensions revolving around the pecking order within the villages do help to explain certain aspects of the crime pattern. The predominantly local nature of crime, the apparent foolhardy commission of thefts locally, and the selection of victims according to the accused's status in the village all indicate that crime was a weapon in the struggles within the village communities.

INTERCLASS CONFLICT AND THE VICTIM
AND ACCUSED RELATIONSHIP

Interclass conflicts are difficult to detect in the ordinary pattern of crime. Yet historical evidence points to tensions that were likely to give rise to felonious activity between classes in medieval England. An observer in England in the 1380s remarked on the divisions among Englishmen and the political problems this caused.

> And as Hannibal saide that the Romayns myghte nought be overcome but in hir owne cuntray; so Englishe men mowe not be overcome in straunge londes, but in hir owne cuntray they beeth lightliche overcome. These men despiseth hir owne and preiseth other menis, and unnethe beeth apaide (content) with hir owne estate; what befalleth and semeth other men, they wooleth gladlyche take to hem self. Therfor hit is that a yeman arraieth hym as a squyer, a squyer as a knight, a knight as a duke, and a duke as a king.[68]

Long before the great revolt of 1381, tensions between the peasantry and nobility gave rise to minor revolts and repressions. The patent rolls and special commissions of oyer and terminer indicate the unrest of the peasantry as do the records in manorial courts, which show that peasants refused to do work for their lords or actually threatened the lords' officials with violence. Evidence also indicates that the lords were often too demanding in their privileges of disciplining the peasantry and extracting services from them and that they frequently treated them with capricious violence. The type of tensions that led to struggles between the peasantry and their overlords—work and money dues, land tenure, restrictions on freedom of movement, wages, and so on—were the sort that had a high potential for ordinary felonies as well as for revolts. Hilton has summed up the sources of conflict between the peasantry and their lay and ecclesiastical lords and has discussed the resistance on the part of the peasantry.[69] But the role that these tensions played in ordinary felony has not been explored. Evidence is scanty because the nobility often sought their own retribution for thefts using means that would not come into the royal courts. The cases that do reflect interclass conflict provide examples of crime being used as a weapon, sometimes very consciously, in repression or revenge.

The crimes of the nobility against commoners show both casual and calculated use of the advantages of their social and political position and their immunity from prosecution in ordinary courts of justice. The arrogance of power is well demonstrated in this case.

> A certain Thomas atte Chirche, esquire to the Earl of Arundel, and a certain unknown man . . . were riding together through "Tamesetrete" towards the Tower, and he came opposite the house of Olive Sorweles, a widow, in the parish of St. Botolph in the Ward of Billingesgate, the said Thomas Atte Chirche nearly threw to the ground with his horse a certain unknown woman carrying a child in her arms, and because the said John de Harwe begged them to ride more carefully, the said Thomas, moved to anger forthwith drew his sword and struck the said John on his right side inflicting a mortal wound.[70]

But the nobility did not always manage to come off so lightly in such encounters. Lord Robert de la More attempted to run down Robert son of John le Taillour with his horse and lance. Although such a heavily armed man on horseback was reckoned to be a match for twelve men on foot, Robert son of John successfully killed Lord Robert. The Yorkshire jurors returned a verdict of self-defense.[71]

Calculated abuse of privilege rather than casual exercise of it seems to have been at the base of many of the criminal actions of the nobility in their relationship to villagers.

> On 3 Dec. (1274) John of Rushall, knight and his esquire Henry of Hastings were entertained at the Parson of Melchbourne's house and Henry took provisions necessary for his Lord's use from many men in Melchbourne. Those whom they owed money for food and oats came and asked for it. John and Henry said that they had no ready money in Melchbourne and asked them to send a man with them to Cambridge and (said) that they should have the ready money there. They unanimously sent Ellis of Astwood with them. Ellis followed them from Melchbourne to "le Rode" where John and Henry and others unknown of John's household cut his throat.[72]

The villagers of Melchbourne were helpless victims of Sir John of Rushall who was eventually acquitted for his part in the theft and murder.

Ever present in the relationship of the peasantry and nobility was the ambiguity of the landlords' dual roles as patrons and oppressors.

The peasantry retaliated against the powerful sway of their overlords by revolts and by crime. A case in Broughton, one of the villages of the Abbot of Ramsey, is an instructive example of the form that these criminal actions could take. In 1294 John Gere, Thomas Gere, John son of Simon Crand, and William son of John Roger were all tried and acquitted for burglary of the Abbot of Ramsey's barn.[73] Undoubtedly, the Abbot's barn was well stocked and, therefore, an appealing target, but the amount of grain stolen would indicate that there might have been a motive other than personal enrichment in the theft. After all, two bushels of grain worth only 15d. to be split four ways was hardly an appealing profit for men who came from the primary families of Broughton. Suspicion that the motive of this burglary was something other than pure greed is heightened by the fact that the Broughton villagers had held a general work strike against the Abbot four years before over the insufficient bread being supplied at the boon work.[74] The theft of 1294 was probably close to the amount of bread the peasants felt had been withheld. It is possible that the Geres and others decided to personally rectify the wrong done. The Geres did have charges of work defaults against them indicating that they had rebelled against the Abbot's labor regulations previously, but their record is no more prominent than that of other villagers.

Some thefts were even more directly rebellious than that at Broughton. Thomas de Burton of Thornton in Spalding was accused of breaking into a box belonging to Lord Thomas de Ros, Lord of Melburn, that contained charters, muniments, and other papers. Another man robbed John Skeet, bailiff of the Hundred of Depwade, of his records and rolls.[75]

Murder of one's master was less common than theft partly because the lords were guarded and partly because the punishment was the torturous one for treason. But Robert Warde of Burnham killed his master. Robert de Hoo of Compton, a shepherd, admitted that he and four other men lay in ambush for the return of their lord, Thomas Goffe, from London and killed him at midnight at "la Knolle" in Windlesham.[76]

Crime as a tool of interclass conflict certainly existed, but the extent to which both sides used it remains unquantifiable. Certainly it played less of a role in the ordinary pattern of crime than did crime among the peasantry. The conditions of society made this obvious. Although the nobility might have been criminous out of all proportion to their numbers in medieval society, as Hilton has claimed,[77] they still comprised less than a tenth of the society, so that they could hardly be the chief criminal threat to the peasantry. The peasants undoubtedly suffered greatly from numerous unrecorded crimes of the nobility, but they were more likely to become the victims of one of their neighbors in the village or town.

Victims with a Special Liability

Some victims encountered in the criminal court rolls stand out as having a special liability for being victimized. They had occupations or physical or psychological traits that made them especially vulnerable to attack. Merchants were engaged in an occupation that put them in a high risk category for robbery. Women were liable to be raped. The sick and handicapped could not resist attack. Still other people brought on their own victimization.

Merchants, who had to move money or goods to and from the markets, made up 16.7 percent of the victims for whom occupations are given. Merchants traveling to or from the fair of St. Ives in Huntingdonshire were primary targets of robbers.[78] The clergy and nobility, who were large landholders with crops and animals as prizes in theft, were victims in 60.2 percent and 8.5 percent of the cases, respectively, where the occupation of the victim was given.[79] It is quite common in the gaol delivery rolls from Huntingdonshire to find cases where the victim, but not the suspect, can be identified as having paid taxes in the lay subsidies. John de Hayle, who paid 2s. 2d. in taxes, was a natural target for a transient pursecutter, Alexander le Whyte of Bristol, because he was obviously a prosperous man with a bulging purse.[80] Langland's observations that wealth invites crime and that the rich man was more in danger of robbery on the road is borne out in numerous cases. I have already cited the famous cases of the cardinals, bishops-elect, justices, and merchants with valuable cargo being waylaid. But the ordinary wealthy traveler also risked attack. William Bere, who paid a 2s. tax in 1327, was robbed of a horse worth 2 marks and goods worth £10 on the road at Berwood and Baneseye.[81]

The handicapped were also likely to be victimized. The mentally handicapped were victims of violence as well as perpetrators. Such was the case in which a Bedfordshire woman murdered her insane husband. She claimed that he suffered a fit of insanity as they were lying in bed and that she believed he was "seized by death." It is curious that rather than letting this hypothesis prove itself, she cut his throat with a small scythe and broke his skull with a bill hook.[82] The ubiquitous lepers of the Middle Ages also appear among the handicapped victims. We have already seen that Margaret Coled of Blithing specialized in robbing lepers who were maintained by charity at the Norwich church doors. Attendants in the leper hospitals also victimized inmates. Henry of Ashbourn in le Pek was a servant in the leper home of Walbeck near Kingsthorp where he murdered two lepers, Richard of Winwich and Roger of Aylesbury, with a hatchet in the middle of the night.[83]

Self-induced physical handicaps such as drunkeness were probably frequent causes of homicidal attacks. Arguments would start in the tavern or on the way home and someone would be killed. One case recounts a group of Irish students drinking in Oxford when a quarrel arose and one clerk was killed.[84] Drunken brawls figured in only 4.3 percent of the rural homicides and in 6 percent of the urban ones, but the influence of drink may have been more important than the records indicate. In one case, the amount of alcohol consumed was specified. Walter of Benington and seventeen of his companions came to the brewhouse of Gilbert of Mordon armed with hoods full of stones, knives, swords, and other weapons. After they had consumed four gallons of beer, Gilbert's wife and his brewer asked them to leave. They refused, saying that they intended to spend their money at that tavern. When their attempt to abduct a young girl from the place was foiled, they attacked the taverner and his brewer with stones. In self-defense, the brewer grabbed a staff and killed Walter.[85]

Victims might precipitate their own death or robbery through negligence or being too charitable. In spite of statutary prohibitions, people took in wanderers either out of charity or because they needed the money lodgers would pay. We have already cited the case of the Bedfordshire family that took in what they assumed was a poor couple in need of charity. During the night the "couple," one a robber dressed as a woman, stole the goods from the house and killed the six-year-old daughter. In another case a woman in Aspley Guise, perhaps a local prostitute, was drinking in a tavern with a man the jurors described as a "ribald stranger." She agreed to "entertain" him in her home. In the morning she was found dead of knife wounds; the fourteenth-century Mack the Knife was never found.[86]

Victim precipitation of felonies appeared most clearly in some of the homicide cases. Many of the self-defense homicide cases might have been victim-precipitated. But with only the testimony of the survivor in a fight, who was to know the truth of who struck the first blow and who the last?[87]

> On Palm Sunday a clerk named David de Northampton, when it was late, was in the street over against his lodging, where he abode in the parish of St. Michael North, beneath the north wall of the town, and as he walked he was saying his prayers and orisons; and John Laurence came there, meeting him, and to cause strife pushed him with his shoulder once and again. And the said David asked him to leave him in peace, and so entered his lodgings, and immediately John came to the door of the lodging and smote upon it twice. And the said David came forth with a staff and smote him upon the head so that he fell to the earth, and beat him with the staff on his shoulders and back and reins and throughout his whole body.[88]

Perhaps John Laurence was a belligerent personality type such as we met with in the last chapter in John le White of St. Ives who was cited in manorial court for five assaults before he finally picked a fatal argument. Other times the jurors testified to long-standing quarrels being at fault. The victim, although he started the argument, did not win the ensuing fight.

In many ways the victims of felonies were very much like the accused. They were predominantly aggressive young males from established village families. In over half the cases the victim and the accused knew each other well since they came from the same village or within a radius encompassing a normal day's social contacts. The Ramsey materials suggest that in picking their victims, each status group chose either from their own group or that immediately above: the primary villagers attacked members of the clergy, the secondary villagers picked the primary villagers, and the intermediate group attacked both the primary and secondary villagers. The selection of victims represented some of the tensions and conflicts within the villages. To someone familiar with modern criminal behavior, the most striking aspect of medieval interactions between victims and accused was that the medieval nuclear family was notably uncriminous toward one another. There is also little evidence of infanticide. Members of certain occupations such as merchants, clergy, and nobility had a particular risk of theft because they traveled with valuable goods or because they had extensive estates to tempt thieves. Some attacks on the nobility and the clergy were undoubtedly interclass conflicts expressed through criminal means. There is also evidence that some victims precipitated their own rape, robbery, or murder. But crime was not always an outgrowth of intracommunity tensions where the victim and the accused knew each other. A number of the accused came from outside the county, particularly robbers, and it is among this group that professional criminals and organized gangs are found.

Chapter Six

Criminal Associations

and Professional Crime

CRIMINAL ASSOCIATIONS and professional criminals evoke mixed responses in both modern and medieval literature and social thought. The Robin Hood ballads of the Middle Ages are paralleled by ballads in our own period about Billy the Kid and Bonnie and Clyde. Books and films on the modern *cosa nostra* are almost as profitable as the syndicate itself. To the ordinary person devoting so much time to the very ordinary pursuits of making a living within the confines of the law, the romance and fantasy of people who gain their livelihood from plunder rather than the sweat of their brows and who subvert justice so that corrupt law enforcers and not themselves are punished have a tremendous appeal. There is, however, another side to the outlaws and their gangs. Not only wealthy members of society and corrupt sheriffs become their victims; sooner or later in the career of the outlaw, ordinary people are victimized and will agree with the relief expressed in the epitaph for one Robin Hood:

> Robert Earle of Huntington
> Lies under this little stone.
> No archer like him was so good:
> His wildnesse named him Robin Hood.
> Full thirteene years, and something more,
> These northerne parts he vexed sore.
> Such out-lawes as he and his men
> May England never know agen.[1]

Modern writers on organized crime reflect the same range of emotions toward their subject as does the general public. Eric J. Hobsbawm in *Primitive Rebels* [2] makes the Robin Hood type of bandit into a virtual welfare agent for the poor, while those writing on more modern organized crime have described the criminal syndicate as both an admirably well-run organization and a very destructive force in our society. Both the view of criminal associations as friends of the poor and as superior corporate organizations leave out the bulk of the ordinary criminals who form associations or who spend most of their efforts procuring a living through criminal means.

Evidence for the organization of crime and for the professional criminals comes from a variety of court rolls and from literary and chronicle references. The system of gaol delivery made some effort to try all people associated in the commission of one crime at the same time. When indictments were made, the jurors presented the names of all members of the gang who committed a crime. The sheriff then tried to arrest them and bring them into court for the same session. Often the justices would not even try a person who had committed a crime in conjunction with others until they all could be rounded up and tried. Other times the records indicate that the person being tried had a number of unidentifiable accomplices. While not naming all members of criminal associations, the gaol delivery rolls supply much insight into their nature. They give accurate information on the types of crimes associations committed; their composition by number, sex, occupation, and kinship; the value and types of goods they stole; and the places where they were most likely to be active. While they give the proportion of crimes tried that were committed by more than one person, this information is more indicative than exact. It was hard for local jurors to identify everyone in a gang crime and difficult for the sheriff to track down and arrest all participants.

Information on habitual offenders is also available both from people who were tried for several crimes at one time and from a sample of twenty years taken from Norfolk where the criminal careers of some people could be traced over the course of a generation or more. Again, information on the number of repeaters, as on the number of crimes committed by criminal associations, is more indicative than exact. First, the offender would be hanged if found guilty and, therefore, unable to repeat his actions. Second, many people managed to elude arrest or indictment for prior or subsequent offenses. The gaol delivery information does permit, however, a description of the sex, occupation, and status of people who were indicted for more than one offense and also indicates the types of offenses they committed and their career patterns in crime.

To go beyond what may be statistically described about organized crime and criminal careers from the aggregate data in the gaol delivery rolls, one must look for individual cases from gaol delivery sessions, coroners' inquests, manorial records, and chronicles and other literature. From sources such as these the motivations of some people for joining criminal associations can be discussed; personal committments to either a career in crime or a stable criminal band emerge; and information about the organization of criminal bands, their function, and their longevity are forthcoming. Although such material is suggestive and speculative rather than based on firm statistical data, it does indicate some of the basic patterns in the organization and professionalization of medieval crime and permits comparisons with later developments in England and elsewhere.

Increasingly, modern criminologists are using the term "organized crime" for the more rational organizations of criminals. In our general discussion of organized crime, however, we will use the term to discuss all associations of people tried together on criminal indictments. Since there are organizational differences between a pair of criminals working together and more formally organized bands of criminals, we will first discuss the general phenomenon of criminal associations and then look at the pecularities of organization in the different types of medieval English criminal associations.

CRIMINAL ASSOCIATIONS

The criminal associations that appear in the medieval records fall within three broad categories: informal associations established for the commission of one or two crimes; more stable bands of outlaws with specific leaders and members who pursued careers in crime; and the highly organized and semi-legal activities of the nobility and their household retainers. The distinctions between these three types of criminal associations have been made on the basis of both the functions the associations performed in the course of their illegal activities and on the degree of organizational rationality and division of labor within the criminal association itself. For instance, a group of peasants who murdered their lord were pursuing one goal within a limited time period, while a band of outlaws who collected extortion money by threats of murder, maiming, and arson were making a career of crime.

The criminologists' distinctions between informal and formal criminal associations are helpful in discussing the three types of criminal associations. The basis for the distinctions is the amount of rationality, cohesiveness, and division of labor involved. In the informal organization there is little rationality of structure. The people who form the criminal group are not linked together or organized around long-term goals such as making a living from crime, fighting enemies or protecting themselves against enemies, performing rituals, or conferring status. They often share particular values about politics or standards of social behavior, but these are incidental to their coming together in a criminal coalition. Their criminal association is usually of short duration and involves only the commission of one or a few crimes. The modern example of the informal criminal association most frequently cited is the juvenile gang.[3] In medieval society a group of villagers coming together for a theft or revenge crime would be a typical example.

The formal criminal organization, on the other hand, has a highly rationalized structure that modern criminologists have likened to bureaucracies, corporations, and even to feudalism.[4] It has a hierarchical structure with specifically defined roles and a chain of command; it limits its membership; it sets up rules of behavior for its members and can punish them if they disobey; it exists to gain power and profit; and, finally, it uses force and all other means at its disposal for insuring its continuity as a unit.[5] Both the outlaw groups and the associations surrounding the nobility give evidence of such rationality in organization.

The distinctions between formal and informal criminal associations provide useful models for looking at the range or continuum of types of criminal associations between those two extremes. They are, however, only guides and cannot provide firm dividing lines. For instance, even the most informal group crimes, such as a husband and wife stealing geese, require some organization, objective, and rational planning. But this type of criminal activity is not on the same level as that of formal gangs with more elaborate organizational systems. A further problem presents itself in that it is often difficult to draw firm lines between the legitimate actions of governments and community groups and the illegal actions of criminals.[6] This problem is particularly difficult for the illegal activities of the nobility in the fourteenth century because they could defend their crimes by saying that they had a time-honored right to fight and to administer justice with the aid of an armed household.

Medieval criminals were a sociable lot showing a preference for committing crimes with one or more accomplices. The court records show that 55 percent of all offenders had accomplices. This figure probably represents underreporting of gang activity since in modern statistics 70 percent to 90 percent of offenders in both Europe and America have accomplices.[7]

The amount of organized crime varied from county to county. In Somerset 69.7 percent of the suspects were indicted with accomplices while in Essex 59 percent were. Both these counties had a heavy concentration of crime in robbery and burglary, crimes that were often committed with associates, so that the high number of indictments for gangs is not surprising. Yorkshire, in spite of its reputation for gangs, had only 39.7 percent of its suspects indicted with accomplices. Yorkshire had some very large gangs that were tried at one time, but the general pattern was for the suspects to be tried alone. The other counties were near the mean: Norfolk, 42.5 percent; Northamptonshire, 44.8 percent; Surrey, 49.5 percent; Herefordshire, 47.7 percent; and Huntingdonshire, 38.9 percent. The Midland counties were similar to Yorkshire; they were not outstandingly high in gang activity despite their reputation for having notorious criminal associations.

The size of both medieval and modern criminal associations tended to be small. The majority of medieval criminals worked in pairs (63.6 percent) or threes (18.8 percent). Only 17.6 percent had four or more associates.[8] Modern studies of criminal associations also show that gangs of two and three predominate, because even in larger gang structures only a few members are involved in a particular criminal act.[9] The size was often dependent upon the particular task the gang was trying to accomplish. If it involved the robbery or ransom of a particularly well-guarded person, such as Sir Gilbert de Middleton's attack on the papal legates and the bishop of Durham or the murder of Roger Bellers, a small army of fifty or more was necessary. Cutpurses and counterfeiters, on the other hand, worked in small groups of two or three. Because the crime pattern differed so much for informal and formal criminal associations, I have arbitrarily designated pairs of criminals as being largely informal criminal associations and groups of three or more as being more likely to be formal criminal associations. This is a very rough designation, but there is a substantial difference in the criminal activities of groups of two and those of three or more members that shows up in the types of crimes committed, the goods stolen, and the places where crimes occurred.

The three crimes that most frequently involved criminal as-

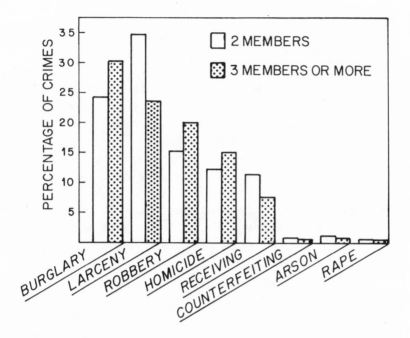

Figure 9. *Comparison of the types of crimes committed by associations of two and three or more.*

sociations were robberies (78.1 percent of all robberies were committed by criminal associations), arson (72.2 percent of all arson cases), and counterfeiting (71.4 percent).[10] That these three crimes had the highest concentration of criminal associations is consistent with the techniques of committing them discussed in chapter 3. Arsonists who were practicing extortion often needed elaborate gangs to get their money. Counterfeiters included both those who made the coins and those who distributed them. Robbery was also more likely to be successful with a gang. The rewards for robbery were so great that it tended to attract more stable outlaw bands. The size of the bands also indicates that robbery was popular among formal criminal associations: 58 percent of the robberies involved three or more persons (see figure 9). Burglary, like robbery, offered high rewards and often demanded more than one person; it, therefore, encouraged the participation of criminal associations (57 percent of all burglaries). Again, there was probably a predominance of formal criminal associations because 55 percent of the burglaries involved three or more persons. Homicide, in which criminal associations committed 59.5 percent of all cases, is an unusual crime to involve more than one person since it tends to result from personal animosities. The category, however, includes cases of robbery and burglary ending in homicide as well as the ordinary disputes. The criminal associations committing homicide tended to be pairs and hence informal associations. Half the rapes were gang rapes. They too include cases of robbery and burglary. Larceny (45.5 percent of all larcenies involved more than one person) and receiving (34.3 percent) were both more individual undertakings. When thieves or receivers did seek accomplices, they tended to use one other person who was within the family or a neighbor. Those who betrayed the king in treason always acted alone.

Felons participating in organized crime selected the most profitable areas, robbery and burglary. The goods they stole reflect this (see figure 10). Cloth was one of the most popular items to steal by force, and criminal associations stole 6.9 percent more cloth than normal. For instance, the Norfolk gang of Ralph of Rockland and John de Sculthorpe were accused of nine robberies involving the theft of cloth.[11] Criminal associations also concentrated more on valuables and industrial products. Like ordinary thieves, they stole livestock most frequently, but they stole fewer animals. They also stole less grain. The most surprising area where criminal associations exceeded the ordinary pattern of theft was in household goods, clothing, and food. The great need for these mundane items suggests that life in the greenwood was not an easy one and that the gangs were often in need of clothing, blankets, pots and pans, and food. They also stole almost as much poultry and pigs as the ordinary felons did. Even the gang of twenty servants of Gaillard Senak was indicted for stealing primarily grain, cloth, meat, and money, and this was a large, well-organized band.[12]

The value of the goods stolen reflects the breakdown of the associations' booty. While ordinarily a quarter of all thefts were 12d. or under, 37.2 percent of thefts by criminal associations were. This is because they were stealing so many low value items among the household goods and clothing. They stole goods worth 1-10s. in 10 percent of the cases, which was similar to the overall pattern. Criminal associations had 26.6 percent of their thefts in the range of 11-20s. compared to the overall 15.6 percent. In cases involving goods over £1 they concentrated 26.7 percent of their thefts compared to 28 percent for the overall figure. The profits criminal associations derived from their crimes were, therefore, not spectacular in most cases. Even

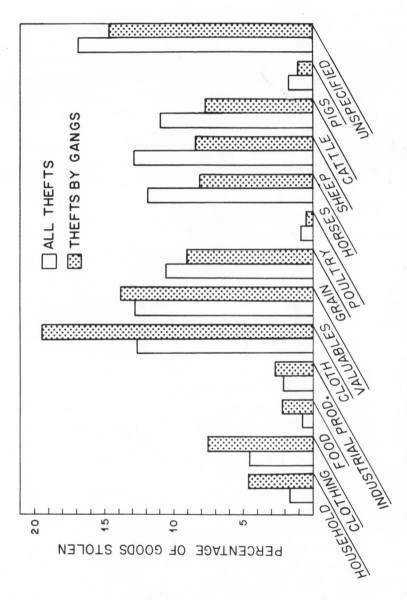

Figure 10. Types of goods stolen by gangs compared to the general pattern of theft.

the outstanding gang crimes could not make up for the numbers of crimes involving small-scale thefts. When the goods were divided two or more ways, the profits were not very great.

Because the criminal associations tended to commit more robberies and burglaries than other felonies, the places they were most likely to meet and attack their victims were in a house, church, field, or street. The victim's home was the scene of 39.3 percent of the criminal encounters and churches were in 14.5 percent, which was similar to the overall pattern. The criminal associations found their victims in fields in 23.2 percent of the cases and highways in a surprisingly low 8.1 percent.[13] Considering the emphasis on robbery, one would expect a higher figure.

The sex composition of the criminal associations followed that of the overall crime pattern: women comprised 10.4 percent of the total membership. They were slightly more common in the pair associates at 11.2 percent of the membership but made up only 9.5 percent of the gangs of three or more. Assuming that the latter gangs were more likely to be professional, the lower participation of women is to be expected. As we have seen in chapter 4, the majority of women committed their crimes with a male associate. The role of the woman in these criminal associations varied greatly depending upon the type of crime and her relationship with the other participants. Women committing crimes requiring physical violence or skill with weapons usually had accomplices. Their role in such associations may have been a passive one such as acting as a decoy. Women, however, appeared as the planners of some of the crimes as well. They might direct the operation without participating in the crime or take the leadership when their associates in crime were related to them.

A key to understanding medieval organized crime, both formal and informal, was the role kinship relations played in forming the core of gang cohesion: 19 percent of all gangs were composed of identifiable kinship groupings. Probably many more of the accomplices were members of the same family, but no identification was recorded. As in intrafamilial crime, those kin that were distinguished in the records were from the immediate nuclear family: spouses and children (see figure 11). Combinations of these groupings were an integral part of both two member and larger gangs. Indeed, the larger associations often contained several family groupings. The Coterel gang included not only the Coterel brothers but also the Bradburn brothers.[14] Henry

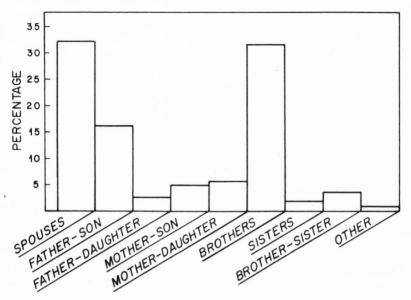

Figure 11. *Types of familial relationships cooperating in crime.*

Underwode and his brother William committed several crimes with Alan de Ousthorp and his son.[15]

The family was a natural social unit to act as an organizational basis for a criminal association, for it had within its structure all necessary elements. It already had established leadership roles, rules of conduct for its members, established procedures for division of labor and profits, and experience working together. When the motivation was present for using this basic organization for criminal purposes, it could be quite effective. The family functioned in medieval criminal associations much as it did in society. Since medieval English society was patriarchal, the father, husband, or older brother tended to dominate and take the leadership role. The father might even coerce his children or wife into criminal acts, particularly receiving. In the cases of sibling gangs such as the Coterels the leadership would fall to the oldest brother. As we discussed in chapter 4, familial cooperation tended to be more common in counties having impartible inheritance. Younger siblings would have to provide a living for themselves after the oldest inherited the estate. Cooperation in crime was one solution. The Folvilles are a classic example of this.

The two kinship relations most frequently found as partners in criminal activity were also the most common in intrafamilial crime—spouses and brothers. Husbands and wives made up 32.3 percent of the familial associations and siblings (with two brothers predominating over other combinations) comprised 37.2 percent.[16] Fathers and sons were the next most popular associates with 16.3 percent. If all parent-child criminal associations were included, they formed 29.6 percent. In most of the criminal associations only two or three family members acted together—a husband and wife, two brothers, or at most parents and several children. Kinship ties were more frequent in pairs of criminals than in the larger gangs. One might expect proportionally more siblings or father-son relationships in the three or more member association, but they participated just as frequently in the pair associations.

More elaborate kinship groupings were less common, but some truly criminal families did appear. Three generations were represented in a family of counterfeiters, the Causbys of Yorkshire. Richard and Albreda were the grandparents. Associated with them were their son John, their daughter Anicia, and their granddaughter Matilda.[17] An even more elaborate familial association was that of the Waraunts of Salle in Norfolk who were in and out of crime for most of the first half of the fourteenth century. Those mentioned in the records include three sisters—Helewisa, Margery, and Matilda—their brother Richard and an older relative, John. John Waraunt appeared in gaol delivery in January 1309 on the charge of having stolen a bundle of goods worth 40s. in the market of St. Mary Magdalene; he was acquitted. Matilda, Margery, and Richard appeared in the session of January 1321 on charges of receiving stolen goods and were acquitted. Helewisa was the next to be tried in June 1321 when she was acquitted for stealing household goods valued at 3s. In July 1321 John Waraunt, who may have been the earlier mentioned John and father of the rest of the family, was convicted and hanged for robbery. He had taken clothes, jewels, and household goods worth 8s. from a fellow townsman in Salle. After the 1321 trials, which ended tragically for one member of the family, the Waraunts stayed out of court, if not out of crime, until 1325 when Helewisa and Matilda were again tried on a larceny charge. They refused to plead for this theft of cloth worth 60s. and were returned to prison *forte et dure*. How they survived this ordeal is not told, but they were tried and acquitted in February 1326 on the appeal of an approver, who said that they had stolen thirty-two cloths in East Dereham. In August 1326 Margery and Helewisa were tried and acquitted of stealing cloth worth 40s. in Salle.[18] With a few exceptions only two members of this family acted together at one time but their careers show that they were capable of interchanging personnel and of carrying off fairly large amounts of valuable property. Helewisa, in particular, showed an increase in the value of goods she took over the period of her career going from household goods worth 3s. to goods worth 40 to 60s.

Occupational information on the composition of gangs would be as informative as that on kinship, but such evidence was only sporadically preserved for the first half of the fourteenth century. Because of the plea of benefit of clergy, the clergy appear to have a disproportionately large role in criminal associations and because of the near immunity of the nobility from prosecution, they appear to have a disproportionately low membership.[19] Although the evidence is sparse, the most interesting professions that appear with some frequency are servants and merchants. Servants had almost a special liability for becoming part of criminal associations either accompanying their masters or executing their orders in criminal pursuits. They were also in an unstable profession and would band together with others of their kind to perform criminal acts. Since merchants were one of the most victimized groups, their presence in criminal associations, particularly those of three or more members, is surprising. Their very occupation, however, made them not only good targets but also likely people to turn a profit themselves from a bit of burglary, highway robbery, piracy, or smuggling. Their contact in the marketplace put them in touch with criminal as well as honest buyers and they had a good knowledge of which houses would be worth a burglary, which merchants would be traveling home from markets with valuable goods or money, and which shipments were expected in port or had shipwrecked on the coast.

Membership in a criminal association depended very much upon the function it performed. Large criminal associations that participated in robberies and extortions tended to be a composite of different occupations and ranks in society. They needed a variety of different contacts who would give them shelter, and they very often needed clerks with an education to write threatening notes. Members of the Coterel gang included a knight, a soldier, bailiffs, peasants, chaplains, vicars, a counterfeiter, and an Oxford don.[20] They were not even of the same political persuasion: some had sided with Edward II and others fought with Thomas of Lancaster in the civil war of 1322. Smaller gangs than the Coterels not uncommonly contained smiths, clergy; brewers, and husbandmen.[21] When a gang came together for a specific purpose, such as the disciplining of a member of the community, however, the gang members tended to be not only from the same occupation but also from the same status. We have seen that the twenty men from Godmanchester who murdered the Parson of Huntingdon were not only established land- and office-holders in the town, but were also socially interconnected.

The mobility of gang members tended to indicate the function of the association and something of its formal or informal status. In organized crime, as in the general pattern of crime, most of the participants were local people. In Norfolk 65 percent and in Northamptonshire 61 percent of the associations were formed from people who lived in the same place. An additional 23 percent in Norfolk and 20 percent in Northamptonshire lived only an average of one to ten miles from one another. The predominantly local connections of members in criminal associations were hardly surprising when one remembers that many of these were family units and that the suspects in general tended to stay close to their home village in committing crimes. Furthermore, most of the criminal associations were informal in nature and thus they tended to be local people banding together for the commission of a particular crime. For instance, fifteen men from Fynele robbed John Bondehowie in Fynele of sixty wooden casks and other goods worth £40; three men from Surlingham committed several burglaries in that neighborhood in 1316; and three men, one from Shipedham, one from Letton, and one from Westfield (all from one to three miles apart) committed a series of burglaries around Surlingham.[22]

An interesting variation on the criminal organizations composed predominantly of local men is that one or a pair might be outsiders. This pattern of membership suggests that a professional criminal or wanderer either incited the action or that local men brought in a consultant and confederate to advise and assist them. For instance, in a gang composed primarily of men from Holcham, one member came from Horsham, almost thirty miles away and another from Walsham, again about thirty miles distance.[23]

Those suspects who found their criminal associates more than eleven miles from their own residence amounted to 12 percent of the gangs in Norfolk and 19.7 percent in Northamptonshire. These people who traveled greater distances may represent the more criminally prone group in the population and may include more of the formal criminal associations than those composed entirely of local people. Of course, people coming from miles apart need not have participated in formal associations. John Margery of Brandon, William Carter of Honingham, and Peter son of Richard of Swanton all lived about thirteen miles from each other but joined to steal clothes and a horse in Norwich.[24] They could have met in a tavern in Norwich and plotted that single crime and then returned home. In other cases, the jurors may have indicted strangers who happened to be in the village at the time and accused them of conspiring to commit a particular criminal act. They may never have known one another before meeting in gaol. Gangs that were composed of people who came from fifty and more miles from each other probably represent a more floating body of criminals and vagrants who traveled together in unstable groups. For instance, John de Hoton in the forest of Ingelwode, John de Shidyerd of Oxford, and John son of Thomas of Bithersthorp originated one hundred miles from each other but were accused of committing a burglary and a larceny in Flegg in Norfolk.[25] The more established criminal associations under the leadership of a particular outlaw or local lord tended to operate within a particular area and to draw their members from that immediate area.

The distance the criminal association traveled to commit its felony is indicative of mobility patterns of organized crime. Again, it is not surprising that most of the criminal associations selected targets either in the same village (34 percent in Northamptonshire) or close by (16.9 percent had residences one to five miles away and 9.5 percent lived six to ten miles away.) The limited mobility of the bulk of criminal associations once again underscores that the gaol delivery rolls present a pattern of local men settling local grudges. However, a greater proportion of criminal associations than individual offenders selected their victims further afield and in different counties. In Northamptonshire, 15.4 percent of the victims resided more than eleven miles from the homes of the accused and 21.2 percent lived in a different county. In Norfolk, the number living in a different county was much smaller because it was a very large county with sea on two sides. Northamptonshire, on the other hand, was easily accessible to a number of other counties and had forests for cover and the Great North Road to attract travelers. These elements made Northamptonshire particularly prone to have criminal associations of the more permanent, outlaw types. They could commit crimes in other counties and retreat across the jurisdictional border. The west Midlands—Warwickshire, Leicestershire, and Oxfordshire—was the home of many of the outlaw bands that appeared in the Northamptonshire gaol delivery rolls. Other suspects were wanted as far away as London and Wiltshire.[26]

The advantages of committing a crime in one county and escaping into another were great for the criminal associations. Pursuit had to stop at the border, and while the next sheriff was getting together a posse, the criminals could escape. Even if caught, they could not be tried until a jury came from the other county. This increased the possibility of escape from gaol and gave the suspects time to arrange pardons and bribes. Most of the criminal associations that crossed county lines were bent on robbery and appeared to be more formal associations, although some neighborhood groups crossed the county line to steal from neighbors on the other side.

INFORMAL CRIMINAL ASSOCIATIONS

By far the bulk of the criminal associations tried in gaol delivery were informal ones composed of neighbors, family, or people such as wanderers and beggars who formed loose ties because of their common circumstances. Individuals came together in various short-lived associations for the commission of specific crimes. They did not consider themselves to be outlaws or professional members of a gang. In this respect, the members of the rural community of all status groups entered into criminal associations very much as a modern criminologist would say that juvenile delinquents become involved in crime. They had day-to-day contact and interaction with one another, they shared values and attitudes, and, where the situation demanded, they moved from this rather loose group into one directed to a specific end. In the cases we are interested in, the ends were felonies. They might be family members sheltering a felonious relative, primary villagers punishing their enemies, poor villagers combining to steal livestock or commit a burglary. Even a criminous family such as the Waraunts of Salle probably only committed crimes to supplement their income or gain an advantage when they saw a good chance for profit. Throughout the book there have been many examples of villagers cooperating in various criminal actions ranging from grain thefts to assassination of their lords. The emphasis of the society and the law was on self-help. It had to be. The members of the community who enjoyed the outlaw ballads knew that in true life, as in the ballads, justice was not always to be gained from the king's courts and officials. They also knew there were no real-life Robin Hoods to solve their problems. It is not surprising, therefore, that these people, who were used to providing their living by the sweat of their brows and cooperating in self-governance and economic production, should also join together in felonious acts.

An analysis of those who acted together in criminal associations in the Ramsey Abbey villages showed that, for the most part, members of different status groups stuck with their own kind in committing crimes. In nineteen instances the primary villagers sought association with each other, and only nine times with secondary villagers. The secondary villagers also formed associations within their own group (twelve intragroup and nine with prominent villagers). All groups associated with outsiders in crime on occasion, but the intermediate group did so exclusively. Perhaps they had a greater affinity for the wanderers of society.

The vagrant population was not so large in early fourteenth-century England as it was to become later nor did the society regard it as the menace that Elizabethan England did.[27] But vagrants were present and they wandered about taking on field work and odd jobs and joining in informal criminal associations. An ordinance of Edward III in 1349 spoke of vagabonds who went through the country "giving themselves to idleness and vice, and sometimes to theft and other abominations."[28] After the Black Death this problem became more severe. The rolls of Parliament for 1377 complained of the able-bodied laborers who "become strong robbers, and their robberies and felonies increase from one day to another on all sides.[29] As in Elizabethan England, the vagabonds tended to form into small groups of unstable membership. A good example of the composition and problems of such gangs is shown in a coroners' roll case.

On 28 April 1272 Adam of Deddington of Oxfordshire, Isabel of Moreton of Buckinghamshire, Walter Scot of Berwick-upon-Tweed and his wife Joan of Stratford outside London came to Dunton and Walter offered a pelt for sale through the whole town. They then sought hospitality through the whole town, but did not find any and later withdrew from the town to "Godeshull," where a quarrel arose between Adam and Walter. Adam struck Walter under the left ear to the throat with a knife called "swytel." Joan immediately raised the hue and the townships came, found Walter dead and arrested Adam and Joan. Isabel heard the hue from the other side of the town and took a (*sic.*) child in her arms and immediately fled to Dunton church, where she stayed until 5 May and then confessed before the coroner that she had stolen a coat of brightly coloured material, a rochet, a veil, a sheet and many other things, that she was in the company of the said thieves and was present at the homicide; she refused to surrender to the king's peace and so she abjured the realm according to law and custom, the port of Dover being given to her.

At the eyre Adam was sentenced to be hanged and was declared a vagabond and in no tithing.[30] The residences of these people make it apparent that they were vagabonds on the move. Walter and Joan came from very distant parts of England and must have met and married in their roamings. The other two people came from counties not far from Bedfordshire. They must have joined briefly in the wanderings and probably ate together the meat of the animal whose pelt they were trying to sell in Dunton. A number of wanderers appeared in the coroners' rolls as both victims and perpetrators of violent deaths.

For the most part these wandering people were not primarily organized for crime but did have the potential for association with other vagabonds or with local people for limited criminal activity. Unlike the more stable criminal bands, they did not work in one specific territory for solely criminal purposes. Most had some capabilities of occupation such as tinkers, carters, or field laborers.[31] Others were beggars and petty thieves such as we met in the play of *The Chicken Pie and the Chocolate Cake*.

The crimes that informal associations committed might involve fairly elaborate planning such as the ambush of a man to murder him, the plotting of a burglary, or the disguise of members of the gang as legitimate messengers. Other informal associations arose out of circumstances of the moment that temporarily united the participants. For instance, when the king's bailiff came from St. Neots to the Prior of the Hospital of Eaton Socon to make an arrest, the prior's hayward and two other servants attacked him and beat him to death with their staffs.[32] The outcome was unintended homicide and the association in the murder was spur of the moment. None of these criminal associations had long stability, rules of behavior for gang members, or expectations of gaining a living by crime. They would either be hanged for their part in a crime or, more likely, they would be released and not appear in court again either singly or with accomplices. While they accepted violence as a way of solving their immediate problems, they did not propose to make a life of such activity as would the outlaw bands.

BANDITS, OUTLAWS, AND HIGHWAYMEN

No criminal traditions are so dear to the hearts of the public and historians as the bandits, outlaws, and highwaymen exemplified by the medieval model, Robin Hood. Robin Hood represents one of the earliest popularizations of a criminal. In idealizing and making acceptable his disregard for life, limb, property, and the law, his actions were rationalized by saying that he only robbed from the rich so that he could give to the poor and when he murdered and maimed he did so in self-defense or as just retribution for injuries done to him. Robin Hood, surrounded by his merry men, is thus rendered not only socially acceptable but, if we are to follow Hobsbawm's idea of social banditry, a veritable welfare agency for the poor and oppressed.

Although ballads similar to those about Robin Hood are found throughout the Western tradition, a historical Robin Hood or even an altruistic outlaw resembling him is difficult to find in any country in any period. Even Hobsbawm must confess to the difficulty of finding a real-life example in peasant societies.[33] The ballads are useful for understanding peasant discontent and fantasies the peasants had about a mythical hero who overcame problems by breaking the law. They are also helpful as a model for analyzing the organization of outlaw bands who sought refuge from the law in the greenwood. These criminal associations were much more stable and structured than the informal associations, but they were also much less common in the overall crime pattern. They had a fairly long-standing membership and clearly defined leadership, lines of command, and rules of conduct for members. The bands either kept to the greenwood or sought protection and sometimes leadership from the local nobility, churchmen, and peasants.

The membership composition of these criminal associations is crucial to understanding them. There has been an active debate over the origins of Robin Hood. Hilton, Keen, and Hobsbawm have maintained that he was a peasant of yeoman rank and that he represents peasant ideals and discontents and is, thus, a primitive rebel. Holt, on the other hand, has said he was a gentleman and the ballads were written for the gentry.[34] The debate is a frivolous one that contributes little to either literary or historical knowledge; it is futile to argue about the class identity of someone who cannot be proved to have existed. In fact, the composition of the gangs in the greenwood and on the highways shows that they included peasants, knights, clerks, and miscellaneous vagrants. The upper nobility virtually never participated in outlaw bands.[35] The gang of Sir John de Colseby and Sir William Bussy included thirty-eight men who committed a series of crimes around Roncliff, Cowick, Ness, Saxton, and other areas of Yorkshire. All were convicted but were able to prove that they were clerks.[36] These men may have been in orders, but as we have suggested previously, they may have only belonged to the lower orders or learned to read so that they could plead benefit of clergy. In a Somerset gang, the members all got benefit of clergy, even though one was identified as a carpenter and another as a smith.[37]

The traditional social bandit, according to Hobsbawm, had a brush with the law and then had no choice but to join or form a criminal band in exile from his village.[38] There was, however, sufficient reason for people to join criminal bands without being driven to it because of previous criminal records. Indeed, Bellamy found that most of the members of the Coterels' large gang had not previously been in trouble with the law.[39] The life of a bandit had a number of attractions, mostly financial, which made for easy recruiting. Membership in the Coterels' gang increased substantially after they went into the highly lucrative area of extortion.[40] For many of the members, temporary financial embarrassments were instrumental in their joining. The civil wars and rebellions of Edward II's reign meant that many of the knights temporarily lost their lands. They joined bands until they were bought off with the return of their property or a royal commission.[41] Others were younger sons who had small inheritances or young men who were waiting until their fathers died and they could take up their land. Both peasants and gentry fell into this group. There were, of course, people from the villages who committed crimes and were outlawed. Some of these simply disappeared until friends and relatives could either buy them a pardon or could fix the jury decision. Others without such influence would join the ranks of wanderers and find work elsewhere or might join an outlaw band. Finally, there were those looking for excitement and for the high living. The English ballads of Robin Hood overlook this obvious motivation for opting for a life in the greenwood. The German peasant epic about Meier Helmbrecht makes the motivation of the young outlaw very clear throughout; he wanted to live like a knight and have all the fine material things a knight has. As Helmbrecht tells his father when he is offered the wealthy peasant's estate:

Whatever, father, be my fate,
I'll not yield now, it's far too late!
Forth I must fare upon the stage,
Now others as your sons engage,
And let them sweat behind your plow.
The cattle such as I drive now
Must bellowing before me flee.
I'd not be here for you to see
Except for lack of nag or steed.
That I can't ride at whizzing speed
Along with others, all on edge,
Go raiding through each peasant's hedge,
And drag him out by head of hair,
That gives me deep regret, I swear.
I'll not endure the pinch of need;
If in three years I should indeed
Raise one poor colt, one cow as well,
Such gain would be a bagatelle.
I'll go a-robbing every day,
That I may gain sufficient prey,
And ample victuals, free of cost;
And that my body from the frost
In winter's kept; unless it be
None buys my captured steers from me.[42]

Young Helmbrecht's attitude is perfectly understandable and consistent with the motivations of those peasants who joined the robber bands and with those who only enjoyed the Robin Hood ballads and thought enviously of the possibilities of the criminal career. The grasping, materialistic peasant who joined the outlaws is no less an expression of peasant discontent than are Hobsbawm's revolutionary bandits.

In selection of victims the real-life bandits were quite different from the ideal. The ideal social bandit was supposed to rob only from the rich in order that he could give to the poor and to kill only when there was just cause. Even Robin Hood and the other ballad heroes did not live up to these impressive standards. Brigands are a rough lot. All the presumed good in the ballads does not disguise the fact that they engaged in a fair number of unjust and brutal slayings. Porters who kept the gates were killed, bodies were maimed so "That he was never on woman born/Could tell whose hed it was," and a child was killed "For ferd lest he should telle."[43] Records of actual burglaries and robberies show that the outlaws could be as brutal to the honest husband and his wife and children as to the oppressors of the people. We have already seen that when gangs of outlaws came into a village for an evening rampage of burglary and robbery, the peasants together with their families and servants were killed by hasty thieves who did not wait to tie up their victims.

The victimization of husbandmen, village craftsmen, and shepherds is not surprising when one recalls that gangs of three or more stole a surprising amount of household goods, foodstuffs, and clothing. A diet of the king's venison alone was not enough to sustain life in the greenwood. Bread, cooking implements, clothing, blankets, and beer were more easily procured from peasant households than from well-guarded nobles', sheriffs', or abbots' residences. Young Helmbrecht made no pretense about the source of his meals and the comfort of his standard of living: "All that the peasants have is mine," he boasted.[44] Something of the outlaws' desperation for the simple articles of life and hence their victimization of the peasantry shows up in a Wakefield indictment.

> Richard del Wyndhill taken as a suspected thief because he came with a message from several thieves to the wife of the late William de Stodlay (begging) victuals for the said thieves and because he threatened the woman to burn her unless she sent food and money by him, and fled when the Earl's foresters tried to attach him for this. He shot at the foresters.[45]

This attempted extortion of goods from an innocent widow occurred at exactly the same period and place where some historians have attempted to identify a historical Robin Hood.[46] If these thieves were associated with a band following the ethics of Robin Hood, they were breaking the rules. For the widow, the foresters, not the outlaws, must have seemed to be the heroes of the day.

There is no reason to assume that bandits will have a more highly developed social conscience than the bulk of the peasantry.

Bandits, like peasants, picked their victims from their own group or the next highest above them. When they needed staples, which was frequently since they were not in a position to carry on ordinary agriculture, they knew that the peasant houses could provide their needs. Sometimes they forced the peasants to receive them into their homes. In a midnight attack in Bedfordshire the sheriffs and posses of Lincolnshire and Huntingdonshire chased a desperate criminal to the home of Roger del Temple. His wife was home and was forced to admit the outlaw. When the bandit leaped to the door to defend himself, he was beheaded. The woman told the jurors that she knew that he was a felon but was afraid to deny him admittance.[47] In another case a husband forced his wife to conceal known felons of his gang who, according to the record, "are now outlaws in Gloucestershire."[48] Undoubtedly, many of the peasants voluntarily received the bandits because they were paid in gifts from the robbers' plunder. It was a highly risky, but also profitable, business to receive outlaws. The outlaws probably also gave gifts freely to the peasantry in the region where they operated in order to bribe them or to buy their goodwill so that they would not indict them.

While the bandits did rely on either cooperation from the peasants or force in taking goods necessary for their survival, larger profits were gained by robbing from the rich rather than the poor. True to the legendary stereotype, gangs of three or more did rob more from churches and churchmen than did the ordinary criminal population. Churches were an obvious target because of the alms, ornaments, and wax candles. The gang of Roger Dalling of Icklingham, Essex, stole ornaments worth 100s. from a Colchester church. Another group under the leadership of Robert Joye and John Skynnere came "armed as for war" to the church at Stanford and took and wounded Godfrey, vicar, and stole goods worth £10.[49] Clergy on the road were also vulnerable, particularly if they looked prosperous. A clerical gang under Chaplain Hugh of Arncliffe and the Dean of Aintree were accused of robbing William Bilet of Malton of money, arms, clothes worth 10s. 3d., and two papal bulls.[50] As we have seen, the gangs did not stop at papal bulls, but took the pope's cardinals and bishops as well. Robin Hood's attacks on the Abbot of St. Mary's were not isolated incidents from romance and indeed pale somewhat in comparison to the reality of attacks on clergy.

The other major source of wealth for traditional attack in the greenwood, on the moors, and along the seacoast were merchants. The cases are so numerous that only a few outstanding examples may be selected. John de Wyghall and John Webster of Beverley with their men held passes on the moors of Blakhouse, Kildale, and Ingelby and robbed several drapers of cloth and money.[51] Merchants were threatened not only on the road, but strong-armed robbers would hold up their stranded ships or rob them in port. As we have seen, two men and their associates held the inhabitants of the port of Whitby under fear from their proclamation and demand of a third of the value of goods from the ships.[52] Robert Boidyn and associates killed thirty-six men on a boat near Hunstanton and took away leather, oil, and money worth £3,000.[53] Merchants and smaller traders were also in danger from large gangs at fairs. Twice in the fourteenth century Scarborough fair was held by outlaws and their bands who defied the king's authority and held the people against their will and for their own profit.[54]

In addition to robbing the peasantry, clergy, and merchants, the outlaw bands also performed criminal acts against the king and his officials and against powerful magnates of the countryside. Some of these actions were in retribution for suffering at the hands of the officials and others were done simply because they, like the wealthy merchants and churchmen, were excellent targets for high profit thefts. Protest against the wealthy and powerful in society is certainly present in some of the acts of the outlaw bands, but more often than not the gang was more interested in profit or personal revenge.

There seems to be little reason to doubt that the murder of Justice Roger Bellers by a federation of west Midlands gangs under the leadership of the Folvilles was a revenge homicide for threats against the notorious outlaws.[55] An argument could also be made that the ransoming of Justice Richard Willoughby was revenge. He had a reputation for selling justice, but so did many of the justices. There seems to be no particular reason to have picked on him except that he was on circuit in the district and was wealthy.[56] If the case was one of revenge, the motivation seems more of an intraneighborhood squabble for power than the symbolic punishment of an oppressive justice. Roger la Zouche, a magnate in the region, was named an accessory in the Bellers case and for complicity with the Willoughby affair,[57] but in 1351 Richard de Willoughby and Roger la Zouche were serving together on a commission of oyer and terminer in the west Midlands.[58] Very possibly the outlaw bands were only hired by Lord Roger for his own political ends.[59] Other examples from the gaol delivery rolls of attacks on officials are equally indecisive about rebellious motivation on the part of outlaw bands. One band was accused of ransoming the king's messenger who was traveling with warrants, but the amount of ransom, 1 mark, leads one to believe that not only money was involved.[60] Other attacks were made on local nobility and on mayors but these too may have been for money rather than for revolution.[61]

In some cases the records specifically state that the accused were acting in insurrection against the king, but these cases, such as the taking of Scarborough or holding the king's messenger, may refer to any attack on the king's authority. Two men who resisted arrest and maltreated Richard Brian at Doncaster were accused of insurrection because he had been sent to arrest them.[62] This was certainly an act directed against the king's justice. A band in Norfolk under the leadership of John son of John Emmes abducted Stephen de Hales, a justice of the king and his fellows.[63] Since no ransom was mentioned, they may have been seeking revenge.

Often the bandits were hired to harass or kill other people's enemies. A common employer of outlaw bands was members of the clergy. The dean and chapter of Lichfield were accused of having received the Coterels and used their services.[64] The Folvilles also had clerical employers.[65] One of the best documented cases is that of the Rector of Weston-sub-Edge in Gloucestershire who hired the notorious Sir Malcolm Musard and his gang to beat up his rival after he was evicted from his living. Musard, his brothers, several clergy, and others came and beat the rival, broke his fish ponds, and did damage in the village.[66] In other criminal exploits, outlaw gangs would work together for a particular prize, as in the murder of Bellers and the ransoming of Willoughby.

A clearly identifiable act of social banditry is difficult to find, although some actions could be interpreted that way. Contrary to the ballads and to Hobsbawm's model for social bandits, the real-life bandits robbed from rich and poor alike. The rich were the most profitable targets, but not necessarily the most common ones. After all, there were few rich people in the stratified rural communities. Revolutionary motivation is difficult to detect in most cases where money was involved. In other cases it is possible that the outlaws may have been working in the pay of local powers who were looking after their own interests.

The bandits' success was very much connected with the degree of their organization: defined leadership, stable membership, rules of conduct, and cooperation with other bands of outlaws. Probably the most crucial single element in their success was an outstanding leader: a Robin Hood. The dominant leader, who was necessary for disciplining group behavior and providing direction in the criminal activities, was a natural outgrowth of the hierarchical organization of medieval society—people expected to be led by an overlord. Outlaws may have escaped these conventional relationships of man to lord by seeking refuge in the greenwood, but their social thinking made it natural for them to form similar allegiances with an outlaw chief. They were conservatives like the peasants who revolted in 1381; they thought that neither the king nor his form of government was bad but that his officials, bureaucrats, and advisers were corrupt. In the Robin Hood legends, the position of sheriff is not abolished, but the king is made to see that Robin Hood would be a better candidate to keep the position honest.

Court roll evidence shows that the conventions of the society were fairly closely followed in selecting the leader. Where there was a knight mentioned, he was usually the leader, and when a family is mentioned, the oldest brother or the father was usually the leader. Those leaders whose origins can be documented came from the gentry, knights, and lower ranks of the nobility. Clergy were also very much in evidence; they too usually came from the gentry. Undoubtedly, some peasants became leaders of bands, but they are difficult to identify. The one medieval bandit, Thomas Dun, to appear in the *Newgate Calendar* was a peasant.[67] The best documented bandit gang made up of servants, tradesmen, and poor tenants was that of William Beckwith whose outlawed relatives and followers held out against the king's justices for five years at the end of the fourteenth century.[68] Most of the gangs, however, seemed to follow the model of the "Meier Helmbrecht" story where a local knight acted as leader and protector of a band of ruffians who terrified the countryside and robbed from rich and poor. There are some notable examples of knights of this sort in the records. Sir Thomas de Heslarton and his relatives, servants, neighbors, and outlaws occupied much of the justices' time in 1352 in Yorkshire, and Sir John de Colseby and Sir William de Bussy were *capitalis de societate* of men who committed a series of crimes in which they netted £3,000.[69] Sir Malcolm Musard was a member of a well-established Gloucestershire family that could trace its lineage back to the Conquest.[70]

The position of the *capitalis de societate* in these criminal associations and the general structure of the rest of the organization is well-illustrated in a letter sent to Richard de Snaweshill, chaplain of Huntington near York in 1336.

Lionel, king of the rout of raveners salutes, but with little love, his false and disloyal Richard de Snaweshill. We command you, on pain to lose all that can stand forfeit against our laws, that you immediately remove from his office him whom you maintain in the vicarage of Burton Agnes; and that you suffer that the Abbot of St. Mary's have his rights in this matter and that the election of the man whom he has chosen, who is more worthy of advancement than you or any of your lineage, be upheld. And if you do not do this, we make our avow, first to God and then to the king of England and to our own crown that you shall have such treatment at our hands as the Bishop of Exeter had in Cheap; and we shall hunt you down, even if we have to come to Corey Street in York to do it. And show this letter to your lord, and bid him to cease from false compacts and confederacies, and to suffer right to be done to him whom the Abbot had presented; else he shall have a thousand pounds worth of damage by us and our men. And if you do not take cognizance of our orders, we have bidden our lieutenant in the North to levy such great distraint upon you as is spoken of above. Given in our Castle of the North Wind, in the Green Tower, in the first year of our reign.[71]

The organization of Lionel's gang is much like that which the Robin Hood ballads describe. Lionel claimed to be a king with a crown and to have an official residence and set of laws that not only governed the behavior within the gang but also set the standards of behavior for outsiders as well. Chaplain Snaweshill was accused of breaking these laws. Punishment of such lawbreakers was to be meted out by the lieutenant of the North, a sort of trusty "Little John." Lionel's gang is classic in structure: a leader with subordinate commanders who could be delegated to oversee activities in the gang's areas of control.

The organization of Lionel's gang closely paralleled that of the central government, thus again showing that the bandits were conservative in their mental outlook. It was natural that the outlaws would turn to the royal government, which they respected, for their models of organization with the king at the top and his captains and henchmen under him to carry out his orders in the field. In the ballads the imitation of the royal system and the respect for the established order is shown in the fact that the gang all wear the Lincoln green livery of their lord, Robin Hood, just as the king's guard or a magnate's household would wear their colors. This royal military scheme of organization may have been very familiar to the outlaws, many of whom had served in the king's armies in Scotland or on the Continent. Even the language in Lionel's letter closely resembles the form of the English king's own letters patent both in the salutations at the beginning and closing giving the residence and the regnal year of the writer. Obviously, Lionel was not an ignorant bumpkin admiring the king from afar; either he or a member of his band was literate and knew what a letter patent looked like and knew how to imitate it. Lionel was not alone in this, for trailbaston and peace commissions speak of criminals writing "as if in a royal style to knights, widows, abbots, priors . . . and others whom they deem wealthy . . . [demanding] stated sums of money by grievous menances."[72]

Not all criminal associations were as flamboyantly or centrally organized as that of Lionel. Many relied upon a single leader and the traditional familial core of members to keep the organization going. As we have observed, the familial unit was already well organized for crime and the lines of authority in the family group were well established. Often the gangs were not monolithic in structure, but had a federation of smaller groups and individuals whom the leader could call upon. The leaders of both the Coterel and the Folville gangs functioned this way.[73] Probably this was a fairly typical way of organizing an outlaw band because of the problems of provisioning and sheltering a large band of men.

When the bands did function as a unit, there were rules of conduct covering such matters as dividing spoils, concealing the name of associates if captured, assisting fellow members to avoid arrest, or helping them escape from prison or gain a pardon or acquittal if caught. When it came to division of spoils, the hierarchy of the band was maintained. In a large gang robbery in 1302 the members of the gang retired to a place of safety and there shared "among the aforesaid mercery and spicery each according to his degree."[74] One gang member, John Drestes, testified that he and nine other men robbed Robin Wyot, a fisherman in Walsham, of cloth and money valued at 50s. John did exceptionally well, getting 17s. for his part. In a three way split of 18s. one man told the justices that he got only 1s. 6d.[75] Exactly what determined the part each person got is not always clear. Perhaps the leader got the most, or the person with the greatest criminal skill, or the person who took the greatest risk, or it could have all been done according to the social status of the members. However it was accomplished, the usual arguments over divisions of the spoils did take place. One thief was killed in an argument over splitting the booty.[76]

Keeping the name of fellow outlaws secret was not always feasible. There were those who either for pay or under threats of duress would reveal the name of their fellows. If captured, keeping silence was particularly difficult since sheriffs and gaolers had no qualms about using torture to force a man to turn approver. Many of the unfortunate men must have given in and betrayed their fellows. Since 96 percent of the approvers withdrew their appeals at the trial, perhaps it was considered adequate for the maintenance of honor to declare innocent all those he had accused under duress. Some approvers tried another strategy. All the people appealed by John Macke, William le Ry of Suffolk, and William de Mendham were already dead.[77]

The well-organized outlaw band provided for warning the members of approaching posses, finding hiding places in forests or in houses of sympathetic property owners, bribing officials, and rescuing gang members from prison or the gallows. When a commission of trailbaston was appointed in 1331 to investigate crime in Nottinghamshire and Derbyshire, the Coterels were forewarned through one or two spies they kept in Nottingham and so were able to escape into hiding.[78] In the outlaw ballads Adam Bell was warned by one of his supporters that a comrade had been captured.[79]

Going into hiding or providing for members of the gang who were being pursued involved considerable planning and contacts. The forests and moors were natural places for retreat, but both ballads and the historical evidence give ample proof that living in the greenwood was not so pleasant as it seems in the Robin Hood stories. A fifteenth century poem describes it well.

> Yet take good hede, for ever I drede, that ye coulde not sustein
> The thorney wayes, the depe valeis, the snowe, the frost, the reyn,
> The cold, the hete; for drye or wete we must lodge on the plan;
> And, us above noon other roue (roof), but a brake, fussh or twayne.
>
> For ye must there in your hand bere a bowe redy to drawe,
> And as the theef thus must ye lyve, ever in drede and awe.[80]

Rather than live continuously in the wilds, most bands relied upon a variety of people to receive them and give them food and shelter. Local people, either for pay or under duress, received outlaws. Magnates who employed the bands frequently sheltered them as well.

But all bands had to keep on the move to elude justice and to avoid offending the countryside to the extent that the peasantry would band together to rid themselves of them. Another solution to the problem of hiding was to go to another county and seek aid from a local outlaw gang. Eustace Folville, when hard pressed, joined the band of Coterels.[81] A Leicestershire outlaw migrated to Essex where he committed a series of lucative crimes in conjunction with local men.[82]

If the pursuit became too hot, then it might be necessary to do more than retreat; the pursuers themselves might have to be attacked. This sort of episode is common in the outlaw legends as when Robin Hood attacked the sheriff who was coming after him. The Coterels captured one of the people sent out to arrest them, Roger de Wennesley, lord of Mappleton. He was forced to agree never to pursue them. Eventually he joined them.[83] Sir Roger Swynnerton of Staffordshire and his supporters closed the doors of the hall where the county court was being held and threatened to kill the sheriff if he tried to start the session.[84]

When all means of avoiding arrest, stopping indictments and trials, or procuring a pardon failed and one of the members of the gang was to be hanged, it behooved the gang to rescue the unfortunate from gaol or from the hangman. In 1318 a group of unknown persons entered Norwich castle gaol and released Richard Phelip who was a prisoner there.[85] In a more desperate rescue, Nicholas Tailor of Gersington, Elliot son of Eve de Lynton, Adam Thresshefeld, and Henry de Plumpton cut down from the gallows Nicholas' brother, Henry, who was being hanged for burglary. They took him to a church where he abjured the realm.[86] In one case in Bedfordshire the gang got there too late. They killed the hangmen instead of saving their companion.[87] With such dramatic historical incidents the tales of Adam Bell's or Robin Hood's rescue of condemned comrades seem plausible.

The bandits who appear in gaol delivery and other criminal records were desperate men and hardened criminals. None seemed to live up to the advice Robin Hood gave to his band.

> Loke ye do no husbonde no harm,
>   That tylleth with his plough;
> No more ye schal no good yeman,
>   That walketh by grenewode shawe.
>
> These bishoppes and these archebishoppes,

Ye shall them bete and binde;
The hye Sheriff of Notyngham,
  Hym holde you in your mynde.[88]

Given the number of poor shepherds and husbandmen who, according to the inquests in the coroners' rolls, were going out to look for their stray chattels and were found the next morning lying in a ditch with bloody wounds and no clothing, it seems unlikely that very many of the bandits had the fine sensibilities attributed to Robin Hood. Why were the tales of Robin Hood so popular when the real-life outlaw bands were more of a scourge to the poor than a help? The answer lies largely in their myth-making potential. The ballad bandits lived daring, flashy lives without toiling at the grinding routines of daily labor. They could even appear to be revolutionaries when their victims were, coincidentally, the same people who oppressed the balladeers.

Ultimately, the outlaws would do more harm than good to the peasants and someone would betray their whereabouts to the sheriff. The populace then reacted very much as did the group of peasants who recognized Helmbrecht and, after tearing him apart, hanged him from a tree. They were peasants whose daughters were raped, who had cattle stolen, who had been beaten and tied up by Helmbrecht and his band. The story teller concludes:

Upon the streets and on the roads
Men could not safely drive their loads;
Their wagons now in peace may fare,
Since Helmbrecht dangles in the air.[89]

But people's memories are short. When outside oppression was greatest, the peasants were willing to forget that the outlaws killed their neighbors and, instead, they glorified the bands' murder of a notable justice, their robbery of the abbot, and their defiance of the sheriff in rescuing an imprisoned comrade. The risks in receiving gifts from the outlaws were forgotten and all that was remembered was that there once were gifts when a person felt needy. Thus the myths were woven around these brutal bandits and were particularly popular just before the revolt of 1381. In real life the peasants were capable of being their own defenders and the real heroes; to argue otherwise is to underestimate them.

The Nobility and Their Household Gangs

A power vacuum remained in the world of organized crime even after one considers the success of the bandits and the proliferation of informal criminal associations. This vacuum involved crimes requiring the use of fixed and fortified residences, the illegal use of power and influence, wealth to buy power and pay armed men to enforce it, and sufficient status in society to defy the ordinary attempts of the government to enforce the law. The barons, counts, and earls of the land filled the gap left by other forms of organized crime as well as usurping the power of the crown to administer justice. The activities of the upper nobility are distinguished from those of the knightly class and the gentry who tended to be involved in direct violence and felonies and to be leaders or protectors of the outlaw bands. The higher nobility had both sufficient social status and power to enter into crimes that boldly defied the king himself. They were a continual disruption to the peace in the fourteenth and fifteenth centuries, culminating in the War of the Roses. As we have seen, the nobles surrounded themselves with armed households that acted in a variety of capacities ranging from administering the nobles' estates to punishing those defying the lord's authority to forming private armies to meet encroachments on their power either by equals or by the king. The age had a term for this practice of the nobility: "livery and maintenance."

The kings found it difficult to control their nobility since they had the power to defy royal justice and ultimately to depose the king and put another in his place. Sending the nobles and their households out of the country to foreign wars, coopting them for peacekeeping commissions, or pursuading them to attack each other were virtually the only means the kings ultimately had for dealing with them. They were particularly difficult to discipline not only because of their armed strength but also because both they and the kings agreed that in some sense their actions were not illegal. Nevertheless, they did break the laws of the land and were one of the chief disruptions to the functioning of the state. On the one hand, the nobles behaved like the elites of crime—the fur collar criminals—on the other hand, they seem more like the Mafia of eighteenth-century Sicily. As elite criminals they used their occupations as warriors and administrators to secure wealth and power in their own hands much as a corporation executive would use his occupation for the same ends. These fur collar criminals did not commit bloody deeds themselves but acted in an executive capacity directing their household members. Their criminal acts included extortion of rights to land and money, jury intimidation, corruption of justice and the royal judicial system, and fighting other nobles who tried to encroach on their power in their territory.

As the prototype of the Mafia, they entered into a patron-client relationship with their peasantry, offering those peasants who put themselves under them protection from their enemies and favorable decisions in the courts. They would intimidate jurors who wanted to indict these protected peasants. In this sense they were serving as power brokers standing between the peasantry and the state officials or other people threatening the villagers. In a period when royal justice did not function smoothly and without corruption, this was a useful service. But the price the peasantry paid was very high and they knew it. If they defaulted on their side of the bargain by not providing the required goods and services, they would end up the victims of their lord's brutality.

The *latifundia* owners and their *bravi* in eighteenth-century Sicily behaved in much the same way as the English nobility of the later Middle Ages and perhaps because of a similar power vacuum situation. They controlled their own territory, defied the king, and provided for their own people. Their criminal activities were blatant subversions of the law of the land, none the less criminal for being done in the open rather than under the cover of the greenwood.[90]

Like other types of criminal associations, the nobles' gangs may be studied for the membership composition and their rationality in organization. The leadership, of course, was always drawn from the higher nobility who held fairly extensive lands and had considerable wealth and prestige both locally and in the country as a whole. The noble had to maintain a fortified residence and have sufficient wealth to provide for his own life-style and for his household retainers. His authority over his retainers and his client peasantry was absolute because he could dismiss a liveried member of his household and could have his peasantry beaten into submission. He was an executive to the gang; the lines of authority were highly rationalized with the leader being distinguished both by his social class and by the power and wealth that he alone could amass.

The household (*familia* or *meinie*) was a mixture of gentry and non-gentry. Having many retainers was both useful and a status symbol to

215

the noble, but they were expensive to maintain, and thus the practice grew up of hiring retainers for special occasions and granting them liveries for short periods rather than life. As we have seen, bandits were often hired for special criminal assaults. When Sir William Stafford got into a dispute he brought in his brother James's criminal gang, while the other side employed Sir William Chutlon's outlaws.[91]

As rationally organized as the nobles' household gangs were in the area of crime, they do not resemble what a modern criminologist would call "organized crime." This is not surprising since the modern criminal syndicates are based on the model of business corporations with all the complexity of corporation politics mixed with the brutality of a secret criminal brotherhood. The nobles' bands of the fourteenth century were based on models of monarchy, feudalism, and familial ties. The nobility were not carving out new and prosperous areas for crime, but were exploiting powers that their position as members of the declining feudal system gave them. Tradition had given them power over their peasants, over the administration, and over private warfare. By the fourteenth century these powers were curtailed, but the lords continued to maintain their dominance through criminal means. They would not have regarded themselves as acting as professional criminals, but as exercising time-honored rights.

Recidivists and Professional Criminals

In assessing the importance of organized crime in the general crime pattern it is necessary to distinguish between the professional criminal and the person who simply repeats criminal acts. Criminology defines the professional criminal as a person who identifies himself as a lawbreaker and pursues crime as a regular day-to-day occupation. He develops the skilled techniques of crime and carefully plans the execution of each offense. The professional criminal makes crime his chief career just as a physician makes medicine his career. This definition does not leave much room for calling many criminals professional. Only "shoplifters, pick pockets, con men, and an upper crust of thieves specializing in large scale thefts could be considered sufficiently skilled and well-established enough to be professionals."[92] Finding a professional criminal in the medieval criminal court records is very difficult, because, although the skills can be established for certain criminals, the professional attitude, ethics, and codes of conduct are only incidental to the records. Although the knights and gentry who had established criminal bands would seem to be the most likely candidates, they and the nobility would identify with their status group in the society rather than consider themselves to be felons. Indeed, most of them did not pursue their criminal ways indefinitely. They often entered the king's service as soldiers or royal officials and disbanded their gangs.

The recidivist commits only a few crimes in his lifetime. He does not support himself by illegal means alone but only resorts to crime if it suits his immediate purposes or if there is a good opportunity to make a quick profit from thefts. He does not identify himself with felons but with his usual status in the community in which he lives.

Recidivists are also difficult to identify in fourteenth-century English criminal records. To simplify the analysis I used a sample of twenty years from Norfolk.[93] Norfolk was a fairly stable county with one of the most efficient law enforcement systems and a less mobile criminal population than that observed for Northamptonshire, so that the repeaters were easier to identify. Presumably, with virtually the only punishment being hanging, there should have been very few recidivists, but, as we have seen, the jurors were lenient and repeaters did come into the courts. In the Norfolk sample 11 percent of those tried were indicted for two or more crimes. Of these 66 percent were indicted for two crimes, 23 percent for three crimes, 3 percent for four, and 8 percent for five or more crimes.

The pattern of crimes and the dates of indictments tells much about the motivation of the repeaters. Most of those committing only two crimes did so in the same year or in consecutive years, thus indicating that they experienced temporary setbacks that required the ready money from thefts or that they fell in with bad company or that they were troublemakers and the community decided either to warn them or to be permanently rid of them. William Mayne and his wife Olive committed a series of small thefts in the famine years.[94] They must have been in temporary straits.

The more serious recidivists do have an identifiable career pattern. They were indicted several times over a period of years, thus showing that they were not compensating for short-term setbacks. The value of the goods they stole tended to increase over the years, perhaps indicating that they were becoming more ambitious and skilled in their thefts. Geoffrey son of Hawise committed several crimes in 1310 and again in 1315, when he was hanged. The record indicates that he had been charged with a number of petty thefts, which must have annoyed the community sufficiently to persuade them to hang him. In 1315 he was convicted because he stole four lambs, a quarter of grain, and because he was a "common thief of sheaves, geese, and chickens."[95] He was certainly a habitual offender, but not a professional. Even more habitual offenders were the Waraunt family of Salle who made part-time crime an ordinary family by-occupation for at least two generations. Finally, there were those repeaters, who, if we knew more about their careers, might have been professionals. They concentrated in the more violent and better paying property crimes and committed crimes over the entire period of the sample. John Hened of Holt, a chaplain, committed a homicide along with robbery; a year later he was charged with diverse robberies committed with other men. Roger Horn committed a series of crimes in 1315 and then was tried again in 1323 for larceny. He eventually became an approver and confessed to a string of crimes. John le Prestsone was accused of eight offenses in three different hundreds and the John Wypes of Dilham, father and son, also had an impressive record.[96] But even people with records such as these may not have been professionals.

The best indication of professional criminal careers comes from the confessions of approvers to the coroners. The approvers may have been forced into their confessions so some of the information is probably false, but the broad outline of the professional's career may be glimpsed in their stories. Some approvers appealed as many as forty or fifty people of aiding them in larcenies, burglaries, robberies, and homicides or having received them or their stolen goods. William Gerland of Somerhouse, for instance, said that two men accompainied him in a robbery of livestock worth 100s. He also appealed seven other men of aiding various larcenies, and he teamed up with four others in two burglaries and a homicide.[97] He is a very typical example. His record shows a diversity in crimes and a pattern of acting as a catalyst to criminal actions. He did not work in a permanent group but sought out a number of different people and groups to work with. In a Norfolk case, a man who followed a similar career pattern was betrayed by three former associates.

> John Arnald of Billingford was taken in the appeal of Alexander of Boughton, approver, for being in his company with other thieves at night when they broke into a hospital in Yarmouth and stole there 13s. in silver and cloth worth 10s. and for killing a man in the hospital. John was also appealed by Simon of Weston, approver, for a certain robbery committed in his company in a field in Felbrigg. They robbed an unknown man of 40s. He was also appealed by

William le Gardener of Bramerton, an approver who died in prison, for being in his company when he robbed at night a certain man in Hardley of three robes worth 40s.[98]

Like the modern professional thief whom Sutherland has studied,[99] the medieval professional moved around the countryside to avoid detection and to sell his criminal experience to locals who wanted to commit crimes. An approver who was caught in Essex, for instance, admitted that he had stolen goods all over East Anglia and had sold them in Surrey where four local men had received him.[100] Taking goods away from the scene of the crime was a typical ploy for the professional. An approver appealed a man for stealing four oxen with him in Herefordshire and crossing the county line to sell them; the approver got a small cut of one-half mark for his efforts. Another approver stole cloth with a woman in Herefordshire and sold it in Leominister to receivers who were probably professionals.[101] Approvers frequently named accomplices living in all corners of England. They were real people who were traced and brought to trial. Andrew Donnes of Walsoken in Norfolk appealed men from Bedfordshire, Kent, and Huntingdonshire, and Thomas LeEspic, who was arrested in Northamptonshire, appealed people who were found in Middlesex, Oxford, and Warwick.[102]

The professional thieves who worked with local people or other professional thieves to commit a particular crime did not necessarily make a large profit. Some claimed that they made none at all. One approver said he got one pig out of the three that were stolen and only 2s. from a horse worth 10s. An approver who was a receiver said he got 5s. profit for selling a horse worth 8s. 4d., but from aiding in the robbery of an ox worth 10s. he got only 16d.[103] For these small-time thieves on the run, the professional life of crime was not particularly profitable, but that corresponds with the experience of modern thieves as well.

Criminals who develop specialization of skills and criminal techniques are more likely to consider themselves professionals. In the medieval world of crime, cutpurses and counterfeiters were the only highly specialized criminals who could qualify in this category. By the Tudor period a number of con men can also be identified as professional criminals, but they are not apparent in the medieval criminal records, for the law did not protect the gullible. According to Ronald Fuller's account, the professionalization of the Elizabethan underworld was so great that each criminal committed only one type of crime.[104] In the Norfolk sample 63 percent of individuals and gangs charged with more than one offense committed the same type of crime and 37 percent were indicted for a variety of crimes. Simon le Miller of Tibenham specialized in burglaries and was convicted of four of them. A group of two men and two women had the speciality of stealing from churches. When they were finally convicted, they had a record of taking goods from three churches.[105]

The famous rookeries of Tudor through Victorian times seemed already to have been established in medieval London and probably in other cities as well. London had great attractions because of the wealth concentrated in one place and because the thieves could find accomplices and a refuge among other thieves. Chaucer described these dives in the *Canterbury Tales.*

> "In slums," he answered, "suburbs are our dwelling;
> We lurk in holes and corners and blind alleys,
> Places where every thief and robber rallies
> By nature, fear-stricken and sacred places
> Where those reside who dare not show their faces."[106]

Jean Bodel in *The Play of St. Nicholas* has a similar description of a ruffians' hangout where they played dice, drank, and plotted their next theft. The characters all go by criminal aliases such as "Clip," "Pinchdice," "Razor," and "Clickett."[107] Reading the Surrey gaol delivery rolls shows that the London suburbs were as big an attraction for criminals as they were in the eighteenth century.[108] Men from Devon, York, Staffordshire, and elsewhere all appear in the records either committing crimes in conjunction with the local people or being received by local people.[109]

At first glance it would appear that organized crime played a large part in medieval crime: over half of all crimes involved two or more criminal associates and the Robin Hood ballads were among the most popular of the day. The bulk of these associations, however, were informal and lacked longevity. The more serious problem in organized crime was the outlaw bands and highwaymen who had a more stable existence and attracted the disaffected from the knights, gentry, and peasantry. They not only committed lucrative crimes on their own, but they were also available for hire to people who wanted crimes committed. But even these more stable groups lasted only about ten to fifteen years before their leaders were coopted by the government into serving in foreign wars or before the leaders were hanged and the gangs split up. The most highly organized criminal associations were those of the barons and their households whose criminal activity fell between that of a white collar criminal and an early Sicilian Mafia type. But they too were often coopted for foreign wars or mobilized in government services and modified their criminal behavior. Very few people participating in organized crime made their sole living from it or would consider themselves to be professional criminals. Instead, they would claim an identity with the status group to which they belonged. The professional criminal population was very low and limited to cutpurses, counterfeiters, and a few professional outlaws. There was not a criminal class. The whole of society appeared to turn readily to criminal solutions to their problems, but they did not easily form a self-concept of criminality. It was fine for a legendary character such as Robin Hood to make his living from crime and those who could get away with it would find a certain amount of social toleration, but there was a lack of real identity with professional outlaws.

Chapter Seven

External Influences on
the Pattern of Crime

THE ANALYZERS of social behavior, be they chroniclers, legislators, historians, or sociologists, observe changes in crime patterns and seek explanations for them. Wars, political disruption, and economic crises tend to be the factors that most readily spring to mind, but demographic changes, delinquent subcultures, racial, physical or psychological characteristics, living conditions, industrialization, and many other factors have been suggested at one time or another to explain patterns of crime. The medieval records permit discussion of only certain hypotheses: psychological and physical influences cannot be measured; there were no racial minority groups and no evidence of a delinquent subculture; and the Industrial Revolution was several centuries in the future. The old standbys of political upheavals, civil and foreign wars, and demographic and economic change, however, can be investigated. Since the records do give a fairly accurate picture of the annual fluctuations in the number of crimes, in the types of crimes and the goods stolen, and in the crimes committed by criminal associations, correlations may be sought between changes in the pattern of crime and the various changes in early fourteenth-century English society.

The pursuit of these correlations is not to establish a single cause of crime: our modern quest for the answer to that problem has been as unsuccessful as the medieval search for the origin of evil. Rather, we will look at the types of societal crises and changes that seemed to intensify the problem of crime or to alter the types of crimes committed and goods stolen. All people committing crimes have personal motivations that contribute to their decision to commit a felony, but external factors such as famines or wars may contribute further impetus for the act.

POLITICAL DISORDER AND CRIME

A long-held popular theory places the blame for high crime rates on bad government and wars. As far back as the first half of the fourteenth century chroniclers and the Commons complained that lax government or veterans of wars were the chief causes of the all-too-prevalent violence. The period certainly did abound in political and military strife. For twenty years Edward II and his barons struggled against each other for control of the central government—a struggle that led to open civil war in 1322 and the king's deposition and murder five years later. A measure of internal political stability accompanied the accession of Edward III to the throne in 1327, but it also brought almost continual warfare, first with the Scots and then with the French in the first phase of the Hundred Years' War. Were contemporary observers correct in placing the blame for increased crime on these political and military crises?

Medieval political theory regarded the responsibility of law enforcement and maintenance of the peace as lying ultimately with the king; indeed, each king swore in his coronation oath to keep the peace and do justice. Felonies were defined as breaches of the king's peace. With the final obligation for supressing crime vested in one person, it is possible that the volume of crime increased during periods of factional strife for control over the monarch (1310-1330) or during his prolonged absences abroad in the French campaigns (1338-1347). Perhaps even the example of the murder of Piers Gaveston and the Despensers increased violence by seeming to condone it. Such crises at the top of the governmental hierarchy might, on the other hand, have had little effect on the people as a whole. Despite the importance of the monarchy as reflected in theory, royal bureaucrats, local authorities, and central court justices actually ran the machinery of law enforcement. If the system of justice ran smoothly despite the lapses of kingship, then perhaps the political crises had little influence on the amount of lawlessness.

We can compare the alterations in the power structure from 1307 to 1330 with the table of crime for the same years (table 12 and figures 12-17). Although Edward I had done much for England during his long reign, he left to his son a large debt and an unfinished war with

Scotland. He also died leaving his heir bitter over the exile of Piers Gaveston, the younger son of a Gascon knight and inseparable friend of the young monarch. As soon as he succeeded to the throne, Edward II recalled his favorite and installed him as Earl of Cornwall. Within the first year of the new reign (April 1308) the magnates united to force Gaveston back into exile. They resented the Frenchmen's influence on their king and their own loss of influence with the central government. But Edward soon won over enough of the barons by gifts and promises to recall Gaveston. By 1310 the barons complained a second time about the evil influence of Gaveston on the monarch. Coming to Parliament armed, they forced the king to accept a reform of his household and exile of his favorite. The barons gained control over the household offices and presented the king with their reform measures and demands in the Ordinances of 1311. Scheming once again gave Edward enough control over his government to bring back Gaveston. Learning of his return in 1312, the chief earl, Thomas of Lancaster, mustered a large force to capture Gaveston. After a hot pursuit across Yorkshire, the favorite surrendered and was carried off to Warwick. The more moderate nobles wanted to hold him for trial, but Lancaster took matters into his own hands and had two of his men kill Gaveston. Horror at this event put the moderate supporters of the king in power until 1314, when Edward's disastrous defeat by the Scots in the battle of Bannockburn discredited them.

The loss of the moderates was Lancaster's gain; he took control of the administration. These years of Lancastrian rule (1315-1317) were the most disordered of the early fourteenth century. The barons, including Lancaster himself, were engaged in private warfare brought on by disputed claims over estates. When Edward tried to lead an army against the Scots, who were raiding the northern counties, Lancaster broke the bridges at York to prevent the king's advance. Worst of all, the country underwent a period of severe famine and accompanying pestilence during these years.

By 1318 Lancaster's failure to govern effectively gave the middle party another chance. They forced Lancaster to accept the Treaty of Leake, which prevented him from sitting in the council. But peace was once more doomed, for by this time the king was under the influence of other favorites—the Despensers, father and son. As in the case of Gaveston, the ambitious Despensers alienated the barons. This time open civil war could not be avoided. Victory at the battle of Boroughbridge in 1322 gave Edward the opportunity to execute Thomas of Lancaster and the other chief rebels.

Despite their success, Edward and the Despensers ruled only until 1326. The Despensers offended the queen, Isabella, who escaped to her brother's court in Paris. Soon afterward Edward sent their son, the heir apparent, to France to do homage for the English possessions there. With young Edward in her control, Isabella planned a coup d'etat. Unable to secure troops from France, she and her paramour, Mortimer of Wigmore, went to Hainault. At the price of a marriage contract between young Edward and Philippa, the daughter of the count of Hainault, they procured mercenaries. On September 23, 1326, they landed in Suffolk. The country, especially London, rose in their favor. They moved west into Herefordshire and executed the Despensers. Edward II became their prisoner, and they forced him to abdicate in favor of his son. Rumors suggested that Isabella had him murdered and that the deed was done through horrible torture. Isabella and Mortimer controlled the government until October 1330, when Henry of Lancaster persuaded Edward III to establish his independence as a monarch. The final drama in this period of violent politics was consistent with the ones that preceded it. Edward and the conspirators burst in on Mortimer and Isabella in their bedchamber and took Mortimer to London in spite of Isabella's pleas. He was tried for treason and drawn and quartered. Isabella was allowed to retire from politics and went to live in Norfolk.

Were these repeated political crimes and murders disrupting enough to produce an increase in crime? A comparison of the power struggles with the annual incidence of crimes for the eight counties (see table 12) shows that in general yearly variations in crime bore only slight relationship to the political events. In the last years of Edward I crime was fairly high but steadily declined after 1302. Crimes increased again in 1309-1310, which corresponds to the period of baronial complaints over Gaveston. The implementation of the Ordinances and the murder of Gaveston, however, coincided with low crime. The annual incidence of crime shot up from 1314-1318, the period of Lancaster's disastrous rule, but this was also a time of famine, Scottish invasions, and private baronial wars. Lancaster's government was probably the least of the curses for the countryside during that period. With the moderates in power in 1319-1322 the level of crime dropped, but between 1323-1326 crime was again high in most counties for which there is evidence. This peak may have been influenced by the civil war and the battle of Boroughbridge, but again there were famines and invasions. The period of the coup d'état saw a leveling off of crime but at a fairly high level. One is tempted to see the slight increases in 1327-1328 as the effect of Isabella releasing prisoners from London and other gaols. The chroniclers complained that this caused incessant outrages in the countryside.[1]

Not all counties were equally involved in the political strife, so that looking at the more disturbed counties might indicate a closer relationship between crime and politics. Yorkshire was continually in the thick of the military maneuverings surrounding the political violence. Gaveston was captured there, York was often the host to legal parliaments and illegal gatherings of barons, and the battle of Boroughbridge was fought in the county. But Yorkshire's pattern of crime is similar to the overall pattern for those years (see table 12). The only specific reference to the civil wars in the gaol delivery rolls is the trial for treason of three of the ring leaders: John de Mowbray, Reginald de Clifford, and Gocelin de Oyville.[2]

Somerset and Herefordshire were also often in the path of rebel's troops as they marched up and down the west country, and Hereford was the scene of some of the major phases of the coup. Somerset's records are sparse but show a similar pattern to the overall one for these years. Herefordshire, on the other hand, has some marked differences. The period of the civil war rather than the famine of 1315-1317 had the highest peak in crime, and in 1329 the county had a much higher incidence of crime than the other counties. The political events of the period probably influenced Herefordshire's pattern of crime in the 1320s. Wigmore had estates in nearby Wales and was stirring up local resentment in the late 1320s just as the Despensers were earlier. This unrest together with the political occurences were crucial for Herefordshire's crime pattern, as Waugh has illustrated.[3] Surrey, Essex, Norfolk, and Northamptonshire all were similar to the general pattern. The slight increase in crimes in Essex between 1328-1329 may be attributable to upsets in London from the coup. Surrey does not have records for the period to substantiate this hypothesis.

It might be argued, however, that the drop in crime following displacements in the ruling elite may merely represent a decline in the efficiency of law enforcement agencies. The effects of discord surrounding the monarchy might have disrupted the administration of justice, thus producing a decrease in the number of cases brought into court. But Tout has shown that, despite the unrest among the barons in the council and the ineffectual authority of the king, the regular machinery of government ran smoothly—perhaps because there was less interference from the top.[4] By the fourteenth century there was a well-established bureaucracy whose best option in times of political unrest was to stay out of the squabbling and do their jobs effectively so that they would be retained. None of the alterations in the council brought about corresponding changes in the administrative personnel.[5] Even Isabella and Mortimer retained the servants of the late king.[6] At the worst period of misgovernment judges went on circuit, courts were held at Westminster or York, and records were kept "just as carefully as if all had been well with the state."[7] Indeed, during the period of 1315-1318 when the gaols were crowded with record numbers of suspects, the government was able to respond immediately and issue extra commissions of gaol delivery and have the justices visit counties as many as five times a year. The fluctuations in the number of crimes per year could not, therefore, represent solely a disruption of the central administration. Some local fluctuations and missing records in counties directly involved in the political maneuverings, however, might represent disruption of the local peacekeeping system.

Another question relevant to the effects of factional strife and state murders on crime is the extent to which these shifts of power interfered with everyday life or set an example of behavior. Aside from periods of civil war, changes among the ruling elite had very few repercussions among the people in the fields. Certainly, most people would know about the violence. The knights and gentry of the shire were frequently called to Parliament to ratify and confirm some power grab or to be told about a treason or a change in the succession. Word of such monumental events would quickly reach the countryside. Lionel, in his threatening letter, alluded to the murder of the Bishop of Exeter in London during the coup. People tended to identify with one side or another and even join in the rebellions if they took place in their territory. The London crowd was always very active in these matters. But did these events influence their own pattern of criminal behavior? Did they assume that if kings and barons could do these things, then it was all right for them as well? As Tout observed, "medieval society was always disorderly and effectiveness of government was so circumscribed that, just as good kings could not make earth an Eden, so bad kings had strictly limited opportunities of doing mischief."[8] The graphs of crimes (see figures 12-19) bear out this conclusion; during the period 1342-1348, when the government was more stable, the number of crimes increased markedly in most counties. Furthermore, with all the examples of political murders in the first third of the century, the proportion of homicides did not increase in relationship to other types of crime.

If the struggles for control over Edward II seldom correlated with peaks in crime, perhaps the long absences abroad of Edward III had more of an influence on the amount of crime. Two possible effects of the king's absence on the number of cases appearing in gaol delivery are either an increase in crime when the figurehead of justice was not present or a decrease in crime if the system for apprehending criminals became more inefficient during his absence.

Contemporaries reacted to the imminent departure of the king on campaigns with the fear that crime was bound to increase while he was away.[9] To quiet these apprehensions, Edward III responded to the urgings of Commons to reinstate the keepers of the peace and even gave them determining powers.[10] He also briefly experimented with making the local communities responsible for the maintenance of order by having them elect their own sheriffs and other officials.[11] Despite these precautions, chroniclers noted unusually serious outbreaks of crime during his first absence in 1338-1340.[12] There are many gaps in the series for these years, but of those counties having records, only Essex and Surrey show a peak of crime for those years. There is no reason that the king's absence should have been more disruptive to them than to other counties because they were near to the bureaucrats of Westminster who could keep an eye on their judicial system. More likely the highs in these two counties represent the presence of troops coming to London. The government was sufficiently worried about the state of the peace when the king planned another absence to recommend to the Commons that they discuss the problem in their sessions. Commons replied that the peace was well enough kept without additional measures.[13] The graphs show, however, that the number of crimes rose during the king's campaigns in the early 1340s. Thus, either the peace was being so well kept that more cases were brought into court or the king's absence or his returning troops resulted in more crime.

We have already dismissed the possibility that reforms brought about a sufficient change in efficiency to have a great influence on the volume of arrests. The impact of the king's absence on the amount of lawlessness cannot be measured. Although the government continued to function, as it did during the upsets of Edward II's reign, we do not know how great a role the physical presence of the symbol of justice played in deterring potential malefactors. Clearly, the absence of the king cannot be the only explanation for increased crime because Edward II was in the country during the abnormal peak in 1315-1318. It is also possible that the strain of carrying on a foreign war, rather than the absence of the king, was responsible for the rise in crime.

Although governmental crises had no clear influence on the number of crimes per year, they could have encouraged other types of crimes and another class of criminal. The powerlessness of the kings to control their barons and their reliance on them for indentured troops in times of war permitted the magnates to build up considerable armies of private retainers whom they put into livery. The Earl of Lancaster maintained a large force that he used at Boroughbridge in 1322 and had used previously in suppressing a revolt in Lancaster and in a private war with the Earl of Warenne.[14] The increase in organized crime resulting from these private armies and returning veterans will be discussed in the next section on effects of war. In addition to encouraging the problems of livery and maintenance the political disorders might have brought about increases in antisocial acts other than felonies. Weakness in the central government could encourage obstruction of justice, corruption of officials, and embezzlement of royal funds. These actions would, however, not fall within the scope of the present study. For the most part, however, the effect of political disruption on crime patterns is difficult to ascertain with any reliability.

WAR AND CRIME

Wars are frequently blamed for increases in crime because it is assumed that looting will occur in the areas disrupted by battles, that the absence of the father from the home will lead his children into delinquency, and, finally, that the veterans of wars return home with a taste for violence and pillaging. Men in the fourteenth century thought that wars were responsible for violence in the countryside. But some modern historians looking back on the composition of medieval armies and the nature of medieval warfare have speculated that the foreign wars might have brought greater peace to the English countryside because they drew of many of the unruly elements of society.

The English armies were recruited in a variety of ways.[15] The two means of recruitment that might have affected the keeping of the peace were the indenture system and the offer of pardons to felons who served in the army. In the indenture system, a noble, knight, or well-known captain contracted with the king to receive payment in exchange for raising troops for the king's campaigns. These troops were not always disbanded upon return to England but instead might be retained in the service of their leader through the practice of livery and maintenance. Outlaws and felons often took service in these troops because they could gain pardons for their crimes from the king in exchange for fighting for him.

Although some of the pay and provisions for the armies came from taxes and purveyance of goods in England, the soldiers made much of their profit and got a large part of their provisions from plundering the country they had invaded.[16] This type of military organization raises a number of questions for the study of crime. Did the foreign wars draw off the unruly elements or did they create more disturbers of the peace? Did veterans continue to make their living by plunder and violence when they returned to England? In addition to foreign wars, England experienced several battles on her native soil as a result of Scottish invasions and two civil skirmishes. Did these battles result in increased crimes of violence and plunder? Does the crime pattern in Yorkshire, which experienced civil war and Scottish invasions, differ from that of the more undisturbed counties?

The dispute between Scotland and England, which led to the Scottish invasions, arose from England's desire to keep Scotland under its hegemony coming into conflict with Robert Bruce's plans to carve out an independent kingdom. Although Scottish raids were almost a continual threat during these fifty years, there were only three periods of serious fighting. The first of these was 1314-1318. In an attempt to curtail the raids, Edward II led an army into Scotland that met a defeat at Bannockburn in 1314, opening the way for unhindered Scottish raids as far south as Richmond in Yorkshire. Five years elapsed before England again tried to check the Scots. Once again the Scots were victorious. While the English army was occupied with a siege of Berwick in 1319, Robert Bruce sent an expeditionary force toward York, where the queen and the central courts were in residence. The Archbishop of York attempted to stop the Scots at Mynton-in-Swaledale with a motley force of clerics, peasants, and townsmen. Routing the untrained Yorkshiremen, the Scots pushed on to Pontefract. This success of the Scots forced Edward into a truce.

The expiration of the truce in 1322 brought another wave of Scottish raids into Yorkshire. Edward made a bid to stop them but soon withdrew when famine and pestilence devastated his troops. Despairing of any protection from the English king, the Yorkshire lords, abbots, and townsmen independently sought peace terms with the Scots. As it was now obvious that the war with Scotland was lost, Edward concluded a thirteen-year truce with Robert Bruce that relieved the north from invasions. After one attempt at fighting the Scots, Isabella and Mortimer agreed to a peace treaty renouncing all English claims to Scotland.

Edward III resented the dishonorable peace and soon broke it by supporting Edward Balliol's claim to the Scottish throne. This action initiated the third period of Scottish wars. Moving his government to York to be nearer Scotland, Edward carried on a series of campaigns between 1332-1337. The wars were costly and, aside from the battle of Halidon Hill in 1333, unsuccessful.

For Yorkshire the Scottish raids and the Lancastrian revolt meant repeated pillage, quartering of troops on the country, purveyance of goods, and levies of local men for the army. In the accepted manner of behavior for armies of the day, the Scots carried off everything movable, burnt buildings and crops, and murdered all who tried to stop them.[17] The only way to avoid the ruinous raids was to pay a fee to the Scots. The raids were so devastating for Yorkshire that its inhabitants had to be exempted from personal property taxes in 1319 and 1322. The North and West Ridings suffered most. Chief taxers of the tenth and the sixth in the North Riding reported that in one hundred and twenty-eight vills no taxable property had been found.[18]

Even the presence of English troops was a burden on the countryside. Although some supplies were brought up from the south, much had to be found in the surrounding countryside through purveyance or outright pillage. Furthermore, the armies brought many disreputable elements into the area. Two hundred of the soldiers who took part in the battle of Bannockburn were pardoned felons,[19] while at Halidon Hill a troop of felons were said to have turned the tide of the battle.[20] The king relied heavily upon Yorkshire men to serve in the armies against Lancaster and the Scots.[21] Thus, if fields were not destroyed by pillage or crops confiscated by native troops, planting might not be accomplished because the tillers were in the army. Perhaps some Yorkshire men, like their neighbors in Northumbria, forsook the plough and followed the Scottish example of ravaging the countryside.[22]

Since Yorkshire bore the brunt of both civil and Scottish wars, the other counties may be used for comparison in evaluating the effects of wars fought on native soil on the volume of crime. The graph of crimes for Yorkshire (figure 13) shows that during the first period of Scottish wars, from Bannockburn in 1314 to the battle of Mynton and the truce in 1319, there was a peak of crimes in Yorkshire. The increase, however, is also found in the other counties, so perhaps the invasions were only an additional irritant to the effects of famine and political crisis that also occurred during these years.

Under the double disaster of civil war at Boroughbridge and fresh and deeply penetrating Scottish raids in 1322, there is a slight decrease in reported crimes in Yorkshire—unless the peak of 1324 represents delayed results. It is possible that the disturbing influence of war prevented normal apprehension and trial of suspects or that the worst effects of the fighting were not felt until a year after the event, when food from interrupted planting or destroyed crops would be most needed. Herefordshire also experienced a sharp rise in this period that may have been related to the civil war. But the number of crimes per year in Norfolk and Northamptonshire also rose in 1323. Both these counties were far removed from the fighting, thus suggesting that the cause of these increases is found elsewhere.

Edward III's Scottish campaigns of 1332-1337, which he conducted from York, coincided with a high level of crime in Yorkshire. The continual presence of troops and levies of Yorkshire men, in addition to the temptations arising from additional wealth brought in by the government at York, must have been factors leading to the high level of crime during these years. In 1334 Edward complained to the mayor and the bailiffs of the city "that several malefactors and disturbers of the peace . . . making assemblies and illicit gatherings both by day and by night in York, its suburbs and neighborhood, go armed and lie in wait for those coming and going to and from that city, and staying there, both the king's ministers and other lieges, and beat, wound and rob them."[23] The problems were peculiar to Yorkshire, for the other counties were generally enjoying a period of low crime.

In general, the influence on crime of fighting in home territory is very difficult to estimate. Dips in the graph, as in 1314, may simply represent the disruption of normal law enforcement procedure, which permitted many felons to escape detection (see table 12). During a raid it was difficult to say whether it was a Scot or a neighbor who drove off the sheep or stole the cow. In two Yorkshire cases in 1321 one man was accused of stealing a cartload of goods worth 40s. and another of robbing a man of 40s. in the turmoil following the retreat of the Scots.[24] Since the graph does show that peaks of crime in Yorkshire generally coincided with periods of fighting, we cannot share Tout's optimism that the peasants were so used to wars that "the marchings and countermarchings of rival armies . . . were not in themselves sufficient to throw the land into confusion."[25] Although there were often other crimes occurring simultaneously, wars must have contributed to the unrest. No community could take heavy taxation for the wars, destruction of crops, driving off of people and cattle, and burning of buildings easily in stride.[26]

In addition to fighting the Scots on home territory, England also became embroiled in a war with France—the Hundred Years' War. The first phase of the war began in 1337 when the French king declared Gascony confiscate and Edward III claimed the right to the French crown. The war was slow in starting. Edward took an army to Flanders and made a series of raids but did not succeed in engaging the enemy. The English navy was more successful. Early in the war France had harassed the English coast and had even burnt Southampton in 1338. The English fleet finally defeated the French at Sluys in 1340. Meanwhile, the inconclusive land war and the debts Edward incurred maintaining his army in Flanders led to a short truce in 1340. By 1342 Edward was fighting in Brittany. Another short truce in 1343 permitted Edward to return to England and make preparations for a larger campaign. The next period of major campaigns, 1346-1347, brought Edward two important victories: the battle of Crécy and the fall of Calais. Peace lasted for nearly a decade after Calais was taken.

The effects of Edward III's foreign wars on England have long been a subject of active debate. The optimistic view argues that the Hundred Years' War stimulated England's economy and brought in wealth through ransoms of French nobles. The war was no financial burden since French possessions bore most of the cost.[27] The armies, far from removing the gainfully employed, drew on unruly nobles and their liveried retainers, vagrants, and felons who wished to obtain pardons by fighting for the king. Although some felons returned to claim pardons, many must have died abroad.[28] Following this argument one would conclude that the number of crimes would decline during the war years.

The opponents of this optimistic view argue that the recruiting drew off 10 percent of the adult male population, which was a heavy burden for an already declining population.[29] The drain on men included many knights, who had served as keepers of the peace or in other local administrative positions, as well as craftsmen such as fletchers, carpenters, smiths, miners, and members of the merchant marine. In addition, the heavy taxes and goods required in purveyance absorbed surpluses that might otherwise have been put to profit and reduced those peasants at subsistance level to begging.[30] This argument sees the foreign wars as having essentially a disturbing influence on society, thus leading to increased disorders. Returning troops, it is argued, added to the lawlessness. With a truce or peace, many of the outlaws returned to England and pursued the same sort of life. In addition, many men, not yet indicted for crime in England, learned pillage, rape, and murder in the wars.[31] Nobles returned with liveried troops that they used to commit crimes or to violently conclude private quarrels, even against the king.[32] And the villagers, oppressed by recruitments, taxes, and purveyances, may well have turned to crime. At least two unwilling recruits rebelled directly through homicide.

> John son of Simon Robert of Cold Ashby, the constable, was found slain at Cold Ashby. He had a wound through the body made with a lance. The jury says that Richard son of William Clerk of Crick and John son of Richard of Ashby were enlisted to serve the king against the Scots at Northampton, and on their way, they came to Ashby, where they found the said John, who had enlisted them. A quarrel ensued in which John was killed. The two assailants fled to the Church of Ashby. The recruits of Northampton arrived and removed them from the church.

In the end they were forced to go along with the army.[33]

Contemporaries certainly blamed the war for the lawlessness of the day. A statute directed the justices of the peace to "inform themselves . . . touching all those who had been plunderers or robbers beyond the seas and are now returned and go wandering and will not work as they were used to."[34] Special measures were apparently needed, for the counties of Wiltshire, Berkshire and Hampshire informed the king that a body of returned soldiers had formed an armed band with other criminals and rode in warlike array robbing, ransoming, and maiming inhabitants.[35]

The evidence from the graphs of the number of crimes per year supports the view that the Hundred Years' War had a deleterious effect on law and order. As an average, the incidence of crime was much higher during the French campaigns of 1342-1347 than they were in the ten preceding years in all counties with records. Even if the War was not the sole cause of the peaks of crime during this period, it certainly cannot be argued that the campaigns brought peace to the English countryside. During the campaigns of Crécy and Calais in 1345-1346, when the largest armies of the Hundred Years' War were shipped across the seas,[36] the number of crimes rose dramatically in Yorkshire and Norfolk.

The gaol delivery rolls, unfortunately, reveal very little on the complaint that returning soldiers formed into armed bands to terrorize the countryside. Since veterans are not identified, the only indication the records can provide is a possible increase in organized crime. The percentage of crimes committed by criminal associations was 55.7 percent between 1340 and 1348, which was quite close to the normal percentage. Of the counties Norfolk, Essex, and Somerset all had large increases in the proportion of crimes committed by criminal associations from 1345 to 1348. This may well represent troops returning through their ports. The southwest of England was particularly plagued with the problem. Many of the activities of these bands were handled through oyer and terminer. There are references in the patent rolls to the depredations of these groups, which included attacks on fairs and on law enforcement officials.[37]

Contemporaries believed that abuses in granting pardons to felons were largely responsible for the increased disorders. In a petition to the king and council in 1347, the Commons complained:

> Many murders, woundings, robberies, homicides, rapes, and other felonies and misdeeds without number are done and maintained in the kingdom because the evil doers are granted charters of pardon . . . to the great destruction of the people. May it please the king to provide a remedy through a statute . . . and order that charters of pardon not be granted without the assent of Parliament.[38]

This protest was made after three previous statutes had failed to remedy the problem.[39] The language of the statutes also reflects the general view that "Murderers, Robbers, and other Felons, be greatly encouraged to offend, by reason that Charters of Pardon . . . have been so lightly granted"[40] . . .

The recruitment of outlaws had two advantages for the king: they had experience with arms and were generally courageous and; it was hoped, their removal diminished the number of criminals at large in England.[41] The assumption underlying pardons was that felons could expiate past deeds by service to the king. As a rule, pardons were not granted until the service had been rendered and attested to by the leaders under whom they had served. Often conditions were specified such as that the felon must stand trial if anyone proceeded against him; that he find people to insure his future good behavior; and that he serve the king for a year if called upon. On these conditions the felon was discharged of all felonies committed before the pardon and allowed to wander freely about the countryside.[42]

It is impossible to know what proportion of felons went into the army and, of those, how many lived to claim a charter. Some idea of the relationship between pardons and military service may be derived from H. J. Hewitt's survey for the years 1339-1340, when at least 850 charters of pardon were issued. In 1346-1347 several hundred grants were made for service in Scotland and France. From these figures Hewitt estimates that from 2 percent to 12 percent of the army consisted of outlaws. The proportion of murderers among the pardoned was considerably above three-fourths.[43]

Was contemporary opinion correct in placing the blame for increased lawlessness on pardoned felons? The gaol delivery rolls, unfortunately, give very little indication. A pardoned felon only stood trial if he was arrested again or if he turned himself over to the sheriff with his pardon. A test sample for Norfolk and Yorkshire did show that the percentage of cases involving pardons increased during the Scottish and French wars.[44] Yorkshire had proportionately more pardon cases because it had more men involved in wars with the Scots and the Lancastrian rebellion. A typical example of a pardon is the case of Walter Osborn of Holcham, John Bryd, John le Speller of Holcham, and John de Bylneye of Holcham, who were accused of piracy in 1327 but produced pardons stating that they had been of service to the king against the rebels and the Scots.[45]

Evidence from the gaol delivery rolls does not make any strong case for an increase of violence either during the fighting or during truces when veterans would be returning from the wars. Violent crimes are homicide, rape, robbery, burglary, and arson (those crimes normally accompanying pillage) as opposed to the nonviolent crimes of larceny, counterfeiting, receiving, and treason. As can be seen from table 9, the proportion of robberies and burglaries to other types of crime was greatest in the beginning of the century, so that war did not appear to be a significant factor. Homicides, however, did increase relative to other types of crimes during the war years. This is particularly interesting since modern studies have indicated this as well, particularly in circumstances where there are troop concentrations or

Table 9. *Percentage of the different types of crimes in five-year averages for all countries, 1300-1348.*

YEARS	LARCENY	BURGLARY	ROBBERY	HOMICIDE	RECEIVING	ARSON
1300-04	32.8	19.9	18.3	17.4	11.2	0.4
1305-09	49.5	18.6	5.2	21.6	4.1	1.0
1310-14	43.9	23.6	9.4	16.9	6.2	0.0
1315-19	38.7	33.2	9.3	10.8	7.3	0.7
1320-24	42.8	23.2	10.4	15.9	6.3	1.4
1325-29	34.4	22.9	15.2	21.5	5.0	1.0
1330-34	37.4	19.5	9.2	26.7	6.7	0.5
1335-39	36.3	19.5	8.0	28.8	5.4	2.0
1340-44	39.3	19.3	11.7	24.7	4.2	0.8
1345-48	42.0	22.3	6.6	25.2	3.5	0.4

a number of returning veterans. Britain in World War II saw a substantial increase of murder, and Monkkonen found a sharp rise in homicide in Columbus, Ohio, during and after the Civil War.[46]

The public of the day seemed more concerned about the effects of war on law and order than about arresting those who gave comfort to the enemy. Of all the cases read for this study, only thirty were indictments for spying.[47] Most of the cases came from Yorkshire during the period 1315-1318, when the Scottish raids were most damaging. The usual charge was spying for the Scots, but Andrew Duketyn of Ravenscar was accused of taking "diverse victuals from the kingdom of England on behalf of the Scots."[48] The accused were all English except for William Scot of Berwick-on-Tweed, who was taken at the port of Yarmouth in Norfolk and tried on November 26, 1313, on suspicion of treason. A Yorkshire woman, married to a Scot, and her daughter were also accused of spying.[49] It is tempting to conclude that then, as now, an enemy national was automatically suspect; but of the many Scots who must have come to the major trading center at Yarmouth, only one was arrested. Furthermore, jurors apparently did not bear a particular grudge against the Scots. When they appear in the records charged with other types of felonies, they were acquitted just as frequently as their English neighbors. Considering how frequently indicted spies were convicted, it is obvious that the villagers were not indifferent to the invasion.[50] One Wakefield villager sued another for slander for calling him "Robert Bruce."[51]

A better argument can be made for the effects of war on crime than political conditions. Political upheavals had little demonstrable effects on the country as a whole or its crime pattern, with the possible exception of Herefordshire. The periods of Scottish wars, 1314-1319, 1322-1323, and 1332-1337, all coincided with rises in crime in Yorkshire, but the famines must also have been a contributory factor. Crime also rose in most counties during the first phase of the Hundred Years' War (1342-1347). Although the hardships of war were probably not the only cause of the increases, war certainly did not siphon off all the unruly elements, leaving the countryside at peace. War also contributed to the problems of the nobles' households and gang activity in general and correlated with increased murder. The Commons were undoubtedly correct in their complaints about the increased horrors of gangs and pardoned felons who were the king's veterans. War, through taxation, purveyance, oppressive recruitment, and pillage, may also have reduced many of the peasantry to a level of poverty and anger that would lead them to make up their losses through criminal means. Taxes got more oppressive through the late 1330s and early 1340s when Edward started the Hundred Years' War. The high levels of crime in the fifth decade may reflect the effects of this oppression. Certainly Yorkshire suffered increased disorders in the second quarter of the century. Eastern England—Essex, Norfolk, Northamptonshire, and Surrey—also bore much of the costs of the wars and had troops passing through on the way to and from France.[52] The wars may have contributed to the crime problems here as well.

ECONOMIC AND DEMOGRAPHIC CHANGE AND CRIME

Because economic and demographic changes have a more measurable effect on the mass of people than political crises, their relationship to crime has been more widely researched. Some studies on the twentieth century have shown that serious crimes tend to increase during economic depressions and fall in periods of prosperity. Economic duress is also likely to cause an increase in crimes against property, especially burglary and robbery.[53] But these attempts to establish a relationship between economic conditions and crime have generally met with much criticism from both historians and criminologists, if not regarding the reliability of criminal statistics, then because of the complexity of economic factors and the existence of alternative, noneconomic explanations for changes in the pattern of crime.[54]

In spite of the hazards of the topic, I feel that two considerations justify a new look at the problem for the medieval period: (1) the relatively greater ease of tracing conditions of social unrest in the simpler circumstances of medieval rural society than in a complex industrial one, and (2) the existence of a large body of information connecting agrarian instability and demographic change in early fourteenth-century England.

Most previous studies have concentrated on the response of crime to economic conditions characteristic of an industrialized society and mostly within an urban setting. The complexity of modern industrial economics, with private and state programs to alleviate distress arising from periods of economic depression, make it difficult to measure the effects of business cycles on the mass of the population. Slumps in the relatively simpler agrarian economy of the Middle Ages, on the other hand, had a more immediate and noticeable effect on the peasant community since life was directly dependent on the outcome of the year's crops. There were few buffers for medieval peasants in years of economic hardship; if the crops were poor for them, they would also be poor for the charitable institutions.

Precisely because the effects of economic contraction on the peasantry of fourteenth-century England have been so well studied, it is an especially appropriate area in which to investigate the relationship between crime and short-run economic change. In a series of articles M. M. Postan and others have established a number of claims about the economic and demographic configuration of late medieval England and its effects on the peasant community. The Postan Thesis is a statement about the relationship between population and food production with its attendant social implications.[55] Briefly, Postan has argued that the population expansion of the twelfth and thirteenth centuries led, by the early fourteenth century, to serious food shortages in most parts of England. The situation was Malthusian; lack of grain and fertile soil on which to produce crops reduced many of the tenant population to living at the subsistence level. In such circumstances, even minor crop failures resulted in death for many people. After the Great Famine of 1315-1317 and the lesser one of 1322-1323, enough of the population had died to relieve the pressure on food resources with the result that grain prices were thereby lowered.

Although many poverty-stricken villagers undoubtedly perished from starvation during the lean years of the early fourteenth century, I would argue that others turned to illegal means of procuring food. Caught between the pincers of growing population and shrinking arable land, some peasants would certainly have turned to crime for a livelihood. Not only the extremely poor elements of peasant society but perhaps also those who experienced only relative deprivation supplemented their incomes feloniously. Overpopulation cut off many of the traditional "stop-gap" measures employed by the medieval poor: the overabundance of laborers made it difficult to find work; begging was probably of limited success under conditions of general food shortage; and service in the king's armies brought its own hazards. It is my contention that enough peasants were turning to criminal activity in those calamitous years of food scarcity to cause significant changes in the statistics of crime, such as we can reconstruct them. After the first quarter of the fourteenth century, however, when the pressure of population on resources was reduced, the volume of crimes would also decrease. In order to test this general hypothesis, three types of indices were studied: the annual volume of crime, the categories of goods stolen, and the types of crimes committed.

One might argue, of course, that rather than following the economic vicissitudes, crime followed the demographic pattern. If the number of crimes per capita remained more or less constant, then the crime curve would follow the population curve. Because demographic information for the first half of the fourteenth century is so imprecise, we cannot show changes by computing the number of crimes per capita per year. We can only compare the crime curve to a tentative population curve. The demographic pattern that Postan proposes is that of an already high and still expanding population at the end of the thirteenth century and the beginning of the fourteenth century with a halt in the population growth coming about the middle of the second decade of the fourteenth century. The easing off of the expansion was caused by general food shortages and particularly by the Great Famine of 1315-1317 and the lesser one of 1322-1323. By the second quarter of the century and before the Black Death in 1349 the population had leveled off at a size that could be maintained on the produce of the land. As table 10 shows, however, only Surrey had a pattern of high crime in 1300-1304 and a steady decrease through the first fifty years of the century. The other counties and the overall

Table 10. *Number of crimes in five-year averages, 1300-1348.*

YEARS	NORFOLK	NORTHANTS.	YORKS.	HUNTS.	ESSEX	SOMS.	SURREY	HEREFS.	8-COUNTY AVERAGE
1300-1304	58	28	61	15	87	82	50	42	53
1305-1309	51	47	*	22	18	*	*	10	30
1310-1314	64	40	74	*	26	*	22	7	39
1315-1319	185	50	236	*	151	159	29	62	128
1320-1324	120	52	128	*	72	*	21	72	77
1325-1329	104	48	114	8	69	38	10	55	56
1330-1334	45	48	163	16	24	28	16	69	51
1335-1339	31	*	98	6	33	42	9	*	37
1340-1344	58	*	171	16	47	75	18	*	64
1345-1348	61	*	230	4	62	79	*	22	73

* Insufficient data.

241

pattern showed a low level of indictments in the first part of the century shooting up in 1315-1319 and remaining fairly high until the 1330s when it dropped. The number of indictments rose again in the late 1340s. The distribution of crimes does not, therefore, strictly follow the proposed demographic curve. Other factors must be looked to in order to explain the peaks and sloughs in the crime pattern.

Figures 12-19 indicate that the changes in the price of wheat correspond very closely with those in the yearly indictments in all counties; so that it is agricultural production that will provide the key to understanding fluctuations in crimes for the early fourteenth century. It is striking that when Postan and Titow plotted deaths among small landholders in the early fourteenth century they found that deaths tended to rise and fall with the price of wheat.[56] Thus the Malthusian situation that Postan suggested had a major social impact both demographically and in social interactions. Although the slump in agricultural production started at different times in different areas of the country, it spread over most of England by the third decade of the century. Declining productivity of the soil was the culprit. Land reclamation had slowed down or stopped by the turn of the century. Marginal land that had been reclaimed earlier deteriorated in productivity. Population expanded nonetheless so that even the smallest adverse growing conditions raised the price of grain and brought real misery to many.

Taking an overview of the first quarter of the fourteenth century, there appears to be a particularly high correlation between the number of criminal cases and wheat prices at a time when population pressure on food supplies was most acute. Lumping together the data from the eight counties yields a correlation coefficient of 0.67 for the period 1330-1335. A further look at the graphs adds to this statistical picture. Norfolk is the best example because it has both the most complete records and the most accurate price data. Figure 12 shows that the number of crimes per year in Norfolk very closely followed the price of wheat. The slight lag in response is, of course, due to the judicial lag of about one year. The period from 1300 to the beginning of the famine of 1315 shows marked fluctuations in both the price of wheat and the incidence of crime. The slight drop in the price of wheat between 1300-1303 is matched by a similar decline in crimes. When the price of wheat rises in 1308-10, crime also rises. In 1311 both drop and remain fairly low until the famine drives up both. During this period, the correlation coefficient between wheat prices and crime was 0.76.

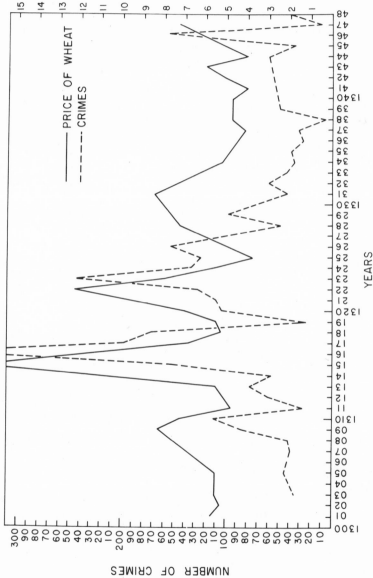

Figure 12. *Comparison of the number of crimes per year and the price of wheat in Norfolk, 1300–1348. (Based on Sir William Beveridge price data at the London School of Economics.)*

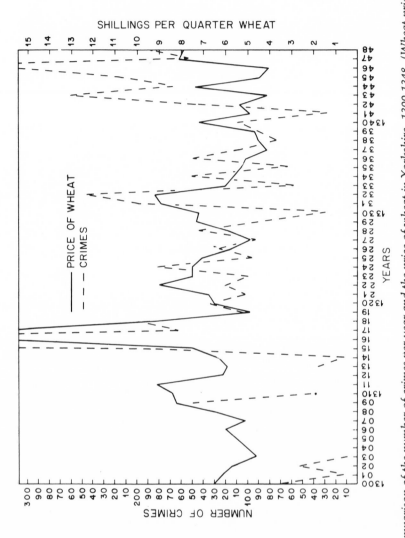

Figure 13. *Comparison of the number of crimes per year and the price of wheat in Yorkshire, 1300-1348. (Wheat prices based on Postan and Titow, "Heriots," table 1. Prices for 1322-1324 from Titow, 98.)*

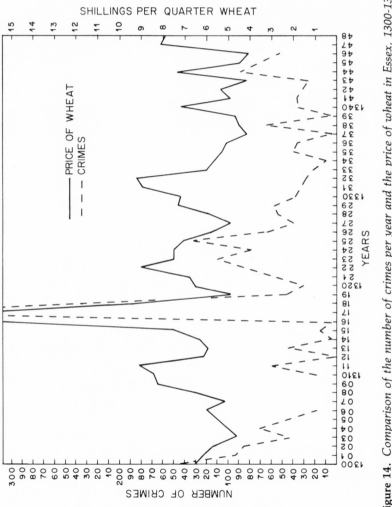

Figure 14. *Comparison of the number of crimes per year and the price of wheat in Essex, 1300-1348.*

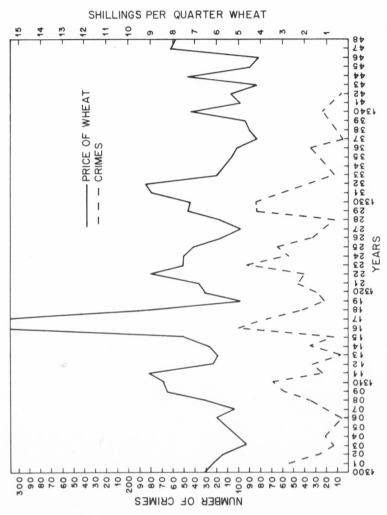

Figure 15. Comparison of the number of crimes per year and the price of wheat in Northamptonshire, 1300-1348.

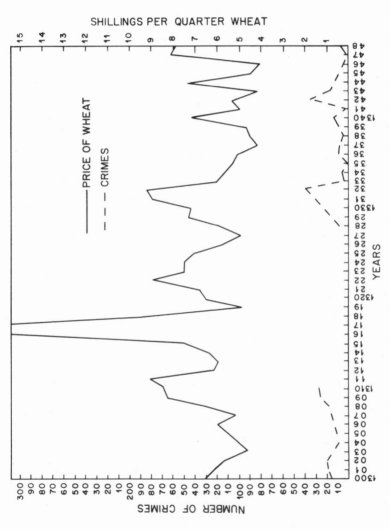

Figure 16. *Comparison of the number of crimes per year and the price of wheat in Huntingdonshire, 1300-1348.*

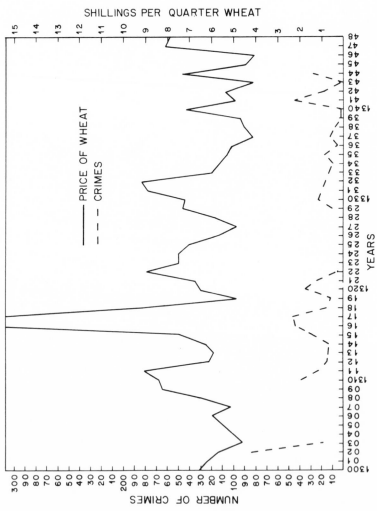

Figure 17. *Comparison of the number of crimes per year and the price of wheat in Surrey, 1300-1348.*

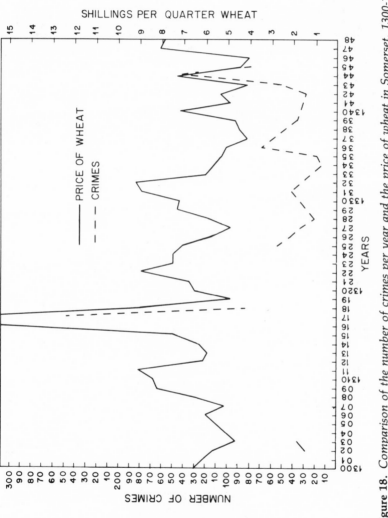

Figure 18. *Comparison of the number of crimes per year and the price of wheat in Somerset, 1300-1348.*

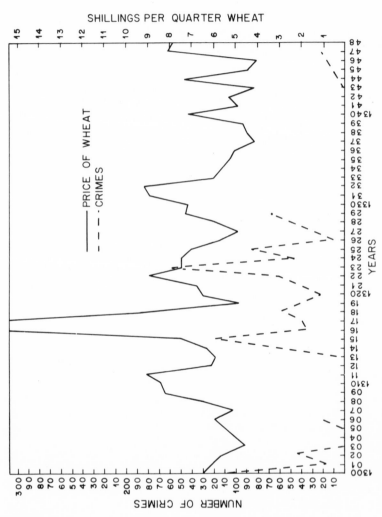

Figure 19. *Comparison of the number of crimes per year and the price of wheat in Herefordshire, 1300-1348.*

Although the evidence is not as consistent, Northamptonshire, Yorkshire, Essex, Surrey, Herefordshire, and Huntingdonshire exhibit a similar pattern, although Surrey, Herefordshire, and Essex differ from the general pattern in that they start out very high in the first years of the century. The close correspondence between the volume of crime and the price of wheat during this decade and a half suggests that the population did respond to famine conditions by turning to crime. Thus there were a series of minor crime waves.

The correlation between the two variables continued close in the crisis years of the Great Famine of 1315-1317 and remained close through the lesser famine of 1322-1323 and roughly through 1325. The effects of famine on crime are easier to measure than those of general economic contraction, for the famines occupy a closely defined period of years (1315-1317, 1322-1323), rather than the long span covering the gradual decline of prosperity. Of the two famines, the first was by far the more severe. Called the "Great Famine" because it spread all over Europe north of the Alps, it was the result of abnormally heavy rainfall and flooding.[57] The chroniclers were almost universal in their observations of the unusual weather conditions.[58] Torrential rains that began in May 1315 continued throughout the summer and autumn. During the next two years harvests were repeatedly bad. The spring rains hindered sowing of oats and barley; the summer rains prevented proper ripening of the grain; and the autumn planting of wheat could not be accomplished. The crop failure forced the price of wheat up from an average of 5s. per quarter to 20s. and higher. The cost of peas, oats, barley, malt, and salt rose proportionately.[59] Because of the grain shortage, livestock was killed and eaten so that it too became scarce. In addition to the woes of famine, cattle and sheep died in large numbers from an epidemic of murrain.[60]

The chronicler Johannes de Trokelowe described in lurid detail the effects of this horrible famine on the people of Suffolk.

Lay magnates as well as religious drew back tightly on their curias, withdrew their customary alms, and reduced their *familia*. Thenceforth these people, who were dismissed, became accustomed to a meager life: they did not know how to dig; they felt ashamed to beg; and because they were unsuited to a life of little food and drink they became parched and thus were led to murder and rapine. The effects of all these things were that the unfaithful did not permit the faithful to live in peace . . . daily many . . . were strangled in thieves' ambushes . . . Horsemeat was so scarce that fat dogs were stolen and many asserted that men as well as women secretly ate their young and strangers . . . Even gaoled thieves devoured, half-alive, recent arrivals among themselves.[61]

In addition to the suffering resulting from the scarcity of grain, people developed dysentery, acute fever, and putrid sore throat.[62] The number of dead was so great that the living, who were weakened with hunger and sickness, could not bury them all.[63] Trokelowe described seeing dirty dead bodies in the wards and lanes of Suffolk.[64]

Another effect of the famine that Trokelowe observed was an increase of crime in the countryside. The members of the lords' households, who had been turned out into the streets, did not know how to earn a living and so resorted to murder and rapine. Trokelowe also claimed that thieves' ambushes became a daily occurrence.[65] H. S. Lucas made an effort to check the veracity of Trokelowe's account by noting the increase in commissions of oyer and terminer enrolled on the patent rolls, but they are not a reliable indicator.[66]

The famine of 1322-1323 was not so severe as the Great Famine and therefore has not been as well studied. Of the chroniclers, only Higden mentioned that Edward II tried to lead an army against the Scots but famine and disease among his troops in Yorkshire forced him to abandon his campaign.[67]

The gaol delivery rolls give very dramatic evidence of a crime wave for the famine years. With the exception of Surrey the number of crimes per year in all the counties for which there is evidence rose dramatically during the Great Famine. Both figures 12-19 and table 10 show that 1315-1319 were extremely high years for crime. The high point was reached in 1316-1317 when crimes increased as much as 200 percent over the previous decade and a half for some counties. Between 1315-1319 crimes increased 223 percent over the average number of crimes for 1300-1314 in Norfolk, 29 percent in Northamptonshire, 247 percent in Yorkshire, 243 percent in Essex, 94 percent in Somerset, and 24 percent in Herefordshire. As the figures show, the volume of crimes increased as the price of wheat went up and fell again with the good harvest of 1319. The return to low grain prices was short-lived, for again with the milder famine of 1322-1323 prices and crime rose in those counties for which there is evidence. The overall correlation coefficient for the famine years was 0.68. For Norfolk, for which there is the best evidence, it was 0.95.

The hardships that the peasantry endured during the famine years are shown not only by the increase in cases recorded in gaol delivery but also in a variety of actions that appear in other court records. For instance, manorial rolls from the famine period evidence a great increase in petty thefts and misdemeanors. Such cases as neighbors stealing vegetables at night or that of Thomas Tailor of Bridgehouse, who broke into the oven of John of Rodes and stole rye bread worth 4d.,[68] seem to indicate the desperate acts of the hungry. Nor do we have to rely solely upon Trokelowe for an understanding of the suffering of prisoners. In the summer of 1316 twenty-three people died in Northampton Castle gaol from a lack of food and drink or from stomach disorders probably arising from starvation. All these people had been imprisoned for thefts.[69] Courts at all levels were busy handling the increased cases. In Wakefield the tourn had to process so many burglary and larceny indictments in 1316 that two juries were required.[70] Perhaps crime was only one way to find food or money in those lean years, for Wakefield manor court was also busy hearing debt and trespass cases. From 1306 to 1313 the average number of debt and trespass cases was 108 per year, in the famine years of 1315-1317 it rose to 222 a year, with 1316 being the most active year.[71] Possibly, when food was scarce, creditors tried to save themselves at the expense of debtors.

The jurors of the hundreds did not react to the increased disorder by drastically increasing the number of convictions. While they did convict a greater percent of the suspects, they seemed content simply to indict the suspects rather than hang them. The crisis did not make them depart from their usual behavior in enforcing the law. Certainly, the jurors were aware of the misery of their fellow villagers during the famine and, as some of the records show, acquitted people for stealing because they were starving.[72] One of these men, Peter le Sknekere, had broken into the house of Godfrey of Geyton and stolen goods worth 2s. 6d. The jurors recommended that the burglary be excused because Peter was suffering from *fame et inopia* at the time of the felony.[73]

After the famine years of the first quarter of the century, the incidence of crime and the price of grain began to level off at a point lower than the pre-famine years. The rise in crime in all counties in the 1340s may, as we speculated, represent the effects of the Hundred Years' War. From 1325 through 1348 grain prices dropped as did population. With fewer people alive after the famines, the terrible crush on resources was reduced. Not only wheat prices slumped during the fourth and fifth decades, but also agricultural prices on products such as legumes, meat, and dairy products. At the same time, wages and the cost of nonagricultural products rose.[74] The agrarian recession had different effects on different segments of the peasant society. For the peasants living on small holdings and near subsistence level, the halt in population expansion, the lowering of land prices, and the rise in wages they received for their labor meant an easing of their situation. For the peasants who had sufficient surplus to sell their wheat and buy industrial goods or hire laborers, the recession was a hardship.[75] These more substantial peasants were receiving less money for their crops while they were paying more money for their equipment and tools.[76]

The effects on the volume of crime of such a gradual change in economic conditions is very hard to measure. Although the economic contraction caused hardships to some segments in the peasant community, it was not as desperate as the circumstances surrounding the famine. Furthermore, in some areas a local industry such as cloth production helped to alleviate the misery. If we look at figure 12, the graph comparing the annual incidence of crime and the prices of wheat per quarter in Norfolk, we see that, aside from the peak in 1346, the level of crime was very low during the period of low wheat prices. The agricultural recession apparently did not force more people into crime in Norfolk. The pattern of crime in Yorkshire (figure 13), however, contradicts the Norfolk evidence, for the level of crime remained very high, despite fluctuations, during the fourth and fifth decades of the fourteenth century. Perhaps Yorkshire suffered more than Norfolk from economic contraction, but it must be borne in mind that this period also coincided with the presence of the central government and troops in Yorkshire, continued Scottish raids, and the first phase of the Hundred Years' War. Norfolk, on the other hand, had always been a more flourishing agricultural area and had a developing woolen industry at Worstead that may have helped to relieve some of the hardship. The other counties for which there is evidence also tended to even out with only a few sharp increases in the 1330s that may indicate local responses to particular conditions or simply reflect unevenness in reporting of crimes. For those who survived the famine, it was now easier to make a living without breaking the law.

In general, the correlation between grain prices and the annual incidence of crime is very strong. For the total data the correlation coefficient was 0.71 (significance level 0.001). Of the counties, only

Herefordshire showed a weak crimes-price relationship with a correlation coefficient of 0.14. Norfolk was the highest with 0.74; Northamptonshire, 0.60; Yorkshire, 0.48; Huntingdonshire, 0.45, Essex, 0.53; Somerset, 0.73; and Surrey, 0.30.[77]

The evidence indicates that the most plausible explanation for the fluctuations in the number of crimes per year was changes in the price of grain. In the first quarter of the century even minor increases in the price of grain were accompanied by increased crime. In the famines of 1315-1317 and 1322-1323 crimes rose dramatically along with the increased grain prices. When population eased off in the second quarter of the century and the price of grain also was reduced, crimes decreased. Those counties such as Herefordshire, Yorkshire, and Surrey that had weaker correlations probably had other factors influencing their crime pattern: Herefordshire was heavily involved in the political struggles of the 1320s and early 1330s; Yorkshire experienced invasions from the Scots and the disruptions of having the king's troops and government in the county.

The influence of economic change is measurable not only by fluctuations in the volume of crime but also by the variety of goods stolen and the types of crimes committed. In some respects the goods stolen is the most sensitive indicator of all, because the data are not subject to the problems of missing records and because thieves always steal those items that are most in demand and that bring the highest prices from receivers. Table 11 gives a very good indication of those goods most valued by medieval thieves and the periods when some of these became more or less popular.

As one would expect from earlier chapters, livestock was the most typical theft. Although the percentage stolen fluctuates over the course of the half-century, these changes bear little relationship to economic changes except perhaps for the high in 1315-1319. The other items on the table, however, varied in popularity with the price movements of the first half of the century. While grain prices were high and there was widespread suffering, foodstuffs (particularly grain), clothing, and household goods were stolen. Throughout the first quarter of the fourteenth century, foodstuffs made up 13.9 percent of the stolen goods, but after 1324 they dropped to 9.9 percent. The highest percentage of foodstuffs stolen was, predictably, in the years of the Great Famine. Clothing and household goods had a similar pattern, starting at 9.1 percent for 1300-1324 and dropping to 6.3 percent after that period.

Table 11. *Percentage of the types of goods stolen in the eight counties, 1300-1348.*

Goods	Norfolk	Yorks.	Northants.	Hunts.	Essex	Soms.	Surrey	Herefs.
Clothing and household	9.7	6.0	11.3	17.3	7.2	6.4	7.3	7.3
Industrial products	6.0	2.4	2.4	7.5	1.7	2.6	3.8	1.8
Cloth	22.0	10.0	11.2	8.3	20.2	6.6	12.3	14.4
Valuables and money	11.7	10.3	11.3	2.2	18.2	12.0	12.9	19.2
Food and grain	12.5	15.7	9.2	12.8	12.1	16.0	11.2	15.5
Livestock	38.1	55.6	54.6	51.9	40.6	56.4	52.5	41.8
Total	100.0	100.0	100.0	100.0	100.0	100.0	100.0	100.0

With the easing of population pressure and the fall of grain prices after about 1325, the just-mentioned items declined somewhat in popularity while industrial goods and luxury items (money and jewels) became more sought after by thieves. Industrial products such as cloth and tools amounted to only 13 percent of the goods stolen in the first part of the century but went up to 20 percent in the period of recovery. There was a similar increase in the percentage of luxury items stolen—from 8 percent to 13 percent. Genicot notes in his analysis of price movements in the fourteenth century that these items rose in price as grain values fell. He speculated that the prices on these goods were driven up either because the wages of laborers employed in making them rose at the same time or because the response to the passing of the years of hardship and famine was to spend the sudden surplus on small luxuries and improved equipment.[78]

Periods of economic setback could have influenced the types of crimes committed as well as the goods stolen. During the period of material privation in the early fourteenth century, one would expect crimes involving theft (larceny, burglary, robbery, and receiving) to increase over other types of crimes. As figure 20 shows, there was a definite tendency for this to happen. The peak for property crimes was reached in the period of the Great Famine at 88.5 percent. After 1329 the percentage of thefts dropped considerably and remained low. One might expect that with the dearth, violent property crimes such as burglary and robbery would increase over simple larceny because goods were more carefully guarded. Table 9 does show that burglary reached its highest point in 1315-1319, but robbery did not. The lean years of the first quarter of the century lead to more thefts generally and to the theft of those goods that could be converted to food.

From the Lay Subsidies of 1334 it is possible to rank the wealth of the various counties in England and thereby determine if wealthy counties attracted more criminals. Norfolk paid £38.9 per thousand acres and was ranked third in wealth. Huntingdonshire, paying £27.6, ranked tenth; Northamptonshire's £26.3 ranked twelfth, Somerset's £19.3 ranked twenty-third; Essex's £18.5 ranked twenty-fifth; Surrey's £17.3 ranked twenty-eighth. Yorkshire was divided into its three ridings for the purposes of its assessment. The North and West Ridings paid £7.0 and £6.5, respectively, and were ranked thirty-sixth and thirty-seventh—two of the poorest regions in England. The East Riding paid £22.2 and was ranked sixteenth. On the average, Yorkshire paid £21.5 per thousand square acres.[79]

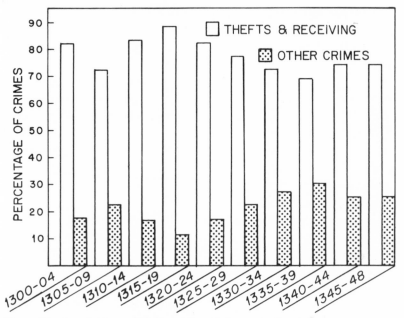

Figure 20. *Comparison of thefts and receiving and other crimes.*

Since the population figures are not available to assess the relative frequency of crime in each county, I have used the number of acres in the counties to have some constant reference point for purposes of comparison. The number of crimes per thousand acres in the various counties shows no relationship to the wealth of the counties. Norfolk, the wealthiest county, had an annual average of 0.06 crimes per thousand acres. Huntingdonshire and Essex had the same number although they ranked tenth and twenty-fifth, respectively. Surrey (0.05 per thousand acres) and Yorkshire (0.04 per thousand acres) were among the poorer counties. The high counties were Herefordshire (0.08 per thousand acres) and Somerset and Northamptonshire (both 0.07 per thousand acres). This group included a range from the moderately wealthy to one of the poorest counties. Wealth, therefore, did not attract criminals nor did poverty in a county create a greater need to make a living through criminal means. The distribution of crimes per acre does not even coincide with the suggested population distribution presented in chapter 2. Norfolk was certainly the most populous county of the fourteenth century, but it had only a moderate amount of crime, whereas Herefordshire, which was sparsely settled, had the highest amount of crime. The distribution of crime indicates that the upset political and social conditions of the west Midlands areas and the southwest were more responsible for the higher density of crime there than were economic conditions.

The types of goods stolen in the different counties also indicates something of the economic influences on crime. All the counties experienced the theft of livestock most frequently, but the percentage was particularly high in Yorkshire, Northamptonshire, Huntingdonshire, Somerset, and Surrey, thus reflecting the emphasis on herding in those counties. In Herefordshire and Essex, which had much herding but also more robbery than most counties, valuables were more frequently stolen than in other counties. The development of the woolen industry in Norfolk and Essex may be seen in the greater percentage of cloth stolen. Huntingdonshire seems to have had a particularly materialistic group of thieves, for they stole more clothing, household goods, and industrial products than were stolen in any of the other counties. Again, the types of goods stolen is a good indicator of economic conditions, for the avarice of thieves follows the market economy.

A final indicator of economic conditions within a particular county is the percentage of thefts (larceny, burglary, and robbery) committed there. Norfolk's crime pattern was dominated by theft—85 percent of all indictments were for theft. Homans' speculation on inheritance laws and landholding in East Anglia may help to explain the extremely high percentage of property crime in Norfolk. Partible inheritance, he argues, broke the land up into units too small to support a family. Norfolk, therefore, early on developed a woolen industry so that families could supplement their insufficient income with a cottage industry.[80] It could also be true that families turned to theft in order to supplement their incomes as well. In the 1381 Peasants' Revolt the Norfolk populace rioted not so much against the taxes and manorial oppressions as they went on a looting binge committing numerous burglaries and robberies under the guise of revolution.[81] The materialistic nature of the Norfolk revolt seemed to be an extension of an already existing mode of criminal behavior that generalized to mob action in 1381. Essex, Surrey, and Somerset also had fairly high levels of property crime (78.3, 79.1, and 76.7 percent, respectively). Essex had the inheritance pattern of Norfolk but did not have the dense population so that the effects of land division were not as severe. The revolts in both Essex and Surrey centered more on the issue of oppression, but their revolutionaries did some looting as well.

259

Herefordshire, Northamptonshire, Yorkshire, and Huntingdonshire (71.5, 69.7, 67.7, and 51.2 percent respectively) tended to have more crimes against the person in relationship to property crimes. Again, the political upsets in at least the first three counties might explain the greater homicide.

In conclusion, the best explanations for changes in the pattern of crime in fourteenth-century England were economic changes and war. In the first quarter of the fourteenth century the number of crimes rose and fell with the price of grain. The Malthusian conditions of expanding population on lands with shrinking productivity meant that many people died of starvation during these twenty-five years while others turned to crime to see them through the crisis. During the Great Famine of 1315-1317 crimes rose as dramatically as the price of grain. When grain prices went down in the 1330s, so too did the number of crimes. By the late 1340s the number of crimes per year again rose although the price of wheat did not. Probably the problems of war—heavy taxation, returning veterans from the continental wars, pardoned felons roaming the countryside, increased practice of livery and maintenance—contributed to the crime peak for those years. Certainly, Yorkshire and Herefordshire, which were most directly involved in the civil war, political struggles, and invasions of the Scots, show a somewhat different distribution of crime than the other counties. The influence of war can also be seen in the proportional increase in homicide in the second quarter of the century. The first quarter, with its problems of food shortage and famine, had more thefts. The types of goods stolen also indicated economic changes. Foodstuffs and grain were more popular items to steal in the first quarter of the century, but when the price of grain fell and industrial products became more expensive, the thieves shifted their preference accordingly. While economic changes correlated very highly with fluctuations in crime and a strong case can be made for the influence of war on crime, political unrest did not seem to modify the behavior of people in the countryside. The political struggles were mostly in the upper echelons of society: the villagers went on indicting and trying suspects and the central court justices were routinely there to hear the cases and pass sentence.

Chapter Eight

The Impact of Crime

on Fourteenth-Century Rural Society

FOURTEENTH-CENTURY rural society was a status conscious one in which there were different social groups vying for control over the local government and economic resources. Although the form of agriculture and the problems of survival forced a good deal of cooperation on the inhabitants, there were also great points of friction that broke out into criminal actions between residents. Conflicts that arose in the competition for power and survival led not only to crime but also to the manipulation of the judicial system: those who had the power used it for their own self-aggrandizement. To sociologists this is more familiar in the guise of conflict theory and refers to the use of law as an instrument of social control.

The village or small-town community was the basic unit for social interactions, for law enforcement, and for producing tensions that would lead to criminal actions. With the exception of robbery, most crimes were local in nature. Larceny and burglary were committed by people who lived in the same village or within a radius that would have permitted frequent contact between the participants in crime. The victims and accused may have had arguments over property that they were settling through felonious acts or they may have simply known who had goods worth stealing. Homicides were also a community phenomenon. Neighbors, rather than family, engaged in the homicidal drama. Most of the murders were the result of arguments that flared up on the spur of the moment or arose *ex odio antiquo*—out of long-standing dislike. The homicides took place in the village fields or in the village streets where men stopped to complain and exchange angry words.

That tensions should arise in the community is hardly surprising given the close contact that life in the village demanded. The strips in the open fields were next to each other, so reaping or plowing another's strip were common offenses. Fodder and pasture for animals was in great demand and animals could be made to trespass on another's crops. Plowing necessitated cooperation in the use of plow teams, but some people's fields would be plowed first and others would have to wait. For the angry victims of such offenses, there was the possibility of settlement in the manorial court, but there also was the ancient and honorable solution of solving problems through assault, homicide, or retributive theft. The emphasis was on self-help. In property law as well, possession was nine-tenths of the law.

The techniques in committing crimes and the seasonal pattern show that community tensions were instrumental in the motivation for most crimes. The criminal techniques exhibited in all crimes, with the exception of counterfeiting and robbery, were very crude and for the most part showed impulsive, angry action rather than careful, premeditated planning. The seasonality of crime tended to follow the agricultural calendar. When people were in the fields from May through September homicides were very high. They then decreased in the winter months. The planting and harvest time were obviously the most tense periods in the communities with arguments over crops, land, and shared responsibilities. The larceny and burglary patterns interwove with each other. In the planting and harvest months when goods were lying around the fields and animals were out to pasture, larceny was high. In the winter months when goods were carefully stored and food getting scarce, the amount of larceny went down and burglary went up. Robbery was a threat throughout the year, but robbers were more likely to be strangers to the community or professional criminals and, therefore, not bound to the agricultural calendar.

Although we tend to call criminal behavior antisocial, in fact, it is often a form of social interaction between the victim and the accused. In the Huntingdonshire villages that were studied in depth for the interactions of the victims and the accused, a distinct pecking order emerged. The primary villagers chose their victims from their own class with whom they would have many contacts leading to arguments and with the clergy who represented the class directly above them. The secondary villagers selected victims from their own ranks and the primary villagers. The intermediate villagers seldom found victims among their own kind but most often among the primary and secondary villagers. Victims, then, came from the groups in the village that were in competition for resources and power with the accused. Crime was apparently used as an instrument of social control and community regulation.

The nobility used their armed households to maintain their power over the villagers. They had a curious relationship with the village communities. They were the chief oppressors because of the control they had over the persons and financial position of the peasantry. They ran the manorial court and could fine or intimidate through violence any peasants who rebelled against their authority. On the other hand, since the king's officials and justices were often corrupt and could not provide fair justice for the villagers, a lord could act as their protector making sure that their enemies were punished and that their cases proceded smoothly in the royal courts. In this role they were very much like a primitive Mafia entering into a patron-client relationship that was mutually beneficial to both parties but that existed as a necessary evil because of the weakness of the central state in providing for its subjects. Some of the criminal activities of the nobility were outgrowths of their social and occupational position, which has led me to compare them to white collar criminals.

While the interclass, inter-status group, and intracommunity conflicts are well represented in the records, intrafamilial crime is not. Family members rarely appeared committing crimes against each other, even homicide. This is one of the most striking differences between medieval and modern criminal behavior. Criminologists assume that the large role that the family plays in modern murder statistics comes about because murder is a crime of passion and family members are among the most likely to become passionately and murderously angry at each other. This leads one to speculate whether the medieval family was a loose group less emotionally involved with each other than with their neighbors or whether they were so closely bound together that they had discovered the secret of family harmony that escapes us. There is insufficient work on the medieval family to establish which of the diametrically opposed hypotheses is correct.

The identity of the suspects also reveals the nature of the power relationships in the village communities. Males dominated both the social institutions and the crime pattern. They were indicted for 90 percent of all crimes and most of the violent ones. Women had a more active role in burglary than do modern women, but that was partly because the goods they most often stole—household items, cloth, and clothing—were more likely to be found in homes and partly because the construction of medieval houses made them very easy to break into. On the whole, however, the passive, noncriminal role ascribed to women in the modern period was already prevalent in the Middle Ages. Women committed crimes with accomplices and played a large role in the passive crime of receiving. The male jurors reacted to female suspects just as do modern law enforcement officials—they indicted and convicted them less frequently than male offenders.

The men who appeared as suspects were predominantly substantial villagers. Those indicted for homicide had enough goods on the average to make them eligible for taxation under the Lay Subsidy of 1334. In the Huntingdonshire sample, the suspects came predominantly from the primary and secondary villagers. Occupational information is sparse in the records, but the number of clergy can be identified because of the plea of benefit of clergy. They appear to be criminous out of proportion to their numbers in the society and, more interestingly, they concentrated on the more violent crimes such as robbery. Very possibly, shrewd professional criminals became clergymen to avoid hanging. But in many respects the clergy acted like the knights and gentry in forming robber bands and settling their disputes through violent and criminal means. They were, after all, often drawn from the same social rank.

The age of the suspects was seldom given in the records. Since the age of majority was twelve, the problem of juvenile delinquency is difficult to identify. Ariès has argued that people did not go through the period of juvenile with all of its attendant modern social characteristics, but, instead, moved directly into the world of adulthood. I have speculated that, in fact, a large proportion of the population was composed of teenagers and young adults and that the general crime pattern of the early fourteenth century is exactly what one would expect from this age group. In modern crime patterns young adult males predominate in property crimes in their teens and early twenties and become involved in homicide in their twenties and early thirties. An unusual sample from the late fourteenth century coroners' rolls placed the average age of the victims of homicides in their early to midthirties.

A few identifiable criminals and bands of criminals fell outside the normal patterns of community conflict. Very few professional criminals could be identified and even recidivists were few. With hanging being the only punishment one might expect no recidivists, but even the number of people indicted more than once was small.

Although the majority of suspects were associated with another person in crime, most of these were informal associations. Some bands, however, consisted of three or more people and exhibited characteristics of bandits or highwaymen. These bands were composed of clergy, knights, gentry, peasantry, and an odd assortment of other people. Their specialities were robbery (robbery and counterfeiting were the only crimes in which strangers to the community predominated), extortion, protection rackets, burglary, and homicide.

The gang structure was very similar to that described in the ballads of Robin Hood. The gangs picked some of their victims from the stereotypes described in the legends, but there the similarity ends. They were not welfare agents for the villagers, indeed, since they had to steal household goods and food from the local population, they were a scourge on the peasants. They sometimes gave the peasantry gifts of plunder, probably to buy their goodwill, and they occasionally attacked the oppressors of the peasantry in their criminal ventures. But, contrary to Hobsbawm's assertions, outlaws who only robbed from the rich to give to the poor and only murdered when they had a just cause are the stuff of legends and myths, not of real life. As mythical heroes they were just as popular with the populace then as now. The balladeers put their social complaints into the ballads, where they well represent peasant discontent. The medieval peasantry, however, did not need heroic figures to rise up and right their wrongs. On many occasions they were their own heroes and revolted against the nobility and the corrupt justices.

The nobility surrounded themselves with bands of household retainers whom they supported through the practice of livery and maintenance. The populace complained about the lords and their household thugs, but the kings found them increasingly impossible to control. Their disputes about territorial rights and control of political power escalated into violence and warfare. In the end they massacred one another in civil war during the Wars of the Roses in the fifteenth century. In some ways this was almost comparable to the St. Valentine's Day Massacre, for the nobility made up the most organized and rationalized element of medieval crime and were in many respects an early Mafia type.

Ordinary tensions within the community produced the bulk of the routine felony actions and charges, but there were also external events that increased the conflicts and brought about crime waves. The Malthusian conditions of the first quarter of the century were particularly influential. Population continued to increase while soil fertility and acreage under production declined. Grain became very scarce, and the price of wheat increased dramatically. In 1315-1317 one of the worst famines in European history struck. A lesser famine occurred in 1322-1323. The effect of the famines and grain shortages was wide-spread deaths; enough that the pressure of population on resources was sufficiently diminished to provide the survivors with adequate food. During those trying years of the first quarter of the century the populace did not hesitate to steal and commit acts of violence in order to survive or simply to maintain the standard of living to which they had become accustomed. Crime increased every time the price of grain increased and dropped with it. The correlation between the two was remarkably close. During the Great Famine the number of crimes per year increased over 300 percent in some counties.

Not only did the annual fluctuations in crime indicate famine conditions but also the types of goods stolen and the variety of crimes committed. Grain was more common as a stolen item in the first quarter of the century than in the second quarter and burglary was more prevalent during that period as well. As the survivors came out of the disaster in the 1330s they demanded more industrial goods and luxuries. The thieves followed the market trends and also stole more of these items.

This close tie between the availability of grain and the annual incidence of crime has important implications for our own future population-food ratios. If, as recent studies indicate, there will be insufficient food to support the world's population by the year 2000 and there will be major famines in some parts of the world, then one might also expect an increase in violence as well. Not every culture reacts in the same way as our Western culture does. In India during recent famines there was not an accompanying increase in crimes. But those cultures whose roots are in the self-help tradition of the Middle Ages, including the United States, would probably react the way their fourteenth-century ancestors did.

The availability of food was not the only factor that appeared to influence the annual number of crimes; the Commons complained that the veterans of the king's wars also caused increased disturbances in the countryside. The character of a medieval army would seem to be proof enough of their complaint. To recruit soldiers the king offered pardons to known felons and outlaws in return for a year of service. Some of these men died in the wars, but many returned to England

and continued to plunder. The king also contracted with nobles and adventurers to provide indentured troops for his campaigns. This increased the problems of livery and maintenance when the nobles brought their private armies home. Fourteenth-century warfare was particularly disastrous for the countryside, since the soldiers were not regularly paid or provisioned and lived from plundering the inhabitants. The Scots who invaded northern England devastated whole areas and the English troops who returned from the continent often continued to live by plunder at home. By the 1340s England had been involved in wars for twenty-five years both against the Scots and the French. There were many veterans in the country particularly in Yorkshire and the Midlands. Crime in general increased in this period, but particularly in the north and west of the country. The influence of war can, perhaps, also be seen in the increase in the proportion of murder to other types of crimes during the period.

The conflicts that produced crimes were carried over into the administration of justice. The evidence from the medieval record does much to confirm the modern criminological theory about law as a powerful instrument whose "control and mobilization can in many ways . . . generate and exacerbate conflicts rather than resolving or softening them."[1] It is further suggested that "the availability of legal resources is in itself an impetus to social conflict because conflicting or potentially conflicting parties cannot risk the possible costs of not having the law—or at least some law—on their side."[2]

The primary villagers used their control over the manorial bylaws and their position as jurors in indictment and trial procedures of criminal law to maintain and further their dominance of the village communities. They indicted members of their own status group and the secondary villagers freely, but seldom convicted them. I argue that indictment was in itself a punishment since it necessitated either a costly stay in gaol while awaiting trial or the expense of a trip to the county gaol for the trial. The jurors could not easily convict members of the established village families for crimes because this was likely to cause a vendetta and they and their family might be indicted and hanged in revenge. The intermediate villagers, on the other hand, had no political power to get back at the primary villagers. Their crime pattern indicates deep resentments, for their homicide victims were among the main village families. They were a potentially obstreperous group in the village, so the primary villagers used their control over the judicial system to indict, convict, and hang them. In so doing they give further evidence of conformity with the behavior predicted in conflict theory that "the party with greater legal as well as non-legal power increases its edge over weaker parties, even to the extreme of excluding the weaker altogether from participation in the legal system" of the villages.[3] The primary villagers were obviously using the judicial system as an elaborate system for warning and punishing villagers in varying degrees. Not only the peasantry but the king, his officials, the barons and their officials, and the church all used their various forms of participation in the judicial system to manipulate it for personal power or financial gains.

With judicial decisions being manipulated for personal political ends, the society did not end up convicting many of the suspects. Less than a third of those tried for felonies were convicted. This meant that the society had to live with a number of robbers, burglars, petty thieves, and murderers in their midst. The high acquittal rate resulted in part from the severity of the punishment. Conviction meant hanging in the bulk of the cases. Pardons, benefit of clergy, and a few lesser punishments staved off death for some, but most were hanged. If the jurors could have decided on the fate of the suspects without sentencing them automatically to death, then perhaps the conviction rate would be over two-thirds, which it was for the clergy who could not be hanged. The medieval experience with punishments too severe to fit the crime is a good counterexample to those today who argue that crime can be curbed through stiffer penalties. Medieval communities were willing to tolerate crime and criminals in their midst rather than convicting them and, although everyone from the king on down complained bitterly about the social cost, no one tried to rectify the situation because they had vested interests in maintaining the status quo.

To be sure, they had some gradations in what they would and would not tolerate, and these distinctions reveal much about their social values. Counterfeiters and spies were usually convicted. There were few of them, but they were regarded as particularly pernicious. Simple larceny, although the most common felony, ended in conviction in the same percentage of cases as the overall conviction pattern. Burglars were convicted more frequently, and robbers were the most detested of those committing property crimes. There were several reasons for this. The robbers were usually strangers to the community who had no claim to ties of friendship and protection. They were frequently members of organized bands who were dangerous to the community and could not be tolerated or regulated within the community system. The villagers distrusted all strangers, particularly robbers, and found it easier to convict and hang these people whom they did not know. There was also less possibility of revenge for the punishment. The people of the Middle Ages from the earliest barbarian law codes through the fourteenth century chose to punish more severely those who committed crimes by stealth, in disguise, or under the cover of night. Ambush and breaking and entering were more dastardly than taking and carrying off goods in simple larceny.

Because they preferred direct action and applauded self-help as a way of settling disputes, jurors were willing to acquit murderers even more freely than thieves. Most murders grew out of arguments that the villagers knew about. They assumed, along with the participants in the homicidal drama, that a good fight was an acceptable way of resolving the conflict. If someone got killed, that was understandable. The society, I argue, did not consider most murderers as dangerous people but rather as successfully aggressive people. If in the practice of national politics the king and his favorites were murdered by the opposition, it did not encourage the people in the countryside to turn more readily to homicide. It was an act that the populace would have considered fairly normal, although they did deplore the secretive way in which Edward II was murdered.

A lingering question is how much impact crime actually had on society. Without population figures this is very difficult to determine, but it is crucial for understanding fourteenth-century English society. If crime was not particularly damaging, then the jurors could very well be lenient about convicting neighbors. Many modern historians, including Hilton, Sayles, Putnam, Gollancz, and Harding, have concluded that the later Middle Ages was outstandingly lawless. The blame for the perceived chaos is laid at the door of the king. Sayles argues that Edward I perverted the law at the end of his reign and that this provided an example for lawlessness. People turned to local protectors and local lords rather than relying on the royal justice; even the king had to use trailbaston commissions because the regular system no longer worked.[4] Harding as well placed the blame on the king for not controlling his "overmighty subjects," the barons and gentry.[5] Hilton has argued that the general brutality of a government that had gallows at crossroads hung with rotting bodies and that nailed heads to city gates encouraged a general brutalization of the population that led to the prevalence of violence.[6]

But where does one find evidence of the prevalence of crime? We have quoted speeches and petitions in Parliament, statutes, ballads, sermons, political songs, and so on all deploring violence, corruption of justice, and lack of peace in the countryside. But these sources are as unreliable for gauging the amount of crime as our modern newspaper headlines and editorial pages. Crime is a political issue that can be trotted out to harass the central government. It was not accidental that many of the Parliamentary complaints came at the time when Edward III was trying to persuade Commons to grant him money for his war in France. Because the members of Commons had a vested interest in getting the office of justice of the peace established, they argued that crime was terrible. Another source is the actual criminal statistics. But, having just presented an entire book of criminal statistics, I still cannot answer the question. One can give the average annual homicides in, say, York, but that does not tell what the risk was for the general population in the city; it only tells the number of people killed. It makes a profound difference if one in 100 or one in 1,000 was at risk annually. Without population figures, the evidence must be indirect.

One thing about medieval crime which is apparent is that it paid quite well by the standards of the day. The mean value of goods stolen in a theft was £1 15s. and the median was 3s. 4d. The profits from theft varied depending upon how much risk the person wanted to take. Larceny paid a mean value of 17s. 11p., burglary £3 8s., and robbery £8 3s. When an annual income of £10-£20 was considered adequate to maintain a knight, when a bailiff of a large estate received a fee of about £10 a year, when an unskilled laborer's wage could be as low as 1d. or 1 1/2 d. for a day's work,[7] and when the 10s. 4d. of movable chattels was considered the minimum for tax purposes, the average theft was most attractive as a supplement.

The evidence also shows that people from all ranks in society turned to crime: nobles, gentry, bureaucrats, members of Parliament, primary villagers, down to vagrants all had criminal records or at least had been indicted for crimes. Furthermore, the chances of being caught and convicted were small. For those who wanted to go into hiding, the policing system gave ample time to escape. Those who remained in their community could use their influence to avoid conviction.

The attractions of crime must be weighed against the inconvenience. Although the outlaw ballads paint a picture of a summer forest with abundant game and ale, in fact, life in the forests was more often hard and uncomfortable. The bandits stole a remarkable amount of ordinary items just to keep alive. Trial and gaol were uncomfortable and expensive even if acquittal was guaranteed. But on the whole, the attractions of committing an occasional crime were fairly great.

Were the inducements to engage in crime sufficient to outweigh the prospects of becoming a victim of a neighbor with the same social attitudes? The impact of crime must be viewed from the victim's perspective. Larceny and/or burglary were the crimes with the most victims. Robbery composed only 10 percent of the cases. Homicide, however, was quite high at 18 percent. Comparisons with modern figures indicate that medieval society did, indeed, have a higher percentage of murders. Although the comparison is not totally accurate, it does give some indication of a greater tendency toward violent solutions to problems than one finds today even in the United States, which is considered to be a violent society. The property loss that the victim would sustain in thefts usually involved livestock— chiefly horses, sheep, and cattle—or else cloth, industrial products, and money or jewels. The most likely place to suffer from a crime was in one's own home, but fields, barns, and highways also could be dangerous. People feared attack and had prayers and verses to ward off thieves.[8]

In assessing the impact of theft on society criminologists sometimes give the value of goods stolen annually. The average value of annual thefts for the first half of the fourteenth century in the eight counties was £111 10s. This was 3 percent of the total taxes the king collected in the Lay Subsidy of 1334 in the counties studied. Criminals, at any rate, could not extract as much money as the king could.

Throughout the book I have tried to measure crime against some constant or to give modern comparisons that would put medieval crime in perspective. I estimated, for instance, that fourteenth-century London had from 5.2 to 3.6 homicides per 10,000 population, which made it very high compared to modern figures. I also showed that in counties that had more crimes per 1,000 acres the impact of crime was greater, but that this was not tied to population size.

The crime pattern of medieval villages and towns can also be compared to that of modern ones to gain some perspective on the impact of crime. Such comparisons are quite instructive. In Bedford, Indiana, a small town near Bloomington with a population of 10,000, there were no murders in 1975 (and only 3 aggravated assaults), 3 rapes, 7 robberies, 182 burglaries, and 703 larcenies.[9] Norwich city, which was of comparable size, in 1313 had 3 homicides, 3 robberies, and 3 larcenies. In St. Ives, a fair town, in 1353 there were 2 homicides, 2 burglaries, 1 robbery, and 1 larceny. In the 1940 *Uniform Crime Report*, a market town of a similar size would have 0.1 murders (1 assault), 0.6 robberies, 4 burglaries, 7 larcenies, and 0.4 rapes.

A rural county in Indiana such as Elkhart that has a population over 25,000 had 2 murders, 7 rapes, 11 robberies, 583 burglaries, and 1,011 larcenies in 1975.[10] Surrey and Herefordshire in pre-plague England might have had a similar population density. Surrey had an average yearly homicide record of 3 homicides, 2 robberies, no rapes, 5 burglaries, and 9 larcenies. Herefordshire had an average yearly record of 10 homicides, 10 robberies, 0.3 rapes, 11 burglaries, and 22 larcenies. What these comparisons seem to indicate is that there must have been a great deal of petty theft through larceny and burglary that was never reported. Some of them may well have been treated as trespasses rather than felonies. Probably, however, there was less property crime in the Middle Ages. The convictions for the various crimes indicated that the taboo against property crimes was greater than against homicide and rape. Not only did jurors convict more people charged with property crimes, but the taboo would be internalized in the society so that fewer property crimes would have been committed.

The comparisons also suggest that the quality of crime was very different in the Middle Ages compared to now. Homicide was much more common and more acceptable in the Middle Ages. One is also struck by the amount of sadistic violence that accompanied some of the homicides, particularly in cases of robbery and burglary. Rather than being tied up, victims were killed. Not one blow, but many and with different weapons were administered. One group of burglars took the time to stop and heat a trivet and sit a victim on it, and another group hamstrung the victims so they could not pursue them. Some of the appeals for homicide indicate torture rather than just killing an enemy.

Rape was an uncommon crime in the first half of the fourteenth century, but that was because it had just been elevated to the rank of a felony fifteen years before. By the 1360s the jurors were indicting about as many men for rape as now, but they were convicting them more frequently. Rape was probably much more common than the reporting indicates. For the most part rape resembled the modern crime, but in some cases the motivation seemed somewhat different. Raping the wife or widow of an enemy was a way of bringing shame on him. It showed that he was too impotent to protect his own property against defilement. Until more is known about the legal position of women in medieval England, it cannot be determined whether rape was more of a personal crime against a woman or a property crime against her husband.

In summary, the inhabitants of fourteenth-century rural England, and this was most of the country, seemed to turn to crime readily as an instrument of conflict resolution. Homicide was very common, and jurors were quite willing to acquit the suspects because their behavior was acceptable in solving conflicts. This did, indeed, make the society a violent one by modern standards. Property crime was less common then than now, but when food was not readily available because of famine and grain shortages, the populace rectified the lack by participating in widespread thefts. All classes of society found crime an attractive supplement to their incomes. There were few professionals and no class that could be called criminal. The population as a whole added to the criminal statistics for the period. All people who had some control over the criminal justice system used that power to resolve private disputes and further their control over others. The criminal law was frequently used as a weapon of social conflict. The prevailing attitude of the society toward crime and law enforcement is summed up in a contemporary poem:

> For why? the good old rule
> Sufficed them,—the simple plan
> That they should take who have the power,
> And they should keep who can.[11]

Appendix A

The Problem of Missing Deliveries

Neither historical nor statistical methods can establish precisely which years have complete records and which are incomplete. Because of the way in which commissions were issued, there is no way to check for missing records from external sources. The original commissions to justices of gaol delivery were recorded on the dorse (back) of the patent rolls, but were not necessarily entered on the plea roll. Since a commission could authorize a judge to go on circuit for an indefinite number of years, a long period could elapse before the issue of a new commission. During this time a judge might miss sessions or lose the records. Furthermore, many commissions were issued that were never acted upon. More reliable would be the writ of *venire facias* to the sheriffs concerning imminent deliveries. These writs are, however, too sparsely preserved to be of much help in identifying lost records. Some evidence indicates that sheriffs were notified by a more informal means than a writ.[1] For external evidence, therefore, we are left with the commissions to the justices on the patent rolls. A study of these rolls did reveal that all gaps of two or more years were because of loss of records. Except in outlying counties such as Cumberland and Northumberland, the central government never allowed a commission to lapse longer than a couple of deliveries.

Internal evidence could, perhaps, reveal more about missing records. Gathering such evidence entails the painstaking process of checking through every person who is returned to prison to see if he reappears in a subsequent delivery. If he does not, then a session might be missing. Even this process cannot be used for all the years because many of the plea rolls do not record those who were returned to gaol without a trial. For real accuracy one would need the calendars, which are only sparsely preserved. Nevertheless, Meekings went through the Bedfordshire rolls to 1351, which are among the most complete, and concluded that all years with two or more deliveries seem to be complete.[2] A further check of the conclusions reached by these means can be made by comparing the number of deliveries per year for all the counties. There is usually a correspondence in the number of deliveries per year in most counties.[3] In this way we know that in 1307, the year of the change of kings from Edward I to Edward II, there was only one delivery in the counties but that it was a particularly full one, so that it was probably the only one held in that year. Likewise, in 1316 there were five deliveries in most of the counties.

In addition to using historical evidence to minimize the effect of missing records, two statistical devices were used on twenty years of Norfolk records. First, I took the modal number of deliveries per year—three—and eliminated all years with less than three deliveries and selected out the three major deliveries from years with more than the modal number. In this way I was able to remove possible distortion caused by missing records. Even holding the number of deliveries per year constant, the graph (figure 21) of the number of crimes per year followed the same pattern as the original distribution plotted from all the surviving records.

The second statistical tool used was the moving average of three years. To arrive at the number of crimes per year by this method, each year's total number of crimes was averaged with the total from the preceding and succeeding years. Thus the number of crimes for 1306 becomes the average of 1305, 1306, and 1307; that for 1307 is the average of the crimes for 1306, 1307, and 1308, and so on. The moving average helps to modify the effects of missing documents by spreading out the deficiencies over several years, thus giving a smoother picture of the pattern of crime on the graph. Like the device of holding the number of deliveries constant, the moving average follows the same pattern as the raw number of crimes.

These statistical devices, therefore, help to confirm the accuracy of the historical evidence. For the purposes of this study, all years having two or more deliveries are used and those having only one delivery are eliminated.

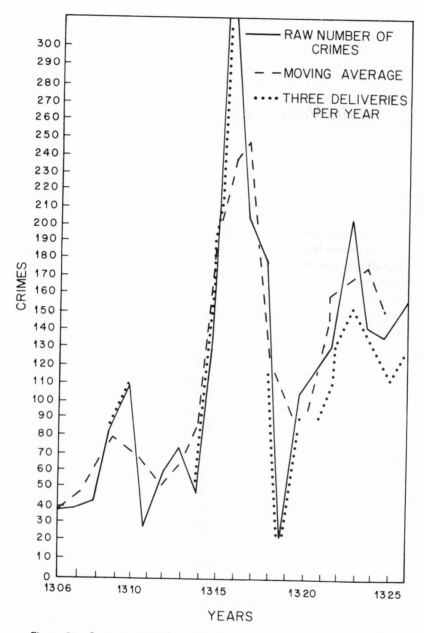

Figure 21. *Statistical devices used to compensate for missing records.*

Appendix B

Influence of the Determining Powers

of the Keepers of the Peace

on the Volume of Cases in Gaol Delivery

Provisions in the peace commissions for keepers of the peace to try cases indicted before them could have caused a drop in the number of cases appearing in gaol delivery. In order to test the effect of a drain of cases from this cause, I compared the years when the keepers had determining powers with table 12 showing the number of crimes per year to see if decreases could be explained by activities of the peace commissioners. The keepers of the peace did not receive permanent power to determine cases indicted before them until 1350. Between 1305 and 1308 the gaol delivery commissions specifically excluded cases indicted before the keepers of the peace. In 1314 and 1326 this provision was again renewed for a year.[1] Supervisors were appointed to hear the cases instead. Putnam concluded that these were special supervisors of the peace, but Meekings has shown that they were actually trailbaston justices who were trying both those indicted by the sheriffs and the keepers.[2] They were part of a government experiment in an attempt to replace gaol delivery but, as Gollancz has pointed out, the gaol delivery and sessions of the supervisors were enrolled together.[3] From March 1329 to November 1330 keepers were given the power to determine cases of those they indicted.[4] The breaks in the records in this year make it difficult to determine the effect of this change. For the month of February in 1332, the keepers again were made justices.[5] There is a decline of cases in gaol delivery in 1332 to 1333, but it is improbable that the sharp decline in Yorkshire, for instance, could have been brought about by one month of cases under a rival jurisdiction. With the impending departure of the king for France in 1338, Parliament requested that keepers again have the power to determine cases.[6] Whatever the drain of cases to the keepers of the peace in those years, the number of cases in gaol delivery rose regardless. From 1344 to 1350 keepers were again appointed but with the provision that they could determine cases only if they were aided by other men "learned in law."[7] A survey of the *Calendar of Patent Rolls* from 1344 to 1348 showed that no commissions to determine cases were issued to keepers of the peace in Norfolk, Yorkshire, or Northamptonshire.

278

Table 12. *Number of crimes per year in the eight counties.*

Year	Nor- folk	Yorks.	North- ants.	Hunts.	Essex	Herefs.	Som.	Surrey
1300	68	69	54	16	143	—	107	—
01	68	12*	26	19	93	—	17	83
02	14*	52	13	20	85	28*	43	18
03	38	9*	21	—	42	136	1*	—
04	26*	—	—	9	70	—	—	—
05	44	—	6*	—	—	—	1*	—
06	42	—	—	—	18	—	20	—
07	40	—	—	—	—	1*	—	—
08	44	—	35	18	—	—	—	—
09	83	149	59	26	—	—	—	—
1310	112	38	68	27	18	—	—	38
11	27	—	24	—	60	—	—	22
12	60	—	33	—	1*	—	—	15
13	76	36	7*	—	45	—	7	—
14	47	12*	35	—	4*	—	—	13
15	144	188	13	—	15*	—	118	28
16	384	661	100	—	4*	—	35	44
17	203	163	75	—	459	248	39	46
18	172	199	42	—	234	84	58	15
19	24	103	22	—	45	—	—	11
1320	105	133	29	—	30	—	22	34
21	116	102	46	—	—	—	—	24
22	133	120	40	—	—	—	60	5
23	240	99	92	—	109	—	158	—
24	141	181	55	—	78	—	47	—
25	136	96	64	—	131	55	85	—
26	152	93	33	—	64	43	12	—
27	91	144	—	—	39	34	—	—
28	50	—	13	8	55	21	—	—
29	93	—	83	—	57	—	69	10
1330	79	29*	84	—	38	—	—	23
31	42	199	—	—	—	42	—	—
32	59	245	—	39	28	—	—	—
33	43	150	13	4	21	—	—	—
34	37	63	—	6	10	15	69	10
35	38	149	—	1*	39	19	—	17
36	29	105	35	9	36	69	—	5

*Data probably missing.

Table 12. (*continued*)

YEAR	NOR-FOLK	YORKS.	NORTH-ANTS.	HUNTS.	ESSEX	SOM.	HEREFS.	SURREY
1337	30	74	5*	8	2*	—	—	12
38	9	—	—	5	84	—	—	8
39	48	—	—	9	5*	37	—	2
1340	—	109	24	13	37	—	—	2
41	—	27*	—	3	38	—	—	44
42	56	146	7*	34	—	29	—	17
43	—	260	—	16	25	52	1*	1*
44	60	167	—	—	88	143	—	28
45	34	213	—	—	—	79	—	—
46	156	367	—	4	52	—	—	—
47	14	153	—	1*	—	—	22	—
48	39	187	—	6	—	—	—	—
Total	3,746	5,485	1,256	301	2,402	1,135	991	575

*Data probably missing.

Aside from the years 1305-1308 in Essex and Herefordshire and 1332-1333, in Essex, Huntingdonshire, Yorkshire, and Norfolk the granting of determining powers to the keepers of the peace did not bring about a decrease in the number of cases appearing in gaol delivery. Even in 1332-1333 the power was only granted for a month; it therefore could not have had much effect.

Appendix C

Influence of Changes

in Law Enforcement Procedures

on the Volume of Cases in Gaol Delivery

Changes in the method of apprehending a criminal or attempts to increase the efficiency of existing law enforcement officials were frequent in the first half of the fourteenth century and may have been responsible for fluctuations in the number of crimes per year. Even during the chaotic reign of Edward II and the long absences abroad of Edward III, there were frequent experiments in law enforcement. The lack of a comprehensive study on the length of time it took for a reform to be put into general practice increases the difficulty of finding evidence that will indicate how long it normally took for a reform to take effect. (In the case of the change of the rape law, implementation took over fifty years.) I assume that the increased efficiency of law enforcement resulting from changes in the administration of justice took one to two years to increase the number of cases in gaol delivery.

The first unique addition to methods of apprehending a felon came in 1308 when the keepers of the peace were given the power to pursue felons from hundred to hundred and from shire to shire.[1] Previously, pursuit ended at jurisdictional boundaries where officials from the next hundred had to take up the chase. It is not known how many felons were apprehended in this way, but the number of cases in gaol delivery did increase in 1309 to 1310 in some counties. Some additional cases may have been the work of keepers of the peace, but by 1310 commissioners were appointed to investigate the keepers because of complaints that they failed to do their job.[2]

In 1314 there was a change of power in the council accompanied by renewed efforts to preserve the king's peace through administrative changes. Again the keepers were singled out for increased powers: the power to hold sworn inquests into suspected felonies and the power of summary arrest of notorious persons who were suspected of felonies but who had not been previously indicted.[3] The increased powers of the keepers corresponded with an increase in the number of cases coming into gaol delivery, but the rise cannot all be attributed to zealous and powerful keepers. First, the increase in court business from an average of 55 cases before 1314 to 384 cases by 1316 in Norfolk, 68 to 661 in Yorkshire, and 38 to 63 in Northamptonshire is too large to be explained solely by granting the power of sworn inquest and summary arrest to two knights in each county. Second, the years 1315 to 1317 were also years of terrible famine, Scottish invasions, and mismanagement in the upper echelons of government, all of which may have brought about an increase in crime. Finally, the government apparently was not convinced of the efficiency of the keepers in matters of summary arrest, at least, for in 1319 they transferred that power to the sheriffs.[4] From 1316 to 1331 there was little change in the procedure of law enforcement except that between 1327 and 1331 the power of summary arrest was suspended altogether.[5] Despite this return to the status quo, crimes peaked again in 1323-1324, apparently independently of changes in enforcement.

Between 1332 and 1337 the government went through another period of experiment in keeping the peace. Commissions of the peace were allowed to lapse. Instead, the government relied on local magnates—given the title of keepers of the county—to see that county and local officials performed their duties and that felons were arrested.[6] During this period gaol delivery business remained at a high level in Yorkshire but declined or remained steady in the other counties. It seems unlikely that these magnates were less diligent than those of Yorkshire unless the king's presence in York spurred his northern barons to greater efficiency. Under the urgings of Commons the keepers again were used extensively in 1338 and thereafter.[7] The increase in court business, however, did not come until the 1340s. On the other hand, the sudden peak of cases in 1346 does not correspond to any new burst of energy on the part of the keepers.

Over the half century the government also tried to increase the efficiency of law enforcement by commissions to investigate local officials, by removal of corrupt officials, and by statute. As we saw in the last paragraph, the commissions of 1310 to investigate keepers of the peace and the commissions to magnates in 1332-1337 had little effect. In 1314 and 1327 Parliament attempted to remove all sheriffs in order to get rid of the corrupt ones. In fact, very few changes of personnel were made at either time.[8] The two statutes that attempted to tighten law enforcement—Northampton (1328) and Westminster (1340)[9]—show little immediate results of drawing more cases into court.

Changes in the procedure of law enforcement and attempts to increase its efficiency show very little verifiable influence on the volume of cases. While there is an increase of court business when justices of the peace are given additional powers in 1308 and 1314, it is questionable whether the correlation is a valid one: since (1) in 1310 the keepers were declared inefficient, they were probably not responsible for the rise in cases, (2) in 1315-1317 and in 1342-1346 the rise is too dramatic to be the work of the keepers alone, and (3) between 1316 and 1331 the level of crime continued to fluctuate even though there were no changes in the administration of justice. In the years 1332-1337, when the counties were placed under the watchful eyes of local magnates, the level of crime goes up in Yorkshire and down in Norfolk. Some local condition in Yorkshire, rather than a reform measure applied equally to all counties, must be looked for to explain the discrepancy. Finally, many of the increases in table 12 correspond to social, economic, and political crises that might have contributed to, or better explain, the increases.

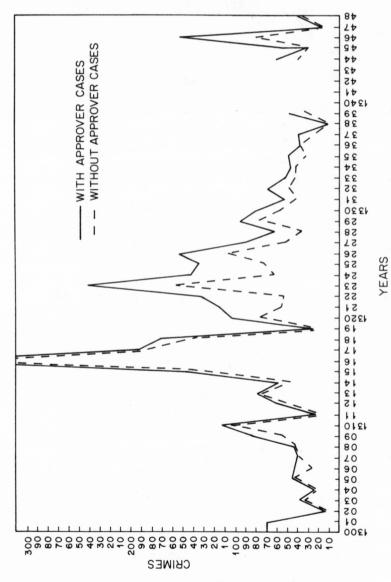

Figure 22. *Effect of approver cases on the distribution of crime.*

283

Appendix D

Judicial Lag

Table 13. *Distribution of cases occurring before and during year of delivery*

TERM	YEAR OF DELIVERY	YEARS BEFORE DELIVERY										TOTAL	
		1	2	3	4	5	6	7	8	9	10+	%	N
Winter	1	37	22	10	8	7	4	3	2	3	3	100	450
Summer	23	33	12	9	8	3	5	1	2	2	2	100	339
Autumn	32	23	11	11	7	7	3	2	2	1	1	100	367
Average for year	18	31	15	10	8	6	4	2	2	2	2	100	1,156

Notes

1 INTRODUCTION

1. *Crime in East Anglia in the Fourteenth Century: Norfolk Gaol Delivery Rolls, 1307-1316,* trans. Barbara A. Hanawalt (Norfolk Record Society, XLIV, 1976), pp. 76-77.

2. John Bellamy, *Crime and Public Order in England in the Later Middle Ages* (London, 1973). James B. Given, *Society and Homicide in Thirteenth-Century England* (Palo Alto, Calif., 1977). Joel Samaha, *Law and Order in Historical Perspective: The Case of Elizabethan Essex* (New York, 1974). Kai T. Erikson, *Wayward Puritans: A Study in the Sociology of Deviance* (New York, 1966). J. J. Tobias, *Urban Crime in Victorian England* (New York, 1972). Eric H. Monkkonen, *The Dangerous Class: Crime and Poverty in Columbus, Ohio, 1860-1885* (Cambridge, Mass., 1975). Douglas Hay et al., *Albion's Fatal Tree: Crime and Society in Eighteenth-Century England* (London, 1975). J. S. Cockburn, ed., *Crime in England, 1550-1800* (Princeton, 1977). L. L. Robson, *The Convict Settlers of Australia* (Melbourne, 1965).

3. F. Pollock and F. W. Maitland, *The History of English Law before Edward I,* 2nd ed. (Cambridge, 1968), II, 466.

4. Ibid.

5. J. F. Stephen, *A History of the Criminal Law of England* (London, 1883), I, 3, gives a more detailed definition.

6. T. F. T. Plucknett, *A Concise History of the Common Law,* 2nd ed. (New York, 1936), p. 374.

7. *Court Rolls of the Manor of Wakefield,* ed. and trans. W. P. Baildon, John Lister, and S. W. Walker (Yorkshire Archaeological Society Record Series, 1901-1945). *Court Rolls of the Manor of Ingoldmells in the County of Lincolnshire,* ed. and trans. W. O. Massingberd (London, 1902).

8. Barbara A. Hanawalt, "Fur-Collar Crime: The Pattern of Crime

among the Fourteenth-Century English Nobility," *Journal of Social History*, 8 (1975), 1-17.

9. Kent would have been a better choice for the southeastern county but it was too large a subject to undertake at the end of the data collection process. It also had some administrative pecularities that made assessment of the data more difficult.

10. In previous articles based on the data for Norfolk, Yorkshire, and Northamptonshire I counted only crimes instead of offenders. Because of this difference in data collection, information on the people involved in crimes—victims and accused—is based largely on data from the other five counties.

11. Bedfordshire has the best preserved records of all the counties and would have been a better choice as a Midlands representative. However, C. A. F. Meekings, Assistant Keeper of the Public Records Office, London, went through the Bedfordshire materials, so I did not wish to duplicate his efforts. They show the same patterns that I found for the other counties.

12. C. A. F. Meekings permitted me to read a manuscript he prepared as an introduction to his *Index to the Medieval Gaol Delivery Rolls*. This material will be hereafter referred to as Meekings, "Manuscript."

13. Marguerite Gollancz, "The System of Gaol Delivery as Illustrated in the Extant Gaol Delivery Rolls of the Fifteenth Century" (Master's dissertation, University of London, 1936), p. 26.

14. Gollancz has suggested that the copy was probably made up a year or so after the sessions. By a statute of 9 Edward III the justices were supposed to deposit the records with the treasurer and chamberlains of the Exchequer every Michaelmas. This was seldom done. Ibid., pp. 36-38.

15. Ibid., p. 46.

16. Meekings, "Manuscript."

17. Meekings, "Manuscript."

18. Gollancz, "System of Gaol Delivery," p. 46.

19. Meekings, "Manuscript."

20. If the senior gaol delivery justice was absent on other royal business, sessions were sometimes missed. Occasionally there is a note in the rolls that no deliveries took place because there were no prisoners or because incursions of the Scots prevented the holding of a session. It is also possible that the central government failed to issue the usual commissions either because of chaos in the council or because there was a lack of competent men to be justices. Gollancz, "System of Gaol Delivery," p. 240.

21. In 1307, for instance, there was only one delivery held in most counties because of the transition between the reigns of Edward I and Edward II.

22. Expanded trailbaston sessions replaced gaol delivery in some counties in 1304-1307 and 1314-1316, Meekings, "Manuscript." Apart from delivering gaols in the county where it happened to be located, the King's Bench did not

have any original criminal jurisdiction until 1323, although it did have the power to review cases from other courts. Even after 1323 little criminal jurisdiction came into King's Bench until well into the fourteenth century. *Select Cases in the Court of King's Bench*, trans. G. O. Sayles, Selden Society, V (London, 1957), pp. xxxvi-xxxviii.

23. J. B. Avrutick, "Commissions of Oyer and Terminer in Fifteenth Century England" (Ph.D. dissertation, University of London, 1967), p. 25.

24. One unusual case appears in *Lathe Court Rolls and Views of Frankpledge in the Rape of Hastings, 1387-1474*, ed. E. J. Courthope and B. E. P. Formoy (Sussex Records Society, XXXVII, 1931), p. 145. "And that William Mellere broke and entered the house of William Croucheman to violate and rape Isabella, wife of William Croucheman, and that he is a common disturber of the peace of the lord King, 20s."

25. *Kent Keepers of the Peace*, trans. Bertha H. Putnam (Records of the Kent Archaeological Society, XIII, 1933), p. xix. Keepers of the peace were pursuing felons from county to county long before they received the specific permission.

26. Tobias, *Victorian England*, chap. 2.

27. E. H. Sutherland and D. R. Cressey, *Principles of Criminology*, 7th ed. (New York, 1966), p. 27.

28. Barbara A. Hanawalt, "Violent Death in Fourteenth- and Early Fifteenth-Century England," *The Journal of Comparative Studies in Society and History*, 18 (1976), 315. Only about 36 percent of the homicides investigated in the coroners' inquests actually came to trial in gaol delivery. Thus, even in the homicide cases the court rolls give only a small portion of those actually committed.

29. Bellamy, *Crime and Public Order*, p. 3.

30. See note 2.

31. Given, *Society and Homicide*, pp. 29-40, tried to arrive at population figures for thirteenth-century England by using the Domesday Book evidence, dubious multipliers, and assumptions about population growth from the late eleventh through the thirteenth century. He did not take into account growth over the thirteenth century. The rates of homicide that he draws from these calculations are not sufficiently reliable to be used for analysis of the incidence of homicide; thus much of the rest of the study can only be viewed with extreme caution. I have preferred to avoid all discussion of rates of crime until, if ever, there is more reliable demographic information for the fourteenth century.

2 THE SOCIAL AND JUDICIAL CONTEXT OF FOURTEENTH-CENTURY CRIME

1. Statute of Winchester, 1285, quoted in William Stubbs, *Select Charters and Other Illustrations in English Constitutional History*, 9th ed. (Oxford, 1913), pp. 466-467.

2. Helen M. Cam, *The Hundred and the Hundred Rolls: An Outline of Local Government in Medieval England* (London, 1930), p. 31.

3. *The Anglo-Saxon Chronicle*, ed. and trans. Dorothy Whitelock (London, 1961), p. 164.

4. Important general, regional, and village studies include: H. S. Bennett, *Life on the English Manor* (Cambridge, 1937). George C. Homans, *English Villagers of the Thirteenth Century* (New York, 1941). Warren O. Ault, *Open-field Farming in Medieval England* (London, 1972). Rodney H. Hilton, *A Medieval Society: The West Midlands at the End of the Thirteenth Century* (London, 1966).

5. For an excellent recent study see Brian K. Roberts, *Rural Settlement in Britain* (Folkstone, Eng., 1977).

6. Charles S. and C. S. Orwin, *The Open Fields* (Oxford, 1938), pp. 61-64.

7. Hilton, *A Medieval Society*, p. 92.

8. Ault, *Open-field Farming*, p. 15.

9. Bennett, *Life on the English Manor*, p. 45.

10. Eleanor Searle, *Lordship and Community: Battle Abbey and Its Banlieu, 1066-1538* (Toronto, 1974), pp. 184-194.

11. Hilton, *A Medieval Society*, p. 131.

12. J. Ambrose Raftis, "The Concentration of Responsibility in Five Villages," *Mediaeval Studies*, 28 (1966), 92-118. In Raftis's work and that of his students, these families are considered to be A families. They are remarkably easy to identify as taking leading roles in the village oligarchy.

13. This category is the most widely interpreted by Raftis and his students. In "Concentration of Responsibility" Raftis divided this group into three categories, B through D, as families disappearing from the village, those appearing in the village, and those continuing in a minor way. Edward J. Britton, "Broughton 1288-1340: A Mediaeval Village Community," (Ph. D. dissertation, University of Toronto, 1973), p. 24, divided the group into B and C families. B families were those who occasionally held office; C families never held office. He used the category of D for outsiders to the village. Edwin B. DeWindt, *Land and People in Holywell-cum-Needingworth* (Toronto, 1972), pp. 208-209, used a similar division for B and C families.

14. Hilton, *A Medieval Society*, pp. 149-166, discusses the sense of community in the west Midlands.

15. William A. Morris, *The Frankpledge System* (New York, 1910), pp. 71, 80.

16. Geoffrey Chaucer, *The Canterbury Tales*, trans. Nevill Coghill (London, 1951), pp. 232-233, has a very good description of living conditions for the poor of the community.

17. Homans, *English Villagers*, p. 228.

18. Josiah Cox Russell, *British Medieval Population* (Albuquerque, 1948),

pp. 24-26. H. E. Hallam, "Some Thirteenth-Century Censuses," *Economic History Review*, 10 (1958), 352. DeWindt, *Holywell-cum-Needingworth*, p. 171, placed the size at 3.8. John Krause, "The Medieval Household: Large or Small?" *Economic History Review*, 2nd ser., 9 (1957), 420, puts the household size at 4.5.

19. *Bedfordshire Coroners' Rolls*, trans. R. F. Hunnisett (Bedfordshire Historical Society, XLI, 1960).

20. See Barbara A. Hanawalt, "Childrearing among the Lower Classes of Late Medieval England," *Journal of Interdisciplinary History*, 8 (Summer 1977), 1-22, for further information.

21. George C. Homans, "The Rural Sociology of Medieval England," *Past and Present*, no. 4 (November 1953), 32-43.

22. Bennett, *Life on the English Manor*, p. 267.

23. J. A. Raftis, ed. "Studies of Peasant Mobility in a Region of Late Thirteenth- and Early Fourteenth-Century England," manuscript.

24. Hanawalt, "Childrearing," p. 6.

25. K. B. McFarlane, *The Nobility of Later Medieval England* (Oxford, 1973), pp. 105, 215.

26. Morris, *Frankpledge*, pp. 152-154.

27. In addition to and paralleling this system for the whole country there were franchisal courts belonging to lords, abbots, bishops, and boroughs. The franchise or liberty was granted by the king and gave the possessor the power to appoint officials, carry out the normal royal law enforcement functions, and collect the revenues arising from them. In some cases the franchisee also had the right to execute felons caught red-handed—*infangthef*. Although hundreds and vills could be under private jurisdiction, the view of frank-pledge, exercised in leet court, was the most common unit. Boroughs often acquired leet jurisdiction with their charters. Since franchise courts and officials were modeled on those of the crown, we may describe them together.

28. Pollock and Maitland, *English Law*, I, 578-579.

29. Just. 3/38 m. 16.

30. Morris, *Frankpledge*, p. 105.

31. Ibid., pp. 70-72.

32. Stubbs, *Select Charters*, 436-459.

33. H. M. Cam, "Shire Officials: Coroners, Constables, and Bailiffs," in *The English Government at Work*, ed. J. F. Willard, W. A. Morris, and W. H. Dunham, Jr. (Cambridge, Mass., 1950), III, 170.

34. Morris, *Frankpledge*, pp. 70-72, 85. The vills were usually composed of several tithing groups, although sometimes they were synonymous. Some parts of the country never had tithing groups. When the frankpledge began to decline after the Black Death, the vill took over its responsibilities.

35. Pollock and Maitland, *English Law*, I, 569.

36. *Wakefield*, III, p. 81. See also pp. 74, 78.

37. Morris, *Frankpledge*, pp. 144-146.

38. See N. D. Hurnard, "Jury of Presentment and the Assize of Clarendon," *English Historical Review*, 56 (July 1941), 374-401, for an early history of the presentment jury.

39. Cam, *The Hundred*, pp. 154-157, 180.

40. Just. 3/176 m. 13.

41. Cam, *The Hundred*, pp. 145-153.

42. Thomas A. Green, "The Jury and the English Law of Homicide, 1200-1600," *Michigan Law Review*, 74: 3 (1976), 422.

43. R. F. Hunnisett, *The Medieval Coroner* (Cambridge, 1961), gives a comprehensive account of the functioning of the office of coroner. The office was created by the Norman kings partly because they wanted to protect the Normans in the countryside from assassination by the native population. A fine called *murdrum* was imposed on the village for all Normans killed. By the fourteenth century the fine was ignored.

44. Bertha H. Putnam, "Transformation of the Keepers of the Peace into the Justices of the Peace, 1327-1380," *Transactions of the Royal Historical Society*, 4th ser., 5 (1920), 23.

45. *Kent Keepers of the Peace*, p. xviii.

46. *Rolls of the Northamptonshire Sessions of Peace*, ed. Margarite Gollancz (Northamptonshire Record Society, XI, 1938), p. xi.

47. *Kent Keepers of the Peace*, p. xix.

48. W. A. Morris, *The Early English County Court* (University of California Publications in History, XIV, no. 2, Berkeley, 1926), pp. 113-114.

49. Hunnisett, *Medieval Coroner*, p. 57.

50. Just. 3/114 m. 10d.

51. F. C. Hamil, "The King's Approvers," *Speculum*, II (April 1936), 253-254. Hunnisett, *Medieval Coroner*, pp. 70-73. Only men could become approvers.

52. Hamil, "King's Approvers," pp. 253-254.

53. Just. 3/48 m. 20. Other approvers appealed people who were dead, Just. 3/49/1 m. 27.

54. Hunnisett, *Medieval Coroner*, p. 69.

55. KB 27/322 m. 28; Just. 3/49/1 m. 39d.; KB 27/273 m. 30; Just. 3/48 m. 9; Just. 1/632 m. 91; and so on. For other complaints about the abuse see *Rotuli Parl.*, II, 9b, 12a.

56. KB 27/334 m. 34.

57. It was highly ineffectual given the acquittal rate and the expense of paying the gaol costs of the approvers.

58. J. J. Jusserand, *English Wayfaring Life in the Middle Ages*, trans. L. T. Smith (London, 1961), pp. 72-86, has an excellent discussion on sanctuaries.

59. Hunnisett, *Medieval Coroner*, pp. 48-49.

60. Just. 3/116 m. 4.

61. Morris, *County Court*, pp. 113-114.

62. Pollock and Maitland, *English Law*, II, 581.

63. Hunnisett, *Medieval Coroner*, pp. 48-49.

64. Just. 3/81/2 m. 16.

65. *Bedfordshire Coroners' Rolls*, p. 20.

66. R. B. Pugh, *Imprisonment in Medieval England* (Cambridge, 1968), pp. 57-86.

67. *Crime in East Anglia*, p. 28.

68. Pugh, *Imprisonment*, pp. 165-191.

69. Ibid., pp. 315-337. Margery Basset, "Newgate Prison in the Middle Ages," *Speculum*, 18 (April 1943), 245-246.

70. Just. 3/176 ms. 13-14.

71. Cam, *The Hundred*, p. 71. Hunnisett, *Medieval Coroner*, p. 161. KB 27/322 m. 28.

72. *Crime in East Anglia*, pp. 55, 60, 66.

73. Ibid., p. 64, is the last appearance of Sapling.

74. William S. Holdsworth, *A History of English Law* (Boston, 1924), IV, 526-527.

75. *Rotuli Parl.*, I, 178a.

76. An example of this writ can be found in *Early Registers of Writs*, ed. E. de Haas and G. D. G. Hall (Selden Society, LXXXXVII, London, 1970), pp. 194-195.

77. Gollancz, "System of Gaol Delivery," pp. 17-18.

78. Ibid., p. 22.

79. *Statutes of the Realm*, 27 Ed. I, St. I, c. 3.

80. M. M. Taylor, "The Justices of Assize," in *The English Government at Work*, ed. J. F. Willard, W. A. Morris, and W. H. Dunham, Jr. (Cambridge, Mass., 1950), III, 239. *Statutes of the Realm*, 4 Ed. III, c. 2.

81. Gollancz, "System of Gaol Delivery," p. 441.

82. *Statutes of the Realm*, 27 Ed. I, St. I, c. 3.

83. Meekings, "Manuscript," contains the most complete discussion of the gaol delivery system. Between 1308 and 1328 any coincidence between gaol delivery and assize commissioners existed only through the activity of individual justices. Local knights or gentry handled gaol delivery when there was no professional justice (Pugh, *Imprisonment*, p. 281). These local men were often the same ones chosen to be keepers of the peace (*Kent Keepers of the Peace*, p. xxxiv). The government twice attempted to return to the assize justices—in the Statute of Northampton in 1328 and in its reaffirmation in 1330 (Meekings, "Manuscript," p. 14). Despite legislation the commissioners were not always assize justices. M. M. Taylor shows that, of the 152 gaol delivery commissions between 1327-1336, only six were sent to the three justices of assize on the circuit in which the gaols were located, forty-five con-

tained at least one or two assize justices, and ninety-eight did not contain one (Taylor, "Justices of Assize," pp. 237-238).

84. Twice in 1334 the Commons petitioned for the enforcement of the provisions (Taylor, "Justices of Assize," p. 238). The government willingly listened but was unable to enforce the statute; justices preferred to do their circuit work in their home district and finish early.

85. Pugh, *Imprisonment*, pp. 308-311.

86. Cam, *The Hundred*, p. 79. Gollancz, "System of Gaol Delivery," pp. 23-24.

87. Stephen, *Criminal Law*, I, 301.

88. KB 27/263 m. 32.

89. Stephen, *Criminal Law*, I, 301.

90. Pollock and Maitland, *English Law*, II, 624-625, 654.

91. Just. 3/48 m. 21.

92. Hamil, "Kings Approvers," pp. 245-247.

93. Just. 3/48 m. 6.

94. *Piene forte et dure* was a designation reserved for women among all the cases I translated for my book *Crime in East Anglia*. It is possible that women underwent a different punishment, perhaps less severe than *ad dietam*.

95. *Vita Edwardi Secundi*, trans. N. Denholm-Young (London, 1957), p. 128.

96. Just. 3/106 ms. 1-2.

97. Leona C. Gabel, *Benefit of Clergy in England in the Later Middle Ages* (Smith College Studies in History, XIV, nos. 1-4, Northampton, Mass., October 1928-July 1929), pp. 31, 61-91.

98. Ibid., p. 60. They could be acquitted through compurgation in the bishop's court or found guilty and be assigned penances for their crimes.

99. Naomi D. Hurnard, *The King's Pardon for Homicide before A.D. 1307* (Oxford, 1969), pp. 68-108, 152-170.

100. W. G. Hoskins, "Murder and Sudden Death in Medieval Wigston," *Transactions of the Leicestershire Archaeological Society*, 21 (1940-1941), 178.

101. Just. 3/100 m. 17; 3/101 m. 1, m. 10, m. 15; 3/102 m. 9.

102. Green, "English Law of Homicide," p. 425.

103. Just. 3/49/3 m. 3d.

104. Just. 3/114 m. 10; 3/74/3 m. 2; 3/49/1 m. 45.

105. M. T. Clanchy, "Law, Government and Society in Medieval England," *History*, 59 (1974), 73-78, takes historians to task for this approach.

106. Maurice Keen, *The Outlaws of Medieval Legend* (London, 1961), p. 91.

107. Donald W. Sutherland, "The Reasoning of Fourteenth-Century Bar-

risters," paper presented at the American Historical Association meeting (December 1976).

108. Keen, *Outlaws*, p. 172.

109. Ibid., p. 87.

110. Thomas Wright, *The Political Songs of England: From the Reign of John to That of Edward II* (London, 1839), pp. 232-236.

111. *Rotuli Parl.*, I, pp. 324a, 365a, 372b (1320, 14 Ed. II), II, pp. 166a (1347, 21 Ed. III), III, 174b, 202a (1347-1348, 21-22 Ed. III).

112. G. R. Owst, *Literature and the Pulpit in Medieval England* (Oxford, 1933), p. 346.

113. Ibid., p. 342.

114. Wright, *Political Songs*, pp. 224-229.

115. Keen, *Outlaws*, p. 87.

116. E. L. G. Stones, "Sir Geoffrey le Scrope (c. 1285-1340) Chief Justice of the King's Bench," *English Historical Review*, 69 (1954), 13-14.

117. Dorothy Hughes, *A Study of Social and Consititutional Tendencies in the Early Years of Edward III* (London, 1915), pp. 183-184.

118. Cam, *The Hundred*, p. 106.

119. Ibid., pp. 70-74. Hughes, *Social and Constitutional Tendencies*, pp. 213-215.

120. Cam, Ibid., p. 106.

121. Ibid., pp. 83-84, 155, 158-159. In Suffolk a clerk was accused of taking bribes from a number of indicted persons to help them either get their names removed from the sheriff's calendar or to pack a jury.

122. Ibid., p. 165.

123. Ibid., pp. 151-152. Complaint about the abuse: *Rotuli Parl.*, II, 26.

124. Hunnisett, *Medieval Coroner*, pp. 120, 122-123.

125. Wright, *Political Songs*, pp. 232-235.

126. Hunnisett, *Medieval Coroner*, p. 36.

127. Alan Harding, *The Law Courts of Medieval England* (London, 1973), p. 92.

128. Just. 1/764 m. 3.

129. Ibid.

130. *Kent Keepers of the Peace*, p. 11. Quoted from *Literae Canturiensis*, I, 120-123.

131. Bellamy, *Crime and Public Order*, p. 29.

132. Ibid., p. 20. McFarlane, *Nobility*, p. 115, has claimed that before 1422 it is hard to find evidence of magnates using armed men to tamper with the courts, but this is obviously wrong.

133. T. F. T. Plucknett, "Parliament," in *The English Government at Work*, ed. J. F. Willard (Cambridge, Mass., 1940), I, 102-103.

134. Harding, *Law Courts*, p. 95.

135. Ibid., p. 93.

136. Ibid., pp. 97-98.

137. Just. 1/764 m. 2.

138. Ibid.

139. *Essex Sessions of the Peace 1351, 1377-89*, trans. Elizabeth Chapin Furber (Colchester, 1953), p. 63.

140. Hilton, *A Medieval Society*, p. 261.

141. Gollancz, "System of Gaol Delivery," p. 235.

142. Owst, *Literature and the Pulpit*, p. 346.

143. *Wakefield*, IV, 167.

144. Gabel, *Benefit of Clergy*, p. 120. Cam, *The Hundred*, p. 79. Hughes, *Social and Constitutional Tendencies*, pp. 216-217.

145. *Essex Sessions of the Peace*, pp. 32-37. Searle, *Battle Abbey*, pp. 432-435. Morris, *Frankpledge*, p. 105. Anne Reiber DeWindt, "Varieties of Peasant Legal Experience: The Huntingdon Eyre of 1286," paper presented at the American Historical Association meeting (December 1977), identified primary villagers, some of villein status, serving on the trial juries of the eyre.

146. Cam, *The Hundred*, pp. 80-81.

147. Just. 3/136 m. 16.

148. *Essex Sessions of the Peace*, p. 65.

149. Just. 3/134 m. 48.

150. Percentages of acquittal of males compared to females: Norfolk 66 percent males, 85.2 percent females acquitted; Northamptonshire 65.1 percent, 84.2 percent; Yorkshire 84.9 percent, 92.6 percent; Huntingdonshire 72.4 percent, 81.5 percent; Essex 62.9 percent, 84.4 percent; Somerset 82.1 percent, 90.4 percent; Surrey 74.6 percent, 83.3 percent; Herefordshire 82.3 percent, 92.3 percent.

151. In New York in 1940 jurors convicted 14 percent fewer women than men. In late nineteenth-century France the male jurors acquitted as many as 20 percent more women than men. O. Pollak, *The Criminality of Women* (Philadelphia, 1950), p. 5.

152. Gabel, *Benefit of Clergy*, p. 32. In York in 1336 five men were tried and convicted of larceny, burglary, robbery, and homicide. They pleaded clergy and managed to pass the literacy test. Just. 3/77/2 ms. 4-5.

153. Gollancz, "System of Gaol Delivery," p. 235. Bellamy, *Crime and Public Order*, pp. 12-21.

154. Walter A. Lunden, *Crime and Criminals* (Ames, Iowa, 1967), p. 162. F. H. McClintock and N. Howard Avison, *Crime in England and Wales* (London, 1968), p. 153.

155. Robson, *Convict Settlers*, p. 8.

156. Lunden, *Crime and Criminals*, p. 163.

157. Just. 3/49/1 m. 37d.

158. 1300-1304, 17.5 percent convictions; 1305-1309, 13.2 percent; 1310-1314, 18.5 percent; 1315-1319, 16 percent; 1320-1324, 20.6 percent; 1325-

1329, 17.8 percent; 1330-1334, 12.8 percent; 1335-1339, 28.6 percent; 1340-1344, 22.3 percent; 1345-1348, 22.6 percent.

159. *Ingoldmells*, pp. 19, 33, 53. Fear of robbers can be traced in place names such as "the Robber's Valey" and "the Robber's Pasture." Hoskins, "Murder and Sudden Death," p. 176.

160. Hanawalt, "Violent Death," p. 298. Given, *Society and Homicide*, pp. 91-105, found a similar low conviction rate in thirteenth-century homicide cases. His treatment of the problems of which way the judgment went depending on the manner in which the accused was charged, his victims, and whether or not he had accomplices is very interesting.

161. "Uniform Crime Reports—1968," in *Crime and Justice*, ed. Leon Radzinowicz and Marvin E. Wolfgang (New York, 1971), p. 138: murder, 43 percent convictions; p. 142: rape, 40 percent convictions; p. 145: robbery, 50 percent convictions; p. 147: burglary, 56 percent, larceny, 71 percent convictions.

162. Austin T. Turk, "Conflict and Criminality," *American Sociological Review*, 31 (June 1966), 338-352. "Law, Conflict and Order: From Theorizing toward Theories" and "Law as a Weapon in Social Conflict" in manuscript. Quote is from the latter, p. 20.

163. Ibid., p. 22.

164. Ibid., p. 21.

3 THE CRIMES: DEFINITIONS, PATTERNS, AND TECHNIQUES

1. T. F. T. Plucknett, "Commentary," in Bertha H. Putnam, *Proceedings before the Justices of Peace in the Fourteenth and Fifteenth Centuries* (London, 1938), pp. cxxxiii-clxi, this quote p. cxxxv.

2. Ibid., p. cxxxvii.

3. Roger Hood and Richard Sparks, *Key Issues in Criminology* (New York, 1970), pp. 25-28.

4. Norfolk, 36.9 percent; Yorkshire, 43.1 percent; Northamptonshire, 45.7 percent; Essex, 32.4 percent; Huntingdonshire, 36.7 percent; Herefordshire, 36.9 percent; Somerset, 35.1 percent; Surrey, 42.1 percent.

5. Stephen, *Criminal Law*, III, 142.

6. Pollock and Maitland, *English Law*, II, 494-500.

7. Jerome Hall, *Theft, Law, and Society*, 2nd ed. (Indianapolis, 1952), pp. 80-109, has one of the clearest discussions of the development of laws that came to encompass our laws of theft. As he points out, medieval society did not undertake to protect the consumer against his own gullibility. The defrauded could bring a civil suit, but the government did not consider duplicity that was freely entered into by both parties as felonious. Fraud by merchants and shopkeepers was controlled to a certain extent through guild regulations. Extortion through threats of violence might be prosecuted under robbery and arson.

8. Plucknett, "Commentary," p. cxxxix.

9. The dates of felonies did not become part of the record until after 1330. The material used here represents a sample drawn from the various counties for after that time.

10. Lunden, *Crime and Criminals,* pp. 27-30. The modern pattern is for a low start from January to April and then a peak in August followed by a return to the April levels for September through December. Larceny is the only property crime, as opposed to personal crimes, that is high in the summer months.

11. Just. 1/765 m. 2.

12. Just. 3/74/3 m. 12.

13. "Meier Helmbrecht," in Clair Hayden Bell, trans., *Peasant Life in Old German Epics* (New York, 1968), p. 69.

14. Ibid., p. 70.

15. Lunden, *Crime and Criminals,* p. 34.

16. "Helmbrecht," p. 68.

17. Just. 3/120 m. 12d.

18. Just. 3/116 m. 3.

19. *The Second Shepherds' Pagent,* in A. C. Cawley, ed., *Everyman and Medieval Miracle Plays* (New York, 1970), p. 91.

20. *Peter Quill's Shenanigans,* in Oscar Mandel, trans., *Five Comedies of Medieval France* (New York, 1970), p. 129.

21. Household goods, 1.2 percent; clothing, 6.1 percent; foodstuffs, 0.5 percent; industrial products, 2 percent; cloth, 10.3 percent; valuables, 3.7 percent.

22. Just. 3/48 m.2.

23. *Wakefield,* II, 129; IV, 94.

24. Just. 3/48/1 m. 37d, 53.

25. *Bedfordshire Coroners' Rolls,* pp. 64, 113-114, 117.

26. Just. 3/105 m. 6d.

27. *The Chicken Pie and the Chocolate Cake,* in *Five Comedies of Medieval France,* pp. 151-158.

28. Ronald Fuller, *The Beggar's Brotherhood* (London, 1936), pp. 146-164.

29. Just. 3/106 m. 3; 3/49/1 m. 49d.

30. Dorothy Chadwick, *Social Life in the Days of Piers Ploughman* (Cambridge, 1922), p. 77.

31. Just. 3/49/1 m. 37d.

32. In the victim's home, 18.6 percent; in fields, 50.8 percent; in barns, 8.3 percent; in streets, 3 percent; in markets, 8.7 percent; in churches, 3.4 percent; other, 7.2 percent.

33. Putnam, *Proceedings before the Justices of the Peace,* p. cxv. It is found mostly in Kent rather than in the other counties whose peace rolls she surveyed. The old term hamsoken was seldom used.

34. The evolution of this definition is discussed in Pollock and Maitland, *English Law*, II, 492-493. Plucknett, "Commentary," pp. cxliv-cxlvi. Harold Schneebeck, "The Law of Felony in Medieval England from the Accession of Edward I until the Mid-fourteenth Century," (Ph. D. dissertation, University of Iowa, 1973), pp. 555-563.

35. Thomas A. Repetto, *Residential Crime* (Cambridge, Mass., 1974), pp. 2-4.

36. Ibid. In modern criminal statistics 3 to 10 percent of all burglaries involved physical violence.

37. Harry A. Scarr, *Patterns of Burglary* (Washington, D.C., 1972), p. 4.

38. H. F. McClintock and N. Howard Avison, *Crime in England and Wales* (London, 1968), pp. 47-51. Lunden, *Crime and Criminals*, pp. 28-29.

39. Scarr, *Patterns of Burglary*, pp. 12, 47.

40. Repetto, *Residential Crime*, p. 30. The modern burglaries involving violence tended to cluster on the weekend. Since these burglaries represented cases of miscalculation about the absence of the owner or may have been motivated by need for drugs or money to celebrate the weekend, this pattern is bound to deviate from the usual burglaries.

41. Modern figures show that 58 percent of the targets of burglary are residential structures. Scarr, *Patterns of Burglary*, p. 10.

42. An additional 7.7 percent were on outbuildings, closes, and such.

43. Repetto, *Residential Crime*, p. 19. In his sample 6 percent were skilled, 82 percent semi-skilled, and 11 percent unskilled.

44. "Helmbrecht," p. 69.

45. Just. 3/125 m. 14d. He was taken off the ship at Yarmouth for trial. When he refused common law, his goods of £7 2s. 2d. were confiscated. Another case of chest breaking was that of Thomas de Burton of Thornton in Spalding who broke into the chest of Lord Thomas de Ros, Lord of Melburn, that contained charters, letters, and muniments. Just. 3/169 m. 27.

46. *Wakefield*, IV, 94.

47. *Statutes of the Realm*, 5 Ed. III (1331), Statute of Westminster, c. 14.

48. Just. 3/48.

49. *Bedfordshire Coroners' Rolls*, p. 116.

50. Ibid., p. 92. Another burglar used a coulter, p. 112.

51. Ibid., p. 14.

52. Just. 2/109 m. 7.

53. *Bedfordshire Coroners' Rolls*, p. 3.

54. Ibid., pp. 45, 91.

55. Ibid., p. 12.

56. Household goods, 2.2 percent; clothing, 3.2 percent; foodstuffs, 1.6 percent; industrial products, 1.7 percent; cloth, 16.2 percent; valuables, 17.7 percent; grain, 17.5 percent; poultry, 0.5 percent; horses, 2.1 percent; sheep, 4.4 percent; cattle, 2 percent; pigs, 0.3 percent; unspecified, 30.4 percent.

57. John E. Conklin, *Robbery and the Criminal Justice System* (Philadelphia, 1972), pp. 1-6.

58. The number of homicides in modern robbery is much lower. F. H. McClintock and Evelyn Gibson, *Robbery in London* (London, 1961), p. 7, shows that in 1957 only 1.3 percent of the cases ended in homicide. It is equally rare in the United States, Conklin, *Robbery*, p. 119. People injured in the Middle Ages were more likely to die than today because of lack of treatment so that the comparison cannot be a direct one.

59. Pollock and Maitland, *English Law*, II, 494.

60. Plucknett, "Commentary," p. cxlii.

61. Ibid.

62. Ibid., p. cxliv.

63. Conklin, *Robbery*, pp. 87-93.

64. Household goods, 1 percent; clothing, 4.9 percent; industrial products, 2.2 percent; cloth, 18.9 percent; valuables, 29 percent; grain, 0.8 percent; horses, 8.5 percent; sheep, 1.4 percent; cattle, 2.4 percent; unspecified, 30.8 percent.

65. Arnold Sagalyn, *The Crime of Robbery in the United States* (Washington, D. C., 1971), p. 4. The modern figure is 57.8 percent.

66. Victim's house, 4.2 percent; accused's house, 3.1 percent; tavern, 1 percent; field, 15.6 percent; barn, 4.2 percent; highway or street; 39.6 percent; church, 28.1 percent; other, 4.2 percent.

67. Stubbs, *Select Charters*, pp. 467-468.

68. Chadwick, *Days of Piers Ploughman*, pp. 77-78.

69. *Bedfordshire Coroners' Rolls*, p. 78. The personal effects of the felon were pathetic; a bow and arrows worth 3d., a coat in poor condition worth 6d., a horn worth 4d., and two knives worth 3½d.

70. Ibid., pp. 22, 1.

71. "Helmbrecht," p. 86.

72. Jusserand, *English Wayfaring Life*, pp. 73-74.

73. E. L. G. Stones, "The Folvilles of Ashby-Folville, Leicestershire, and their Associates in Crime," *Transactions of the Royal Historical Society*, 5th ser., VII (1957), 91-116.

74. John G. Bellamy, "The Coterel Gang: An Anatomy of a Band of Fourteenth-Century Criminals," *English Historical Review*, 79 (October 1974), 698-717.

75. A. E. Middleton, *Sir Gilbert Middleton and the Part He Took in the Rebellion in the North of England in 1317* (Newcastle-on-Tyne, 1918), pp. 28-29.

76. Just. 3/81/2 m. 16.

77. Just. 3/78 m. 20. See also the ransoming of a king's messenger for 1 mark in KB 27/319 and Just. 3/78 m. 24d. Thomas Parson of Ingelby was held for £20 and Just. 3/78 m. 21 where the victim was abducted from his home.

78. Just 3/145 m. 14, similar case on m. 21. A potential robber was killed by Maurice Seley who was a servant traveling with Lord Walter and others when he tried to rob them at a pass on the way to Colneye, Just. 3/134 m. 12.

79. Just. 3/78 m. 47.

80. Just. 3/78 m. 46; 3/125 m. 9d.

81. Just. 3/79/1 m. 1.

82. Just. 3/81/2 m. 55; 3/176 m. 12.

83. Just. 3/80/1 m. 6.

84. Just. 2/111 m. 16.

85. *Wakefield*, IV, 2-3.

86. Just. 3/49/1 m. 34. For another example see Just. 3/49/1 m. 36 and m. 17.

87. Just. 3/119 m. 3.

88. Just. 3/49/1 m. 17. See also Just. 3/47/3 m. 6.

89. Just. 3/49/1 m. 36.

90. *Bedfordshire Coroners' Rolls*, p. 7. Similar cases appear on pp. 12, 22 and 101.

91. Ibid., pp. 29-30.

92. Just. 3/116 m. 1.

93. Just. 1/764 m. 1.

94. Bellamy, "Coterels," p. 706.

95. Essex, 0.7 percent; Somerset, 0.4 percent; Surrey, 1.2 percent; Herefordshire, 0.6 percent; Norfolk, 0.6 percent; Northamptonshire, 1 percent; Yorkshire, 0.9 percent.

96. Just. 3/136 m. 1d.

97. Just. 1/607 m. 11.

98. Just. 3/47/3 m. 5.

99. Just. 1/764 m. 3.

100. *Wakefield*, IV, 146.

101. Just. 3/145 m. 1.

102. Bellamy, *Crime and Public Order*, pp. 95, 102.

103. Bellamy, "Coterels," p. 706.

104. Just. 3/76 m. 7.

105. Just. 1/376 m. 83. Given in Schneebeck, "Law of Felony," pp. 514-520.

106. Huntingdonshire, 20 percent; Essex, 7.4 percent; Somerset, 2.7 percent; Surrey, 7.1 percent; Herefordshire, 9.7 percent; Norfolk, 4.8 percent; Northamptonshire, 4.6 percent; Yorkshire, 5.9 percent.

107. A large number of approvers appealing receivers could throw off the data in Huntingdonshire because the sample size is so small.

108. Pollack and Maitland, *English Law*, ignored the problem. Hall, *Theft, Law, and Society*, pp. 52-58, has the best analysis of receiving.

109. Plucknett, "Commentary," pp. clxi-clxii.

110. Just. 3/99 m. 1 gives one example among many.

111. Just. 3/78 m. 43.

112. Just. 3/99 m. 5.

113. *Wakefield*, II, 128-129.

114. *Second Shepherds' Pagent*, p. 93. For a real case see *Wakefield*, V, 13.

115. Just. 3/78 m. 43.

116. Just. 3/51/2 m. 3; 3/134 m. 49d. See also Just. 3/24/4 ms. 3d., 5, 7.

117. Just. 3/49/1 m. 35.

118. Just. 3/114 m. 13.

119. Just. 3/116 m. 1d.

120. "Helmbrecht," p. 49.

121. Just. 3/78 m. 43; 3/51/2 m. 12.

122. Just. 3/99 m. 1d. Another example is at Just. 3/114 m. 12, in which a man received a gang of twelve.

123. Jusserand, *English Wayfaring Life*, p. 74.

124. Andrew F. Henry and James F. Short, Jr., "Status and the Relational System," in Marvin E. Wolfgang, ed., *Studies in Homicide* (New York, 1967), pp. 268-269.

125. Hanawalt, "Violent Death," pp. 299-300, has a discussion of the preservation of the coroners' records.

126. The preservation of early fourteenth-century rolls in Northamptonshire and not in most other counties is perhaps the result of the Northamptonshire Eyre of 1329-1330.

127. *Records of Medieval Oxford, Coroners' Inquests, the Walls of Oxford, etc.*, trans. H. E. Salter (Oxford, 1912).

128. *Calendar of Coroners' Rolls of the City of London, A.D. 1300-1378*, trans. R. R. Sharpe (London, 1913).

129. See Hanawalt, "Violent Death," p. 301, for details.

130. Plucknett, *Common Law*, p. 445. For a full discussion of pardons see Hurnard, *King's Pardon for Homicide* and Thomas A. Green, "Societal Concepts of Criminal Liability for Homicide in Medieval England," *Speculum*, 47, no. 4 (1972), 669-694. The coroners' roll evidence shows that the jurors were making decisions on some of the accidental homicides and not bringing criminal indictments against the killers. In a Northamptonshire case a clerk was shooting arrows at a target and accidentally struck a three-year-old girl who was behind it. The inquest jurors called this a case of misadventure, Just. 2/107 m. 2. In another case one boy accidentally killed another while they were playing and the jurors did not classify it as a homicide, Just. 2/114. There is also a case in London, *Coroners' Rolls of the City of London*, p. 83. If the jurors were softening the definition of homicide at the indictment level, they were probably also doing so at the trials by returning verdicts of innocent. In other words, the jurors were making distinctions in practice that did not become statute law until the close of the fourteenth century.

131. Plucknett, *Common Law*, p. 445.

132. J. M. Kaye, "The Early History of Murder and Manslaughter, Part I," *The Law Quarterly Review*, 83 (July 1967), 365-395, has an excellent discussion of the early distinctions and the history of the 1390 statute.

133. *Uniform Crime Reports* (Washington, D.C., 1965), p. 51. In calculating this figure, I have left out auto theft and aggravated assault since they were not felonies in fourteenth- and fifteenth-century England. However, since it is possible to argue that more assaults ended in homicide in the Middle Ages because of the ineffectiveness of medical care, I also did a calculation including aggravated assaults with homicides and arrived at 8 percent—still considerably lower than medieval England. Given, *Society and Homicide*, pp. 33-40, failed to take higher mortality from homicide into account, thus making medieval society appear even more murderous. Marvin E. Wolfgang, *Patterns in Criminal Homicide*, (Philadelphia, 1958) pp. 116-118, has observed that the rising of assault and the lowering of homicide in Philadelphia is a result of the influence of better medicine during the twentieth century. In modern England the percentage of homicides compared to all other felonies is 0.2 percent, T. Morris and L. Blom-Cooper, *A Calendar of Murder; Criminal Homicide in England since 1957* (London, 1964), p. 277.

134. L. O. Pike, *A History of Crime in England* (London, 1873), I, 254-255.

135. Russell, *British Medieval Population*, pp. 285-287, finds from the 1377 poll tax a population of 35,000 and guesses that the population before the plague was nearer to 60,000. The lowest figure would certainly be in excess of 33,000 as Sylvia L. Thrupp points out in *The Merchant Class of Medieval London* (Ann Arbor, 1962), p. 52. By using ranges of population here, I have avoided some of the problems Given, *Society and Homicide*, ran into trying to establish absolute homicide rates for the thirteenth century.

136. *Uniform Crime Reports* (Washington, D.C., 1965), p. 51.

137. Paul Bohannan, "Patterns of Homicide among Tribal Societies in Africa," *Studies in Homicide*, ed. Marvin E. Wolfgang (New York, 1967), p. 218.

138. For a modern comparison see Morris and Blom-Cooper, *Calendar of Murder*, p. 277. In England between 1900-1949 there were only 7,500 murders or only about 1,500 more murders than the yearly number of people killed on the road.

139. See Hanawalt, "Violent Death," pp. 318-320, for the figures for this and other conclusions based on the Northamptonshire, London, and Oxford data.

140. Wolfgang, *Criminal Homicide*, p. 99. Lunden, *Crime and Criminals*, pp. 27-29. J. Cohen, "The Geography of Crime," *Readings in Criminology and Penology*, ed. D. Dressler (New York, 1964), p. 230.

141. The distribution of homicides by months in Northamptonshire, London, and Oxford is as follows. Northamptonshire: Jan. 7.0 percent, Feb. 6.5,

March 10.7, April 10.1, May 8.3, June 10.8, July 8.8, Aug. 10.7, Sept. 7.4, Oct. 4.5, Nov. 7.6, Dec. 7.6. London: Jan. 7.0, Feb. 10.0, March 8.0, April 6.0, May 11.0, June 11.0, July 8.0, Aug. 10.0, Sept. 6.0, Oct. 6.0, Nov. 11.0, Dec. 6.0. Oxford: Jan. 3.7, Feb. 13.0, March 5.6, April 13.0, May 11.1, June 11.1, July 7.4, Aug. 1.8, Sept. 7.4, Oct. 7.4, Nov. 7.4, Dec. 11.1. The material appears in tabular form in Hanawalt, "Violent Death," p. 318. For a fuller and more recent discussion of the Oxford homicide pattern see Carl I. Hammer, Jr., "Patterns of Homicide in a Medieval University Town: Fourteenth-Century Oxford," *Past and Present*, no. 78 (1978), pp. 2-21.

142. Wolfgang, *Criminal Homicide*, pp. 106-107.

143. Lunden, *Crime and Criminals*, pp. 27-29.

144. The Northamptonshire coroners' roll data show knives being used in 41.7 percent of the homicides, axes and hatchets in 13.6 percent, swords in 5.9 percent, bow and arrow in 5.8 percent, lances in 0.2 percent, pitchforks in 1.9 percent, staffs in 26.7 percent, fists or feet in 0.6 percent, hammers in 2.7 percent, and other implements in 0.9 percent. The information appears in tabular form in Hanawalt, "Violent Death," p. 319. In modern England 33 percent of the murderers use sharp instruments. Evelyn Gibson and S. Klein, *Murder 1957 to 1968: A Home Office Statistical Division Report on Murder in England and Wales* (London, 1969), p. 24. In Africa 30 percent to 71.4 percent of the murderers use sharp instruments. Bohannon, "Patterns of Homicide," p. 227.

145. Just. 2/110 m. 13.

146. Gibson and Klein, *Murder*, p. 24. In modern England 17.4 percent use blunt instruments. Among African tribes, 11.8 percent to 51 percent use blunt instruments. Bohannon, "Patterns of Homicide," p. 227.

147. *Coroners' Rolls of the City of London*, p. 170.

148. Victim's home, 17.1 percent; accused's home, 10 percent; tavern, 1.4 percent; field, 12.8 percent; barn, 4.3 percent; highway or street, 30 percent; market or shop, 4.3 percent; church, 15.7 percent; other, 4.3 percent.

149. Schneebeck, "Law of Felony," p. 269.

150. Thomas R. Forbes, "Life and Death in Shakespeare's London," *American Scientist*, 58 (1970), 520.

151. Emile Durkheim, *Suicide*, trans. John A. Spaulding and George Simpson (New York, 1951).

152. *Bedfordshire Coroners' Rolls*, p. ix.

153. Just. 2/111 m. 27.

154. Just. 2/113 m. 7.

155. Just. 2/113 m. 14.

156. Just. 2/113 m. 28.

157. Just. 2/111 m. 15.

158. Schneebeck, "Law of Felony," p. 270.

159. Rodney H. Hilton, "Peasant Movements in England before 1381," in

Essays in Economic History, ed. E. M. Carus-Wilson (London, 1962), p. 90.

160. *Medieval Oxford*, p. 26.

161. *Bedfordshire Coroners' Rolls*, p. 114.

162. Mayhem was reduced to a civil plea in 1285.

163. Schneebeck, "Law of Felony," pp. 466-467.

164. Ibid.

165. Ibid., pp. 486-505. Sue Sheridan Walker has been exploring this difficult problem of abduction. See her article "Violence and the Exercise of Feudal Guardianship: The Action of *'Ejectio Custodia'*," *American Journal of Legal History*, 16 (1972), 320-333.

166. Schneebeck, "Law of Felony," pp. 434-505. One curious point he brings out is that the legal opinion held both in treaties and in practice that if the woman conceived during rape, she had to have voluntarily entered into sexual relations with her attacker. Conception, they maintained, was impossible without the woman's consent.

167. Ibid., pp. 482-486.

168. "Unified Crime Reports—1968," p. 134. Again I have removed the auto thefts and assaults from the calculation.

169. Just. 3/79/1 m. 50d. Other cases in Just. 3/79/3 m. 8 and Just. 3/78 m. 7.

170. Just. 3/80/1 m. 2. For others see Just. 3/77/4 m. 11 and Just. 3/78 m. 1.

171. Just. 3/78 m. 27; 3/80/5 m. 14d, 17.

172. Just. 3/81/2 m. 9.

173. Andreas Capellanus, *The Art of Courtly Love*, trans. John Jay Parry (New York, 1972), p. 24.

174. Schneebeck, "Law of Felony," pp. 477-478, gives too much emphasis to this point. We know far too little about medieval marriage practices to assume that this was common enough to influence criminal statistics.

175. *Calendar of Patent Rolls, 1317-1321*, p. 477.

176. Ibid., pp. 197, 290.

177. Ibid., p. 560.

178. *Bedfordshire Coroners' Rolls*, pp. 27-28.

179. Just. 3/78 m. 10; 3/80/1 ms. 9d., 7.

180. Just. 3/78 m. 31.

181. Just. 3/80/1 m. 6.

182. Just. 3/80/1 m. 13d.

183. *Calendar of Patent Rolls, 1317-1321*, p. 485.

184. Menachem Amir, "Patterns of Forcible Rape," in *Criminal Behavior Systems*, ed. Marshall B. Clinard and Richard Quinney (New York, 1967), p. 65. He found that force was used in all but 15 percent of the rapes but that nearly half of them were "non-brutal beatings" and choking.

185. *Coroners' Rolls of the City of London*, Roll A.

186. Ibid.

187. Just. 3/78 m. 21.

188. Schneebeck, "Law of Felony," p. 478-79.

189. *Robin and Marion*, in *Five Comedies of Medieval France*, trans. Oscar Mandel (New York, 1970), p. 87.

190. Ibid., pp. 93-95.

191. Just. 3/80/4 m. 14.

192. Just. 3/78 m. 13d. On m. 14 a single rapist kept a woman for a week.

193. Just. 3/80/1 m. 6.

194. Amir, "Forcible Rape", pp. 67, 69-73.

195. Just. 3/81/2 m. 3. Similar cases, Just. 3/78 ms. 12d., 16d.

196. Huntingdonshire, 1.3 percent; Essex, 0.2 percent; Somerset, 0.2 percent; Surrey, 0.2 percent; Herefordshire, 0.9 percent; Norfolk, 0.6 percent; Northamptonshire, 0.7 percent; Yorkshire, 0.5 percent.

197. Bellamy, *Crime and Public Order*, p. 49, expressed the opinion that the king wrongly used treason charges in this case, but in fact in this and other cases Edward II was acting in a boldly innovative way.

198. Pollock and Maitland, *English Law*, II, 505-506.

199. Just. 3/49 m. 39d.

200. Just. 3/47/3 m. 4.

201. Just. 3/110 m. 5; 3/106 m. 3.

202. Just. 3/75 m. 34. See also Just. 3/117 m. 15.

203. T. F. Tout, "Medieval Forgers and Forgeries," *Bulletin of the John Rylands Library, Manchester*, 5 (1919), 217.

204. KB 27/334 m. 35. See also Just. 3/75 m. 11.

205. Just. 3/75, m. 11.

4 THE SUSPECTS

1. Bertha H. Putnam, "Shire Officials: Keepers of the Peace and Justices of the Peace," *The English Government at Work*, III, ed. J. F. Willard, W. A. Morris, W. H. Dunham (Cambridge, Mass., 1950), p. 217.

2. Huntingdonshire, 9.5 percent women; Essex, 9.3 percent; Somerset, 6.6 percent; Surrey, 8.7 percent; Herefordshire, 10.3 percent; Norfolk, 14.5 percent; Northamptonshire, 10.4 percent; Yorkshire, 7.6 percent.

3. Samaha, *Law and Order*, p. 27. J. M. Beattie, "The Criminality of Women in Eighteenth-Century England," *The Journal of Social History*, 8 (1975), 80, found that in Surrey the proportion was 1 woman to 8 men.

4. Hermann Mannheim, *Comparative Criminology*, 2nd ed. (Boston, 1967), p. 697.

5. Dorie Klein, "The Etiology of Female Crime: A Review of the Literature," *Issues in Criminology*, 2 (1973), 3-30. This review is highly critical of the emphasis on sexuality among the various male interpretors of female behavior.

6. W. A. Bonger, *Criminality and Economic Conditions,* ed. A. T. Turk (London, 1969), p. 64.

7. Carol Z. Wiener, "Sex Roles and Crime in Late Elizabethan Hereford-shire," *The Journal of Social History,* 8 (1975), 308-312, is an excellent analysis of the sex-role stereotyping in society and in criminal roles.

8. Gwynn Nettler, *Explaining Crime* (New York, 1974), pp. 102-103. Be-tween 1960 and 1969 overall violent crimes have increased 142 percent for men and 231 percent for women and overall property crimes have increased 73 percent for men and 211 percent for women.

9. D. M. Stenton, *The English Woman in History* (London, 1957), Eileen Power, *Medieval Women,* ed. M. M. Postan (Cambridge, 1975), and Susan Mosher Stuard, ed., *Women in the Middle Ages* (Philadelphia, 1976).

10. Hanawalt, "Childrearing," pp. 7-8.

11. Henry Kramer and James Sprenger, *Malleus Malificarum,* trans. Montague Summers (London, 1928), p. 44.

12. Wolfgang Lederer, *The Fear of Women* (New York, 1968), pp. 92-98, used a Freudian framework to explain women's low participation in crime, but the evidence upon which he bases his claim is drawn from an Agatha Christie mystery. In the end he proves nothing except that he fears that women do conceal crimes. Pollak, *Criminality of Women,* p. 10, explained the differences between men and women and their criminal participation through an analysis of the sex act: men cannot conceal a failure at orgasm while women can. He never explains what the connection is between a sex act and a criminal act. This type of psychological argument reflects the subjective views of the authors and is based on no research data.

13. Klein, "Female Crime," p. 23. She argues that this "chivalrous" treatment of female offenders is extended to middle class white women only, not to poor and Third World women. But her own statistics indicate that this is incorrect. All women are indicted less frequently than men. In fact, chivalry has little to do with it since the attitudes we are studying are among the peasantry.

14. Lunden, *Crime and Criminals,* p. 102. Women committed 19 percent of all larcenies. In modern America, of all the homicides, robberies, burglaries, and larcenies women committed, 87.6 percent were larceny.

15. Beattie, "Criminality of Women," p. 91.

16. Lunden, *Crime and Criminals,* p. 102, as adjusted for the four felonies.

17. Just. 3/74/2 m. 11.

18. Lunden, *Crime and Criminals,* p. 102. In the modern figures 7.7 percent of the males were arrested for robbery compared to 2.7 percent of the females.

19. Just. 3/77/2 m. 3. For other cases see Just. 3/75 ms. 13-16.

20. Just. 3/76 ms. 3-3d.

21. *Wakefield,* II, 57.

22. Lunden, *Crime and Criminals,* p. 102, 18 percent of the murderers arrested were female.

23. Ibid., 14 percent of all arrests for assault are women.

24. Veli Verkko, "Static and Dynamic 'Laws' of Sex and Homicide," *Studies in Homicide,* ed. Marvin E. Wolfgang (New York, 1967), p. 42, develops a law to predict the lower appearance of women in crimes against life: "In countries of higher frequency of crimes against life the participation of women in these crimes is small." Although this law has been justly criticized for leaving out a variety of other factors that might explain the differences in rates between men and women, nevertheless, it does fit the medieval statistics. His second law that, "If the frequency of crimes against life in a country tends to increase, the increase primarily affects the number of male criminals," is also borne out, particularly in the hundred years of Northamptonshire coroners' roll evidence.

25. Pike, *Crime in England,* II, 527.

26. Just. 3/125 m. 9d.

27. *Bedfordshire Coroners' Rolls,* p. 14.

28. Carol Z. Weiner, "Is a Spinster an Unmarried Woman?" *The American Journal of Legal History,* 20 (1976), 27-31. Valerie C. Edwards, "The Case of the Married Spinster: An Alternative Explanation," *The American Journal of Legal History,* 21 (1977), 260-265.

29. For examples see Just. 3/18/5 ms. 15, 35 and 3/129 m. 12 where the wife is hanged but the husband is not.

30. Just. 3/125 m. 9d.

31. Just. 3/78 m. 46. See also Just. 3/79/1 m. 2d.

32. Just. 3/51/4 m. 3d.

33. Holdsworth, *English Law* III, 372, puts the age of criminal responsibility after fourteen years old. Hurnard, *King's Pardon,* p. 152, found no pardons for thirteen-year-olds and concluded that they were presented as twelve-year-olds. The gaol delivery cases, however, are explicit in stating that the accused was guilty but should be excused "because he is under 12 years of age." See Just. 3/50/2 m. 5 for one example.

34. *Bedfordshire Coroners' Rolls,* p. 51.

35. Just. 3/136 m. 16.

36. Philippe Ariès, *Centuries of Childhood,* trans. Robert Baldick (New York, 1962).

37. N. J. G. Pounds, *An Economic History of Medieval Europe* (London, 1974), pp. 155-156, is an excellent summary of the data.

38. Nettler, *Explaining Crime,* pp. 98-100. Tobias, *Victorian England,* p. 60, describes the problems of increased crime in Victorian London as the effect of a demographic bulge early in the nineteenth century.

39. *Coroners' Rolls of the City of London,* p. 83.

40. *Wakefield*, IV, 168.

41. Just. 3/48 m. 32. See also Just. 3/48 m. 43 where a ten-year-old boy stole goods worth 11s. 6d. and Just. 3/49/1 m. 3.

42. Just. 3/49/1 m. 49d.

43. *Bedfordshire Coroners' Rolls*, p. 33.

44. Just. 2/109 m. 2.

45. W. G. Hoskins, *The Midland Peasant* (London, 1957), p. 78.

46. *Early Huntingdonshire Lay Subsidy Rolls*, ed. J. Ambrose Raftis and Mary Patricia Hogan (Toronto, 1976), pp. 13-27. A further problem with the subsidy rolls is that they do not include all family members such as sons or wives and daughters.

47. R. B. Pugh, "Some Reflections of a Medieval Criminologist," *Proceedings of the British Academy*, 59 (London, 1973), 20. Given, *Society and Homicide*, pp. 68-70 also makes the mistake of assuming that the low value of convicted felons' chattels indicates that they are the poor of society.

48. Hunnisett, *Medieval Coroner*, pp. 31-33.

49. *Wakefield*, IV, 167.

50. Pugh, *Imprisonment*, pp. 316-317.

51. DeWindt, *Hollywell-cum-Needingworth*, p. 267, found that 46 percent of the trespasses were committed by this group. Britton, "Broughton," pp. 235-250.

52. Just. 3/24/1 m. 2.

53. DeWindt, *Hollywell-cum-Needingworth*, p. 267, and Britton, "Broughton," pp. 235-250, found a similar pattern in the manorial courts for secondary villagers.

54. Just. 3/24/4 m. 4d.

55. Just. 3/24/4 m. 3d.

56. Britton, "Broughton," p. 23, DeWindt, *Hollywell-cum-Needingworth*, pp. 209-210.

57. Just. 3/24/1 m. 2.

58. Britton, "Broughton," p. 239.

59. Ibid., p. 242. In manorial court records Britton found that all cases of theft were A families. This may indicate that the A group was able to demote their theft cases to the manorial level while others were less likely to be able to do so.

60. Just. 3/136 m. 16.

61. Raftis, "Concentration of Responsibility," pp. 116-117.

62. Bellamy, "Coterels," pp. 716-717, found that the peasants receiving them were all in the lay subsidy rolls, and therefore, well off.

63. Raftis, "Social Structure in Five East Midlands Villages," *Economic History Review*, 2nd ser. 18 (1965), 87-90. There were forty outsiders who committed crimes with known villagers or in the village in the Ramsey sample. This is similar to the number of outsiders committing trespasses and assaults.

64. *Bedfordshire Coroners' Rolls*, pp. 118, 32.

65. Hans von Hentig, *The Criminal and His Victim: Studies in the Sociology of Crime* (New Haven, 1948), p. 308.

66. *Statutes of the Realm*, II, I Henry V, St. 1 c. 5. The labels used to identify the suspects were not reliable even then.

67. Just. 3/49/1 m. 36; 3/125 m. 14d.

68. Just. 3/48.

69. Just. 3/78 m. 46.

70. Just. 3/79/3 m. 1.

71. Norfolk, 5.1 percent; Yorkshire, 3 percent; Northamptonshire, 5 percent; Huntingdonshire, 5 percent; Essex, 3.7 persent; Somerset, 4.7 percent; Surrey, 4.7 percent; Herefordshire, 5.5 percent.

72. Walter Rye, *History of Norfolk* (London, 1885), pp. 180-181.

73. Household goods, 0; clothing, 5.8 percent; foodstuffs, 0; industrial products, 2.2 percent; cloth, 9.8 percent; valuables, 37.3 percent; grain, 4.9 percent; poultry, 0; horses, 21.6 percent; sheep, 4.3 percent; cattle, 7.2 percent; pigs, 0.

74. 1-12d., 38.5 percent; 1-10s., 5.5 percent; 11-20s., 21.3 percent; over £1, 35.1 percent.

75. Stones, "Folvilles," pp. 117, 129.

76. Just. 3/75 ms. 13-17.

77. Just. 3/48 m. 5.

78. Just. 3/74/3 ms. 6-7.

79. Just. 3/48 m. 5.

80. Just. 3/107 m. 1. Another case Just. 3/48 m. 39.

81. Hanawalt, "Fur-Collar Crime."

82. Edwin H. Sutherland, *White Collar Crime* (Bloomington, Ind., 1949), p. 9.

83. Stones, "Folvilles" and Bellamy, "Coterels." Even in his book *Crime and Public Order*, Bellamy drew his examples almost solely from the upper classes. There are also numerous articles in local history journals about the crimes of the aristocracy.

84. Hilton, *A Medieval Society*, p. 254.

85. This figure is certainly not representative of the number of nobility who were tried in gaol delivery but only those identified by title. Others without titles or younger sons could be present but not easily identified except by someone acquainted with the names of the county nobility.

86. *Kent Keepers of the Peace*, pp. xxix-xlii.

87. *Statutes of the Realm*, 37 Ed. III, c. 8-12.

88. McFarlane, *Nobility*, pp. 6-8.

89. *Select Cases from the Coroners' Rolls, 1265-1413*, ed. C. Gross (Seldon Society, IX, London, 1896), p. 58.

90. *Rotuli Parl.*, II, p. 64.

91. M. M. Postan, Lecture at the University of California, Los Angeles, March 1974. S. L. Waugh, "The Profits of Violence: The Minor Gentry in the Rebellion of 1321-1322 in Gloucestershire and Herefordshire," *Speculum*, 52 (1977), 843-869.

92. Just. 3/74/4 ms. 1-2. See also Just. 3/49/2 m. 4 and KB 27/248 m. 10.

93. Just. 3/51/3 m. 6d.

94. Just. 1/764 ms. 1-10.

95. Just. 1/764 m. 1, m. 2.

96. Just. 3/48.

97. Just. 1/764 ms. 2d., 3.

98. Clanchy, "Law, Government and Society," pp. 73-78, pointed out that these historians tend to be "king's men" and look at history with the hindsight of Tudor absolutism rather than feudalism as their model of government.

99. *Calendar of Patent Rolls*, 1301-1307, p. 349.

100. For a more complete discussion on the relationship of the king to his barons in punishing them for their crimes see Hanawalt, "Fur-Collar Crime," pp. 9-14.

101. *Essex Sessions of the Peace*, p. 65.

102. Just. 3/134 m. 49.

103. Just. 3/24/4 m. 5.

104. Just. 3/24/3 m. 1d.

105. Nigel Walker, *Crime and Insanity in England*, I (Edinburgh, 1968), 27-28. Hurnard, *King's Pardon*, p. 159.

106. Walker, *Crime and Insanity*, I, 24-25.

107. Ibid., pp. 27-28. Walker cites only *non sanae mentis* and *furiosus*, but all the forms mentioned appear in the gaol delivery rolls.

108. A. C. Crombie, *Medieval and Early Modern Science*, I (New York, 1959), 237. See also Thomas F. Graham, *Medieval Minds: Mental Health in the Middle Ages* (London, 1967).

109. Just. 3/48 m. 24d; 3/119 m. 14d. Other examples: Just. 3/48 m. 22 and 3/125 m. 10.

110. Just. 3/48 m. 4d.

111. Just. 3/125 m. 4d.

112. Just. 3/48 m. 10. Other cases: Just. 3/48 ms. 13, 20, and 24d.

113. KB 27/327 m. 36d. Because of her general ill health and debilitation she was bailed while she awaited pardon.

114. Just. 3/76 m. 17.

115. Just. 3/47/3 m. 14.

116. Just. 3/48 m. 10.

117. KB 27/327 m. 36.

118. Just. 3/78 m. 48.

119. Just. 3/119 m. 14d.

120. Just. 3/51/3 m. 13.

121. Just. 3/48 m. 6.

122. Just. 3/49/1 m. 40.

123. Just. 3/48 m. 10.

124. Just. 3/48 m. 4d; m. 20; m. 8.

125. KB 27/355 m. 29.

126. H. Weihofen, *Mental Disorder as a Criminal Defense* (New York, 1954), p. 15; W. C. Sullivan, *Crime and Insanity* (New York, 1924), pp. 89-100.

127. Mannheim, *Comparative Criminology*, I, 251.

128. Sullivan, *Crime and Insanity*, pp. 131-149. Sullivan uses the old term of dementia praecox rather than schizophrenia. Weihofen, *Mental Disorder*, pp. 116-117, gives a brief description of the schizophrenic killer. "The catatonic schizophrenic displays a sweeping abandonment of conventional behavior . . . Indecent exposure, outrageous sexual proposals or attacks, brutal assaultiveness, gross destructiveness, threats, murder, etc. may be carried out with reckless abandon."

129. Just. 3/48 m. 11.

130. Just. 3/74/3 m. 14.

131. Walker, *Crime and Insanity*, I, 29.

132. Rotha M. Clay, *The Medieval Hospitals of England* (London, 1909), pp. 32-33. As leprosy died out as a disease, many of the leper hospitals were transformed into hospitals for the insane.

133. Ibid., p. 31.

134. G. Rosen, *Madness in Society: Chapters in the Historical Sociology of Mental Illness* (London, 1968), pp. 140-141.

135. Just. 3/48 m. 13.

5 THE RELATIONSHIP BETWEEN THE VICTIM AND THE ACCUSED

1. *Piers Plowman* in J. B. Ross and M. M. McLaughlin, eds., *The Portable Medieval Reader* (New York, 1949), p. 198.

2. Hentig, *Criminal and His Victim*, p. 384. Hentig was one of the first to identify the relationship. The administrators of justice are concerned in these cases with watching who in this intimate relationship first broke the law and also with the motivations for the act that might well have been incited by the victim himself.

3. Israel Drapkin and Emiliano Viano, eds., *Victimology* (Lexington, Mass., 1974).

4. M. J. C. Hodgart, *The Ballads* (New York, 1962), pp. 92-93.

5. Just. 3/81/2.

6. Just. 1/258 m. 9.

7. *Wakefield*, II, 93.

8. Just. 3/48 m. 4d.

9. Just. 3/110 m. 5.

10. *Medieval Oxford*, p. 27.

11. Holdsworth, *English Law*, IV, 501.

12. Hurnard, *King's Pardon*, p. 169.

13. Richard H. Helmholtz, "Infanticide in the Province of Canterbury during the Fifteenth Century," *History of Childhood Quarterly*, 2 (1975), 384. This is the best summary of the synodal legislation and its application.

14. Ibid., p. 382.

15. Ibid., pp. 380-382. He feels that more might have been heard at the local level than appear in the bishop's court.

16. Ibid., p. 384.

17. *Wakefield*, V, 82.

18. Emily R. Coleman, "L'infanticide dans le Haut Moyen Age," *Annales: économie, société, civilisations*, 29 (1974), 315-335. Richard C. Trexler, "Infanticide in Florence: New Sources and First Results," *History of Childhood Quarterly*, 1 (1973), 98-116.

19. *Accidents Facts, 1968 Edition*, National Safety Council (Chicago, 1968), p. 14.

20. Albert P. Iskrant and Paul V. Joliet, *Accidents and Homicide* (Cambridge, Mass., 1968), p. 14.

21. *Second Shepherd's Pagent*, p. 95.

22. Johannes de Trokelowe, *Annales (Chronica Monasterii S. Albani)*, ed. H. T. Riley, Rolls Series (London, 1866), p. 95, claims that in 1316-1317 mothers killed their children and ate them.

23. Just. 3/169 m. 9.

24. The sample used here was 99 cases taken from Just. 2/102 and 119A.

25. Marvin Wolfgang, "Victim-Precipitated Criminal Homicide," *Studies in Homicide*, Marvin E. Wolfgang, ed. (New York, 1967), pp. 77-78. Age heaping, or rounding to the nearest ten years, may account for the slightly higher mean age.

26. Just. 2/119A m. 5.

27. Just. 2/119A m. 1; m. 5.

28. Morris and Bloom-Cooper, *Calendar of Murder*, p. 280. In Philadelphia it was 29.2 percent, Wolfgang, *Criminal Homicide*, p. 209. Given, *Society and Homicide*, pp. 41-60, found that the thirteenth-century homicide pattern among family members was similar to that which I found for the fourteenth century.

29. In nonfamilial actions only 21.6 percent were involved in assaults, with 67.4 percent in property disputes.

30. Just. 3/48 m. 13.

31. Just. 3/23 m. 1.

32. *Ingoldmells*, pp. 119-120, has examples on nonhomicidal disputes between brothers.

33. Ramon H. Myers, *The Chinese Peasant Economy: Agricultural Development in Hopei and Shantung, 1890-1949* (Cambridge, Mass., 1970), pp. 164-166.

34. *Wakefield*, II, 140, 141. In another case, a mother got the better of her son by holding the land he was to inherit eighteen years beyond the time he reached majority, *Ingoldmells*, p. 98.

35. Hoskins, "Murder," pp. 179-183.

36. *Wakefield*, III, 34, 41, 51.

37. *Bedfordshire Coroners' Rolls*, p. 10.

38. Just. 3/48 m. 29.

39. *Wakefield*, III, 108. See also 109 and IV, 33.

40. Ibid., III, 45.

41. Just. 3/24/1 m. 2.

42. Just. 3/78 m. 2.

43. *Bedfordshire Coroners' Rolls*, p. 13.

44. R. H. Helmholtz, *Marriage Litigation in Medieval England* (Cambridge, 1974), pp. 74-111. Michael M. Sheehan, "The Formation and Stability of Marriage in Fourteenth-Century England: Evidence of an Ely Register," *Mediaeval Studies*, 33 (1971), 249-252. A mitigating factor in the stiff divorce laws was that the marriage contract was fairly loose. Consent of the parties and subsequent consummation were all that was necessary for a valid marriage. Parental consent and a church ceremony were not necessary. Thus there were a fair number of bigamy cases coming into the ecclesiastical courts.

45. *Bedfordshire Coroners' Rolls*, p. 19.

46. *Wakefield*, V, 18.

47. Just. 3/107 m. 7.

48. Quoted in Mannheim, *Comparative Criminology*, p. 306.

49. Wolfgang, "Victim-Precipitated Criminal Homicide," p. 74.

50. Just. 3/108 m. 1.

51. *Bedfordshire Coroners' Rolls*, p. 73.

52. Dennis Chapman, *Sociology and the Stereotype of the Criminal* (London, 1968), p. 156, places a large emphasis on Oedipal slayings in modern crime.

53. Bohannon, "Patterns of Homicide," pp. 223-225.

54. J. Ambrose Raftis, "Town and Country Migration," in "Studies in Peasant Mobility," unpublished manuscript. Raftis found that five miles or less was the usual radius of a day's business or pleasure contacts. In Norfolk, which was a more settled agricultural area than Northamptonshire, 31.4 percent of all crimes occurred in the village of the accused.

55. In Northamptonshire with its many borders, there was a larger number of suspects from outside the county, but where villages in other counties were contiguous, the residents would have known each other although official contacts would have been less in law enforcement areas.

56. Just. 3/49/1 m. 17.

57. Hanawalt, "Violent Death," p. 309.

58. Wolfgang, *Criminal Homicide,* p. 191.

59. *Select Cases from the Coroners' Rolls,* p. 69.

60. Again there is a problem in cheating in the subsidy rolls and, therefore, this figure undoubtedly indicates an underrepresentation. DeWindt, *Holywell-cum-Needingworth,* p. 71, found that the major families were victims in 31 out of 77, or 40 percent, of the acts of violence recorded in manorial courts so that perhaps the figure is not too far off.

61. Just. 3/136 m. 13d.

62. This information was provided by John Beattie of the University of Toronto who is working on a study of seventeenth and eighteenth century English crime.

63. Just. 3/24/4 m. 2.

64. Just. 3/24/2 m. 2.

65. Britton, "Broughton," p. 247. The secondary villagers assaulted the prominent villagers, defamed them, and raised the hue and cry against them more frequently than the opposite occurred.

66. Just. 3/25/1 m. 6.

67. Just. 3/24/4 m. 1d.

68. *Higden's Polychronicon,* trans. John Trevisa, in R. B. Dobson, ed., *The Peasants' Revolt of 1381* (London, 1970), pp. 53-54.

69. Hilton, "Peasant Movements in England before 1381," pp. 73-90.

70. *Coroners' Rolls of the City of London,* pp. 34-35.

71. Just. 3/214/4 m. 9.

72. *Bedfordshire Coroners' Rolls,* p. 82.

73. Just. 3/94 m. 9d.

74. Britton, "Broughton," pp. 370-372.

75. Just. 3/169 m. 27; 3/175 m.2.

76. Just. 3/49/1 m. 50; 3/129 m. 58.

77. Hilton, *A Medieval Society,* p. 166.

78. Just. 3/24/4 m. 5d., m. 4d.

79. Sample of 246 cases. The prominence of the clergy as victims is particularly significant since there was no benefit of clergy in being a victim. It probably is a further indication of the resentment of the villagers against the clergy's wealth.

80. Just. 3/134 m. 49d.

81. Ibid.

82. *Bedfordshire Coroners' Rolls,* p. 102.

83. Just. 3/49/1 m. 37d; 2/113 m. 11.

84. *Medieval Oxford,* p. 9.

85. *Coroners' Rolls of the City of London,* pp. 114-116.

86. *Bedfordshire Coroners' Rolls,* p. 42.

87. Green, "Criminal Liability," has discussion of this problem.

88. *Medieval Oxford*, pp. 3-4.

6 CRIMINAL ASSOCIATIONS AND PROFESSIONAL CRIME

1. Hodgart, *Ballads*, p. 68. This was a seventeenth-century claim for the epitaph of one "historical" Robin Hood.

2. Eric J. Hobsbawm, *Primitive Rebels* (Manchester, 1959), pp. 13-29.

3. Donald R. Cressey, *Criminal Organization: Its Elementary Forms* (London, 1972), p. 11.

4. E. W. Burgess, "Summary and Recommendations: Illinois Crime Survey," quoted in Marshall B. Clinard and Richard Quinney, *Criminal Behavior Systems* (New York, 1967), p. 383.

5. Cressey, *Criminal Organization*, pp. 11-12.

6. Ibid., p. 14.

7. Hood and Sparks, *Key Issues in Criminology*, p. 87.

8. Two members, 63.6 percent; three members, 18.8 percent; four members, 7.4 percent; five members, 3.7 percent; six members, 2.7 percent; seven members, 1.1 percent; eight members, 0.5 percent; nine members, 1.7 percent; ten members, 0.1 percent; eleven or more members, 0.4 percent.

9. Hood and Sparks, *Key Issues in Criminology*, p. 87.

10. These figures were derived from Huntingdonshire, Essex, Somerset, Surrey, and Herefordshire, which had more complete information because of a difference in data gathering. The percentages are, therefore, high, reflecting the Essex and Somerset predominance in criminal associations. Given's *Society and Homicide* chapter, "The Entrepreneurs of Violence," pp. 106-133, cannot be taken as an accurate description of organized crime in general since it is dealing with only those cases of burglary and robbery that ended in homicide, which account for only 8 percent of all burglaries and robberies. Given's data do not include information on gangs involved in thefts not ending in homicide although this comprises the great bulk of the crimes committed by gangs. His discussion leaves out the bulk of the informal criminal associations and gives a picture of medieval gangs much more sinister than it actually was.

11. Just. 3/49/1 m. 41.

12. KB 27/248 m. 10.

13. Victim's home, 39.3 percent; accused's home, 2.6 percent; tavern, 0.8 percent; field, 23.2 percent; barn, 8.1 percent; highway, 8.1 percent; market, 2.6 percent; church, 14.5 percent; other, 0.8 percent.

14. Bellamy, "Coterels," p. 700.

15. Just. 3/77/2 m. 4.

16. Barbara Hanawalt Westman, "The Peasant Family and Crime in Fourteenth-Century England," *Journal of British Studies*, 13 (1974), 14, has a more complete discussion. Given, *Society and Homicide*, found a similar pattern of

family participation in criminal associations for homicide cases. The overall participation of family associations in the homicide cases was 20.2 percent, p. 126, and thus was very close to the family participation in all types of cases in the fourteenth century.

17. Just. 3/75 m. 34.

18. Just. 3/48 m. 5d., 3/49/1 ms. 35, 36, 39, 3/117 ms. 10, 15.

19. The data are based on the five county sample: clergy, 98 mentioned; butchers, 4; millers, 6; servants, 13; craftsmen, 7; shepherds, 3; merchants, 20; nobles, 8; officials, 3; tailors, 10.

20. Bellamy, "Coterels," pp. 712-713.

21. Just. 3/104 m. 18d. and 3/23 provide examples.

22. KB 27/271 m. 29; Just. 3/48 ms. 38d., 32.

23. Just. 3/48 m. 32.

24. Just. 3/49/1 m. 37d.

25. Just. 3/48 m. 13.

26. Forty of the gang members came from other counties to commit crimes in Northamptonshire: 3 from Buckinghamshire, 4 from Oxford, 9 from Warwickshire, 1 from Middlesex, 4 from Huntingdonshire, 9 from Leicestershire, 1 from Gloucestershire, 2 from Rutland, 1 from Bedfordshire, 2 from Lincolnshire, 1 from London, 1 from Staffordshire, 2 from Wiltshire.

27. A. L. Beier, "Vagrants and the Social Order in Elizabethan England," *Past and Present*, no. 64 (1974), pp. 3-29.

28. Jusserand, *English Wayfaring Life*, p. 149.

29. Ibid.

30. *Bedfordshire Coroners' Rolls*, p. 48.

31. Beier, "Vagrants", p. 14.

32. *Bedfordshire Coroners' Rolls*, pp. 75-76.

33. Hobsbawm, *Primitive Rebels*, p. 13.

34. Keen, *Outlaws*, pp. 226-227. Maurice Keen, "Robin Hood, A Peasant Hero," *History Today*, 8 (1958), 684-689. J. C. Holt, "The Origins and Audience of the Robin Hood Ballads," *Past and Present*, no. 18 (1960), pp. 89-110. J. C. Holt, "Robin Hood, Some Comments," *Past and Present*, no. 19 (1961), pp. 16-18. R. H. Hilton, "The Origins of Robin Hood," *Past and Present*, no. 14 (1958), pp. 30-34. T. H. Aston, "Robin Hood, Communication," *Past and Present*, no. 20 (1961), pp. 7-9.

35. Bellamy, *Crime and Public Order*, pp. 72-73.

36. Just. 3/74/4 m. 1-2. A thirty-seven member gang with a similar composition worked around Knaresborough, Just. 3/74/4 m. 1.

37. Just. 3/104.

38. Hobsbawm, *Primitive Rebels*, p. 15.

39. Bellamy, "Coterels," p. 705.

40. Ibid., p. 706.

41. Ibid., pp. 704-705, 715-716.

42. "Helmbrecht," p. 67.
43. Keen, *Outlaws*, p. 4.
44. "Helmbrecht," p. 70.
45. *Wakefield*, III, 148.
46. Keen, *Outlaws*, pp. 183-187.
47. *Bedfordshire Coroners' Rolls*, pp. 20-21.
48. Just. 3/99 m. 1.
49. Just. 3/18/4 m. 3; 3/164 m. 37.
50. Just. 3/81/2 m. 13.
51. Just. 3/45 m. 21. See also Just. 3/78 m. 47, where a pass at Berngestan was held for four days, or Just. 3/145 m. 14, where a pass in Newberg Park was held and merchants robbed.
52. Just. 3/79/1 m. 19.
53. Just. 3/49/1 m. 34. See also Just. 3/47/3 m. 6 and 3/49/1 m. 17.
54. Just. 3/81/2 m. 55, Henry de Roston of Scarborough and six other men of the city were tried for it and in 1391 William March of Scarborough and his band were accused of the same, Just. 3/176 m. 122. William of Coventry, a famous outlaw, and his band took over Foxele market, Just. 2/111 m. 16.
55. Stones, "Folvilles," p. 119.
56. Ibid. pp. 122-123. Willoughby himself was on the panel of justices at the trial where the one person connected with his abduction and ransoming was tried and acquitted. Bellamy, *Crime and Public Order*, p. 78, expresses the opinion that it was a revenge and intimidation.
57. Stones, "Folvilles," pp. 119, 123. A relative of Lord Roger was accused of the actual murder.
58. Hoskins, "Murder," p. 177.
59. If they were only hitmen for Lord Roger, this would explain why the Coterels got so little from the ransom money for their pains. Bellamy, "Coterels," p. 706, was puzzled about this.
60. KB 27/319.
61. Just. 3/176 m. 12; Bellamy, "Coterels," p. 706.
62. Just. 3/183 m. 1.
63. Just. 3/164 m. 37.
64. Bellamy, "Coterels," p. 711.
65. Stones, "Folvilles," p. 121.
66. Hilton, *A Medieval Society*, pp. 256-258.
67. J. L. Rayner and G. T. Crook, *The Complete Newgate Calendar* I, (London, 1926), 1-7.
68. Carolly Erickson, *The Medieval Vision* (New York, 1974), p. 150.
69. Just. 3/79/1 ms. 5-9; Just. 3/74/4 ms. 1-2. For other examples see KB 27/248 m. 10; Just. 3/78 m. 44; KB 27/334 m. 29; Just. 3/49/2 m. 4.
70. Hilton, *A Medieval Society*, pp. 255-258.

71. Ibid., Stones, "Folvilles," pp. 134-35. Original in KB 27/307, m. 27.

72. Stones, "Folvilles," p. 134.

73. Bellamy, "Coterels," p. 705.

74. Jusserand, *English Wayfaring Life,* p. 37.

75. Just. 3/49/1 m. 43d; 3/51/3 m.2.

76. Hunnisett, "Pleas of the Crown and the Coroner," *Bulletin of the Institute of Historical Research,* 32 (1959), 117-137.

77. Just. 3/49/1 m. 27.

78. Bellamy, "Coterels," p. 709.

79. Keen, *Outlaws,* pp. 124-125.

80. Jusserand, *English Wayfaring Life,* p. 142.

81. Bellamy, "Coterels," p. 707.

82. Just. 3/18/4 m. 6.

83. Bellamy, "Coterels," p. 710.

84. Bellamy, *Crime and Public Order,* p. 19.

85. Just. 3/49/1 m. 30. See also Just. 1/632 m. 96.

86. Just. 3/75 ms. 13-16. Also see Just. 3/49/1 m. 44d.

87. *Bedfordshire Coroners' Rolls,* p. 109.

88. Keen, *Outlaws,* p. 101.

89. "Helmbrecht," p. 89.

90. Henner Hess, *Mafia and Mafiosi: The Structure of Power,* trans. Ewald Osers (Lexington, Mass., 1973), pp. 17-18.

91. Bellamy, *Crime and Public Order,* p. 26.

92. George B. Vold, "The Organization of Criminals for Profit and Power," in Clinard and Quinney, *Criminal Behavior Systems,* p. 396.

93. It was impossible to transcribe all the names of the offenders and the victims when compiling the criminal data. Furthermore, since the spelling of an individual's name could vary radically from one entry to another, it would have been difficult to computerize the information.

94. Just. 3/48 m. 26d.

95. Just. 3/48-49.

96. Ibid.

97. Just. 3/75 ms. 11-12.

98. Just. 3/48 m. 32.

99. Edwin H. Sutherland, ed., *The Professional Thief: By a Professional Thief* (Chicago, 1937).

100. Just. 3/112 m. 18.

101. Just. 3/116 m. 1.

102. Just. 3/102 m. 9; 3/100 m. 17.

103. Just. 3/51 m. 14d; m. 5.

104. Fuller, *Beggar's Brotherhood,* p. 26.

105. Just. 3/48 m. 25; m. 30d.

106. Chaucer, *The Canterbury Tales,* p. 470.

107. Jean Bodel, *The Play of St. Nicholas*, in Mandel, *Five Comedies of Medieval France*, pp. 56-64.

108. J. M. Beattie, "The Pattern of Crime in England, 1660-1800," *Past and Present*, no. 62 (1974), pp. 47-52.

109. Just. 3/129.

7 External Influences on the Pattern of Crime

1. Thomas Walsingham, *Historia Anglicana* (London, 1863) p. 183; Adam Murimuth, *Continuatio Chronicarum* (London, 1883) p. 49; *Chronicon de Galfridi le Baker de Swynbroke* (Oxford, 1889) p. 24.

2. Just. 3/76 m. 23; Yorks., 24 Mar. 1322. The inclusion of these trials in the gaol delivery sessions is an anomaly because of the noble birth of the offenders and their offense of high treason. One wonders if the justices of gaol delivery happened to be conveniently near or whether it was a final degradation to the offenders to stand trial like an ordinary felon. A description of their part in the revolt may be found in *Chronicle of Lanercost* (Glasgow, 1913), pp. 229-230, 233-237.

3. Waugh, "The Profits of Violence," pp. 843-869.

4. T. F. Tout, *The Place of the Reign of Edward II in English History*, 2nd ed. (Manchester, 1936), p. 22.

5. Ibid., pp. 26-27.

6. T. F. Tout, *Chapters in the Administrative History of Medieval England*, III (Manchester, 1920), 10, 30.

7. Tout, *Place of Edward II*, p. 214.

8. Ibid., p. 213.

9. Putnam, "Transformation of the Keepers," p. 23. Hughes, *Early Years of Edward III*, p. 227. Both authors raise this point but do not give their sources.

10. Putnam, "Transformation of the Keepers," pp. 41-48.

11. M. McKisack, *The Fourteenth Century, 1307-1399* (Oxford, 1959), p. 158.

12. Hughes, *Early Years of Edward III*, p. 227. Again she gives no source.

13. *Rotuli Parl.*, II, 140.

14. McKisack, *Fourteenth Century*, pp. 50-51.

15. M. Powicke, *Military Obligation in Medieval England* (Oxford, 1962). A. E. Prince, "The Indenture System under Edward III," *Historical Essays in Honour of James Tait*, ed. J. G. Edwards et al. (Manchester, 1933), pp. 283-297. A. E. Prince, "The Army and Navy," *The English Government at Work*, I, ed. J. F. Willard and W. A. Morris (Cambridge, Mass., 1940), 332-393. N. B. Lewis, "The Organization of Indentured Retinues in Fourteenth-Century England," *Transactions of the Royal Historical Society*, 4th ser., 17 (1945), 29-39.

16. McKisack, *Fourteenth Century*, p. 246. D. Hay, "The Division of

Spoils of War in Fourteenth-Century England," *Transactions of the Royal Historical Society*, 5th ser., 4 (1954), 91-109. J. R. Maddicott, *The English Peasantry and the Demands of Crown, 1294-1341*, Past and Present Society Supplement 1, 1975, gives an excellent summary.

17. Edward Miller, *War in the North* (Hull, Eng., 1960), gives an appraisal of the damage done to northern England as a result of the Scottish raids. Maddicott, *English Peasantry*, pp. 10-14, 36-37, shows effects of purveyance, taxation, and recruitment in Yorkshire.

18. J. F. Willard, *Parliamentary Taxes on Personal Property* (Cambridge, Mass., 1934), pp. 122-125.

19. A. E. Prince, "The Strength of the English Armies in the Reign of Edward III," *English Historical Review*, 46 (July 1931), 354.

20. J. E. Morris, "Mounted Infantry in Medieval Warfare," *Transactions of the Royal Historical Society*, 3rd. Ser., VIII (1914), 93. R. Nicholson, *Edward III and the Scots* (Oxford, 1965), p. 130.

21. W. Page, ed., *Victoria County History of Yorkshire*, III (London, 1913), 404.

22. Walsingham, *Historia*, p. 150.

23. *Calendar of Patent Rolls, 1333-1337*, pp. 294-295.

24. Just. 3/76 m. 26, Yorks.

25. Tout, *Place of Edward II*, p. 213.

26. Miller, *War in the North*, pp. 7-8. *Chronicle of Lanercost* (Glascow, 1913) pp. 205, 221, 238, and passim., also tells the painful story that accompanied each raid. Maddicott, *English Peasantry*, pp. 67-75, summarizes the disastrous effects for the peasantry of the heavy taxation and purveyance during the wars.

27. K. B. McFarlane, "England and the Hundred Years' War," *Past and Present*, no. 22 (July 1962), pp. 9-10.

28. Ibid., p. 5. Hughes, *Early Years of Edward III*, pp. 235-236.

29. M. M. Postan, "The Cost of the Hundred Years' War," *Past and Present*, no. 27 (April 1964), p. 37.

30. Ibid., pp. 37-39. See Maddicott, *English Peasantry*, for a more detailed discussion.

31. H. J. Hewitt, *The Organization of War under Edward III* (Manchester, 1966), pp. 173-175.

32. Prince, "Indenture System," pp. 283-284.

33. *Select Cases from the Coroners' Rolls*, pp. 74-75.

34. C. G. Crump and C. Johnson, "The Powers of the Justices of the Peace," *English Historical Review*, 27 (1912), 227.

35. Ibid., p. 236, from Patent Roll, 27 Ed. III, Pt. II, m. 8d.

36. McFarlane, "The Hundred Years' War," p. 5.

37. *Calendar of Patent Rolls, 1345-1348*, pp. 317-406; *1348-1350*, p. 574.

38. *Rotuli Parl.*, II, 172.

39. *Statutes of the Realm*, Statute of Northampton 2 Ed. III, c. 2; 10 Ed. III, st. I, c. 2-3; 14 Ed. III, st. I, c. 15.

40. Ibid., 10 Ed. III, st. I, c. 2-3.

41. Hewitt, *Organization of War*, p. 173.

42. Ibid., pp. 29-30.

43. Ibid. Figures arrived at by Hughes, *Early Years of Edward III*, p. 219, place the proportion at about two-fifths.

44. Norfolk: 1300-1309, 0.5 percent; 1310-1319, 2 percent; 1320-1329, 2 percent; 1330-1339, 4 percent; 1340-1348, 5 percent. Yorkshire: 1300-1309, 2 percent; 1310-1319, 1 percent; 1320-1329, 2 percent; 1330-1339, 4 percent; 1340-1348, 3 percent.

45. Just. 3/119 m. 3, Norfolk, 15 Sept., 1327. Other examples: Just. 3/78 ms. 13, 20, 22, 48.

46. Lunden, *Crime and Criminals*, p. 84. Monkkonen, *Dangerous Class*, pp. 53-54.

47. Just. 3/75 ms. 34, 3, 4; 3/48 m. 24d.; 3/76 ms. 36, 26, 7d.; KB 27/355 m.50.

48. KB 27/355 m. 50: *"duxit diversa vitualia ex regnum regis angle in partibus Scotie."*

49. Just. 3/48 m. 24d.; 3/75 m. 4.

50. Just. 3/75 m. 34.

51. *Wakefield*, II, 71.

52. Maddicott, *English Peasantry*, pp. 17, 29, 32-33, 38, 63-64, 68.

53. Bonger, *Criminality and Economic Conditions.* D. S. Thomas, *Social Aspects of the Business Cycle* (London, 1925).

54. For a good summary of the problems in correlating crime with business cycles see T. Sellin, *Research Memorandum on Crime in the Depression* (New York, 1937). Economic interpretations of fluctuations in crime is again gaining a certain popularity among criminologists and those concerned with law enforcement.

55. M. M. Postan, "Medieval Agrarian Society in its Prime: England," *Cambridge Economic History of Europe*, I, 2nd ed. (Cambridge, 1966), 549-659. "Some Economic Evidence of Declining Population in the Later Middle Ages," *Economic History Review*, 2nd ser., 2 (1950), 221-246. M. M. Postan and J. Z. Titow, "Heriots and Prices on Winchester Manors," *Economic History Review*, 2nd ser., 11 (1959), 392-411. J. Z. Titow, *English Rural Society, 1200-1350* (London, 1969), Ian Kershaw, "The Great Famine and Agrarian Crisis in England, 1315-1322," *Past and Present*, no. 59 (1973), pp. 3-50. A recent and comprehensive summary may be found in M. M. Postan, *The Medieval Economy and Society* (London, 1972). Not all scholars have accepted this thesis. Edward Miller, "The English Economy in the Thirteenth Century: Implications of Recent Research," *Past and Present*, no. 28 (1964), pp. 21-48 and "England in the Twelfth and Thirteenth Cen-

turies: An Economic Contrast?", *Economic History Review*, 2nd ser., 24 (1971), 1-14, has put the economic decline back into the thirteenth century. Barbara Harvey, "The Population Trend in England between 1300-1348," *Transactions of the Royal Historical Society*, 5th ser., 16 (1966), 23-42, and D. G. Watts, "A Model for the Early Fourteenth Century," *Economic History Review*, 2nd ser., 20 (1967), 543-547, have argued that Postan's price evidence was inconclusive and that good harvests and a healthy land market continued up until the Black Death. W. C. Robinson, "Money, Population and Economic Change in Late Medieval Europe," *Economic History Review*, 2nd ser., 12 (1959), 63-67, argued that the influx of bullion rather than overpopulation caused price fluctuations in the first half of the century. Both economic evidence, such as shrinkage of the land under cultivation and increased wages, and direct evidence of reduction in replacement rates of the population are strong enough to warrant the acceptance of the theory for the purposes of this study. Sylvia L. Thrupp, "The Problem of Replacement Rates in Late Medieval English Population," *Economic History Review*, 2nd. ser., 18 (August 1965), 101-119.

56. Postan and Titow, "Heriots," pp. 392-411. It might be argued that a comparison between wheat prices and crime is misleading, since peasants actually depended upon beans, peas, barley, and oats for their daily bread and grew wheat for a cash crop. Their circumstances could hardly be considered desperate if they had an abundance of everything but wheat. J. Longden has disposed of this objection in a statistical note accompanying Postan's and Titow's article on heriots: "Statistical Notes on Winchester Heriots," *Economic History Review*, 2nd ser., 2 (1959) 415-416. In the present study, wheat prices were used because they indicate the fluctuations of all grain prices and because they are more reliable. Because they were a cash crop, a record of their yearly sale price was kept. Using the less reliable prices from J. E. Thorold Rogers, *Six Centuries of Work and Wages* (London, 1884), for oats and beans, a correlation coefficient of 0.55 and 0.60, respectively, was found when comparing the yearly fluctuations in their price with crime. See Barbara A. Hanawalt, "The Economic Influences on the Pattern of Crime in England, 1300-1348," *The American Journal of Legal History*, 18 (1974), 281-297.

57. H. S. Lucas, "The Great European Famine of 1315, 1316 and 1317," *Speculum*, 5 (October 1930), 343-377.

58. *Annales Paulini*, I, 278. *Vita Edwardi Secundi*, p. 64. *Chronica Monasterii de Melsa*, II, 332. *Annals of Loch Cé*, I, 579. *Chronique de London*, p. 38. Adam Murimuth, p. 24. Johannes de Trokelowe, *Annales*, pp. 92-96. *Chronicle of Lanercost*, p. 233. *Chronicon de Galfridi le Baker de Swinbroke*, p. 9.

59. Lucas, "European Famine," pp. 351-352.

60. Ibid., p. 355.

61. Trokelowe, *Annales*, pp. 92-96.
62. C. Creighton, *A History of Epidemics in Britain, AD 664-1866* (Cambridge, 1894), p. 48.
63. Lucas, "European Famine," p. 357.
64. Trokelowe, *Annales*, p. 94.
65. Ibid., pp. 93-94.
66. Lucas, "European Famine," p. 360.
67. Creighton, *Epidemics* p. 49.
68. *Wakefield*, IV, 85.
69. Just. 2/108B.
70. *Wakefield*, IV, p. xiii.
71. The data come from four volumes of Wakefield manor court records: vols. 2-5.
72. Just. 3/48 m. 42; 3/49/1.
73. Just. 3/48 m. 36d.
74. L. Genicot, "Crisis: From the Middle Ages to Modern Times," *Cambridge Economic History of Europe*, I, ed. M. M. Postan (Cambridge, 1966), tables on p. 682. See also pp. 683-694. Postan, "Medieval Agrarian Society," p. 567.
75. Postan, ibid., p. 630. Titow, *English Rural Society*, p. 65.
76. Genicot, "Crisis for the Middle Ages," p. 689.
77. Significance levels: Herefordshire (p 0.3); Norfolk (p 0.001); Northamptonshire (p 0.05); Yorkshire (p 0.002); Huntingdonshire (p 0.02); Essex (p 0.07); Somerset (p 0.001).
78. Genicot, "Crisis," pp. 692-694.
79. R. S. Schofield, "The Geographical Distribution of Wealth in England, 1334-1649," *Economic History Review*, 18 (1965), 504.
80. Homans, "Rural Sociology," pp. 38-39.
81. A. Réville, *Le soulevement des travilleurs d'Angleterre en 1381* (Paris, 1898).

8 The Impact of Crime on Fourteenth-Century Rural Society

1. Turk, "Law as a Weapon in Social Conflict," p. 31.
2. Ibid., p. 20.
3. Ibid., p. 21.
4. *Select Cases in the Court of King's Bench*, Selden Society, VI, (London, 1965), liii, lv-lvi.
5. Alan Harding, *A Social History of English Law* (London, 1966) p. 86.
6. Hilton, "Origins of Robin Hood," p. 36.
7. Titow, *Rural England*, pp. 46-47.
8. J. D. Vann. "Middle English Verses against Thieves: A Postscript," *Speculum*, 34 (1959), 636-637.
9. The statistics for some other rural Indiana towns with about 10,000

population are Carmel: no murder (2 assaults), 1 rape, 1 robbery, 68 burglaries, 220 larcenies. Connersville: no murder (66 assaults), no rape, 2 robberies, 66 burglaries, 627 larcenies. Beech Grove: 1 murder (12 assaults), 2 rapes, 11 robberies, 160 burglaries, 549 larcenies.

10. Bartholomew county, Indiana, had no murders, 3 rapes, 7 robberies, 257 burglaries, and 1,011 robberies. It also had a population of 25,000 or over.

11. L. B. Larking, "On the Heart Shrine in Leyburn Church," *Archaeologia Cantiana*, V (1963), 143.

APPENDIX A THE PROBLEM OF MISSING DELIVERIES

1. Gollancz, "System of Gaol Delivery," p. 23.
2. Information supplied by C. A. F. Meekings.
3. Ibid.

APPENDIX B INFLUENCE OF THE DETERMINING POWERS OF THE KEEPERS OF THE PEACE ON THE VOLUME OF CASES IN GAOL DELIVERY

1. *Northamptonshire Sessions of Peace*, pp. xv-xvi.
2. *Kent Keepers of the Peace*, p. xx; Meekings, "Manuscript."
3. *Northamptonshire Sessions of Peace*, p. xvi.
4. Putnam, "Transformation of the Keepers," p. 27.
5. Ibid., p. 28.
6. Ibid., p. 34.
7. Ibid., p. 41.

APPENDIX C INFLUENCE OF CHANGES IN LAW ENFORCEMENT PROCEDURES ON THE VOLUME OF CASES IN GAOL DELIVERY

1. *Kent Keepers of the Peace*, p. xvii. *Northamptonshire Sessions of Peace*, p. xi.
2. Ibid.
3. *Kent Keepers of the Peace*, pp. xviii-xix. Putnam, "Transformation of the Keepers," p. 23.
4. Ibid.
5. Putnam, "Transformation of the Keepers," p. 36. *Northamptonshire Sessions of Peace*, p. xx.
6. Putnam, "Transformation of the Keepers," pp. 29-32.
7. Ibid., pp. 41-48.
8. Morris, "The Sheriff," pp. 47-49.
9. *Statutes of the Realm*, pp. 257-261, 281-289.

Bibliography

MANUSCRIPTS

Great Britain. Public Record Office. *Assize Rolls* (Just. 1).
Great Britain. Public Record Office. *Coroners' Rolls* (Just. 2).
Great Britain. Public Record Office. *Gaol Delivery Rolls* (Just. 3).
Great Britain. Public Record Office. *King's Bench Rolls* (KB 27).
Great Britain. Public Record Office. *Patent Rolls* (C66).

PRINTED DOCUMENTS

BEDFORDSHIRE CORONERS' ROLLS, trans. R. F. Hunnisett. Bedfordshire Histori-
cal Society, vol. 41 (1960).
CALENDAR OF CLOSE ROLLS, 1302-49, 12 vols. London: Public Record Office,
1892-1954.
CALENDAR OF CORONERS' ROLLS OF THE CITY OF LONDON, A.D. 1300-1378,
trans. R. R. Sharpe. London, 1913.
CALENDAR OF PATENT ROLLS, 1301-1350, 14 vols. London: Public Record Of-
fice, 1891-1916.
COURT ROLLS OF THE ABBEY OF RAMSEY AND THE HONOR OF CLARE, ed. Warren
O. Ault. New Haven, 1928.
COURT ROLLS OF THE MANOR OF INGOLDMELLS IN THE COUNTY OF LINCOLNSHIRE,
ed. and trans. W. O. Massingberd. London, 1902.
COURT ROLLS OF THE MANOR OF WAKEFIELD, ed. and trans. W. P. Baildon,
John Lister, and J. W. Walker. The Yorkshire Archaeological Society
Record Series, vols. 29, 36, 47-48, 109 (1901, 1906, 1917, 1930, 1945).
CRIME IN EAST ANGLIA IN THE FOURTEENTH CENTURY: NORFOLK GAOL DELIVERY
ROLLS, 1307-1316, trans. Barbara A. Hanawalt. Norfolk Record Society,
vol. 44 (1976).
EARLY HUNTINGDONSHIRE LAY SUBSIDY ROLLS, ed. J. Ambrose Raftis and
Mary Patricia Hogan. Toronto, 1976.

EARLY REGISTERS OF WRITS, ed. E. de Haas and G. D. G. Hall. Selden Society, vol. 97. London, 1970.

ESSEX SESSIONS OF THE PEACE, 1351, 1377-1379, trans. Elizabeth Chapin Furber. Essex Archaeological Society, Occasional Publications, no. 3, Colchester, 1953.

EYRE OF KENT, 3 vols. trans. W. C. Bolland. London: Selden Society, 1910, 1912, 1913.

KENT KEEPERS OF THE PEACE, 1316-1317, trans. Bertha H. Putnam. Records of the Kent Archaeological Society, vol. 13 (1933).

LATHE COURT ROLLS AND VIEWS OF FRANKPLEDGE IN THE RAPE OF HASTINGS, 1387-1474, ed. E. J. Courthope and B. E. P. Formoy. Sussex Records Society, 1931.

LEET JURISDICTION IN THE CITY OF NORWICH DURING THE THIRTEENTH AND FIFTEENTH CENTURIES, trans. W. Hudson. Sheldon Society, vol. 5., London, 1892.

RECORDS OF MEDIEVAL OXFORD: CORONERS' INQUESTS, THE WALLS OF OXFORD, ETC., trans. H. E. Salter. Oxford, 1912.

ROLLS OF NORTHAMPTONSHIRE SESSIONS OF PEACE, ed. Margarite Gollancz, Northamptonshire Record Society, vol. 11. 1938.

ROTULI PARLIAMENTORUM UT ET PETITIONES ET PLACITA IN PARLIAMENTO, 6 vols. London, 1832.

SELECT CASES FROM THE CORONERS' ROLLS, 1265-1413, ed. C. Gross. Selden Society, vol. 9, London, 1896.

SELECT CASES IN THE COURT OF KING'S BENCH, 6 vols., trans. G. O. Sayles. London: Selden Society, 1936, 1938, 1939, 1957, 1965.

STATUTES OF THE REALM, 11 vols., ed. A. Luders, T. E. Tomlins, J. Raithby, London, 1810-1828.

CHRONICLES

THE ANGLO-SAXON CHRONICLE, ed. and trans. Dorothy Whitelock. London, 1961.

ANNALES PAULINI (CHRONICLES OF THE REIGNS OF EDWARD I AND EDWARD II), ed. W. Stubbs. Rolls Series, no. 76, London, 1882.

ANNALS OF LOCH CÉ, ed. and trans. W. H. Hennessey. Rolls Series, no. 54, London, 1871.

THE ANONIMALLE CHRONICLE, ed. V. H. Galbraith. Manchester, 1927.

CHRONICA MONASTERII DE MELSA, ed. E. A. Bond. Rolls Series, no. 43, London, 1867.

CHRONICLE OF LANERCOST, ed. H. Maxwell. Glasgow, 1913.

CHRONICON DE GALFRIDI LE BAKER DE SWYNBROKE, ed. E. M. Thompson. Oxford, 1889.

CHRONICON HENRICI KNIGHTON; VEL CNIGHON, MONACHI LEYCESTRENSIS, 2 vols., ed. J. R. Lumby. Rolls Series, no. 92, London, 1889-1895.

Bibliography

CHRONIQUE DE LONDON DEPUIS L'AN 44 HENRI III JUSQU'A L'AN 17 EDOUARD III, ed. G. J. Aungier. London: Camden Society, 1844.

Murimuth, Adam. CONTINUATIO CHRONICARUM, ed. E. M. Thompson. Rolls Series, no. 93, London, 1883, 1889.

Trokelowe, Johannes de. ANNALES (CHRONICA MONASTERII S. ALBANI), ed. H. T. Riley. Rolls Series, no. 28, London, 1866.

VITA EDWARDI SECUNDI (CHRONICLES OF THE REIGNS OF EDWARD I AND EDWARD II), ed. W. Stubbs. Rolls Series, no. 76, London, 1883.

Walsingham, Thomas. HISTORIA ANGLICANA, 2 vols., ed. H. T. Riley. Rolls Series, no. 28, London, 1863.

BOOKS AND ARTICLES

Abbiateci, A. F. Bilacois, Y. Castan, S. Petrovitch, Y. Bongert, and N. Castan. Crimes et criminalité en France 17e-18e siècles. Paris, 1971.

Accident Facts, 1968 Edition. National Safety Council. Chicago, 1968.

Amir, Menachem. Patterns in Forcible Rape. Chicago, 1971.

——— "Patterns of Forcible Rape." In Criminal Behavior Systems: A Topology, ed. Marshall B. Clinard and Richard Quinney, pp. 60-75. New York, 1967.

Ariès, Philippe. Centuries of Childhood: A Social History of Family Life, trans. Robert Baldick. New York, 1962.

Aston, T. H. "Robin Hood: Communication." Past and Present, no. 20 (1961), 7-9.

Ault, Warren O. "By-Laws of Gleaning and the Problems of Harvest." Economic History Review, 2nd ser., 14 (1961), 210-217.

——— Open-field Farming in Medieval England. London, 1972.

——— Open-field Husbandry and the Village Community: A Study in Agrarian By-laws in Medieval England. Philadelphia, 1965.

——— Private Jurisdiction in England. New Haven, 1923.

Avrutick, J. B. "Commissions of Oyer and Terminer in Fifteenth Century England." Ph.D.dissertation, University of London, 1967.

Baker, A. R. H. "Evidence in the 'Nonarum Inquisitiones' of Contracting Arable Lands in England during the Early Fourteenth Century." Economic History Review, 2nd ser., 19 (1966), 518-532.

Baldick, R. The Duel: A History of Dueling. London, 1915.

Bartholomew, J. The Survey Gazetteer of the British Isles. Edinburgh, 1950.

Bartlett, J. N. "The Expansion and Decline of York in the Later Middle Ages." Economic History Review, 2nd ser., 12 (1959), 17-33.

Basset, Margery. "Newgate Prison in the Middle Ages." Speculum, 18 (April 1943), 233-246.

Bean, J. M. W. The Decline of English Feudalism, 1215-1540. Manchester, 1968.

Beard, A. The Office of Justice of the Peace In England, and Its Origin and

Development. New York, 1904.

Beattie, J. M. "The Criminality of Women in Eighteenth-Century England." *The Journal of Social History*, 8 (1975), 80-118.

―――― "The Pattern of Crime in England, 1600-1800." *Past and Present*, no. 62 (1974), 47-95.

Beier, A. L. "Vagrants and the Social Order in Elizabethan England." *Past and Present*, no. 64 (1974), 3-29.

Bell, Clair Hayden, trans. *Peasant Life in Old German Epics: Meier Helmbrecht and Der Arme Heinrich.* New York, 1968.

Bellamy, John G. "The Coterel Gang: An Anatomy of a Band of Fourteenth Century Criminals." *English Historical Review*, 79 (October 1964), 698-717.

―――― *Crime and Public Order in England in the Later Middle Ages.* London, 1973.

Bennett, H. S. *Life on the English Manor.* Cambridge, 1937.

Bercé, Y. M. "Aspects de le criminalité au XVIIe siècle." *Revue Historique*, 239 (1968), 33-42.

Beresford, M. *The Lost Villages of the Middle Ages.* London, 1965.

Beveridge, W. "Materials for a Price History." Unpublished manuscript at the London School of Economics.

Blatcher, Marjorie. "The Working of the Court of King's Bench in the Fifteenth Century." Ph.D.dissertation, London University, 1935.

Bohannan, Paul. "Patterns of Homicide among Tribal Societies in Africa." In *Studies in Homicide*, ed. Marvin E. Wolfgang, pp. 211-237. New York, 1967.

Bolland, W. C. *The General Eyre.* Cambridge, 1922.

Bonger, W. A. *Criminality and Economic Conditions*, trans. H. P. Horton. Boston, 1916. Another edition, ed. A. T. Turk. London, 1969.

Bridbury, A. R. *Economic Growth: England in the Later Middle Ages.* London, 1962.

―――― *England and the Salt Trade in the Later Middle Ages.* Oxford, 1955.

Britnell, R. H. "Production for the Market on a Small Fourteenth-Century Estate." *Economic History Review*, 2nd ser., 19 (1966), 380-387.

Britton, C. E. *A Meteorological Chronology to A.D. 1450.* Meteorological Office, Geophysical Memoirs, vol. LXXX. London, 1937.

Britton, Edward J. "Broughton 1288-1340: A Mediaeval Village Community." Ph.D. dissertation, University of Toronto, 1973.

Buckatzsch, E. J. "The Geographical Distribution of Wealth in England, 1086-1843." *Economic History Review*, 2nd ser., 3 (1950), 180-202.

Bühler, C. E. "Middle English Verses against Thieves." *Speculum*, 32 (1958) 371-372.

Cam, H. M. "The General Eyres of 1329-1330." *English Historical Review*, 39 (1924), 241-249.

―――― *The Hundred and the Hundred Rolls: An Outline of Local Government in Medieval England.* London, 1930.

Bibliography

────── "Shire Officials: Coroners, Constables, and Bailiffs." In *The English Government at Work*, vol. III, ed. J. F. Willard, W. A. Morris, and W. H. Dunham, pp. 143-183. Cambridge, Mass., 1950.

────── "Some Early Inquests before 'Custodes Pacis.' " *English Historical Review*, 40 (1925), 411-419.

────── *Studies in the Hundred Rolls, Some Aspects of Thirteenth Century Administration.* Oxford Studies in Social and Legal History, 11, Oxford, 1921.

Capellanus, Andreas. *The Art of Courtly Love*, trans. John Jay Parry. New York, 1972.

Cartwright, Desmond S., Barbara Tomson, and H. Schwarts. *Gang Delinquency.* Monterey, Calif., 1975.

Carus-Wilson, E. M. *Medieval Merchant Venturers. Collected Studies.* London, 1954.

────── "The Woollen Industry." *Cambridge Economic History*, vol. II, ed. M. Postan and E. E. Rich. Cambridge, 1952.

Cawley, A. C., ed. *Everyman and Medieval Miracle Plays.* New York, 1959.

Chadwick, Dorothy. *Social Life in the Days of Piers Ploughman.* Cambridge, 1922.

Chamblis, William J. *Sociological Readings in Conflict Perspective.* Reading, Mass., 1973.

────── and Robert B. Seidman. *Law, Order and Power.* Reading, Mass., 1971.

Chaney, C. R. "The Punishment of Felonous Clerks." *English Historical Review*, 51 (1936), 215-236.

Chapman, Dennis. *Sociology and the Stereotype of the Criminal.* London, 1968.

Chaucer, Geoffrey. *The Canterbury Tales*, trans. Nevill Coghill. London, 1951.

Chesler, Phyllis, *Woman and Madness.* New York, 1972.

Clanchy, M. T. "Law, Government and Society in Medieval England." *History*, 59 (1974), 73-78.

Clay, Rotha M. *The Medieval Hospitals of England.* London, 1909.

Clinard, Marshall B. *Sociology of Deviant Behavior.* New York, 1963.

────── and Daniel J. Abbott. *Crime in Developing Countries: A Comparative Perspective.* New York, 1973.

──────. and Richard Quinney. *Criminal Behavior Systems: A Typology.* New York, 1967.

Cockburn, J. S., ed. *Crime in England, 1550-1800.* Princeton, 1977.

Cohn, Norman. *Europe's Inner Daemons: An Enquiry Inspired by the Great Witch-Hunt.* New York, 1975.

Coleman, Emily R. "L'infanticide dans le Haut Moyen Age." *Annales: économie, société, civilisations*, 29 (1974), 315-335.

Conklin, John E. *The Impact of Crime.* New York, 1975.

―――― *Robbery and the Criminal Justice System*. Philadelphia, 1972.

Cox, J. C. *The Sanctuaries and the Sanctuary Seekers of Medieval England*. London, 1911.

Creighton, C. *A History of Epidemics in Britain, A.D. 664-1866*, 2 vols. Cambridge, 1894.

Cressey, Donald R. *Criminal Organization: Its Elementary Forms*. London, 1972.

Crombie, A. C. *Medieval and Early Modern Science*, 2 vols. New York, 1959.

Crump, C. G., and C. Johnson. "The Powers of the Justices of the Peace." *English Historical Review*, 27 (1912), 226-238.

Darby, H. C. *The Medieval Fenland*. Cambridge, 1940.

―――― ed. *Historical Geography of England before 1800*. Cambridge, 1936.

Davenport, F. G. *The Economic Development of a Norfolk Manor, 1086-1565*. Cambridge, 1906.

Davis, J. C. *The Baronial Opposition to Edward II. Its Character and Policy*. Cambridge, 1919.

Denholm-Young, N. *The Country Gentry in the Fourteenth Century with Special Reference to the Heraldic Rolls of Arms*. Oxford, 1969.

―――― *Seignorial Administration in England*. London, 1937.

Denisoff, R. Serge, and Charles H. McCaghy. *Deviance, Conflict, and Criminality*. Chicago, 1973.

DeWindt, Anne Reiber. "Varieties of Peasant Legal Experience: The Huntingdon Eyre of 1286." Paper presented at the American Historical Association meeting, Dallas, December 30, 1977.

DeWindt, Edwin B. *Land and People in Holywell-cum-Needingworth*. Toronto, 1972.

Dobson, R. B. *The Peasants' Revolt of 1381*. London, 1970.

Dodwell, B. "Holdings and Inheritance in Medieval East Anglia." *Economic History Review*, 2nd ser., 20 (1967).

Douglas, D. C. *The Social Structure of Medieval East Anglia*. Oxford Studies in Social and Legal History, vol. IX. Oxford, 1927.

Drapkin, Israel, and Emiliano Viano, eds. *Victimology*. Lexington, Mass. 1974.

Dressler, D., ed. *Readings in Criminology and Penology*. New York, 1964.

DuBoulay, F. R. H. *The Lordship of Canterbury: An Essay on Medieval Society*. New York, 1966.

Durkheim, Emile. *Suicide*, trans. John A. Spaulding and George Simpson. New York, 1951.

Edwards, Valerie C. "The Case of the Married Spinster: An Alternative Explanation." *The American Journal of Legal History*, 21 (1977), 260-265.

Erickson, Carolly. *The Medieval Vision*. New York, 1974.

Erikson, Kai T. *Wayward Puritans: A Study in the Sociology of Deviance*.

New York, 1966.

Forbes, Thomas R. "Life and Death in Shakespeare's London." *American Scientist*, 58 (1970), 511-520.

—— "London Coroner's Inquests for 1590." *Journal of Medicine and Allied Sciences*, 28 (1973), 376-386.

Foss, E. *The Judges of England*, 9 vols. London, 1870.

Fuller, Ronald. *The Beggar's Brotherhood*. London, 1936.

Gabel, Leona C. *Benefit of Clergy in England in the Later Middle Ages*. Smith College Studies in History, vol. XIV, nos. 1-4. Northampton, Mass., October 1928-July 1929.

Genicot, L. "Crisis: From the Middle Ages to Modern Times." In *Cambridge Economic History*, vol. I, ed. M. M. Postan, pp. 660-742. Cambridge, 1966.

Gibson, Evelyn, and S. Klein. *Murder 1957 to 1968: A Home Office Statistical Division Report on Murder in England and Wales*. London, 1969.

Gillis, John R. "The Evolution of Juvenile Delinquency in England 1890-1914." *Past and Present*, no. 67 (1975), 96-126.

Given, James B. *Society and Homicide in Thirteenth-Century England*. Palo Alto, Calif., 1977.

Glassock, R. E. "The Distribution of Wealth in East Anglia in the Early Fourteenth Century." *Transactions of the Institute of British Geographers*, no. 23 (1963), 113-123.

Goebel, Julius. *Felony and Misdemeanor: A Study in the History of English Criminal Procedure*. New York, 1937.

Gollancz, Marguerite. "The System of Gaol Delivery as Illustrated in the Extant Gaol Delivery Rolls of the Fifteenth Century." Master's dissertation, University of London, 1936.

Graham, Thomas F. *Medieval Minds: Mental Health in the Middle Ages*. London, 1967.

Gras, N. S. B. *The Evolution of the English Corn Market*. Harvard Economic Studies, vol. XIII. Cambridge, Mass., 1915.

Gray, H. L. "The Commutation of Villein Services in England before the Black Death." *English Historical Review*, 29 (1914), 625-656.

—— "The Production and Exportation of English Woollens in the Fourteenth Century." *English Historical Review*, 39 (1924), 13-35.

Green, Thomas A. "The Jury and the English Law of Homicide, 1200-1600." *Michigan Law Review*, 74, no. 3 (1976), 414-499.

—— "Societal Concepts of Criminal Liability for Homicide in Mediaeval England." *Speculum*, 47 (1972), 669-694.

Guenée, Bernard. *Tribunaux et gens de justice dans le Bailliage de Senlis á la fin du moyen age*. Strasbourg, 1961-1963.

Hall, G. D. G. "The Frequency of General Eyres." *English Historical Review*, 74 (1959), 90-92.

Hall, Jerome. *Theft, Law, and Society*, 2nd ed. Indianapolis, 1952.

Hallam, H. E. "Population Density in Medieval Fenland." *Economic History Review*, 2nd ser., 14 (August 1961), 71-81.

────── *Settlement and Society: A Study of the Early Agrarian History of South Lincolnshire*. Cambridge, 1965.

────── "Some Thirteenth-Century Censuses." *Economic History Review*, 10 (1958), 340-361.

Hamil, F. C. "The King's Approvers." *Speculum*, 11 (April 1936), 238-258.

────── "Presentment of Englishry and the Murder Fine." *Speculum*, 12 (July 1937), 285-298.

Hammer, Carl I., Jr. "Patterns of Homicide in a Medieval University Town: Fourteenth-Century Oxford." *Past and Present*, no. 78 (1978), 1-23.

Hanawalt, Barbara A. "Childrearing among the Lower Classes of Late Medieval England." *Journal of Interdisciplinary History*, 8 (Summer 1977), 1-22.

──────"Community Conflict and Social Control: Crime in the Ramsey Abbey Villages." *Mediaeval Studies*, 39 (1977), 402-423.

────── "The Economic Influences on the Pattern of Crime in England, 1300-1348." *The American Journal of Legal History*, 18 (1974), 281-297.

────── "The Female Felon in Fourteenth-Century England." *Viator*, 5 (1974), 253-268.

────── "Fur-Collar Crime: The Pattern of Crime among the Fourteenth-Century English Nobility." *Journal of Social History*, 8 (1975), 1-17.

────── "The Peasant Family and Crime in Fourteenth-Century England." *Journal of British Studies*, 13 (1974), 1-18.

────── "Violent Death in Fourteenth-and Early Fifteenth-Century England." *The Journal of Comparative Studies in Society and History*, 18 (1976), 299-320.

Harding, Alan. *The Law Courts of Medieval England*. London, 1973.

────── "The Origins and Early History of the Keeper of the Peace." *Transactions of the Royal Historical Society*, 5th ser. 10 (1960), 85-109.

────── *A Social History of English Law*. London, 1966.

Harriss, G. L. "The Commons' Petitions of 1340." *English Historical Review*, 78 (1963), 625-654.

Hartung, Frank E. *Crime, Law, and Society*. Detroit, 1965.

Harvey, Barbara. "The Population Trend in England between 1300-1348." *Transactions of the Royal Historical Society*, 5th ser., 16 (1966), 23-42.

Hatcher, John. *Rural Economy and Society in the Duchy of Cornwall, 1300-1500*. Cambridge, 1970.

Hay, Denys. "The Divisions of Spoils of War in Fourteenth Century England." *Transactions of the Royal Historical Society*, 5th ser. 4 (1954), 91-109.

Hay, Douglas, Peter Linebaugh, Cal Winslow, John G. Rule, E. P. Thompson. *Albion's Fatal Tree: Crime and Society in Eighteenth-Century England*.

London, 1975.

Heard, Nigel. *Wool: East Anglia's Golden Fleece.* Lavenham, Eng., 1970.

Heaton, H. *The Yorkshire Woollen and Worsted Industries.* Oxford Historical and Literary Studies, vol. X. Oxford, 1920.

Helmholtz, Richard H. "Infanticide in the Province of Canterbury during the Fifteenth Century." *History of Childhood Quarterly,* 2 (1975), 382-389.

—— *Marriage Litigation in Medieval England.* Cambridge, 1974.

Hentig, Hans von. *The Criminal and His Victim: Studies in the Sociology of Crime.* New Haven, 1948.

Hess, Henner. *Mafia and Mafiosi: The Structure of Power,* trans. Ewald Osers. Lexington, Mass., 1973.

Hewitt, H. J. *The Organization of War under Edward III, 1338-1362.* Manchester, 1966.

Hilton, Rodney H. *Bond Men Made Free: Medieval Peasant Movements and the English Rising of 1381.* London, 1973.

—— *The Decline of Serfdom in England.* London, 1969.

—— *The Economic Development of Some Leicestershire Estates in the Fourteenth and Fifteenth Centuries.* Oxford, 1947.

—— *The English Peasantry in the Later Middle Ages.* New York, 1975.

—— *A Medieval Society: The West Midlands at the End of the Thirteenth Century.* London, 1966.

—— "The Origins of Robin Hood." *Past and Present,* no. 14 (1958), 30-43.

—— "Peasant Movements in England before 1381." In *Essays in Economic History,* ed. E. M. Carus-Wilson, vol. II, pp. 73-90. London, 1962.

—— ed. *Peasants, Knights, and Heretics: Studies in Medieval English Social History.* Cambridge, 1976.

—— and H. Fagan. *The English Rising of 1381.* London, 1950.

Hoare, C. M. *The History of an East Anglian Soke.* Bedford, 1918.

Hobsbawm, Eric J. *Primitive Rebels.* Manchester, 1959.

Hodgart, M. J. C. *The Ballads.* New York, 1962.

Holdsworth, William S. *A History of English Law,* 11 vols. Boston, 1924.

Holt, J. C. "The Origins and Audience of the Ballads of Robin Hood." *Past and Present,* no. 18 (1960), 89-110.

—— "Robin Hood, Some Comments." *Past and Present,* no. 19 (1961), 16-18.

Homans, George C. *English Villagers of the Thirteenth Century.* New York, 1941.

—— "The Rural Sociology of Medieval England." *Past and Present,* no. 4 (November 1953), 32-43.

Hood, Roger, and Richard Sparks. *Key Issues in Criminology.* New York, 1970.

Hoskins, W. G. *The Midland Peasant: The Economic and Social History of a Leicestershire Village.* London, 1957.

—— "Murder and Sudden Death in Medieval Wigston." *Transactions of the Leicestershire Archaeological Society*, 21 (1940-1941), 176-186.

Hudson, William. "The Assessment of the Townships of the County of Norfolk for the King's Tenths and Fifteenths, as Settled in 1334." *Norfolk Archaeology*, 12 (1903), 243-297.

—— "Norwich and Yarmouth in 1332, Their Comparative Prosperity." *Norfolk Archaeology*, 16 (1907), 177-196.

Hughes, Dorothy. *A Study of the Social and Constitutional Tendencies in the Early Years of Edward III.* London, 1915.

Hunnisett, R. F. *The Medieval Coroner.* Cambridge, 1961.

—— "The Medieval Coroners' Rolls." *The American Journal of Legal History*, 3 (1959), 95-124, 205-221, 324-359.

—— "Pleas of the Crown and the Coroner." *Bulletin of the Institute of Historical Research*, 32 (1959), 117-137.

—— "Sussex Coroners in the Middle Ages." *Sussex Archaeological Collections*, 95 (1957), 42-58.

Hurnard, Naomi D. "Jury of Presentment and the Assize of Clarendon." *English Historical Review*, 56 (July 1941), 374-401.

—— *The King's Pardon for Homicide before A.D. 1307.* Oxford, 1969.

Inciardi, James A. *Careers in Crime.* Chicago, 1975.

Iskrant, Albert P., and Paul V. Joliet. *Accidents and Homicide,* Cambridge, Mass., 1968.

Jenkinson, H., and M. H. Mills. "Rolls from a Sheriff's Office of the Fourteenth Century." *English Historical Review*, 43 (1928), 21-32.

Jeudwine, J. W. *Tort, Crime, and Police in Medieval Britain.* London, 1917.

Johnston, H. *Edward of Carnarvon, 1284-1307.* Manchester, 1946.

Jusserand, J. J. *English Wayfaring Life in the Middle Ages,* trans. L. T. Smith. London, 1961.

Kaye, J. M. "The Early History of Murder and Manslaughter, Part I." *Law Quarterly Review.* 83 (1967), 365-395, 569-601.

Keen, M. *The Outlaws of Medieval Legend.* London, 1961.

—— "Robin Hood, A Peasant Hero." *History Today*, 8 (1958), 684-689.

—— "Robin Hood, Peasant or Gentleman." *Past and Present*, no. 19 (1961), 7-15.

Kellaway, William. "The Coroner in Medieval London." In *Studies in London History*, ed. A. E. J. Hollaender and William Kellaway, pp. 75-91. London, 1969.

Kershaw, Ian. "The Great Famine and Agrarian Crisis in England, 1315-1322." *Past and Present*, no. 59 (1973), 3-50.

Klein, Dorie. "The Etiology of Female Crime: A Review of the Literature." *Issues in Criminology*, 2 (1973), 3-30.

Kramer, Henry, and James Sprenger. *Malleus Maleficarum,* trans. Montague Summers. London, 1928.

Krause, John. "The Medieval Household: Large or Small?" *Economic History Review*, 2nd ser., 9 (1957), 420-432.

Langbein, John H. *Prosecuting Crime in the Renaissance: England, Germany, France*. Cambridge, Mass., 1974.

Larking, L. B. "On the Heart Shrine in Leybourne Church." *Archaeologia Cantiana*, 5 (1863), 133-145.

Leadman, A. D. H. "The Battle of Mynton." *Yorkshire Archaeological and Topographical Journal*, 8 (1883-1884), 117-122.

Lederer, Wolfgang. *The Fear of Women*. New York, 1968.

Lennard, Reginald. *Rural England: A Study of Social and Agrarian Conditions*. Oxford, 1959.

Lesser, M. A. *Historical Development of the Jury System*. London, 1894.

Le Strange, H. *Norfolk Official Lists*. Norwich, 1890.

Levett, A. E. *Studies in Manorial History*. Oxford, 1963.

Lewis, N. B. "The Organization of Indentured Retainues in Fourteenth Century England." *Transactions of the Royal Historical Society*, 4th ser., 27 (1945), 29-39.

Lipson, E. *The Economic History of England*, 3 vols. London, 1937.

Longden, J. "Statistical Notes on Winchester Heriots." *Economic History Review*, 2nd ser., 11 (1959), 412-417.

Lucas, H. S. "The Great European Famine of 1315, 1316 and 1317." *Speculum*, 5 (October 1930), 343-377.

Lunden, Walter A. *Crime and Criminals*. Ames, Ia., 1967.

McClintock, F. H. *Crimes of Violence: An Enquiry by the Cambridge Institute of Criminology into Crimes of Violence against the Person in London*. London, 1963.

—— and N. Howard Avison. *Crime in England and Wales*. London, 1968.

—— and Evelyn Gibson. *Robbery in London: An Enquiry by the Cambridge Institute of Criminology*. London, 1961.

MacDonald, John M. *Rape: Offenders and Their Victims*. Springfield, Ill., 1971.

McDonald, Lynn. *The Sociology of Law and Order: Conflict and Consensus Theories of Crime, Law, and Sanctions*. London, 1975.

Macfarlane, Alan. *Witchcraft in Tudor and Stuart England: A Regional and Comparative Study*. London, 1970.

McFarlane, K. B. "England and the Hundred Years' War." *Past and Present*, no. 22 (July 1962), 3-13.

—— *The Nobility of Later Medieval England*. Oxford, 1973.

McKisack, M. *The Fourteenth Century, 1307-1399*. Oxford, 1959.

Maddicot, J. R. *The English Peasantry and the Demands of the Crown: 1294-1341*. Past and Present Society Supplement 1. Oxford, 1975.

Maitland, F. W. *Forms of Action at Common Law*. Cambridge, 1962.

—— *Township and Borough*. Cambridge, 1898.

Mandel, Oscar, trans. *Five Comedies of Medieval France*. New York, 1970.
Mannheim, Hermann. *Comparative Criminology*, 2nd ed. Boston, 1967.
—— *Social Aspect of Crime in England between the Wars*. London, 1940.
—— *War and Crime*. London, 1941.
Meekings, C. A. F. "Index to the Medieval Gaol Delivery Rolls." Unpublished manuscript in the Public Record Office, London.
Middleton, A. E. *Sir Gilbert Middleton and the Part He Took in the Rebellion in the North of England in 1317*. Newcastle-on-Tyne, 1918.
Miller, Edward. "England in the Twelfth and Thirteenth Centuries: An Economic Contrast?" *Economic History Review*, 2nd ser., 24 (1971), 1-14.
—— "The English Economy in the Thirteenth Century: Implications of Recent Research." *Past and Present*, no. 28 (1964), 21-48.
—— *War in the North*. Hull, Eng., 1960.
Milsom, S. F. C. *Historical Foundations of the Common Law*. London, 1969.
Mitchell, S. K. *Taxation in Medieval England*. New Haven, 1951.
Monkkonen, Eric H. *The Dangerous Class: Crime and Poverty in Columbus, Ohio. 1860-1885*. Cambridge, Mass., 1975.
Morris, Albert. *Homicide: An Approach to the Problem of Crime*. Boston, 1955.
Morris, J. E. "Mounted Infantry in Medieval Warfare." *Transactions of the Royal Historical Society*, 3rd ser., 8 (1914), 77-102.
Morris, T. and L. Blom-Cooper. *A Calendar of Murder; Criminal Homicide in England since 1957*. London, 1964.
Morris, William A. *The Early English County Court*. University of California Publications in History, vol. 14, no. 2. Berkeley, 1926.
—— *The Frankpledge System*. New York, 1910.
—— *The Medieval English Sheriff to 1300*. Manchester, 1927.
—— "The Sheriff." *The English Government at Work*, vol. 2, ed. W. A. Morris and J. R. Strayer. Cambridge, Mass., 1947.
Myres, Ramon H. *The Chinese Peasant Economy: Agricultural Development in Hopei and Shantung, 1890-1949*. Cambridge, Mass., 1970.
Nettler, Gwynn. *Explaining Crime*. New York, 1974.
Nicholson, R. *Edward III and the Scots: The Formative Years of a Military Career*. Oxford, 1965.
Oman, Charles. *The Great Revolt of 1381*. Oxford, 1969.
Orwin, Charles S., and C. S. Orwin. *The Open Fields*. Oxford, 1938.
Osborne, Bertram. *Justices of the Peace, 1361-1848*. Shaftesbury, 1960.
Owst, G. R. *Literature and the Pulpit in Medieval England*. Oxford, 1933.
—— *Preaching in Medieval England: An Introduction to Sermon Manuscripts in the Period, 1350-1450*. Cambridge, 1926.
Page, W., ed. *Victoria County History of Yorkshire*, III. London, 1913.
Palmer, Stuart. *The Violent Society*. New Haven, Conn., 1972.
Pelham, R. A. "Fourteenth-Century England." In *Historical Geography of*

England before 1800, ed. H. C. Darby, pp. 230-265. Cambridge, 1936.

Perroy, E. "Les profits et rancons pendant la Guerre de Cent Ans." *Mélanges d'Histoire du Moyen Age à la Memorie de Louis Halphen*. Paris, 1951.

Pike, L. O. *A History of Crime in England*, 2 vols. London, 1873.

Platt, A. M. "The Criminal Responsibility of the Mentally Ill in England." Masters dissertation, University of California, Berkeley, 1956.

Plint, Thomas. *Crime in England: Its Relation, Character and Extent as Developed from 1801-1848*. London, 1851.

Plucknett, T. F. T. "Commentary." In *Proceedings before the Justices of Peace in the Fourteenth and Fifteenth Centuries*, by Bertha H. Putnam. London, 1939.

—— *A Concise History of the Common Law*, 5th ed. New York, 1956.

—— *Edward I and Criminal Law*. Cambridge, 1960.

—— "Parliament." In *The English Government at Work*, ed. J. F. Willard, vol. I, pp. 82-128. Cambridge, Mass., 1940.

Pollak, O. *The Criminality of Women*. Philadelphia, 1950.

Pollock, F., and F. W. Maitland. *The History of English Law before Edward I*, 2 vols., 2nd ed. Cambridge, 1968.

Postan, M. M. "The Costs of the Hundred Years' War." *Past and Present*, no. 27 (April 1964), 34-53.

—— "Medieval Agrarian Society at Its Prime: England." In *Cambridge Economic History of Europe*, 2nd ed., vol. 1, ed. M. M. Postan, pp. 549-632. Cambridge, 1966.

—— *The Medieval Economy and Society*. London, 1972.

—— "Note." *Economic History Review*, 2nd ser., 12 (1959), 77-82.

—— "Some Economic Evidence of Declining Population in the Later Middle Ages." *Economic History Review*, 2nd ser., 2 (1950), 221-246.

—— "Some Social Consequences of the Hundred Years War." *Economic History Review*, 12 (1942), 1-12.

—— and J. Z. Titow. "Heriots and Prices on Winchester Manors." *Economic History Review*, 2nd ser., 11 (1959), 392-411.

Pounds, N. J. G. *An Economic History of Medieval Europe*. London, 1974.

Powell, Edgar. *The Rising in East Anglia in 1381*. Cambridge, 1896.

Power, Eileen. *Medieval Women*, ed. M. M. Postan. Cambridge, 1975.

—— *The Wool Trade in English Medieval History*. Oxford, 1941.

Powers, E. *Crime and Punishment in Early Massachusetts, 1620-1692: A Documentary History*. Boston, 1966.

Powicke, M. *Military Obligation in Medieval England: A Study in Liberty and Duty*. Oxford, 1962.

Prince, A. E. "The Army and Navy." In *The English Government at Work*, vol. 1, ed. J. F. Willard and W. A. Morris, pp. 332-393. Cambridge, Mass., 1940.

—— "The Indenture System under Edward III." *Historical Essays in Hon-*

our of James Tait, ed. J. G. Edwards, V. H. Galbraith, and E. F. Jacob, pp. 283-297. Manchester, 1933.

———— "The Strength of the English Armies in the Reign of Edward III." *English Historical Review*, 46 (July 1931), 353-371.

Pugh, R. B. *Imprisonment in Medieval England*. Cambridge, 1968.

———— "The King's Prisons before 1250." *Transactions of the Royal Historical Society*. 5th ser., 5 (1955), 1-22.

———— "Some Reflections of a Medieval Criminologist." *Proceedings of the British Academy*, 59, Oxford, 1973.

Putnam, Bertha H. "Ancient Indictments in the Public Record Office." *English Historical Review*, 29 (1914), 479-505.

———— *Proceedings before the Justices of the Peace in the Fourteenth and Fifteenth Centuries*. London, 1938.

———— "Shire Officials: Keepers of the Peace and Justices of the Peace." In *The English Government at Work*, vol. 3, ed. J. F. Willard, W. A. Morris, and W. H. Dunham, Jr., pp. 185-217. Cambridge, Mass., 1950.

———— "Transformation of the Keepers of the Peace into the Justices of the Peace, 1327-1380." *Transactions of the Royal Historical Society*, 4th ser., 5 (1920), 19-48.

Radzinowicz, Leon, and Marvin E. Wolfgang, eds. *Crime and Justice*. New York, 1971.

Raftis, J. Ambrose. "Changes in an English Village after the Black Death." *Mediaeval Studies*, 29 (1967), 158-177.

———— "The Concentration of Responsibility in Five Villages." *Mediaeval Studies*, 28 (1966), 92-118.

———— "Social Structure in Five East Midlands Villages: A Study of Possibilities in the Use of Court Roll Data." *Economic History Review*, 2nd ser., 18 (1965), 83-100.

———— *Tenure and Mobility: Studies in the Social History of the Medieval English Village*. Toronto, 1964.

———— *Warboys: Two Hundred Years in the Life of an English Mediaeval Village*. Toronto, 1974.

———— ed. "Studies of Peasant Mobility in a Region of Late Thirteenth- and Early Fourteenth-Century England." In manuscript.

Rayner, J. L., and G. T. Crook. *The Complete Newgate Calendar*, 5 vols. London, 1926.

Redstone, V. B. "Some Mercenaries of Henry of Lancaster 1327-1330." *Transactions of the Royal Historical Society*, 3rd ser., 7 (1913), 151-166.

Repetto, Thomas A. *Residential Crime*. Cambridge, Mass., 1974.

Réville, A. *Le soulèvement des travilleurs d'Angleterre en 1381*. Paris, 1898.

Roberts, Brian K. *Rural Settlement in Britain*. Folkstone, Eng., 1977.

Robinson, W. C. "Money, Population and Economic Change in Late Medieval Europe." *Economic History Review*, 2nd ser., 12 (1959), 63-76.

Bibliography

Robson, L. L. *The Convict Settlers of Australia: An Enquiry into the Origin and Character of the Convicts Transported to New South Wales and Van Dieman's Land, 1787-1852.* Melbourne, 1965.

Rogers, J. E. Thorold. *Six Centuries of Work and Wages.* London, 1884.

Rosen, G. *Madness in Society: Chapters in the Historical Sociology of Mental Illness.* London, 1968.

Ross, J. B., and M. M. McLaughlin, eds. *The Portable Medieval Reader.* New York, 1949.

Ruggiero, Guido. "Sexual Criminality in the Early Renaissance: Venice 1338-1358." *Journal of Social History* (1975), 18-37.

Rusche, George, and Otto Kirchheimer. *Punishment and Social Structure.* New York, 1939.

Russell, Josiah Cox. *British Medieval Population.* Albuquerque, 1948.

Rye, W. "Crime and Accident in Norfolk in the Time of Henry III and Edward III." *Norfolk Antiquarian Miscellany,* 2 (1883), 159-193.

―――― *A History of Norfolk.* London, 1885.

―――― "Notes on Crime and Accident in Norfolk Temp. Edward First." *Archaeological Review,* 2 (1889), 210-215.

Sagalyn, Arnold. "The Crime of Robbery in the U.S." In *Crime and Justice, 1970-71,* ed. Jackwell Susman. New York, 1972.

―――― *The Crime of Robbery in the United States.* Washington, D.C., 1971.

Salzman, L. F. *English Industries of the Middle Ages.* Oxford, 1923.

―――― *English Trade in the Middle Ages.* London, 1964.

Samaha, Joel. *Law and Order in Historical Perspective: The Case of Elizabethan Essex.* New York, 1974.

Sayles, G. O. *The Court of the King's Bench in Law and History.* Selden Society Lecture. London, 1959.

Scarr, Harry A. *Patterns of Burglary.* Washington, D.C., 1972.

Schafer, Stephen. *Theories in Criminology: Past and Present Philosophies of the Crime Problem.* New York, 1969.

Schneebeck, Harold, "The Law of Felony in Medieval England from the Accession of Edward I until the Mid-fourteenth Century." Ph.D. dissertation, University of Iowa, 1973.

Schofield, R. S. "The Geographical Distribution of Wealth in England, 1334-1649." *Economic History Review,* 18 (1965), 483-510.

Schove, D. J., and Lowther, A. W. G. "Tree-rings and Medieval Archeology." *Medieval Archeology,* 1 (1957), 78-95.

Schur, Edwin. *Labeling Deviant Behavior: Its Sociological Implications.* New York, 1971.

Searle, Eleanor. *Lordship and Community: Battle Abbey and Its Banlieu, 1066-1538.* Toronto, 1974.

Seebohm, Frederic. *The English Village Community Examined in its Relations to the Manorial and Tribal Systems and to the Common or Open Field Sys-*

tem of Husbandry. London, 1913.

Sellin, T. *Research Memorandum on Crime in the Depression.* New York, 1937.

Shannon, E. F. "Medieval Law in *The Tale of Gamelyn.*" *Speculum,* 26 (1951), 458-464.

Sheehan, Michael M. "The Formation and Stability of Marriage in Fourteenth-Century England: Evidence of an Ely Register." *Mediaeval Studies,* 33, (1971) 228-263.

Short, James F., and Andrew Henry. "Status and the Relational System." In *Studies in Homicide,* ed. Marvin Wolfgang, pp. 255-270. New York, 1967.

Stenton, D. M. *The English Woman in History.* London, 1957.

Stenton, F. M. "The Road System of Medieval England." *Economic History Review,* 1st ser., 7 (1936), 1-26.

Stephen, J. F. *A History of the Criminal Law in England,* 3 vols. London, 1883.

Stones, E. L. G. "The Folvilles of Ashby-Folville, Leicestershire, and Their Associates in Crime." *Transactions of the Royal Historical Society,* 5th ser., 7 (1957), 91-116.

—— "Sir Geoffrey le Scrope (c. 1285-1340) Chief Justice of the King's Bench." *English Historical Review,* 69 (1954), 1-17.

Stuard, Susan Mosher, ed. *Women in the Middle Ages.* Philadelphia, 1976.

Stubbs, William. *Select Charters and Other Illustrations of English Constitutional History,* 9th ed. Oxford, 1913.

Sullivan, W. C. *Crime and Insanity.* New York, 1924.

Sutherland, Donald W. "The Reasoning of Fourteenth-Century Barristers." American Historical Association, 1977.

Sutherland, Edwin H. *White Collar Crime.* Bloomington, Ind., 1949.

—— ed. *The Professional Thief: By a Professional Thief.* Chicago, 1937.

—— and D. R. Cressey. *Principles of Criminology,* 7th ed. New York, 1966.

Szabo, D. *Crimes et villes, étude statistique de la criminalité urbain et rurale en France et en Belgique.* Paris, 1960.

Taylor, M. M. "The Justices of Assize." In *The English Government at Work,* vol. 3, ed. J. F. Willard, W. A. Morris, and W. H. Dunham, Jr. Cambridge, Mass., 1950.

Terry, S. B. *The Financing of the Hundred Years' War, 1337-1360.* London, 1914.

Thomas, D. S. *Social Aspects of the Business Cycle.* London, 1925.

Thompson, I. A. A. "A Map of Crime in Sixteenth Century Spain." *Economic History Review,* 2nd ser., 21 (1968), 244-267.

Thrupp, Sylvia L. *The Merchant Class of Medieval London.* Ann Arbor, 1962.

—— "The Problem of Replacement Rates in Late Medieval English Population." *Economic History Review*, 2nd ser., 18 (August 1965), 101-119.

———"A Survey of the Alien Population of England in 1440." *Speculum*, 32 (1957), 262-273.

Titow, J. Z. *English Rural Society, 1200-1350.* London, 1969.

——— "Evidence of Weather in the Account Rolls of the Bishopric of Winchester 1209-1350." *Economic History Review*, 2nd ser., 12 (1960), 360-407.

——— *Winchester Yields: A Study in Medieval Agricultural Productivity.* Cambridge, 1972.

Tobias, J. J. *Crime and Industrial Society in the Nineteenth Century.* London, 1967.

——— *Urban Crime in Victorian England.* New York, 1972.

Tout, T. F. *Chapters in the Administrative History of Medieval England,* 4 vols. Manchester, 1920.

——— *The History of England from the Accession of Henry III to the Death of Edward III.* London, 1920.

——— "A Medieval Burglary." *Bulletin of the John Rylands Library, Manchester,* 2 (1915), 348-369.

——— "Medieval Forgers and Forgeries." *Bulletin of the John Rylands Library, Manchester,* 5 (1919), 208-234.

——— *The Place of the Reign of Edward III in English History,* 2nd ed. Manchester, 1936.

Trexler, Richard C., "Infanticide in Florence: New Sources and First Results." *History of Childhood Quarterly,* 1 (1973), 98-116.

Turk, Austin T. "Conflict and Criminality." *American Sociological Review,* 31 (1966), 338-352.

——— "Law as a Weapon in Social Conflict." In manuscript.

——— "Law, Conflict and Order: From Theorizing toward Theories." In manuscript.

Ullmann, Walter. *The Medieval View of Law.* London, 1946.

Uniform Crime Reports. Washington, D.C., 1965.

"Uniform Crime Reports—1968—U.S." In *Crime and Justice,* ed. Leon Radzinowicz and Marvin E. Wolfgang. New York, 1971.

Vann, J. D. "Middle English Verses against Thieves: A Postscript." *Speculum,* 34 (1959), 636-637.

Verkko, Veli. "Static and Dynamic 'Laws' of Sex and Homicide." In *Studies in Homicide,* ed. Marvin E. Wolfgang, pp. 36-44. New York, 1967.

Vinogradoff, Paul. *English Society in the Eleventh Century: Essays in English Medieval History.* Oxford, 1908.

Vold, George B. "The Organization of Criminals for Profit and Power." In *Criminal Behavior Systems,* ed. Marshall B. Clinard and Richard Quinney, pp. 394-398. New York, 1967.

Walford, C. "On the Famines of the World: Past and Present." *Journal of the Royal Statistical Society,* 41 (1878), 433-526; 42 (1879), 79-265.

Bibliography

Walker, Nigel. *Crime and Insanity in England*, vol. 1. Edinburgh, 1968.

Walker, Sue Sheridan. "Violence and the Exercise of Feudal Guardianship: The Action of 'Ejectio Custodia.' " *The American Journal of Legal History*, 16 (1972), 320-333.

Watford, A. H. "Calendar of the General and Special Assize and General Gaol Delivery Commissions on the Dorses of the Patent Rolls: Richard II (1377-1399)." Unpublished manuscript in the Public Record Office. London, 1966.

Watts, D. G., "A Model for the Early Fourteenth Century." *Economic History Review*, 2nd ser., 20 (1967), 543-547.

Waugh, S. L. "The Profits of Violence: The Minor Gentry in the Rebellion of 1321-1322 in Gloucestershire and Herefordshire." *Speculum*, 52 (1977), 843-869.

Wedermeyer, Ellen. "Social Groupings at the Fair of St. Ives." *Mediaeval Studies*, 32 (1970), 27-59.

Weihofen, H. *Mental Disorder as a Criminal Defense*. New York, 1954.

West, Donald J. *Murder Followed by Suicide*. Cambridge, Mass., 1966.

Westlake, H. F. *The Parish Gilds of Medieval England*. London, 1919.

Westman, Barbara Hanawalt. "A Study of Crime in Norfolk, Yorkshire, and Northamptonshire, 1300-1348." Ph.D. dissertation, University of Michigan, 1970.

—— For other references to Westman see Hanawalt.

Whyte, William Foote. *Street Corner Society. The Social Structure of an Italian Slum*. Chicago, 1965.

Wiener, Carol Z. "Is a Spinster an Unmarried Woman?" *The American Journal of Legal History*, 20 (1976), 27-31.

—— "Sex Roles and Crime in Late Elizabethan Hertfordshire." *The Journal of Social History*, 8 (1975), 308-312.

Willard, J. F. "Inland Transportation in England during the Fourteenth Century." *Speculum*, 1 (1926), 361-374.

—— *Parliamentary Taxes on Personal Property*. Cambridge, Mass., 1934.

—— "The Scottish Raids and the Fourteenth-Century Taxation of Northern England." *University of Colorado Studies*, 5 (1908), 373-420.

—— "The Taxes upon Movables in the Reign of Edward II." *English Historical Review*, 29 (1914), 317-321.

—— "The Taxes upon Movables in the Reign of Edward III." *English Historical Review*, 30 (1915), 69-74.

Wolfgang, Marvin E. *Patterns in Criminal Homicide*. Philadelphia, 1958.

—— ed. *Crime and Culture: Essays in Honor of Thorsten Sellin*. New York, 1968.

—— ed. *Studies in Homicide*. New York, 1967.

—— Leonard Savits, and Norman Johnston, eds. *The Sociology of Crime and Delinquency*. New York, 1962.

Bibliography

Wright, E. C. "Common Law in the Thirteenth-Century English Royal Forest." *Speculum*, 3 (1928), 166-191.

Wright, Thomas. *The Political Songs of England: From the Reign of John to That of Edward II.* London, 1839.

Zehr, Howard. *Crime and Development of Modern Society: Patterns of Criminality in Nineteenth Century Germany and France.* Totowa, N.J., 1976.

Index

Abduction, 104, 106-110, 171. *See also* Ransoming

Abjuring the realm, 36, 37, 200, 212

Accomplices, 124-125, 185, 187-188, 189-190, 192, 219, 264. *See also* Approvers; Criminal associations

Acom, Peter de, 93

Adam of Deddington, 199-200

Adam son of Richard of Saham, 89

Adam the Waynwright, 128

Adultery, 164-165

Age: of suspects, 115, 125-128, 150, 264; of victims, 124, 154-158, 264

Agnes daughter of William Neilesone, 153

Agnes of Weldon, 69

Agnes widow of Robert de Abberford, 110

Agnes wife of John le Smithesson, 102

Aintree, dean of, 205

Alcohol, and homicide, 144, 181

Ale tasters, 24-25

Alexander of Broughton, 218

Aliases, 220

Alice daughter of Roger de Walton, 43

Alice daughter of Simon de Hepworth, 164

Alice niece of the vicar of Depsham, 42

Alice widow of Adam Broun, 163

Alice wife of John Kyde, 154

Amyas, William, 92

Anglo-Saxon Chronicle, 20

Angot, Robert, 146, 147, 148, 149, 150

Annotsen, John, 34

Appeals, 4, 36-37, 40, 41-42, 48

Approvers, 17, 36-37, 40, 44, 48, 49, 53, 57, 61, 93, 137, 149, 170, 194, 211; hanging of, 36, 42; and trial by combat, 40, 41-42; and professional criminals, 218-219; and crime rate, 283

Ariès, Philippe, 126-127, 264

Armed bands, *see* Outlaw bands

Arnald, John, 218

Arrest, 34, 35, 36, 37, 44; summary, power of, 281-282

Arson, 3, 64, 77, 90-92, 189; convictions for, 59, 60; indictments for, 66, 67; suspects, 118, 136, 138, 170; and insanity, 147, 148; victims of, 153, 169; rates of, 236, 237

Art of Courtly Love, by Andreas Capellanus, 106

Arundel, earl of, 51-52

Assault, 4-5, 7, 23, 24, 78, 123, 130, 150, 158, 174, 262, 272; within the family, 159, 160, 162, 163

Assize of Arms (1181), 33

Assizes, 5, 40, 49, 52

Bail, 37, 39, 48

Bailiffs, 31, 33, 34-35, 37, 40, 44; corrupt, 48, 51-52

Baker, John and Richard, 163

345

Bakere, Robert le, 57, 74
Baldwin, Laurence, 176
Balliol, Edward, 231
Ballok, John, 33
Bandits, 7, 60, 139, 201-213, 215, 265.
    See also Outlaw bands
Barbur, Adam le, 111
Barker, Thomas le, 176
Basoun, Richard le, 74
Baurserman, Robert le, 165
Bayl, Robert, 93
Beadles, 24, 25
Beaufitz, Hugh, 103
Beaumont, Sir Henry, 87
Beckwith, William, 208
Bedel, Walter le, 165
Bedford, Indiana, 271-272
Bedfordshire, 28, 80, 81, 94, 212;
    records, 28, 275, 288n11; robbery in,
    89, 181; homicide in, 134, 180-181;
    child mortality in, 155-156
Beggars, 73-74, 133
Bell, Adam, 211, 212
Bellamy, John, 17, 202
Bellers, Roger, 188, 206
Bello Monte, Alainore de, 41
Benedict son of Walter, 170
Benefit of clergy, 40, 42-43, 54-55, 268,
    269
Benne, John, 122
Bere, Emma le, 104
Bere, William, 180
Bernard, John, 176
Beruglby, Robert de, 100
Bevetoun, William, 80
Bigamy, 4, 167, 312n44
Bilet, William, 205
Bird, William, 54, 145
Black Death, 8, 199, 240
Bodel, Jean, *The Play of St. Nicholas*,
    220
Boidyn, Robert, 88, 206
Bolle, Maud, 80
Bondehowie, John, 196
Bonger, W. A., 116
Bonis, Andrew, 174

"Bootless" crimes, 4
Bordesle, Henry, 103
Borough English, 28
Boroughs, 6, 97, 289n27
Bot, 4
Boteler, Cecilia le, 50
Bovetoun, Ralph, 82
Bracton, Henry de, 64
Bradburn brothers, 192
Bradshaw, Sir William, 50
Brendel, Margery, 95
Brente, Lord Robert de, 142
Brethale, Hugh de, 103
Brett, Lady Juliana la, 142
Bretton, John, 102
Brewester, Agnes le, 74
Brian, Richard, 207
Britten, treatise writer, 64
Brodish, William de, 137-138
Bromyard, John, 47, 52
Broughton, Hunts., 130, 131, 132, 175,
    179. *See also* Ramsey Abbey villages
Broughton, John de, 130
Broun, Richard, 163
Bruce, Robert, 9, 230, 231
Bryd, John, 236
Brydand, John, 89
Buleyn, Adam, 170
Burglary, 3, 64, 66, 67, 76-78, 84, 218,
    219, 261, 272; convictions for, 59,
    60, 62, 268-269; goods stolen, 71, 75,
    82-83, 270; seasonality of, 78-79,
    112, 262; techniques, 79-82; and
    rape, 105-106, 107-108, 153; by
    women, 118-119, 120, 122, 263-264;
    suspects, 127, 128, 132-133, 141-142,
    150, 169, 170, 173; by clergy, 136,
    137, 138; victims of, 153, 154, 158,
    169, 271; by criminal associations,
    189-190, 192, 195, 200, 204, 265;
    rates of, 236, 237, 238, 253, 257, 259,
    266, 272
Burning, 44
Burton, Thomas de, 179, 297n45
Bussy, Sir William, 142, 202, 208
Bylaws, of villages, 25, 31, 53, 175

Index

124, 151, 152-154, 160, 161, 163, 165-166, 273

Woodwards, 24, 25

Wormbridge, Richard de, 95

Wounding, 78, 104

Writs, 13, 39, 48, 275

Wyghall, John de, 205

Wylughby, Sir Richard de, 47, 87, 206, 207

Wyndhill, Richard del, 204

Wyot, Robin, 210

Wypes, John, father and son, 218

Wyryng, John, 72

Wyt, Reynold le, 89-90

Year Books, 64, 65

York, archbishop of, 230

Yorkshire, 10, 11-12, 67, 112, 115, 226, 236, 257, 259, 267; records, 8, 13, 278; Scottish invasions of, 9, 12, 56; settlement pattern of, 21; conviction rate in, 56, 60; spying in, 59, 110, 237; larceny in, 65-66, 67; burglary in, 67, 76, 119; robbery in, 67, 83, 84, 88; receiving in, 67, 95-96; homicide in, 67, 98, 162-163, 178, 260, 270; rape in, 67, 105, 153; inheritance in, 162-163; organized crime in, 188, 194, 202, 208; crime rate for, 266, 230-233, 235, 238, 241, 244, 251, 252, 254, 255, 258, 260, 279-280, 282, 283

Zouche, Roger la, 206